EXTENDING HORIZONS

Psychoanalytic Psychotherapy with Children, Adolescents, and Families

EXTENDING HORIZONS

Psychoanalytic Psychotherapy
with Children, Adolescents,
and Families

edited by

Rolene Szur
and
Sheila Miller

with a preface by
Rolene Szur

Karnac Books

London   1991   New York

To the memory of
Jess Guthrie
Martha Harris
Sara Rosenfeld

First published in 1991 by
H. Karnac (Books) Ltd.
58 Gloucester Road
London SW7 4QY

Distributed in the United States of America by
Brunner/Mazel, Inc.
19 Union Square West
New York, NY 10003

British Library Cataloguing in Publication Data

Extending horizons: psychoanalytic psychotherapy with
   children, adolescents, and families.
   1. Psychotherapy
   I. Szur, Rolene
   616.8915

ISBN 0–946439–88–5

Printed in Great Britain by BPCC Wheatons Ltd, Exeter

CONTENTS

ACKNOWLEDGEMENTS

The editors wish to thank Lisa Miller for her early interest and support, Mary Boston for reading and offering her helpful comments on a number of chapters, and Jill Hodges for some interesting discussions when the book was first planned. We are grateful to all the authors who have so generously contributed their work, and also to the many, necessarily anonymous, patients with whom the therapeutic endeavour was shared.

We take this opportunity of thanking the Child Psychotherapy Trust for their generous help in financing the technical aspects involved in the preparation of the manuscript. We wish also to express our sincere appreciation to Cesare Sacerdoti of Karnac Books and to Klara King for many thoughtful and helpful suggestions.

Muriel Maseyk, who was responsible for typing and re-typing many drafts of many manuscripts with both patience and interest, deserves all our thanks.

The royalties from this book will go to the Child Psychotherapy Trust, 27 Ulysses Road, London NW6 1ED. This is dedicated to ensuring that enough child psychotherapists are trained to work within the NHS to provide help for children and families who suffer from emotional problems, some of which, in varying degrees and circumstances, are described in the following pages.

CONTRIBUTORS

The authors who have contributed to this volume each present an experience and an approach that is to some extent individual to the case and to the practitioner, while at the same time remaining within the broad spectrum of the psychoanalytic tradition, viewed as a constantly growing and developing study of the complex variants of human experience and relationships.

ANNE ALVAREZ is a Principal Child Psychotherapist in the Child and Family Department of the Tavistock Clinic. She has a book currently in preparation on her special interest, entitled, *Live Company—Psychoanalytic Psychotherapy with Psychotic Borderline, and Deprived Children.*

JAMES ASTOR is a Training Analyst at the Society of Analytical Psychology, a member of the Association of Child Psychotherapists, and a Chartered Psychologist in private practice.

MARIA BERGER initially worked as a child psychologist in Europe and Australia before coming to England and qualifying as a Child Psychotherapist at the Anna Freud Centre, where she was the first Chairman of the Research Group on Adoption.

MARY BOSTON is a child psychotherapist and former Senior Tutor at the Tavistock Clinic, who now lives and works in North Devon. She is co-editor with Rolene Szur, of *Psychotherapy with Severely Deprived Children* (Routledge and Kegan Paul, 1983), and co-editor with Dilys Daws of *The Child Psychotherapist and Problems of Young People* (Karnac, 1988). She is currently engaged, with Dolly Lush and Eve Grainger, in a research project at the Tavistock Clinic, on adopted and fostered children in psychotherapy.

JONATHAN BRADLEY has a background in psychology and is now a Principal Child Psychotherapist at the Tavistock Clinic and in Hackney.

BETA COPLEY, formerly a Principal Child Psychotherapist and now a visiting teacher at the Tavistock Clinic, has also taught in Rome. She co-edited, with Sally Box and others, *Psychotherapy with Families: An Analytic Approach* (Routledge & Kegan Paul, 1981), and with Barbara Forryan, *Therapeutic Work with Children and Young People* (Robert Royce, 1987). She is founder and tutor of a multi-disciplinary course on individual therapeutic work in Birmingham.

FRANCIS DALE is a Principal Child Psychotherapist in Torbay, Devon, where he has also organized a brief course of training in psychoanalytic psychotherapy within the National Health Service.

DILYS DAWS, a Principal Child Psychotherapist, previously at the Child Guidance Training Centre and now at the Tavistock Clinic, is the author of *Your One-Year-Old* (Corgi Books, 1969) and *Through the Night: Helping Parents and Sleepless Infants* (Free Association Books, 1989); she co-edited with Mary Boston *The Child Psychotherapist and Problems of Young People* (Karnac Books, 1988).

HELÉNE DUBINSKY is a Principal Child Psychotherapist in the Adolescent Department of the Tavistock Clinic; her interests also include working with groups of mothers suffering from post-natal depression, and joint work with mothers and young children.

PETER FONAGY is Freud Memorial Professor of Psychoanalysis (designate) at University College, London, and research co-ordinator at the Anna Freud Centre. A member of the British Psycho-Analytical Society and on the editorial board of the *International Journal of Psychoanalysis,* he is currently training in child analysis at the Anna Freud Centre. His major research interest is the application of systematic research strategies to theoretical and technical issues in psychoanalysis.

ERNA FURMAN is a distinguished member of the Cleveland Centre for Research in Child Development in the United States and an international authority on the subject of bereavement in childhood.

GENEVIEVE HAAG, psychiatrist, psychoanalyst, and associate member of the Paris Psychoanalytic Society, has a special inter-est in child analysis, infant development, and autistic organiza-tions. She has published a number of papers on these topics in books, psychiatric and psychoanalyic journals, and reviews.

MARTHA HARRIS was a psychoanalyst and child psychotherapist who followed Esther Bick in the task of organizing child psycho-therapy training at the Tavistock, and whose creative imagina-tion led to the evolution of the pre-clinical observation course with 'work discussion' seminars, an increasing expansion of the numbers of students, and the founding of a number of similar trainings abroad. Her writings have been published in *Collected Papers of Martha Harris and Esther Bick,* edited by Meg Harris Williams (Clunie Press, 1987).

JILL HODGES, a research child psychologist before training in child psychoanalytic psychotherapy, is now a Senior Child Psy-chotherapist at the Hospital for Sick Children, Great Ormond Street, and at the Anna Freud Centre. She has worked with Professor B. Tizard on a longitudinal study of children who have spent their early years in institutions (*Journal of Child Psychology and Psychiatry,* January 1989).

MARGARET HUNTER is Principal Child Psychotherapist at Camberwell Child Guidance Clinic and formerly worked for Greenwich Social Services. Her experience has been mainly with separated, adopted, and fostered children, particularly those with traumatic early lives. Helping them to come to terms with their experience has been the core interest of her analytic work.

ROSALIE JOFFE is a child and adult analyst who trained at the Anna Freud Centre and at the British Institute of Psycho-Analysis. She is in private practice, works at the Brent Consultation Centre for Adolescents, and is Chairwoman of the B.A.P. Child Psychotherapy Training Committee.

ISOBEL MENZIES LYTH is a Training Psychoanalyst in work with children and with adults; formerly a consultant at the Tavistock Institute of Human Relations, she is currently teaching and practising in Oxford. She has a special interest in the care of children in institutions. A collected edition of her writings has been published by Free Association Books.

SHEILA MILLER is a Top Grade Child Psychotherapist and Clinical Tutor at the Tavistock Clinic. She has worked in Child Guidance Clinics in Essex and Hertfordshire and has a special interest in adoption and fostering and in the development of child psychotherapy outside London. She is currently organizing a course on 'Growing up in a Multi-Ethnic Society'.

GEORGE MORAN is the Director of the Anna Freud Centre, a child psychotherapist, and honorary reseach fellow at University College London. He is editor of the *Bulletin of the Anna Freud Centre* and has contributed to research on juvenile-onset diabetes and development psychopathology.

ELIZABETH MUIR is a New Zealand-trained child psychotherapist now working in Toronto, Canada, as a clinician and teacher in the C. M. Hincks Treatment Centre; she is also a member of the faculty of the C. M. Hincks Institute.

MARGARET RUSTIN, who is currently the elected head of the Child Psychotherapy Discipline in the Tavistock Clinic and Co-ordinating Tutor of the Clinical Training has worked in a number of National Health Service settings in London and has taught child psychotherapy in Italy and the United States. She is the author with Michael Rustin of *Narratives of Love and Loss* (Verio, 1987), and one of the co-authors of *Closely Observed Infants* (Duckworth, 1989).

ISCA SALZBERGER WITTENBERG, formerly a Top Grade Child Psychotherapist, is now a visiting teacher at the Tavistock Clinic, holds a Visiting Professorship at Turin University, and teaches in a number of countries in Europe and overseas. Previous publications include *Psycho-Analytic Relationships and Insight* (Routledge & Kegan Paul, 1970), *The Emotional Experience of Learning and Teaching* (Routledge & Kegan Paul, 1983), contributions to *Explorations in Autism,* edited by Donald Meltzer et al. (Clunie Press, 1975), and *The Child Psychotherapist and Problems of Young People,* edited by Dilys Daws and Mary Boston (Karnac Books, 1988).

ALAN SHUTTLEWORTH is a Principal Child Psychotherapist at Waltham Forest and Senior Clinical Lecturer in Social Work in the Child and Family Department of the Tavistock Clinic.

VALERIE SINASON is a Principal Child Psychotherapist at the Tavistock Clinic Day Unit and Child and Family Department, where she co-convenes the Mental Handicap Workshop. She is co-convenor of the Mental Handicap Section for the Association for Psychoanalytic Psychotherapy (APP) in the National Health Service and a member of the Child Abuse Research Group for the Association for Child Psychology and Psychiatry (ACPP). She is also a poet (*Inkstains & Stilettos,* Headland Press, 1987).

ROLENE SZUR was formerly Principal Child Psychotherapist at the Hospital for Sick Children, Great Ormond Street, and at the

Tavistock Clinic, where she is now a visiting teacher, and has also taught courses in Rome. She is co-editor with Mary Boston of *Psychotherapy with Severely Deprived Children* (Routledge & Kegan Paul, 1983) and contributed to *The Child Psychotherapist and Problems of Young People,* edited by Dilys Daws and Mary Boston (Wildwood House, 1977) and to *Child Abuse, the Educational Perspective,* edited by Peter Maher (Blackwell, 1987).

FRANCES TUSTIN is an international authority on autism and as a Child Psychotherapist worked for 30 years directly with autistic children. Before her retirement she was head of the Child Psychotherapy Department in the Child Guidance Training Centre at the Tavistock Clinic. She is an Honorary Affiliate of the British Psycho-Analytic Society and Honorary Member of the Association of Child Psychotherapists. Among her publications are *Autistic Barriers in Neurotic Patients* (Karnac Books, 1986), *The Protective Shell in Children and Adults* (Karnac Books, 1990).

GIANNA WILLIAMS, a Top Grade Child Psychotherapist in the Adolescent Department of the Tavistock Clinic and Organizing Tutor of the Observation Course, founded the Ethnic Minorities Workshop in 1984. She initiated and taught a number of Tavistock Model courses in Italy and one in Brazil. Previous publications include her contributions to books on child psychotherapy, severely deprived children, and emotional aspects of learning.

MARGARITA WOOD is a Principal Child Psychotherapist with a special interest in art, and she has contributed to *Art as Therapy,* edited by T. Dalley (Tavistock, 1984).

INTRODUCTION

Rolene Szur

This book brings together a wide range of issues in the field of psychotherapy with children, young people, and their families. A number of chapters focus on developments or special areas of clinical work and related theoretical or technical issues and concerns. One or two explore the application of psychodynamic understanding in fields other than the directly or indirectly clinical. (In reports on clinical work, care has been given to the protection of confidentiality, and all names of patients and families mentioned are pseudonyms.)

The growth and development of work of this kind, with children and families within the wider community, is founded on and deeply indebted to the pioneering work of the Child Guidance Clinics set up in earlier years and to the initiatives and discoveries of Anna Freud, Melanie Klein, and Margaret Lowenfeld during the 1930s and 1940s. Its history included the emergence of multi-disciplinary teams and the birth of the new discipline of child psychotherapy, with a *Journal of Child Psychotherapy* being founded during the 1950s. This provided a possibly unique local and international forum for presentations over a wide spectrum of professional interests and orientations within the fields of child and family psychotherapy. Contributions from psychoanalysts, psychiatrists, and psychologists and from medical practice have, over the years, helped to enrich the work and in this sense represented also a preservation of the multi-disciplinary concept. We are grateful to the Journal for the role it has played and for some of the material that we have included here.

It is hoped that the following chapters may offer other workers and students in the field some areas of interest in the current thinking and practice of psychoanalytic psychotherapy. These include developments that have helped to promote considerable flexibility of approaches and so enhanced the quality of professional responsiveness to the particular need or special problem as it is presented. The four chapters in part one, which describe varied clinical problems and their treatment, may serve to illustrate this.

Child psychotherapy, with its special focus on the individual inner world, and family therapy, with its principal focus on the environment of the family group, have in more recent years mutually sought and found ways of living together, though not always without difficulties. (It is tempting to reflect on how far the extent of these difficulties may have represented a certain polarization and re-enactment of the universal childhood conflicts involved in the struggle to find a proper balance between retaining the sense of individuality yet remaining within the family.) However, it is very heartening to find in chapters four and five many different lines of creative thinking and of clinical developments that have arisen out of these struggles.

Further, the psychoanalyst and family therapist, John Byng-Hall (1986), writing on his interesting concept of 'family scripts', comments on the need for child psychotherapists and family therapists to collaborate. It is his view that in some instances children who are not able to respond to family therapy may 'do dramatically well in child psychotherapy', and that family work in general may also provide 'a good launching pad' for individual psychotherapy with a child.

Although the use of the term 'psychotherapy' in this book assumes a common basis in a psychoanalytic orientation and training, it is interesting to note that among those who have trained as child psychotherapists there will be a number of former graduates from disciplines other than psychology, thus bringing experience from other professions, including social work, teaching, other arts and sciences, medicine, and law.

The part played by psychotherapy may vary from one case to another. In cases of mental and physical handicap and of child abuse, for example, while the roles of education and social work have generally been taken for granted for some time, it is only in more recent years that an increasing recognition of the major importance of these children's 'special needs' in terms of their internal worlds (Martin & Beezley, 1977; Lynch & Roberts, 1982; Boston & Szur, 1983) has begun to receive appropriate response.

The failure to recognize the relevance of mental and emotional understanding and support in some depth for mentally and physically handicapped children and young people has only fairly recently been remedied. (In fact, the Warnock Report, 1978, failed to mention this at all.) The neglect of this aspect has been particularly true of mental handicap, and chapter twelve provides some insights into the fears and anxieties that may underpin or intensify conditions of handicap. Increased recognition of cases of children suffering from seriously deprived or damaging family environments and of the need for psychotherapeutic help for them within the context of the social services, and for their families, has also led to a considerable increase of referrals in this area. The painful complexities of working with such children are discussed in part four, under the heading, 'Deprivation and Damage'.

In terms of the 'treatment approaches' described in part one, the most traditional pattern of psychoanalytic psychotherapy is that presented in chapter one, insofar as it represents a 'one-to-one relationship' with the patient, who is attending intensively—that is, more than once or twice a week—and in this is also most closely linked with what is standard psychoanalytic practice. However, fresh theoretical explorations and insights that are introduced into the nature and quality of the psychotherapeutic alliance and its development in both therapist and patient over time bring a new dimension to this case study.

While the work of child psychotherapists continues to be mainly with individual children, a number of new modalities have entered into the technical resources of the discipline, many of which are described here. This has happened partly in response to new settings and situations in which psychoanalytic understanding of both group and individual relationships could be appropriately brought together. This is most immediately evident in working with the family group, and many fertile developments in these terms are illustrated and discussed in part one.

Another important development that has been considerably extended is working within the context of the group in institutional settings, such as schools and hospitals, for example (Hartnup, 1986), as well as within the professional network and the circle that consists of 'the referrers and the referred' themselves, which may also constitute a group of its own (Dyke, 1987). The theoretical thinking about and the structuring of such work is outlined by Isobel Menzies Lyth in chapter twenty-three.

A further direction in which advances are currently being made is psychoanalytically informed work with small groups of children. This began partly in response to the need to extend precious resources and therefore with expedience in mind, but it has been found to be the method of choice with some children. This group work is being developed by Susan Reid, who considers that children who have problems in peer relationships benefit from work in a small group. Also for some children, in particular for children who lack early nurturing experience, it can initially feel too persecuting to be seen individually. A group experience, usually offered weekly for periods of up to one year or longer, can be a solution in itself, or it can be the prelude to individual psychotherapy. Group work with the siblings in a family is particularly useful in cases where the referred child is the focus for problems shared by all the siblings. Sibling group work is also undertaken with children who have experienced a shared trauma, such as bereavement or a murder in the family.

The overall developments taking place in the field of analytic psychotherapy have therefore included increasing extensions of theoretical and technical responses to the needs of children and young people, within the specific areas of environmental stress and damage, and to those with physical or mental disability and disease. Simultaneously, considerable initiatives and developments have been taking place in the theory and practice of working with families in terms of psychoanalytic understanding, as discussed in chapters three and four. Widespread interest in Wilfred Bion's thinking on groups has been addressed to understanding and responding to problems arising in institutional settings.

Together with an increasing application and confidence in extending along these paths, there has also been a vigorous movement to bring psychoanalytically oriented work further into the area of research and to design new ways of doing so that are appropriate to the complexities of psychoanalysis, while taking into account the more standard models of scientific investigation. The final chapters, therefore, present fresh thinking in terms of theoretical approaches and original designs for undertaking further research.

While it is thus the concluding section that is devoted specifically to theory and research, this does, we hope, express the important theme that clinical work, theory, and research need to be understood in terms of a creative interaction. In this sense all clinical work may be read not only as offering a live history of the progress of an individual or a family, but as a shared journey of discoveries.

PATIENTS, FAMILIES, AND TREATMENT APPROACHES

P art one focuses on the differing approaches or techniques that may be selected in response to the specific needs and circumstances presented by each referral. The chapters include, therefore, examples of individual work with a child or patient, work with a family, and combinations of these. There are also examples of short-term treatment programmes that are available for troubled adolescents, one case of the indirect treatment of a young child via his mother, and a description of the ways in which exploratory procedures with families may be linked to the therapeutic process.

[R.S.]

PATIENTS, FAMILIES, AND TREATMENT APPROACHES

CHAPTER ONE

Intensive child psychotherapy: working with Matthew towards understanding

Alan Shuttleworth

This opening chapter is an account of intensive long-term psychotherapy with a young child. In this sense it offers an example of the classical experience of psychoanalytic child psychotherapy from which so many of the developments described in later chapters have sprung. The boy, Matthew, referred to the clinic in his sixth year, was thus attending during the period of his latency years and was, in terms of age, therefore, representative of a major group of child referrals. (The children presented in the following chapters by Erna Furman and by Elizabeth Muir were also seen during different phases of latency development.)

Matthew was referred with severe learning difficulties, but eventually he did very well at school. Of special interest in this study are the theoretical and clinical issues that are explored as the therapist struggles to find a way to the child, and eventually to consider how far he had been failing to think 'with' the child and thinking 'at' him instead.

[R.S.]

In this chapter I try to give a picture of what sort of experience psychoanalytical child psychotherapy is for patient and therapist. The case I describe was intensive; at the beginning, the child came five times a week. The experience of such intensive treatment is not fundamentally different from that of the more common once- or twice-weekly therapy. It is simply that intensive therapy gives patient and therapist alike more time together in which to explore the patient's feelings, and a more intimate sense of contact characteristically develops as a result. The general points I make in this chapter about the experience of child psychotherapy apply as much to the one form as to the other.

Of course, this is not an account of child psychotherapy in general. It is an account of the work of a Kleinian child psychotherapist who has been influenced by the work of Bion—or, to be more accurate, of someone who was then a rather inexperienced Kleinian child psychotherapist, beginning to experience the enormous impact of Bion at the same time he was also feeling the impact of the particular child, Matthew, whose therapy is described in the second half of this chapter. I put it in this way not to disown the therapist I was then, but, rather, to express an identification with him. His, at times, clumsy stumbling towards understanding a particular child, with the help and sometimes hindrance of changing ideas, is for me what going on thinking is like. Different child psychotherapists would have approached Matthew with different initial ideas. I hope to have written in a way that may nevertheless convey something general about the experience of child psychotherapy.

Child analysts and therapists have, on the whole, emphasized the continuities between child and adult work and have demonstrated similar emotional processes at work in both. This has borne a great fruit of understanding. I hope this chapter will also convey the flavour of the difference. For the conversation of adult with child is different from that of adult with adult. Though intensely serious because it is a way of bringing relief to suffering, it is also true that, like many encounters between an adult and a child, its unavoidable off-balance lop-sidedness gives child psychotherapy a certain inherent comedy as well.

The human studies

It was a major achievement of the British object-relations school of psychoanalysis that it has become possible to see clearly that psychoanalysis needs to be grasped, not only through its links to natural science, but also as part of a broad humane tradition of inquiry into human experience (Winnicott, 1971; Milner, 1957; Rycroft, 1968). It is linked most closely, perhaps, to the novel, the portrait, and other arts, as well as to a certain kind of history, anthropology, and sociology, in which the sense of life being lived, with different presences and voices, is recovered. This recovery is not achieved through processes characteristic of the natural sciences. A different sort of study, dependent on a strong, lively interest in this aspect of the world, is required. A source of evidence must be found which allows some access to the lived experience of the person(s) we are studying. A particular method, such as the study of primary sources in history, needs to be brought to bear in order to allow close attention to be paid to the fine details of particular human situations. This needs to have at its centre sensitivity to emotional experience and a capacity for identification. Characteristically such study involves a phase of being immersed in and overwhelmed by the complexity of encountering some actual bit of life. Understanding grows out of this kind of immersion. The reliance on this distinctive sort of study has tended to mark off psychoanalysis and the other human studies from their natural science neighbours.

In some of the human studies—in history, for example—the attempt is to understand the lives of others at a distance: what we can then achieve is to *think about* them. In psychoanalytic work, in contrast, the effective thinking is done in their presence. It is a collaborative process. When it goes well, therapist and patient *think with* each other; otherwise they *think at* each other. It is the story of my collaborative thinking with one child and its vicissitudes that I hope to convey—how we moved from a situation where I was often thinking at him to one where we were sometimes thinking together.

Thinking, phantasy,
and new emotional experience

Thinking, collaborative or otherwise, is not the only thing that goes on in psychoanalytic inquiry and certainly not in child psychotherapy. Following, in the main, Bion's work, one can say that three different kinds of mental process are encountered in the therapy room—*thinking, phantasy,* and *emotional experience.* Different kinds of communication between patient and therapist are associated with each.

First, there is *thinking,* referred to by Freud as the *secondary process;* the work of the *ego* in attending to and getting to know the world, discriminating what is real from what is wished or feared. This conscious waking thought, deliberate empirical inquiry, is referred to by Bion (1962) as *K,* by which he means the process of getting to know something, as *attention* and *inquiry,* and as *Reason.* What is distinctive about psychoanalytic inquiry is that, having made a commitment in common with many other approaches to try to offer help to those experiencing emotional disturbance, it sets out with no other means than the determination to go on thinking about feelings. We will see in Matthew's case that there was a long period when no thinking seemed possible. This was followed by another long period in which thinking was only allowed if it kept well away from feelings and experiences. In the end he agreed that we should 'go on—with thinking'. Such thinking characteristically speaks in its own prose voice.

Freud's central discovery was that a different kind of mental process, *powerful primitive phantasy, generated in early life, driven by instinctual forces, subject to the 'primary process',* makes a continuous, often unconscious, dominating contribution to all mental life. Freud's main thrust was to show that such phantasy, under the rule of hallucinatory wish-fulfilment, continuously threatened reason with subversion. Klein argued that the emotions of very early life give rise to phantasy and phantasied *objects.* These objects are real presences, continuously affecting all our awareness of things. In Matthew's case, for instance, his play about savage biting animals—a horse in an

early session, a wolf–dog and a machine–mouth in a later one—
seems to be an attempt to represent a phantasy of this kind.
Klein argued that a mostly unconscious, phantasied *internal
world,* inhabited by *internal objects,* is generated as part of the
process of early individual development. It dominates our psychosomatic state and, through projection, all our apprehension
of and thinking about the world. The psychoanalytic framework
is designed precisely to receive the speech of this dimension of
the mind. Freud argued that dreams were its clearest speech. In
psychoanalysis its voice is sought through free association; in
child psychotherapy, through free play.

Bion has helped us see more clearly that new emotional
experience continuously pours like a tide into whatever mental/
emotional containers thinking and phantasy have created. The
process of receiving fresh experience and the feelings it generates
may be said, in Bion's (1962) account, to be the third major
dimension of mental life encountered in the therapy room. He
goes on to argue that such experience may be mentally/emo-
tionally *digested,* or it may remain *undigested.* It is digested, he
argues, when the existing containers of reason and phantasy are
able to expand to receive the new experience and follow its con-
tours. In this process experience and feelings are imaginatively
transformed, so that images with a sense of intimacy, life, feeling, and truth are created. Where this occurs, there is a sense of
play, of lateral thinking, of a free-floating conversation developing, following an unplanned course, throwing up an unexpected
image that gathers things together.

Where the experience is, in some way, too disturbing for this
to happen, it may get stuck in the mind in an undigested form.
One thinks of survivors of disasters who are stuck with an
experience they cannot absorb, where memory rewinds and
rewinds the events and overwhelming feelings seem stuck. Disturbing undigested experiences may become linked in complicated ways (that differ from creative transformation) with
primitive phantasies to produce powerful unconscious ag-
glomerations, centres of turbulence. When these feel overwhelming, they may generate panic, resisting and disrupt-
ing conscious thought, creative imaginative transformation,

and emotional digestion. Rigid pathological defensive structures may develop to keep their disruptive force under control.

In Matthew's case, it seems likely that he did not have an early environment that would have helped him digest very early shocks he received. A rigid defensive structure was put in place instead. When he came to therapy, one of the concerns was that he seemed to have no way of emotionally digesting current experiences.

A primitive form of communication—*projective identification*—is seen as the way in which the mind tries to rid itself of and/or communicate to others such disturbing undigested emotional states. Projective identification is their speech. It is argued that such states of mind and feeling are somehow directly pushed into other people. Thus there are recipients of such states as well as transmitters. Emotional atmospheres are generated and received. The recipient's own mental and emotional state is directly affected below the level of conscious awareness and may produce impulsive acting-out if not understood. When it is understood, the process can be grasped as a form of communication in which the receiver is being made to feel directly something of the communicator's experiences.

A conversation of different voices

There are different dimensions to the mind with different kinds of speech. Psychoanalysis studies the 'conversation'[1] among these voices. If the individual feels that a setting (a conversation, a collaboration, or a container, to use Bion's term) is available to him or her, externally or internally, which has the width and generosity to include these different kinds of voice and so expand and change in response to them, then rigid defences against the disruptive power of undigested experience and phantasy can be relaxed. Frightening centres of feeling can then be released into a conversation that is able to bear the pressures generated by the meeting of straightforward thinking, primitive phantasy, and disturbing emotional experience. Within conversations that have this sense of a receptive space, creative imaginative transformation of a kind that aids the growth of an individual sense of meaning may occur. Psychoanalytic inquiry aims to study, and offers assistance in nurturing, the capacity for such internal conversation.

This is a difficult task, since the voices speak in different languages or modes. Each has radically different ways of constructing reality. It is as if only one were really like a voice talking, one more like a dance than a voice, and another more like a fight than either. All are struggling within a strange communication. The psychoanalytic psychotherapist tries to enter into this complex communication, bringing his voice into it, with its own language and registers. We will see in the material presented that, at the beginning, a dream-like play seems to develop under its own pressure, separate from me, brushing against my thinking voice, making some use of what I say to develop itself. Later we see a ritualization of the sessions, both defensive and celebratory, seizing on the repetitiveness of my thinking voice to enfold it within its rites. Later still, a war is taking place, with an explosive, expulsive force, intent on the demolition of all traces of thinking. Later again, a thinking voice joins a conversation with mine, on strict condition that both voices avoid precisely those registers that are able to open out into talk of feelings and internal matters. Only late in the therapy will a conversation take place that allows a fluid movement between various voices. These processes of thinking together emerge out of a background that has been less like a conversation and more like a tragi-comic stumbling, bumping into and missing each other.

Bion has helped to clarify the way this conversation within the mind itself comes under attack. This clumsy, backwards-and-forwards, aproaching-and-evading, bumping-and-barging process of conversation generates anxiety because its complexity, and the incoherence from which it starts, is alarming. It also causes anxiety since the experiences with which the conversation is struggling to deal are themselves disturbing. Such anxiety may inhibit and attack thinking, leaving instead fragmented bits of what could have been coherent directions of thought. For example, for a long time Matthew told me nothing about his life outside. When he began occasionally to do so, I was not at first aware that this was happening. Such sessions would begin with a jumbled burst of talk emerging under pressure, in which we seemed to be in the middle of a situation that was never explained: fragmentary bits and pieces, whose connections I could not fully grasp, emerged from it and often seemed mixed up with fragments from his previous play in the room. The talk did not form into coherent wholes; it was like the broken bits of what would have been sentences and sometimes of what would have been words. I began to think that I was getting the bits of a whole account of something that had really happened to disturb him, broken up because the pressure of anxiety was too great. I began to say that I thought he was wanting me to know something had happened that had upset him a lot. In time, I thought he came to find that sort of comment helpful, and, gradually, more coherent accounts of real experiences began to emerge.

What Winnicott (1960) called a *holding capacity* and Bion (1962) *containment* helps individuals sustain themselves through such experiences. It leads to growth and enables them to gather a conversation out of such fragments. Such containment depends on bringing together in a fruitful way intellectual capacities that are in the service of truth and emotional capacities for affection, concern, and care. In infancy and childhood such containment is primarily provided by real parental care, which may be internalized and lead to the growth of a containing capacity within the child's own mind. It seemed that Matthew was someone whose parents had, at a crucial time, not been able to provide the containment he needed. Instead of his experiences being understood and modulated by them, he had felt flooded with theirs and responded by 'switching off', trying to become rigid to shut out experience, feelings, and thinking.

Recent work by child psychotherapists in the Kleinian tradition, influenced particularly by Bion, Bick, and Meltzer, has stressed the importance of recognizing projective identification as a form of emotional communication. Recognizing rigid defensive structures against primitive catastrophic anxiety, attending to the question of containment, and recognizing disturbances of thinking have deepened therapeutic work with children. This has led to an enormous expansion in the range of children seen for psychoanalytic psychotherapy well beyond the confines of the supposedly traditional 'verbal, insightful', neurotic child—for instance, autistic children (Tustin, 1972, 1981, 1986; Meltzer, 1975), severely deprived children (Boston & Szur, 1983), and mentally handicapped children (Sinason, 1986). These ideas have not only helped in the therapy of children unable to talk about their feelings or engage in symbolic play, they have also thrown new light on the particular world opened by any attempt to think with children about their feelings.

It is a strange, often uncomfortable domain, in some ways different from that opened up in work with adults on that same task. It is often a world of apparent indifference to the adult-defined task of thinking. Compelling, evocative images may be produced in the course of play or drawing, but the child may seem quite unwilling to think with the therapist about their meaning. All the time, there is the evoking of moods, atmospheres, climates of thought and feeling 'in the room' and in the therapist. The child psychotherapist attempts to approach the middle of this always complex, often fragmented conversation/dance/warfare that is taking place within the child and to bring a sustained interest and a capacity for attention and thought to bear on the task of unravelling it. It is both the sheer amount of sustained interest and attention that the child psychotherapist brings and the single-mindedness of the commitment to *think* with the child about what is going on in the child's feelings that characterizes child psychotherapy. Out of this, over time, shared collaborative thinking between adult and child grows.

Use and abuse of theory

What primarily characterizes psychoanalytic work, as Bion clarified this, is not that it brings a distinctive body of theory to bear on the same things that are explained by others more straightforwardly. What it has introduced is a new instrument of observation, something like the microscope, which allows a particular dimension of reality to be seen and thought about more clearly, in a more sharply focused and sustained way than was possible before. This area of interest is individual emotional experience. The 'microscope' is the psychoanalytic setting, a fixed time in which, without interruption, the psychotherapist can focus with the patient entirely on the task of thinking about the patient's feelings. Within this setting an immersion in the complexity and detail of a particular life can occur. It is the argument of psychoanalysis that the processes of observation and thought by which we ordinarily understand one another, when brought to bear through this particular microscope, reveal extraordinary phenomena. The accumulated study of these phenomena has generated the complex, articulated framework of understanding and theory that now exists.

The theory throws light on this strange, uncomfortable domain. However, when it is theory we have in our minds rather than the patient, we will see theory through the microscope and not the patient. We may feel we are ahead of the patient and end up thinking *at* him or her. In contrast, when it is the patient we have in mind, we may endeavour to follow into their world and be able to begin thinking *with* them. The theory may then be illuminating. Bion has drawn attention to the dangers of using theory in omnipotent ways that distance us from the patient and from the task of collaborative thinking that is the *raison d'être* of the work.

In much of psychoanalytic psychotherapy we are trying to gather the points of maximal coherence of meaning. The danger lies in isolating such moments of achieved coherence from the non-understanding and active misunderstanding that surround them, out of which they have emerged. Accounts of such moments often have something of a magical, effortless quality to them. To try to write an account that avoids this danger, however, is difficult. No one relishes presenting their clumsiness or over-theoretical anticipations of meaning or slowness. However, that is what I shall attempt here. My intention is not to sum up my understanding of Matthew, nor to focus on the content of what I said. It is, rather, the emergence of our collaborative thinking out of earlier vicissitudes during which something else was going on that I want to attend to. In this way I would like to throw light on what sort of thing the therapy was, the experiences it held for Matthew, and the stumbling, anxious, humbling experiences it held for me.

MATTHEW

Referral

Matthew was referred for a consultation aged 5½, with serious difficulties. There seem to have been signs of autistic features at some stage, though these were no longer clearly to be seen during the therapy itself. I saw him for six years—five times a week for the first three, tapering off to once a week by the end.

Before going any further with what Matthew would often have said was my 'usual gibberish', I feel I should let him have his own say first. One of the things I learnt from him, painfully and slowly, was to gather my thoughts together into a statement only after first submitting, for much longer than I liked, to listening to him, endeavouring to think my way step by step into his point of view. On good days towards the end of therapy he sometimes said that part of him did love therapy. But earlier he would also, I think, have wanted me to quote him as saying, 'Look, just shut up, don't ask any more stupid questions, sit still and listen', and 'When can I stop coming? I hate coming. It's so boring. It's been five years. It's nearly half my life, you know.'

He was referred just before starting formal schooling because there was acute anxiety as to whether he could function in an ordinary school. Speech development was slow, and he never made spontaneous conversation. At 'news time' in the nursery he repeated the same sentence week after week. For a long time he screamed if he wanted anything, but eventually he learnt to ask, though using single words, not sentences. His hand control was poor, and his resultant frustration would lead to screaming and banging. His painting was very immature, but he had good visual perception, he was good at puzzles, and he had a normal concept of number for his age.

We learnt about lapses into long periods of 'withdrawal' at home, accompanied by a tendency to stare into space. 'He has difficulty in starting a sentence in answer to a simple question and will repeat "I was . . . I was . . . um . . . um" while trying to concentrate on what the question was and then just withdraw.' He would also hold food in his mouth for long periods. Withdrawal also showed over major external events such as his birthday, or a visit to the circus. He would neither anticipate them with excitement nor remember them with interest. In summary, he was referred because of a difficulty that inhibited learning, communicating, feeling, and thought.

Matthew had a brother three years older, who had no serious difficulties. His mother, largely overwhelmed by and overwhelming with her many anxious preoccupations, moved quickly from one worry to another. Father was overshadowed. Matthew had been born with the cord twice around his neck and had a forceps delivery, followed two weeks later by minor surgical intervention. During his first year mother's eyes had required bandaging for lengthy periods when she suffered recurring eye ulcers. The family were under acute external and financial stress during this whole period. When Matthew was about four, his adenoids were removed—his parents thought this had corrected serious earlier hearing loss.

Clear diagnostic assessment on this evidence is not easy. It may well be that intense parental anxiety, particularly acute during Matthew's infancy, was an important contributory factor. A degree of early deafness alone would not, I think, have caused his overall developmental difficulties but may have been an important factor, making his very early traumas less digestible and thus exacerbating developmental problems. Whatever the contributory factors, major pathological defensive reactions seem to have ensued, with obsessional mechanisms used to bring things so rigidly under control that many areas of emotion and mental life were seriously inhibited.

There was great anxiety that when he started school he would be unable to learn, and, indeed, for about the first three years of therapy, his rate of learning remained painfully slow, falling further and further behind his peers. At the heart of what happened in the therapy was that Matthew gradually made me feel the enormous force of whatever it was in him that was resistant to learning, so that I felt impotent in the face of it. It was through weathering that experience of feeling defeated that I began to learn how to learn from Matthew. As I did so, he began to improve; we were able to think together, and he showed increasing signs of being able to learn. He made me aware of the crushing force of his learning difficulty: more than this, he made me *have* his learning difficulty. I had to become an impossibly slow learner if I was really to know what it was like to be Matthew. I had good warning this was in store for me when, in the first year of therapy, we had this interchange:

'You're a dumbhead, Mr Shuttleworth.'

'What's a dumbhead?' I asked.

'It's because your head's been split.'

'What splits it?' I asked.

'Oh shut up, you're stupid, you're a dumbhead. . . . You're the most dumbhead I've ever seen. . . . You'll never grow up and go to secondary school.'

I would like to convey a sense of the overall pattern of six years of therapy, which began about a year after the initial referral, by dividing it roughly into a number of stages. I hope in this way to show the turmoil of the therapy. We will see Matthew getting better and also see him move from being essentially a pre-latency child through a kind of latency onto the threshold of adolescence.

Stage one:
brushing against my thinking

In the first three weeks of therapy there was a flow of extraordinary, vivid material that communicated, I thought, an urgent preoccupation with trying to achieve the imaginative transformation both of very early experience and of current anxieties. My experience of the thinking relationship between us in relation to this flow of material was that Matthew needed to make a statement, perhaps in order to get this material out of his mind and into mine. His main use of my interventions seemed to be to construe them as encouragements or discouragements to go on with this flow. They led to brief moments of us thinking together about the material that was emerging, but the overall feeling was of my receiving a flow rather than thinking collaboratively together.

In the very first session there was this: 'When I was nought, I was in my Mummy's tummy. It was dark. I was eaten by an animal. I was bitten by it. It was a horse.' In the fourth session of that week, Matthew again referred to being nought and being in Mummy's tummy in the dark. He then enacted this scene with the toys. The horse pressed its head down onto the boy who was lying on the ground, and Matthew had a squeezing murderous look on his face. The boy was saying pathetically, 'Oh, please don't eat me. . . .' The horse did the same to the baby with a more murderous feeling, and it seemed the baby had been squeezed to death. The Mummy said, 'Don't do that', as if the horse had been mildly naughty. The Daddy doll then told the horse off, in a similarly mild way, but the horse pressed its nose hard into the Daddy's genitals with the same squeezing murderous look on Matthew's face. I said, 'There's a wish for the Mummy and Daddy to be able to stop the dangerous horse, but there's also a worry about whether they are really strong enough to do it.' At this point he put the horse back into the farm pen and turned to repetitive play with the bricks and the car.

In the third week of the therapy, he made a tower out of bricks, with a staircase up the side. He stood the cow on the top of the tower and, in a voice that I took to be the cow's, commented tremulously on how tall it was, how high up. Earlier he had seemed attentive when I made an interpretation about a greedy baby Matthew wanting to be king of the castle. I said, 'I think this is about the baby Matthew lying on the floor looking up at Mummy's face and Mummy's breasts and wishing to be up there but feeling they're a long way away.' He then enacted a scene in which the cow was very frightened about being so high up and in the dark. A reassuring camel who seemed to be a Daddy came up, calmed her, and led her down carefully. I started to make an interpretation about the baby Matthew and he interrupted me to say, 'No, the baby Mummy!' I said, 'You are telling me that baby Matthew was afraid that Mummy on her own was a baby Mummy who was frightened, who couldn't see in the dark. The baby Matthew felt it was all right while Daddy was there; Daddy would look after Mummy. But what would happen to baby Matthew if Daddy was not there, if he was on his own in the dark with a frightened Mummy?' 'I don't know', he replied. Daddy went on top of the tower to show it was safe.

Stage two:
ritual enfolds thinking

There was a growing ritualization of the sessions, which developed its fullest form by the middle of the first term and lasted into the middle of the second year. The routine was a developing one that could, from time to time, respond to events in the room that took his fancy and fold them into the pattern, while other bits got dropped. It was a way of penetrating the room in a way that will, I think, become clear.

At its most elaborate the ritual went something like this: Matthew would assemble a four-sided farm pen and put two animals into it, not always the same two but always of different species. He would then turn to the bricks. At first they would be placed around the pen in a formal pattern of some kind. They would then emerge from that pattern and sometimes be said to constitute a train of big bricks, with little bricks on top as passengers that travelled round the pen, looking at the animals or being licked by them. When it was a train it became a means of travelling further afield in the room. For a long time a tower of big bricks was arranged in a special colour sequence and then transferred in the same order to a small table-top. They would then be transferred to the table by the window, and here it was vital to carry them *en bloc* and spill them with a clatter. At one period, they were then given 'a jolly good stir' and, with a rhythmic chant, dismissed one by one by a strict Daddy/teacher voice punishing the naughty children. The pen and animals were re-assembled on top of the filing cabinet by the window ledge. Matthew was now at 'home'.

Once there, he had a repertoire of things he could play. One consisted of rhythmically chanting, 'I'm the king of the castle, get down you dirty rascal'. By the middle of the first term this routine also included a visit along the corridor to the toilet at some point before he reached the window ledge. The routine also always included a visit to the beaker of water I'd provided for a drink. The whole routine would take about twenty minutes to perform. For a period there was also a shorter ending ritual.

Looking at this routinization from the point of view of collaborative thinking, what chiefly strikes me is that its primary function was not to communicate something to me so that we could think together about it, but to enable him to *be* something in the room: at the beginning, to be safe; later on, to be in control.

On bad days, when Matthew seemed subdued, listless, depressed, the function of the ritualized play, particularly with the bricks, seemed dispiritingly anti-thinking. There was no opening towards thinking together in those sessions I was able to perceive. I became aware these were bricks he was playing with—objects with minimal intrinsic meaning—rather than dolls or animals. He was unwilling to talk around the play. Sometimes in such sessions there would be listless, endlessly repetitive play with the bricks. On good days, when he was in a lively mood, Matthew could enjoy interpretations about the routine, happily agree to them, and incorporate them with delight. For instance, I soon found myself repeating the interpretation that he wanted to make a good safe place that stayed the same. He liked the interpretation and wanted to include it in the routine, and if I did not say it, being reluctant to repeat myself, he would cast anxious glances at me and sometimes say, 'You aren't saying anything.' When I did say it, I was conscious of a repetitive quality of intoning a litany and his enjoyment of this. After a holiday break we began in this way, and he exulted, 'You said same, same, same, same, same . . .' In other words, Matthew has perceived that my thinking ('my usual gibberish') was a part of me. He welcomed it, not because it was thinking that he could join in, but because of its constancy, which was (at this stage) welcomed.

Stage three:
attacking thinking

There was gradually mounted what I came to experience as a terrific attack on my thinking. This led to a mounting tension in me and to a period of intense mutual persecution, in which my sadism as well as his was provoked. Part of a mid-week session from the third term of therapy illustrates this. He was late. In the waiting room his mother handed me a letter about a forth-coming session they would miss. As I was reading it in the therapy room, Matthew stood in front of me and said in a strict voice, 'Read the letter! Think!' I said he was being a Daddy Matthew, speaking to a silly little boy me. Matthew began to sing in a chanting way, 'Now I'm fifty, coming on sixty. Now I'm sixty, coming on seventy . . .'. He started to count: 'Lon, loo, lee, lor, live . . .', up to 'lenty-leven'. I said I thought he was turning ordinary thoughts about numbers, about times of sessions and dates of holidays, into secret nonsense.

He went to the toilet and, as he often did, hummed behind the door, mimicking the effort of defecation, 'la–ah–ah–ah'. Back in the room, he lay sprawled along the window ledge, looking out in a dreamy state. At one point he opened and closed the window with his teeth. He found a cigarette stub and some ash in the ashtray. He tipped these out of the window, chanting, 'Barber . . . Barber . . . Barber'. I said I thought he was tipping the traces of a Mummy or Daddy who brought other children to see me out of the window. He began to perform what he once referred to as his 'band', and it was clear this was done to distress me. He sat on the window ledge, banging his heels on the metal radiator cover, noisily opening and shutting the window, chanting, 'Ah! Ah! Ah! Ah!' The noise, with which I was familiar, was deafening and piercing.

He repeatedly spat into the ashtray and held it upside down, so that the spit dripped to the floor. He took a drink and drib-bled that into the ashtray and onto the floor. At one point he stopped to try to tie up his shoe-lace, which he found difficult. I said he spent a little bit of time in the ordinary world, saying ordinary things and learning to do ordinary things like tie up his shoe-laces, but most of the time he spent in a special secret world where he was boss. I was interrupted by his cry of 'shut-up!' and he began singing raucously, 'One man went to mow . . .'. He continued all the way to ten men went to mow, though he had difficulty counting back from the higher numbers.

As he tipped the wastepaper bin upside down, I saw with regret that a plastic cup from the coffee machine and a newspaper had been left inside. He said, 'It wasn't an accident, I did it on purpose, you're not listening and I won't listen'. I said, 'You want to turn the therapy thoughts into rubbish like poos. You want to spit the therapy thoughts out of your mouth and poo them out of your bottom.' He cut up the plastic cup and threw the pieces towards the door. One hit me in the eye and hurt considerably. He said, 'I didn't mean to hit you in the eye, I'm sorry.' He shredded the newspaper and scattered it over the floor.

Reflecting now, I do not have much quarrel with the content of these interpretations (although, in this session, I failed to get hold of the fact that he felt dropped by me in relation to the special communication I received from his mother about missing a session). I do find myself uneasy with the feelings that attach to them. I think one can detect these attitudes:

1. a desire to make and insist on interpretations of a kind I already have in mind before the session begins because of my previous experience with him and because of my theories;
2. anxiety in the face of Matthew's feelings, which makes me want to use interpretations to seize what is happening and control it because I am afraid that, otherwise, the therapy will tumble into a chaotic meaningless jumble;
3. a wish to use interpretations to hurt Matthew as he is hurting me.

Stage four:
the defeat of thinking?

It became increasingly clear to me that my sadism was provoked by these sessions. I would have liked to force my thoughts on him. His resistance to me/attacks on me were only heightened by this. There seemed no future I welcomed along that road, so, in effect, I at least partly withdrew from my insistence on trying to think. There was a long period, lasting on and off for nearly two years, in which I often felt his attack on my thinking had succeeded so that my capacity to think and pay full sustained attention to him were only present intermittently.

The material I would like to cite from this period of therapy concerns the state of his toy box. For the first year or so it had been tidy. It now became a sort of pudding. All the toys were regularly immersed in water play and dropped back into the box. The paper had all been shredded. A damp, smelly nest-pudding filled the box and was stirred, sometimes for an unendurably long time, until the toys he needed floated to the surface. He showed no frustration at this, no desire to look more systematically or cut through the mess.

This box is an image for the state of my mind at times during this period, and the stirring is an image of the only attempts I could mount to find meaning. At the worst moments I felt hopeless about my capacity as a therapist and that if Matthew's parents and my colleagues knew what was happening, they would withdraw their support. I felt Matthew had exposed my reliance on a rigid brick-like structure of cliches and preconceptions that I defended with rage. Without my theories I felt I was left with a useless inert pudding of a mind.

He frequently appeared vacant and mindless in the session. At other times he would enact long complicated stories with the toys for six or more sessions, involving prolonged repetitive chases, killings, rescues in which all sense of who was a goody and a baddy or stood for what quality was lost to me, and I could barely stand taking any of it in. When that happened, I found myself 'switching off', withdrawing attention, no longer trying to follow but thinking about something else of interest only to me. I felt I was betraying my calling.

Strangely, it was during this period that his parents began to report, in our termly meetings, signs of slow but steady improvement in Matthew. During this period, also, the massive ritualization of the sessions was gradually dropped. At that time I did not have a complete grasp of the sense I would now make of this whole experience: that is, that Matthew had succeeded in communicating to me by projective identification the nature of the problem that he was bringing. He had pushed his learning difficulty into me so powerfully that I experienced it vividly as my own. I had become, truly, a dumbhead Mr Shuttleworth. He found this helpful. Once that had happened, it seemed that learning could begin.

Stage five:
the growth of 'straightforward' thinking

By the third year of therapy, in some sessions, when I was able
to abandon not only the wish to make interpretations but also
the despair at my failure to do so, I was sometimes able to pay
sustained attention in a different, *disinterested* way, not self-
consciously as a psychotherapist but as an unusually interested
and attentive adult might to a child. When I was able to do this,
we were sometimes able to have brief conversations about what
he was doing, and for the first time in the therapy he would
sometimes refer to his life outside. These conversations were
only tolerable to him if they were absolutely non-interpretative
and without that quality that the novelist, Elizabeth Taylor
describes like this in *The Sleeping Beauty*: '[The boy] felt again
that the man was like a psychiatrist asking questions which
were really not those questions at all, but deeper ones.' I had to
stick to the facts as presented and show no desire to make anything deeper of them: he was, in my view, an accurate reader of
my intentions in this respect. Matthew seemed to require me at
this time to show I was willing to meet him on the ground of
straightforward thinking alone. These were the first really
enjoyable conversations we had. I was still anxious about where
this was going, whether this was therapy, but was more hopeful.

Stage six:
thinking together about his inner world

Matthew remained acutely sensitive for a long time to the question of whether I was willing to wait and listen for long enough
first and be 'disinterestedly interested' in understanding him. It
then began to be possible for our thinking together to go
beneath the surface and to deal with what he was feeling and for
him to feel that interpretations were sometimes in the service of
that process. Previously, any reference to feeling or thinking
had been drowned out by noise.

I would like to present material from a session of this kind
towards the end of the therapy, in which, for a time, Matthew

and I begin thinking creatively together about deeper things. In the course of this, two images (a *machine mouth* and a *whirlpool*) that seem important emerge.

He enacted a 'horror film' with the toys, and at the end of it, as at the end of a field trip at school, I was tested to see how attentive I had been. A 'wolf–dog' was pursuing, catching and savaging a 'man–monkey'—that is, when the man was attacked by the wolf–dog, a monkey seemed to appear out of his chest and run away. (These characters were familiar to us.) The monkey joined in fighting the wolf–dog and could also go back into the man and seemed, in doing so, to bring him back to life. The story ended with the monkey and the man together killing the wolf–dog. This was a much shorter and more comprehensible version of the interminable stories that had filled session after session previously. 'I'll finish it now', Matthew said, 'It's a short one today.'

He then asked me questions that required me to have observed closely and to think clearly about the meaning of small clues. I kept saying I was not sure of the answer. He wanted me to guess and was annoyed I would not. He would then explain what the clues to the correct answers were, and each time I could see that at my most alert I might well have got them right. I said I could see what he meant, and there were clues I had missed; it was not just a question of paying attention and looking to see all the time what was going on, it was also a question of thinking hard about what it meant. 'Yes, of course!' said Matthew.

At some point, he said the wolf–dog attacked the monkey and the man because he could not make out whether there was one monkey or two, and he felt annoyed he was being fooled. A little later he asked if I thought the wolf–dog was a goody or a baddy. I was not sure (having this recent explanation of his in mind). He was annoyed, telling me that of course he was a baddy because he killed the first monkey and the man. Again I was told off for not paying proper attention. I was struck by the contrast with the amoral quality of the earlier interminable stories in which all sense of who was good and bad was lost.

In this session, so far, he has begun with an imaginative theme that, in its preoccupation with a biting attack, echoes much of his previous material. He has required us to explore this in terms of straightforward thinking that stays on the surface. This has opened out quite interestingly into more general discussion about the qualities of that kind of thinking, such as close sustained attention and inference. It develops further, as we go on below, into a conversation that begins to explore the feelings connected with these images. It seems clear we are building on the previous communication by projective identification, which had dominated many difficult months. A conversation that includes within its span these very different aspects of mental functioning starts to unfold. My impression is that it was not any crucial interpretation of mine that led to the change; rather, it was more my capacity to bear not interpreting for a long period, to go on to show genuine interest in the surface of his conscious preoccupations and then respond once more in an interpretative way when he was ready.

He put the things back into the box and moved round restlessly. Taking a pair of scissors, he put the handles into his mouth so that the blades stuck out in front. He sat facing me, manipulating the handles with his tongue, so that the blades opened and closed. He made as if to cut his finger, opening and closing the scissors on it. He drank some water, apparently sucking it up along the blades of the scissors, making a throaty noise as he did so. He held it inside his mouth, with the scissors still in place, making a bubbling noise. As he went back to the table I asked if he was imagining anything as he drank and made these noises. (At one time such a question would have been anathema to him.) He indicated that he was not. I said I had noticed him doing something I had not seen before—that is, manipulating the scissors with his mouth to open and cut them on his finger. 'Like this?' He showed me again and said, 'I'll show you how I do it. I put my tongue underneath and then do this.' But as the scissors were back in his mouth I could not see what he was doing. He made the noises in his throat again and started to explain about it, but because of the scissors in his mouth I could not tell what he said. I said so, and he took them out, explaining, 'It needs petrol—no, water. Water is its petrol. When it makes that noise it's getting rusty and needs water. When it makes that other noise it's getting the water and it's not rusty then and it doesn't need any more for a while and can lie still.'

I commented that if water was its petrol then it was a kind of a machine. 'Yes', he said, 'a machine–mouth.' He carried on this game, backwards and forwards. I struggled to formulate an interpretation for what seemed to me to be crucial material, his imagination openly at work in what was clearly a central area for him. I said that he had explained it was a machine–mouth, needing water as its petrol to stop it getting rusty. I said it made me think of the wolf–dog, which used its teeth for biting and feeding just as the machine–mouth used the scissors for cutting and drinking. At first he shook his head in disbelief at this idea but then changed his mind and said, 'Yes, all right', as if there might be something in that. I reminded him of asking me if the wolf–dog was a goody or a baddy and my saying I was not sure. If the machine–mouth was similar to the wolf–dog, then the same question arose about the machine–mouth. Was *it* a goody or a baddy? The problem was: it might well be a baddy, just as he had said the wolf–dog was. But the wolf–dog had felt tricked. Suppose someone—the machine–mouth or the wolf–dog—needed to feed, needed water for his petrol, and yet felt it was dangerous or it might be tricked, it might feel it needed scissor–teeth to protect itself while it was feeding.

I felt this was an occasion when I needed to try to get hold of things, so I went on. I thought baby Matthew might have felt something like that. That feeding, drinking milk from Mummy, was dangerous. (He gave me a 'groan–groan' look.) In that case he might have needed a machine–mouth with wolf–dog scissor–teeth to protect him while he fed—because he had to feed. When he came here and I paid attention to what he was feeling and thinking, he felt he got something important from me, like a kind of feeding. Yet he felt this was dangerous, so he came here, too, with a machine–mouth with scissor–teeth to protect him-self by, for example, switching off, or never replying, or saying, 'Boring'.

He took me by surprise by responding in a way that felt like lateral creative thinking, producing what seemed to be a dream-image. He said, 'What I've been thinking about is what makes a whirlpool.' I asked about this, and he was reluctant to go on, saying he did not know why he was thinking about this, he just was. He did say his thoughts about whirlpools were that people get pulled down into them and killed and that in the TV series *Terrahawks* the spaceship comes up out of a whirlpool safely because it is a spaceship. I thought the whirlpool was important and perhaps was telling us what a baby, say, might feel was dangerous in feeding: that the milk might have a whirlpool that would suck the baby down. An ordinary baby couldn't survive, so it would need to become a machine–mouth, spaceship–mouth, strong and powerful with controls, to survive. Initial scepticism was followed by, 'You mean the milk's like a kind of sea, so there's a whirlpool in that.' I said, 'Yes.' Then, with a bit of excitement, he said, 'The baby could drink lots of milk coming up to the edges of the whirlpool, without going into the dangerous middle of it, and get really fat and then spit the milk out again'.

He asked if I thought it had been a horror film. I was not sure. He said it was, sort of. I said sometimes when he called it a horror film it was because everyone was killed. 'Or else it's about the born-baby and everyone trying to kill it throughout the film', said Matthew. I agreed with him that that was the other reason.

It seems clear an outsider might still feel I have my Kleinian theories but might also feel that these have now become for Matthew a manageable and even interesting and helpful part of the way I think. At the same time, I am interested for a sustained period in what Matthew is thinking, following him on his terms, before turning aside to my thoughts. Matthew, in turn, is willing to follow my thinking, which, he recognizes, is related to, but different from, his. He is now thinking in a lively way. We are able to think together in a conversation, and interesting, unpredictable things emerge which surprise us both.

Stage seven:
thinking together about worries

I conclude with material towards the end of therapy, when he was 12, when Matthew and I were thinking together about his feelings towards me in the room as connected to his feelings about his life outside. By this time he had already shared with me the terrible painfulness of being mocked by others, particularly children of his own age, for being a 'dumbhead'. This painful experience, which had for so long been forcibly projected into me, was now often owned as his own.

He came in explosively angry with me and began to go on about stupid, boring therapy and wanting to stop. This was very familiar before and after holiday breaks but not usual in the middle of term. I said I thought something must have happened that had upset him. He was persistent that I answer why he had to come. Eventually I tried to frame an answer, stumbling hesitantly into it. 'Oh, can't you just get on and answer, without all that thinking!' I said I wondered if he found it easy to answer difficult questions with someone standing over him, saying, 'Come on, answer, yes or no, now'. He answered, 'No, I suppose not. O.K., go on then—with thinking'. I did then manage to talk about the difficulty in learning he had when he started therapy. I reminded him how he had introduced and often used the phrase 'switching off' to describe the way he went absent in the sessions and linked this with the learning difficulties. There was some discussion about this, and he seemed more peaceful. He thanked me for answering his question. I said I was still wondering if something had happened to upset him.

He said, 'Well, something has upset me. We overslept this morning by twenty minutes, and so we missed the right bus and had to wait half an hour in the cold, and that made me angry. Another thing is that yesterday cross-country (which he loves) was cancelled, and we had to listen to music instead, and it was really boring. What's really upsetting me is that exams are starting on Monday, and they'll be going on all week. I'm bloody worried about it, you know. I'm always worried about exams. I don't know how I'll manage with all the exams in the future—O levels, A levels, Degree. I'm going to revise all weekend and get my parents to lock me in the sitting room, but I'm worried about those exams you can't revise for, like English. Writing a story or a description about something isn't too bad, but I'm hopeless about comprehension. The other thing is that I find it very hard to revise or do homework because I get bored all the time and keep wanting to play while I'm sitting there, supposed to be doing my homework.'

Later I heard from his parents that he did revise over the weekend, without the door being locked, and that he did quite well in the exams. The principal anxiety, which originally led to therapy, was whether he could learn and also whether he could communicate, want, feel, and think. The difficulty in learning has now become an anxiety that *he* can think, feel, and communicate about. He has continued to do quite well in his exams, and in other ways, too. He comes now occasionally when there is something he is particularly worried about that he wants to think about with me. After all, he has known me for a long time.

NOTE

1. The notion of a conversation is, I think, central to Bion's view of mental life. It does not perhaps become fully explicit until *A Memoir of the Future* (1990), written as a long internal conversation. The notion of a conversation, as distinct from a *causal chain* or a *system*, is the fundamental model of human interaction in the symbolic interactionist school of sociology: the argument is that the conversation/debate/struggle about the meaning to assign to things is the fundamental human process that takes on locally shaped, essentially unpredictable form.

CHAPTER TWO

Treatment-via-the-parent: a case of bereavement

Erna Furman

In contrast to the direct intensive work described in chapter one, this account introduces us to a treatment procedure that enables the child's mother to provide him with appropriate support and counselling during a period of particular stress. Both the general and the specific indications for this choice of

---

From the Cleveland Centre for Research in Child Development and the Department of Psychiatry, School of Medicine, Case Western Reserve University. This paper was presented to the Seattle Psychoanalytic Society in March 1977, and to the New York Psychoanalytic Society in January 1979, on the occasion of receiving the 1976 Heinz Hartmann award for the book, *A Child's Parent Dies* (New Haven: Yale University Press, 1974); it was published in the *Journal of Child Psychotherapy*, 7 (1981), No. 1, pp. 89–103, and is reprinted by permission. I am grateful to Steven's mother for her permission to publish this account of our work in the hope that it may benefit other bereaved children and parents. I am also indebted to Ms Lois D. Archer, Educational Director, and the teachers of the Hanna Perkins School for their help in our work.

treatment are outlined, together with a description of the child's progress over a period of some three years.

STEVEN

I n this chapter I portray three crucial years of Steven's development, from the time of his father's death—just prior to Steven's third birthday—up to the beginnings of latency at age 6. I focus on tracing how aspects of the father's illness, death, and the subsequent fatherless years affected Steven's development. He was helped by his mother, with whom I worked throughout this period in a weekly treatment-via-the-parent, and by the teaching staff of the Hanna Perkins Therapeutic Nursery School and Kindergarten, which Steven had attended since he was 3 ½ years old (Furman & Katan, 1969). The therapeutic work was based on the mother's and teachers' observations, augmented by my own weekly visits at the school.

Although we kept open the option of individual analysis for Steven, during this period of work we considered treatment-via-the-parent to be the treatment of choice, for several reasons: in spite of phase-appropriate difficulties, some neurotic manifestations, and a tendency to instinctual regression under stress, Steven maintained a progressive development. His defences had not calcified to the point of rigidity, nor had they been inadequate to binding his anxieties. Thus no serious inner obstacles interfered with access to his psychic life. The mother–child relationship was characterized by age-appropriate closeness and empathic mutual understanding as well as a shared knowledge of the past. Even at the height of distress at the beginning of our work, the mother functioned well in her parental role, and she was familiar with emotional development and its handling and keen on actively helping her boy. Aware of some of her weaknesses, she struggled valiantly to overcome them and largely succeeded. Apart from these more usual indications for treatment-via-the-parent, it seemed particularly important that, following the loss of the father, the mother–child relationship should not be interfered with by the introduction of an outsider—which the analyst inevitably is—unless it proved absolutely necessary.

Initial picture

Steven's mother contacted me about two weeks after the father's death, on her return with Steven from a brief stay with her family and just before Steven's third birthday. Her main concern was prophylactic, although Steven was showing some behavioural difficulties: he had recently become very afraid of aggressive people, especially a girl with whom he sometimes played, but, at other times he also provoked 'potential' aggressors, such as his older teasing cousin and their own gentle but huge dog. Steven had periods of getting 'high': excited, loud, and somewhat hyperactive, especially when visitors came to the home. This difficulty had preceded the father's death, and the mother had linked it then with times when she and her husband had tense arguments. Judging by their content, however, Steven's most recent 'high' episodes appeared also linked to experiences with a neighbour, a policeman who often had his police car with blaring radio parked near their house and who liked to regale the children on the street with excited accounts of his cop-and-robber activities. Further, Steven had started to withhold bowel movements and occasionally urine, a difficulty that had been much less in evidence during his toilet training a year earlier. There was occasional night wetting. Steven was also quite concerned about any separation from mother. We learned later that, occasionally and since about 18 months of age, Steven had suffered from *pavor nocturnus,* during which he could neither be woken nor be comforted. It usually started with his crying in distress and walking towards the door that led to the bathroom, but sometimes he ended up rocking on his rocking horse. He always wet himself at these times either before, during, or after leaving his bed. He had no memories of these episodes, and neither original onset nor current occurrences could be linked to known events.

In general, however, Steven appeared age-appropriately developed in the early phallic phase, bright and very verbal.

History

Steven is his young parents' first and only child, and the mother eagerly looked forward to his arrival. The father, in spite of a successful professional career and loving relationship with his wife and son, struggled with a self-destructive depressive illness. The mother learned that he had been quite depressed before she had known him, but she became aware of his difficulty only during Steven's first year and, increasingly, in the latter part of Steven's second year. Periodic bouts of withdrawal coupled with misuse of alcohol and drugs showed at times of stress. To Steven the father's illness manifested itself at first in sleeping, not being available when Steven wanted him, not responding to him, and, occasionally, in teasing. By the time Steven was two, the mother realized the seriousness of the father's illness. At that time she also had to undergo a breast operation for removal of what turned out to be a benign tumor. It was a period of great anxiety plus several days of physical separation from Steven, the only one he experienced. The grandmother cared for Steven and noted his overt sadness and listlessness in spite of many phone and gift contacts with the mother. But he felt immediate relief when mother returned. Steven's third year was chaos as father's health deteriorated, unalleviated by psychiatric treatment, which he reluctantly accepted but never utilized. Mother never knew when or in what state father would return home, whether she might be called to pick him up at work, or whether they would have to cancel and change all plans if he was not well. Although the parents tried strenuously to protect Steven from the impact of the father's illness and from their quarrels about it, the tension mounted. Mother, who tended to be loud, angry, and controlling when very anxious, felt that Steven often bore some of the brunt of her mood. She tried to discuss her trouble with him but could not alter her behaviour. She finally decided to get a divorce.

The mother told Steven only that he and she would, the next day, go for a short vacation to his aunt's family. When she informed the father of her wish for a divorce and plans to leave town, he reacted with an irrational fit of fury in which he bodily threw her against the wall. Steven watched the scene and pleaded with father to leave Mummy alone. At that point the mother decided to leave with Steven at once, 'to go to grandma to be safe'. While they were getting ready the father, demented, threw furniture and houseware into the street, as if to get rid of wife and child, while Steven anxiously yelled at him to spare his and Mummy's things. The paternal grandmother came to stay with the father, and his doctor was informed, but Steven did not know that. The next day, when the mother returned alone for some of her belongings, she found the father dead, called the police, and, since she had to stay on for official business, she called Steven to say that she would be late. On returning to Steven, she told him that Daddy had died. Steven asked, 'Did the police come?' and mother affirmed this. Steven stayed with a family friend during the funeral and burial and was told of all the details except for the cause of death. Later autopsy proved it to have been caused by an injection of cyanide. The suicide took place after both the paternal grandmother and the doctor assumed that the father had calmed down and left him, according to his wish. After the funeral mother and Steven visited the aunt as had originally been planned and then returned to their house, which has remained their home.

It has been our experience that the exact circumstances of the parent's death play an important part in the child's understanding of the event (Furman, 1974). This was confirmed in the case of Steven, where each detail proved to be significant.

Coping with the death and mourning

The initial months of work focused on clarifying with Steven the concept of death, the circumstances and cause of the father's death, and on helping him to differentiate himself from the father's fate.

Steven knew from his earlier experiences with small dead animals that dead meant the absence of the functions of living, such as motility, eating, or feeling pain; he even knew about burial and bodily decay. His many questions showed how he applied this knowledge to his father's body: 'Do the worms eat him?' 'Can one dig him up and see?' 'Does it hurt him?' He wondered, 'Did every part of him die?' and asked specifically whether father's penis was dead too, which the mother confirmed. He worried whether all this would happen to his mother and to him, either now or when he would become a Daddy. His fear intensified on later visits to the grave when he noted how many graves there were, but he also used these occasions to master his concerns.

Steven asked reproachfully why someone had not stayed with Daddy and was relieved to learn that the paternal grandmother and the doctor had indeed been called in. Steven became very aware of what made other people or animals die but did not question the cause of his father's death. However, he repeatedly turned to gun and police play. When the mother wondered with Steven about this play, he brought out that he thought the police had come because Daddy was out of control and had killed him; hence his initial question—'Did the police come?'—which the mother had affirmed because she had misinterpreted its meaning. Over a period of time Steven absorbed the information that Daddy had suffered from a mind sickness which had muddled up his thinking and had made him want to die—so different from healthy people—and that it had made him give himself a shot of stuff that made the body die. He learned that the father had been calm when he was left alone on the fatal night and that the police were called the next morning by mother to take Daddy to the hospital so that the doctors could either help him or officially pronounce him dead and that this was a doctor's special job. Later, in connection with many remembered episodes, the earlier signs of father's illness were discussed as well as related issues—the proper and improper use of medicine, the unusual and noninfectious nature of father's illness, and how father's aggressive behaviour differed from the anger of healthy people.

Steven's withholding of bowel movements and urine yielded to interpretations of a mix-up between bowel movements and 'Daddy feelings', and his wish to control things inside him because he had not been able to control what happened outside. Nightwetting, although it persisted longer, was related to 'big feelings', which Steven could gradually verbalize—helplessness, sadness, and especially anger. Steven's excited teasing behaviour was linked primarily to an identification with the aggressors—the anxious mother who had been defensively angry and the fearsome uncontrolled father. There were many recountings of the scene of the attack that had overwhelmed Steven and his mother with fear for their bodily safety.

During this period Steven's *pavor nocturnus* recurred. The mother was able to help Steven become aware of this symptom, and when the first content reached consciousness it was seen to relate to Steven's recent observation of his little girl-friend's nudity during a beach outing. This led to clarification of sexual differences and conception but also increased Steven's phallic sadistic behaviour with big sticks and pretend guns with which he attempted to poke holes into objects. He felt very badly about this and feared that big men would be angry at him. In pursuing this concern with Steven he reminded his mother that, already as a little toddler, he used to be in the bathroom with Daddy when the latter shaved and urinated. He described father's genitals in detail, confessed that he had always wanted to take Daddy's big penis, and, after his death, had hoped that now he could be able to have it for himself—hence his earlier question—'Are all parts of Daddy dead, even his penis?'—which had not struck the mother as so meaningful at the time.

Steven's *pavor nocturnus* subsided after these discussions and did not recur, although the underlying experiences and feelings were to reemerge in later years, attached to new development concerns.

As Steven came to grips with the realities concerning the father's death, mourning proper began with great intensity and lasted unremittingly for well over a year and, episodically, throughout the second year, comparable to but not imitative of his mother's mourning. In words, actions, and activities Steven remembered and longed for all the gratifying aspects of the father–child relationship. He tolerated deep prolonged sadness and even considerable anger. Over and over he bemoaned the fact that nothing could be done to help Daddy. When he saw children play a particular game, he began to cry, as it reminded him of Daddy playing it with him. He could not join in because it would be no fun without Daddy. Several months later he did join in, saying he liked to play this game because it reminded him of how nice it was when he played it with Daddy. Strikingly, both longing and identification repeatedly took the form of performing previously shared activities and keeping joint interests, with very little need for concrete reminders and hardly any magical identifications of the more primitive pre-oedipal kind. He utilized well his relationships with an older neighbour and with his grandfather, without substituting them for the father. For Steven, as for other under-fives with an immature sense of time, anniversaries were not of great significance. Rather, he missed his father during daily routines (mealtimes, going-to-bed stories), when visiting places where father had been with him (the park, picnics), and with new developmental steps (starting nursery school). Steven was acutely sad when other fathers visited the school. When he was told that his Daddy knew the Hanna Perkins School and would have been glad for Steven to attend there, he sighed, 'Now I can like my school'.

Steven also experienced the loss of the father as a narcissistic depletion. In comparing himself with other children he felt he was inadequate because he had no Daddy at home, no big power to bolster his boyish self-esteem. He felt insignificant in having no Daddy to talk about or to show to his peers, although he referred proudly to his father's profession and to memories of times with him.

As we were to learn, Steven's cathexis of the father remained strong throughout the oedipal period and affected his superego formation, although by that time the acute mourning of the real father had subsided and he had sought and enjoyed relationships with potential fathers.

Some effects of the father's death on Steven's phallic phase

When Steven was 3½ years old, about seven months after his father's death, the mother began to prepare him for entry to the Hanna Perkins Nursery School. With this news, and with mother occasionally going out in the evenings, Steven developed severe tempers around separations, even in the home, especially at bedtime. He provoked his mother with his disobedience and several times ran away from her just after she returned. When she interpreted this as a passive into active defence, Steven began to express his anger at her verbally and complained that he felt very 'left out' when she was not with him. We learned that his anger was also a defence against his feeling of utter helplessness in the face of loss of object and against a deep narcissistic hurt at the imagined rejection that loss implied for him. Steven's separation difficulty subsided with this work and never recurred, but the feelings of being alone, helpless, and rejected continued to manifest themselves in other areas.

In the initial weeks of nursery school, during a very gradual separation from the mother, Steven achieved a good intellectual mastery of the new environment, but he kept himself aloof emotionally from the teachers, preferring independence to relying on their help whenever possible and using the school rocking chair rather than the relationship with the teacher to comfort himself when he missed his mother. Although eventually he formed a close relationship with his teachers, Steven remained aloof with people to the point of rejecting their friendly overtures and rarely initiating contacts. The mother brought this to his attention, and once when he ignored a family friend's gracious greeting she pointed out to him how much he had hurt the man's feelings. Steven was surprised and chagrined. He empathized acutely with the man, saying, 'Oh, he felt all alone', and added, wistfully, 'I have known that feeling for a long time'. A next step in understanding came when it was observed how much even minor rebuffs hurt Steven's feelings. One time he felt deeply and permanently rejected when his little friend refused to play with him just then because he was busy. Steven could appreciate that his reaction to the friend's 'no' was unrealistic and perhaps belonged to another situation. He could also be shown in many instances that he warded off his painful 'all alone' feeling by rejecting others. This brought memories of times when his father had, in his illness, withdrawn from Steven, rejecting his overtures. With much work on this topic Steven's identification with the father lessened, but it was not till Steven's fifth birthday that he was able to integrate his 'all alone' feelings fully with his experience with his father. Many friends and relatives over-celebrated Steven's fifth birthday in an attempt to make up for the missing father, but when the nice party was over Steven wept inconsolably for his Daddy and at feeling rejected by him through the latter's death. The mother and he could then discuss the 'all alone' feelings Steven had so often experienced due to father's illness and which had culminated in the father killing himself and thus seemingly rejecting his child. This helped Steven considerably. As we were to learn, however, his propensity to feel rejected coloured Steven's attitudes to gentlemen friends of the mother and made the mother's oedipal rejection of him especially difficult to tolerate.

I have already mentioned the narcissistic depletion Steven experienced with the loss of the father. Steven's feeling of phallic adequacy was no doubt threatened much earlier, when he enviously viewed the father's penis, but a number of events during the phallic phase further enhanced his concerns. Just prior to the start of nursery school Steven had a swollen testicle, which led to a traumatic hospital visit where a surgeon physically overwhelmed him. The swelling later subsided without treatment. He also had a dead tooth, which caused intermittent pain and interfered with eating. In addition, there were repeated colds and ear infections during the first year of school. This resulted in considerable hearing loss, with anxiety about the possible need for an operation, like the one his little girl-friend had to undergo. Actually, conservative but tiresome medical measures corrected the condition. All these factors affected Steven's feeling of competence in the nursery. Whereas at home he was quite skilful and interested in a variety of activities, at school he avoided them or expended minimal effort. Sometimes he scribbled up or destroyed his work and, instead of using his own creative ideas, he imitated others. At times he turned to 'high' teasing fantasy play to ward off his fear of not measuring up to tasks. When the mother paid a morning's visit at school, however, Steven's self-esteem was enhanced, and he took greater interest and pride in his achievements.

Likewise, Steven used the mother initially as a protector against her fears of the 'bigger boys'. This prolonged his need for her at the time of entry. Actually, only a few other boys were physically bigger and more capable, but Steven viewed all of them as superior, displacing onto them his feelings about the father. Steven's conflicts manifested themselves in provocative teasing behaviour. It was observed that he generally teased potentially aggressive or teasing men and boys. When his defence of identification with the aggressor was interpreted, Steven could express his fear of these people and could be shown that he overreacted to them because they reminded him of the times when his father's disturbed teasing had frightened him. Steven vividly recalled many such occasions. Likewise, Steven often became silly and teasingly excited when something unusual happened—for example, when their car was almost mired in a muddy parking place. At other times Steven annoyed adults by 'copying' the naughty behaviour of others: for instance, when a peer turned off the lights, Steven immediately followed suit. When the mother discussed these and similar incidents with Steven, it gradually emerged that he became acutely anxious when people or events surprised him or appeared out of control. The mother helped Steven by linking this to his earlier fears of his father's outbursts and unpredictable moods. To some extent Steven's defences also represented an identification with his mother, who reacted in a somewhat loud, excited, and controlling fashion when helpless—both with the sick father of the past and with Steven in the present when his teasing behaviour reduced her to helplessness and made her anxious. The mother struggled hard to exercise conscious control over this difficulty within herself, discussed it with Steven, and told him she hoped he would be able to cope differently.

In his second year of nursery school Steven mastered his phallic narcissistic difficulties to a considerable extent. He invested his activities and achievements independently and could utilize and enjoy his good potential. His aloofness and provocativeness subsided, and his relationships improved and deepened. With the other boys he was able to compete and show off his skills appropriately. The positive aspects of his earlier experiences with his father found their way into friendship with peers and ever more satisfying times with his grandfather and adult men friends, with whom he engaged in a comfortable working-together relationship. These hard-won masteries were, however, short-lived as oedipal conflicts intensified and revived earlier experiences in a new context.

Steven's oedipal phase

When Steven was almost 5 years old, the intense period of mourning came to an end for his mother and him. Steven began to wish for a new Daddy. The mother dated a man, Mr A, who loved Steven as the son he had always wanted, and Steven soon reciprocated with genuine fondness. Increasingly, however, Steven's teasing and provoking of old returned. With the teachers he defied requests, ignored admonitions, and indulged in excited doll corner play and misuse of toy materials. We learned that at home Steven's similar baiting of his mother usually ended up with her giving him a couple of smacks on the bottom. In this way she provided regressive gratification of an oedipal nature, which further stimulated his excitement. The mother came to recognize how unhelpful this was. She explained to Steven that she would no longer smack him because she did not love people in a toddler way and wanted to help him to grow up so that one day he would be able to love a lady his own age in a grown-up way too. Steven reacted to the mother's oedipal rejection first with fury and increased determination, then with a desperate feeling of depletion and helplessness, a return of the 'all alone' feelings. He began to have a problem with wriggling and inability to sit still. When the mother wondered with him about this, he confessed very guiltily that he was withholding faeces and urine because 'it feels nice'. Steven had used this auto-erotic gratification at earlier stressful times during the height of the father's illness and again immediately following his death. For Steven, as for other fatherless boys, it was especially painful to recognize that whereas he wooed his mother as the ideal loved partner, she sought out a newcomer, apparently spurning what her boy offered her. When Steven, his mother, and her friend planned a joint spring vacation trip, the following incident took place on the day before they left.

Steven was hunched down sitting in the sandbox in the park adjacent to their home. He was joined by a man who hunched down next to him. The mother observed the two from her kitchen window, eventually went out, found the man to be a stranger who at once tried to 'pick her up' and she quickly left with Steven. When she asked him what he and the man had been doing, Steven told her that the man rubbed Steven's penis and asked him to show it, which Steven did not do. Steven hugged his mother, said how glad he was she had come and taken him away because he had been so scared. The mother sympathized, told him that the man had a trouble and that Steven should always call for her to help him.

During the subsequent trip there was no reference to the incident or behavioural reaction. Steven acted very grown-up, tried to identify with manly behaviour in many ways, but, towards the end, complained bitterly at not being allowed to share his mother's single hotel room. On their return, when the boyfriend gave the mother a goodbye kiss, Steven kicked her. During the following weeks Steven was exceedingly angry, excited, and defiant. Some of this was clearly related to his oedipal disappointment in his mother and anger at her, some of it related to the seduction. The mother overheard Steven tell his friend, the policeman's son, about it. The boy suggested they go to 'look for the man to see if he is still in the park', and Steven was ready to join in. The mother stopped them and later told Steven that he must have got very excited by the man's touching of him and perhaps felt badly that his excitement had kept him from running away and calling Mummy at once. She related Steven's recent persistent excited behaviour at home and school to this, 'I can't stop myself and I don't want you to stop me'.

Steven's reactions to the trip and seduction were overshadowed and confused by the fact that his mother's relationship with her boyfriend changed to a mere friendship, and she began to go out with a new man, Mr B, a widower with two prepubertal sons. Mother and Steven spent a great deal of time in activities with this family. Mr B was fond of Steven and enabled him to share in many of his and his boys' interests, but he was more reserved than Mr A (the previous boyfriend) and less in need of a son. Steven felt keenly how little he was compared to these three tall males and considered himself rejected and left out. He endowed Mr B with his own father's negative attitudes, just as he had attributed his father's positive aspects to Mr A. Although Steven again tried to be very grown-up and manly on the joint family outings, his anger and excitement manifested themselves at school and in seeking renewed regressive gratification from his mother. Steven also became quite curious about sexual matters but refused verbal explanations. 'Don't give me that talk, I want to see', he insisted. One day he revealed a 'secret' to another boy while both were using separate closed stalls in the nursery-school bathroom. Steven said he had been using the dressing room at Mr B's club and seen adult men urinate. He was greatly relieved when the teachers reported this secret to his mother, and he then confided to her that he had tried to use the urinal but could not reach. In discussing the incident with Steven it could be linked to his recent excitement and anger, to how little and 'teased' he felt when he compared himself to men. His wish to see was related back to the seduction in the park when the man wanted to see Steven's penis and Steven perhaps wished to see the man's. Steven himself brought up his memories of seeing his father nude when he was a toddler. He added that when he saw his father's penis he took it. The mother questioned this, and Steven surprised himself when he explained, 'I think I was so little that seeing and taking was like the same thing. I just didn't know then that they are different.'

Steven's oedipal feelings reached their crest during the summer, when, on a brief joint vacation, Mr B and Steven's mother shared a room. Steven had always reacted strongly to his mother's private times with her men friends—delaying going to bed, coming down from his room with needless requests, checking used ashtrays and glasses in the morning, and being outspokenly angry at his mother before and after she would go out for an evening—but he had never had to face proof of his mother's adult intimacy with her friend. Now he was both furious and deeply hurt, and he behaved accordingly. However, he managed quite well during a later vacation week with Mr B, which they spent with Steven's aunt's family.

On their return, a week prior to the start of school, Steven had a severe anxiety dream: 'A big bird flew down from the sky.' He later added vaguely that maybe the bird tried to pick up or hurt a little boy who lived nearby. Steven was anxious for several nights after that, feared going to his room to sleep and wakened a few times. With the start of school Steven's anxiety subsided markedly, except for wanting his light on 'because monsters are on the walls when it's dark'. Almost from the first day Steven misbehaved in the Hanna Perkins Kindergarten. He was uninterested in learning activities, could not settle down to play or work, and spent his time either imitating a couple of uncontrolled boys' outbursts or provoking them to lose control. When isolated, he always asked whether the other boy was back in control, and only when the answer was affirmative did Steven calm down. He was impervious to and defiant of the teachers' admonitions and requests and acted as though he had forgotten all school rules and means of self-control.

In talking with his mother, Steven was only aware of his fear of the uncontrolled 'bigger boys' and complained that 'nobody can stop them'. The mother suggested to Steven that the turmoil he saw in others might really be his own and that, when the others were not around, this very turmoil appeared on the walls of his room at night. As Steven began to enlist himself in working on his trouble, many aspects could be understood. He displaced his anger at his mother's nights with the boyfriend to the teachers and, with his omnipotent defiance, made them feel helpless in order to ward off his own helplessness in the face of his mother's rejection and of his imagined inadequacy at school tasks. He did not try to learn, for fear of not being able to compete with other boys successfully. Steven managed to be nice and obedient with adult men by displacing his oedipal competition to the classroom situation, projecting his own anger to his peers, and controlling, through provocation, their feared retaliatory outbursts. When Steven faced his underlying anger at men sufficiently to voice it to his mother, she suggested he tell his feelings to Mr B. Steven whispered in terror, 'But I could never tell a big man that I'm mad at him. The bigger the man, the less you can be mad at him.' Why? Apparently the consequences were unspeakable. Nevertheless, the mother arranged a meeting between Steven, Mr B, and herself to give Steven a chance to discuss his specific complaints of being left out. Steven plucked up all his courage and stated his feelings. Mr B assured him that he was not angry back and said he well remembered when his own boys and even he as a child had felt that way. Steven was greatly relieved.

Other layers of his difficulty now became accessible. Steven recognized from his descriptions of the out-of-control schoolmates' behaviour that they reminded him of his father's outbursts, which had preceded his death. In his own anger Steven also identified with the father—he was unstoppable and devastating. He was finally able to associate his earlier anxiety dream, recalling some events that had precipitated it: he had attended a museum talk about birds of prey with live specimens; during their visit to the aunt he had learned that her dog had been killed by a car; and on a visit to the village cemetery there he had read the inscription of a child's tombstone, '. . . and the angel of the Lord came down from heaven and touched him'. The bird who flew down from the sky in Steven's dream represented the killer–avenger father. Steven again went over the father's outburst and asked if Daddy had been mad at him because he, Steven, called to him to leave his mother alone. In retrospect he interpreted events differently: mother had chosen him, Steven, to go away with, and when Daddy found out about that he felt so left out and angry that he lost his temper and wanted to kill them and killed himself. This helped to clarify Steven's fear of his own left-out feelings and of expressing anger at men. It was also his masturbation fantasy, as we learned that one aspect of Steven's explosive behaviour at school related to his renewed withholding of urine and increased touching of his genital.

Steven's negative oedipal conflict and its passive antecedents had manifested themselves periodically. Although Steven's withholding of faeces and urine had many active and masculine aspects, there were also passive ones. Steven knew that his passing a large motion probably precipitated the swelling of his testicle, which in turn led to his being overpowered by the surgeon who examined him. Minor swellings had occurred a couple of times since then without necessitating medical attention. Steven felt discomfort along the canal to the testes at these times, and it was unclear whether his withholding was designed to anticipate or control these feelings. Steven had the earlier experience of being teased by his father and later provoked and teased men and boys who appeared unpredictable to him. He provoked his mother to smack his behind. He had his penis rubbed by the stranger in the park. Steven often 'appropriated' Mr A, his mother's boyfriend. His feelings came to the fore most clearly at a later point when the mother informed him that she had decided against marrying either Mr A or Mr B, although she liked both of them. Steven was very upset, but only with much help could he finally express his great anger at the mother for depriving him of these potential fathers as well as of his own father, as though she had been responsible for his death.

The beginnings of latency

Steven's anxiety dream and subsequent school problem represented not only the latter phase of his oedipus complex but also the first superego internalizations. When Steven's school behaviour improved, his anxieties at going to bed increased, and he still dared not sleep without the lights on. Focusing on this problem, Steven described his fear that the monsters of the dark would come and do bad things to him. Why? Steven answered by drawing the teachers' attention to his excited water play with the taps in the school bathroom, and the mother became aware of how long it took Steven to bathe in the evening as he splashed around in the tub. It was now possible to show Steven that he felt very guilty over his play with his own body–tap and over the genital excitement he felt from holding back urine—so guilty that it seemed safer to pass on to the grown-ups the job of knowing the rules and of controlling him than to listen to his own conscience. But when he was alone at night, the guilty feelings caught up with him, as though they were monsters and threatened to punish him. Steven's newly harsh introject was evidently modelled on the killing angry father.

The concomitant working-through of Steven's memories of the father's aggression in the context of his current oedipal anger at men seemed to help Steven modify his superego sufficiently to tolerate and utilize its injunctions more comfortably. He gradually involved himself more in his schoolwork, took pride in learning and achieving, and especially enjoyed his gift in mathematics. Peers became friends and partners in play and work. He could structure his free time better with more available neutral energy and heeded the adults' reminders to check with himself whether this or that really seemed the right thing to do when Steven appeared to be on the verge of wrong-doing or loss of control. The withholding of urine stopped, and he bathed more quickly. Steven thought ahead much to his first year in primary school, where he wanted to do well and be a regular schoolboy. At home he managed nicely, pursued new interests, and no longer needed his night light.

Follow-up

Steven has progressed well during his latency years. When he was about 8 years old, his mother shared with me this conversation, which she had happened to overhear between Steven and his new friend while the boys looked at toys and mementos in his room:

'You don't have a Dad, do you?'

'That's right. My Dad died.'

'I know he died, but how did he die?'

'He had a mindsickness.'

'You mean he died of that mindsickness?'

'No, his mindsickness made him so mixed up that he made himself die. The doctors tried to help his mindsickness, but they couldn't.'

'Your Dad was a great swimmer, wasn't he?'

'Yes, this is one of the trophies he won. He was a great swimmer.'

It is too early to gauge whether Steven resolved his conflicts in such a way that they will not encroach upon his development or encumber his adolescence. His mother knows he may experience difficulties and may need an analysis at a later point.

CHAPTER THREE

Exploration and therapy in family work

Beta Copley

The role and influence of the family in relation to the difficulties being experienced by a child or an adolescent may
vary widely and depend on many complex factors—both
within the individual and within the family. In chapter two it
was a member of the young child's family, his mother,
through whom the therapist felt the boy could be appropriately helped and supported. This chapter explores family
work in terms both of its diagnostic and its therapeutic potential. The latter may emerge as being of particular relevance
either to the individual or to the family as a group. A number
of clinical examples illustrate these processes, and a number
of approaches to family therapy are discussed.

[R.S.]

This chapter draws on two earlier papers by the author, in which
clinical material is described in more detail, namely: 'Work with a
Family as a Single Therapist with Special Reference to Transference
Manifestations', *Journal of Child Psychotherapy, 9* (1983), and 'Explorations with Families', *Journal of Child Psychotherapy, 13* (1987), no. 1.

Families in distress can be bewildered in their search for help; services may need to ponder the best way to intervene. Initial explorations can be useful. These can take different forms and have varied outcomes. An initial contact with a family can range from a short consultation to a more dynamic brief intervention. It may or may not be an introduction to further work, either with the family as a whole or with individual members. The term 'exploration' seems preferable to that of 'assessment' because it has a more dynamic connotation, allowing for the possibility of something being accomplished within such a process itself. 'Exploration' also lends itself more readily to the idea of a two-way process. Feelings within a family about the nature of the service and the institution offering it may need to be thought about openly. 'Assessment' can carry both passive and persecutory connotations, with implications of being assessed 'for' something—and possibly found wanting. Here I first discuss some psychoanalytically informed exploratory work with families, followed by a longer-term intervention; with these in mind I outline underlying concepts and indications for this method of work. I then consider this approach in the context of other schools of family therapy.

The Field family:
a family consultation

Mr and Mrs Field requested a private consultation for themselves and their 18-year-old son, Ken; they were concerned about him in general, but sought help following his two recent convictions for travelling without a rail ticket. (Although this was a private consultation, the issues discussed here are also relevant to work in a clinic.) Ken (the only child living at home) was not seeking help himself, but he was willing to be seen with his parents, and I offered a few exploratory sessions in which we could consider together whether more help, and of what kind, was needed.

The father was a professional man, and the mother made jewellery at home. Shame in relation to the publicity which Ken's conviction had received locally had led the parents to seek a consultation at some distance. Father voiced his disappointment at Ken not attempting to follow an academic path, as he himself had done. Mother was more silent on this point. Ken was taciturn but agreed with his parents' view that he was not ill and had some social life. His morose yet disengaged presence felt heavy in the session, and this did not seem solely attributable to the ticket episode. At the time of the offences he had been 'travelling nowhere in particular'. Ken's older half-sister, Liz, had left home to study, and the house was pointedly described as being quieter without her. She joined the exploration at my request.

The atmosphere changed when she came. Rivalry between Liz and her mother was apparent, as was tension between the parents when it became clear that the mother enjoyed Ken's presence at home in the day time, contrasting with the father's emphasis on how he should be away at university. But there was also a more hopeful feeling in the room, and Ken was active in the discussion of the issues for all the family around both children leaving home. In the discussion the mother became tearful, and Ken became protective towards her. I recognized with them that my intervention was being experienced as stirring conflict. It seemed that the family had allowed some of their difficulties to surface but felt too threatened to embark on any longer-term work. After an agreed interval they let me know that Ken had obtained a place at a polytechnic (less prestigious than the university attended by father). It seemed that there had been some movement, and though we do not know the meaning of this for Ken personally, there was a chance that he now might be able to begin a journey in his own right to 'somewhere in particular'.

Meltzer (1986), in a chapter on 'Family patterns and cultural educabilility', refers to the classification described by Harris and himself in which individuals within a family may be seen to occupy certain psychic roles and fulfil certain functions, such as: generating love, promulgating hate, promoting hope, sowing despair, containing depressive pain, emanating persecutory anxiety, thinking, and creating lies and confusion. In this family Liz may have held some of the containing, thoughtful, and hopeful functioning. (The use here of the term 'containing' will be elaborated later in the chapter.) I may have been able to gather some indication of this possibility from experiencing a stagnation of thinking in the first session, followed by leavening of the heaviness when Liz was mentioned. Of course more came out when she came, as with Pandora's box, than just hope, as some of the more controversial family feelings were also associated with Liz. The exploration was based on an acknowledgement of the feelings that led to help having been sought, and a minimal exploration of family dynamics and resources. Recognition was given to the family's wish to hold the experience near the level of what might be called a consultation to the institution of the family.

The Wood family:
a brief dynamic exploration

The experience with the Woods was very different. Dirk, a trendily dressed 15-year-old adolescent whose clothes, hair-style, and hair colour varied each time, came for four exploratory sessions with his mother, who had sought help after he had been involved in a minor burglary. Dirk was the child of an extramarital relationship of mother's; his seventeen-year-old sister, Peg, a child of the marriage, was about to leave home. Mother had had psychiatric treatment some years ago. Only the mother and Dirk in fact came, although the whole family was invited. The dynamic issues as to the places in the family of father and son came immediately to the fore. Mother maintained that father might be too embarrassed to come; he was promiscuous— unlike her, she said, who had only briefly become involved with the man who had made her pregnant with Dirk. She hardly knew this man—he was immature and not very bright. But she had told her husband (who was referred to within the family as 'Father') from the beginning, and he had accepted the situation. I asked Dirk if he knew all this, or whether it was a shock. Mother said he did; Dirk said he had only known about some of it. Throughout our contact I found myself attempting to make space for Dirk's feelings in relation to the mother's outpourings.

Father was said to have 'broken the door down' in anger when Dirk was convicted of the burglary and fined. Dirk said he wanted to fight Father, but outside. The account had the flavour of an American Western film, with father now being described as doing the 'breaking and entering', with no picture of a perhaps understandably angry father. I said it sounded as if they were talking about a problem of having two men in one house, Dirk being described as a man. The mother agreed, but made a verbal slip, calling father 'son', to which I drew their attention, commenting on the closeness at times between mother and Dirk; the mother now referred to Dirk as 'a good boy' and talked of his improved attendance at his new school; Dirk said he wanted to study more but felt mixed up. We can see how a shift to a more ordinary manifestation of a mother–son relationship could take place, followed by more contact with personal anxieties. I questioned their feelings of coming to this, for them, new clinic. The mother relaxed and started to cry and spoke of worries having led to her being admitted to mental hospital at one time. Here it seemed appropriate to take up whether or not we in this clinic were felt able to relate constructively to such feelings of worry.

In a further session the mother said Dirk was now back with her parents, because the father liked a quiet evening. She had often stayed there with the children when they were little, the father visiting on Saturday evenings and sleeping on the sofa. Dirk said he had sometimes thought his grand-parents were his parents, and that he looked like mother's brother. He claimed there was no room for both father and himself, and that his mother was better off without him. The subject of the broken door came up again, with an implication that the sole problem was the father's lack of forgiveness. I took up the changing views as to which side of the door the violence lay, Dirk's side or the father's. Dirk said Father was not his father and that he could not forgive him, because he went around with others. I said that we had heard that his mother had 'been around' with someone else, and this long-term family problem was difficult to think about. Maybe Father was now being blamed for not being the father who had created Dirk with mother.

I wondered if the quiet evening with father linked with a wish mother had expressed for the 'adolescent phase' to be over. Mother said thoughtfully to Dirk that he did go out with the girls. I took up the notion of *unfaithfulness*, mother with father (!), Dirk with the girls, and how we had also heard that Peg was about to leave home and that sooner or later this could also happen with Dirk. Somewhere here I mused how father or Dirk were somehow on the 'wrong side' of the door when violence was around; could this have anything to do with breaking in when feeling shut out; if so, this might have some link in feeling with the 'breaking and entering' of burglary. Shortly after this we heard how father and Dirk together had tried to keep knowledge of the burglary from mother to protect her from a possible risk of breakdown, so it was now possible to take up a protective pairing of the males, as opposed to other combinations of relationships that had been mentioned.

We heard in the third session that Peg had been a lot of trouble earlier and something about a better relationship between father and Dirk prior to adolescence. I commented how problems were presented as if they were due largely to some defect in father, although there seemed, paradoxically, to be some idea of potential change with time after 'this adolescent stage'. Dirk had brought with him an impressive school biological project, which he showed to me with pride, so it was possible to comment that the description of 'not very bright', which had been applied to his biological father by mother, need not apply to him.

This was obviously a volatile and chaotic family under particular stress in responding to adolescence, influenced, as we have seen, by the relationship between mother and Dirk, both in its current strength and possible future changes. Major family crises led to missed sessions, despite mother's attempts to attend. We do not know at first hand about father or Peg. Dirk was clearly unmotivated for any longer-term therapy, and the chances of mother being able to accept, attend, and use insight therapy with benefit to the whole family did not seem high. Of course the family's oedipal turmoil around inter-generational love, strengthened by the feelings around Dirk's conception and the role of father, would be liable to continue, exacerbated under the stimulus of Dirk's adolescence. On the other hand Dirk and his mother did move towards some experience and recognition of the nature of the problems in the sessions and attempt to think together about them. Perhaps our contact might lessen, though hardly remove, the amount of recourse to immediate action. It may seem strange that I have taken an example of family work where only two members were present, but in so doing I hope to have conveyed something of an approach that also relates to absent members within the dynamics of the session, and how a brief exploratory process may have some therapeutic potential.

The Tree family:
a family exploration leading to individual work

Individual therapy for one or more members can also follow a family exploration. This was the case in the Tree family, where Anna, a 17-year-old anorexic girl, was first seen together with her parents and two sisters by a colleague and myself. Anna, still at school, was an extremely emaciated adolescent, mostly silent, often rubbing her finger against her cheek in a manner reminiscent of a baby. She had already been hospitalized twice and had expressed herself unwilling to have individual therapy; she only reluctantly attended with her family, claiming that mother was over-concerned. Anna's sisters, both apparently cheerfully involved in their work and studies, withdrew after the first interview, followed by Anna herself after four exploratory sessions, repudiating any sense of need. We maintained the focus of a family exploration with the parents for four further sessions, taking up what we experienced as the family's mistrust of our approach and how they felt us to be as unhelpful as the earlier hospitals. Some recognition of their criticism of each other as parents followed.

Both the amount and nature of mother's fears that Anna could die became apparent, some of these seemingly stemming from Anna herself, despite Anna's earlier disclaimers to us. We explored how much this was felt to be due on the one hand to mother being an over-willing absorber of family pain, as if this was a superior aspect of maternal functioning for which no husbandly help was necessary, or, on the other hand, to a lack of emotional contact between the parents. We gradually got in touch with mother's feelings of having been neglected by father, but how she also found it difficult to call on his help. Father spoke of having felt anxious himself about Anna from babyhood. Despite some acrimony, both parents seemed to experience relief in spontaneously reflecting on some events in Anna's infancy and some of their own life experiences with us.

Mother especially remained dissatisfied with our failure to provide 'answers' about Anna's anorexia. However, our non-critical attention, and, we thought, our willingness to bear and think about their feelings, including a now quite openly expressed disbelief about our capacity to relate to their needs, seemed to help them to feel that we were to some extent open to experiencing their distress. This seemed relevant to a reap-praisal, in which Anna now sought individual therapy. It seemed that within the family father had been helped to be more in touch with his own anxieties and responsive to those of his wife. Also, and probably related to this, mother may have become less willing to soak up Anna's distress. This small lessening of the entanglement between Anna and her mother may have helped Anna to feel some need for help on her own account. We agreed that it seemed right to attempt to meet this need with individual work, especially in view of the infantile component we have observed in it.

The Bush family:
a family exploration leading to longer-term family work

Sean, a 14-year-old boy, was referred by his mother on account of school problems in which she also seemed involved. Sean, his mother, and his seventeen-year-old sister, Dawn, were invited to attend for an initial exploration. The parents had been divorced for some years, and the older children of the marriage lived in Ireland. Contact with father was currently non-existent. In the second session Sean lay on the floor in a regressed manner at mother's feet, winding and unwinding a scarf reminiscent of an umbilical link between mother and baby, and we heard about family difficulties at the time of his birth. I tried to relate to these unexpected events not to establish a history of 'causes', but, rather, to lead into trying to understand current feelings. The partly sensuous bond that was revealed between Sean and his mother also included an 'agreement' that Sean would obey his mother, with the proviso that she would not ask him to do something like putting his hand in the fire! Soon we were in the midst of heated family rows, Sean withdrawing behind a paper and then trying to take charge, mother being called a liar, Dawn adjudicating between Sean and mother but also speaking to a feeling of desperation.

Sean seemed disturbed, but lacking in motivation for individual therapy. There were also strong indications for family work. There was the sensuous quasi folie-à-deux quality between Sean and mother, the possibility that Sean carried a lot for the family in his enactment of a false 'super-dad' role, and the undermining of adulthood in the family rows. The drive for therapy also lay mainly in mother, and the feeling of need in Dawn. We agreed to meet for a term and then to review. The work in fact extended over two years.

Much of the therapy evidenced the inability of the family to bear doubt, anxiety, or individual differences, which were often met by bitter, envious attacks, and an attempt to destroy meaning. Thus Dawn to her mother, politely: 'You begin.' Mother: 'What shall I say?' Dawn: 'That's a bloody silly way to begin.' In this longer-term work I sought to draw out and make use of their relationship with me as a means of understanding what was happening, and as a potential vehicle of change. I was soon subject to mockery by the adolescent children, with no real parental protest, any point that I made being attacked and made meaningless. Attempts were made to set up alternative subjects of alleged importance and interest, such as the state of Sean's smelly feet! An initial view that the indexed patient, Sean, was the prime emanator of confusional and persecutory anxiety seemed to be confirmed: he also seemed to be the chief protagonist for 'an envious assumption of moral superiority without any morals' (Bion, 1962). But he was not alone in this, and it was important to offer space for disentangling a view of him as the sole problem. The family frequently behaved as if it were living in the world of Sartre's (1965/1982) *Huis Clos* and enjoying its experience of Hell. But it was sometimes possible to get in touch with an idealized view of family life, such as a description of a childhood scene of holding hands and repeating 'we are a family', although this was also denigrated. Gradually some change took place from what had seemed interminable mockery of me, and at times I was seen as someone who was able to keep them in mind and to *think* about pain, contrasting with their painful pleasure of 'passing the parcel' of hurtful attack around to each other. Sometimes there was a perception within the family of me in a softer, often quite infantile way. Mother referred to Dawn having thought of me as a loving mother who could take my children camping, and Sean was heard to chant my name in soft, lalling tones. Dawn referred to an appreciation of coming to my nice room with nice plants; it seemed that at these moments there was some feeling of being in touch through the therapy with a world very different from their Hell of *Huis Clos* and a willingness to move out of a gang state of mind.

Gradually it became possible for some actual anxieties to be owned, such as that of Dawn being left alone at night, and to discuss difficulties such as Sean's attitude to homework. The children also became able to reinitiate contact with their father and reassess their relationship with him anew for themselves. Individual therapy unusually became available through the school for Sean and also for his mother, and was accepted. Dawn, who had to a large extent been burdened as the holder of any potential thinking and depressive pain for the family, now seemed able to own more of both her own hostility and need and transferred to individual therapy in our clinic. Both Sean and Dawn, despite setbacks, were heard to be making progress some time later. The recognition and disentanglement of family involvements seemed to be a necessary first step before individual members could see individual help as meaningful.

The nature of this approach

A major feature is that of containment in the sense developed by Bion (Bion, 1962). He draws on the notion of a distressed baby conveying a part of himself in pain to his mother, so that this is now 'contained' in her. He describes this taking place by means of the mechanism defined as projective identification by Klein (Klein, 1946). The mother, in what Bion calls her 'reverie', reflects on the infant's distress and in due course reconveys it to the baby in a form that has more meaning and is more possible to bear. This is a two-sided communication about mental pain, which can go wrong through difficulties on either side. When things go well, the infant takes in and identifies with the containing process and develops his own containing potential. Similarly, the family's experience of the relationship with the worker can result in a helpful process of introjection. We glimpsed in the Tree family how a child's anxiety could be over-absorbed by a mother, blocking development, but how some containment of anxiety by the father could help. We also saw how a family exploration might help to restore the containing process. (This approach is elaborated in Box, Copley, Magagna, & Moustaki, 1981).

The therapist provides mental and emotional space for thinking about feelings in the family, in particular those of distress, conflict, or others that may in some way be felt to be unacceptable. The therapist both 'holds' and thinks about what is happening, conveying her thoughts to the family when it seems appropriate. In this work it seems desirable to comment in terms of what individuals may be expressing in the context of the family, rather than couching interventions in a way that could be felt to smack of personal remarks made in public. Being clear with a family about the time available, and thus when and for how long contact is proposed, is also relevant to the containing process. As we have seen, relationships with absent members are also important. Such a way of working implies active involvement by the therapist in relating to what could be expressed by all family members, including silent ones; over-passivity could be felt to indicate an unwillingness to contain conflict.

Such work also draws on Bion's theory of groups (Bion, 1961), again using the concept of projective identification within the family. This mechanism serves to convey more than pain; unwanted feelings and aspects of the self can be projected in omnipotent phantasy onto others; we saw how Dirk Wood located some of his own violence in his father by this means, and that this was irrespective of whether the father was or was not actually a violent man. A member may accept such a projection and thus speak unconsciously on behalf of others, as Mrs Tree initially did about Anna's disowned suffering. A member can also carry a function for the family, as we saw in the case of Liz Field. If the worker couches her response as much as possible in terms of what is happening within the family, she may be able to gather in some of the projections, understand more of the roles carried, as well as the intrinsically different and maybe fluctuating points of view among members. In the Wood family I tried to draw in and hold Dirk's feelings about his conception beside those voiced by his mother, and also the fluctuating views expressed about father: violent, odd man out on the sofa, the one who liked a quiet evening with mother, the one who formed a protective couple with Dirk for mother's sake, and so on. When it seemed that mother and Dirk were aware that I was trying to accept and think about their feelings, I attempted to make links with Dirk's violence and projections—about the door, for example. Earlier material may usefully be evoked when linking is appropriate; the reference concerning Dirk's heredity and the school biological project is an example. In this family, space was needed to look at the projections, couplings, rivalries, and feelings about heredity in the context of adolescence and a minor delinquent crisis. The hope would be that the family might be able to introject and identify with at least a modicum of this containing process.

A worker may not, however, be experienced as a benign 'container', as I did not appear to be by the Field family when I touched on some of the differences within the family. Such feelings need to be recognized. In exploratory family work it is often less important to relate to personal aspects of the transference to the therapist than to the family's feelings about the institution to which they have come and the here-and-now functioning of the therapist within it; this may well be coloured by 'pre-transference' feelings within the family about what sort of place they are coming to and what reception they are likely to get. We saw how Mrs Wood's feelings about having been in a mental hospital resonated with her anxieties about approaching our clinic; in the same way the Tree family brought suspicion with them.

How a family responds to our recognition of such feelings can help to decide how to proceed in the intervention. The Trees felt relieved at our acceptance of their suspicion, and the work went ahead; the Fields felt understanding to be too invasive, and the work was held at the level of a consultation. In longer-term work, manifestations of transference feelings may of course become more personal to the worker, as with the Bush family.

It is often by one's own feelings in relation to the family, the countertransference, that one becomes aware of the communications within the family, especially perhaps those reaching the therapist by projective identification. The feelings of frustration aroused in me by Mrs Wood's accounts of the missed sessions helped me to take the possible conflict surrounding the chaos seriously. With the Field family my feelings of heaviness made me aware of some of the difficulties; later, when I was led to feel I was being 'a stirrer of conflict', I was able to share something based on this with them. This in turn helped me to reach a decision about an appropriate limit to the exploration.

The work I describe is often carried out by co-therapists, often seen to represent an image of a parental couple. The various family members may well have different perceptions of each of the therapeutic pair, and the therapists will thus need to be prepared to think about possible disagreements arising between them, which could be a consequence of how they are related to by the family and the different projections they receive, both positive and negative. A therapist working individually may need to relate to family feelings about an absent partner. Individual work can, however, also lead to a deepening of the relationship with the therapist and allow work with feelings that have a very infantile root to take place, as in the case of the Bush family.

Indications for family explorations

Unless contra-indicated, an initial family exploration may have much to offer. A simple indication is apparent when one member or members of a family are carrying worry or concern, but another is seen as 'needing treatment'. This is relevant to our four families and is particularly relevant in adolescence, when parents may be worried but no longer are able to insist that their 'child' attend individually. The adolescent, may, however, as we have seen, be willing to attend with parents, whom he may see as needing help.

A crisis situation, and problems experienced in direct relationship to the family, are other indications. A 7-year-old boy, Bill, was referred for bad behaviour at school shortly after his father had suddenly left the family. His 8-year-old sister, Tania, seemed very calm. Intervention revealed how much she was identified with her mother's quiet, withdrawn behaviour, which attempted to put a brave face on things but failed to help the children with their feelings. Some of Bill's 'bad' behaviour could, when looked at in detail, be understood as trying to get rid of the family distress. A family intervention in which these responses could be brought together, contained, and thought about in the context of father's leaving seemed appropriate.

Indications of considerable fusion between family members, or of splitting, projective identification, and possible scapegoating within the family could also call for family exploration, as with the Bush family. Although there are outstanding instances where a family intervention may be called for, it is not necessarily possible to be aware of this from the referral, and firm indications may in fact only emerge in the course of the initial exploration; Sean's difficulties could have been taken at face value as a school problem. On the other hand, there are of course cases where a family intervention could clearly be intrusive to individual privacy, as for example with an adolescent actively seeking a sequestered setting.

Family explorations can allow families such as the Fields and Woods, who are unlikely either to be offered or to accept what might be termed ongoing therapy, to have an experience where their needs can be related to and thought about in a way they can use; this could be in a more consultative (as with the Fields) or dynamic (as with the Woods) style, depending on the family. By such means therapeutic insights derived from psychoanalytic understanding may be usefully shared over a wider population than might otherwise benefit. A family may be helped to draw some kind of metaphorical map as to where they are and as to what road they wish to take. With the Wood family, for example, one could relate to how the problems surrounding Dirk's conception were still live issues for them. These could be discussed in terms of the family's current experiences during Dirk's adolescence; the problems were also relevant to the impending break-up of this nuclear family unit as Dirk grew towards adulthood. Such a map hopefully has more of the qualities of a globe than a page in a book, allowing for some experience of depth and cross-currents of feeling.

One can see from the Tree family how work involving both parents was relevant to Anna being able to accept therapy. Even a non-attending father, such as Dirk's, could be used as part of the work in his absence. An intervention involving siblings, as with Liz in the Field family, can aid understanding. Dawn's more depressive and hopeful stance may have helped the Bush family to attend, but the undermining effect both of her pseudo-maternality and her collusion with her brother's negative approach to understanding needed teasing out for all their sakes.

My main examples have been drawn from adolescence, and I am grateful to Mary Boston in allowing me to refer here to observations she made about families with younger children when we both discussed family interventions at a meeting of The Association of Child Psychotherapists in London in 1986. She also underlines the value of keeping options open when the therapeutic team does not know what is likely to be required. This allows for the possibility of continuing with further family meetings or dividing into a different combination. Two therapists could, for example, continue to work separately with parents and a child or children. The therapists in this case have the opportunity of making their decisions on the basis of observed family dynamics and not just from hearing about the child from the parents. Family information, such as that about a child's babyhood, becomes accessible and is then shared knowledge between the child and a therapist who continues to work with him. Preliminary family interviews in this case also make it easier for small children to separate and go with the therapist; older children, too, can feel more in the picture about the referral. If the therapy is to be with a different worker than the initial one, a child can be seen without establishing too much of an individual transference relationship. Mary Boston also agrees that a family consultation can be therapeutic in its own right, and if short-term work only is available, as in many clinics, then a few family interviews may make the best use of limited resources.

As regards what might be called the decision-making component of such explorations, the very nature of the joint meeting makes for more open appraisal as to what may be wanted by family members and thought appropriate and possible by the therapists.

Different methods of family work

So far we have been looking at a psychoanalytically informed approach to family work, but as there may be a number of models of family work within a clinic, there is a need to think about problems of difference and co-operation. This involves thinking about both how our work is seen by colleagues and our own need to understand something about their methods.

Sometimes differences of approach may seem greater than they in fact are. What we think of ourselves as doing and what somebody else thinks we do are not necessarily the same thing. Hoffmann (1981) views the psychodynamic model as being conceived in 'linear' terms and the purpose of psychodynamic treatment being to enable patients recover memories of repressed events and re-experience accompanying buried emotions. She contrasts this with 'circularity', central to the systems epistemology of family therapy, stressing the inter-relationship of one person's response to another. Her description of here-and-now multiple dynamic relationships in fact reflects more closely the version of family work I try to follow than does her description of psychodynamic method. As touched on in the discussion of the Bush family, I see any discussion of history as bearing on the understanding of current family relationships, rather than a search for linear causation or the re-experience of buried emotion as such. As workers in a multi-disciplinary team we probably need not only to read some of the literature of other approaches, but also to discuss it with colleagues.

Contact between different approaches may further understanding, despite very different methods of intervention. In the structuralist approach (Minuchin, 1974; Minuchin & Fishman, 1981), we can follow the skilled observation and appraisal of the 'here and now' of the session and the extensive thinking devoted to families and subsystems within them. We can also see processes with which we are familiar described in different words, and so get a sense of a widely used family therapy language that can ease communication with colleagues. In the structuralist approach understanding is actively conveyed to the family from the standpoint of someone who has clear goals for them, and who responds to events in the session, including the countertransference, in what may be a very personal style. In the systemic 'Milan' approach as described by Palazzoli (Palazzoli et al., 1978), psychoanalytic understanding has a place in the background, but possible intrapsychic reality is put to the side in favour of therapeutic interventions designed to provoke change and often consisting in the giving of ritual tasks or paradoxical prescriptions. It is important to appreciate that these are theoretical tenets leading to the concerted attempt to disturb what is seen as essentially false communication within the family, even if we feel uneasy with a method where a partial truth may be taken as representing the whole, or where an activity with anti-developmental components is overtly given a purely positive connotation.

The approach, then, of some schools of family therapy are overtly goal-oriented, actively didactic, and provocative of change, and the therapists are seen as conveying their expertise to the family. Does this pose a problem for co-operation and, if so, how? To raise this question is not intended as a criticism of such approaches. But there is a difficulty. Our own intrinsic definition of ourselves and the kind of work we seek to do may lead us to stand aside, not from family therapy, because many of us do engage in this, but from certain kinds of family therapy. Of course our way of working may also be unacceptable to a school of thought that relies on its own tightly knit and thought-out way of working. The model of containment described here implies that the therapist's willingness to think about feelings brought to her is also a potential model for the family to take in, identify with, and use themselves. A child psychotherapist may have a particular contribution to make in relation to the communications of the children, but it does not make her someone who 'knows' what is right for the child or family. In fact, a vital aspect of our primary professional role as psychoanalytical psychotherapists is to work from the point of view of 'not knowing', and it is this essential professional attribute, relevant to our work with all our patients, that could be at risk if we actively engage in certain kinds of family therapy or participate in consultations that lead one to accept a certain kind of expert role and move away from a state of mind of being 'with' the patient.

The feasibility of joint work probably needs to be examined with one's colleagues with actual interventions in mind. The psychodynamic psychotherapist may be able to work with some flexibility if the approach of the team sanctions an open and non-didactic response to the family's perceptions of the clinic and therapists, both positive and negative. What is fundamental is the intrinsic professional need to offer a service that relates openly to the family's experience. I should like to end with a reference to a piece of family work by Harris (Harris & Carr, 1966), referred to in the Introduction to part two, which underlines the value of 'expert' help, not in the form of instructions based on superior knowledge, but, rather, providing an experience of relating to and thinking *with* the family.

CHAPTER FOUR

Integrating individual and family therapy

Elizabeth Muir

This chapter explores issues that may arise in situations where a child's participation in family therapy may seem to present some risk to the need for a secure experience of confidentiality within the child's individual psychotherapy. A fresh approach to these parallel processes is described and examined in terms of psychoanalytic theory and of outcome in the case history of a young girl.

[R.S.]

In establishing an integrated approach to individual and family therapy, we are thinking in terms of a partnership between two equally valid and complementary concepts. This would begin with an assessment of both the individual child as the referred patient, and of the family. The form of treatment approach would then be determined by the formulation reached and also by the family's perception of the problem.

The outcome of an assessment frequently results in a child being taken into individual psychotherapy while the family is

65

seen collaterally in family therapy. In practical terms, undertaking collateral work with an individual child and with the family might seem in itself to be using an integrated approach. However, in contrast to a tradition that approaches the two processes as separate though parallel, we have frequently found it most helpful to work towards an active integration of the two experiences. In order to do this it is necessary to focus on some of the elements that are common to both individual psychoanalytically oriented psychotherapy and family group psychotherapy.

It was Freud (1912b) who suggested that (paraphrased) in the final analysis every conflict has to be fought out in the sphere of the transference. Certainly the transference is the cornerstone of psychoanalytic psychotherapy, and therefore it is important for the child psychotherapist to understand the specific use of transference in collateral individual child and family therapy; to be able to describe how the transference can be used to facilitate the integration of the therapeutic work with the individual child with that of the family group.

With the adult patient the transference is the displacement onto the therapist of unresolved conflictual aspects of an early primary object relationship; it represents an unconscious attempt to work through, within the new attachment, conflicts originating in the earlier parent and/or sibling relationships. With children the unresolved conflicts are both past and current; the objects are living and being lived with (A. Freud, 1966; Sandler, Kennedy, & Tyson, 1975). There has been much controversy in the literature about the transference in child therapy; whether it occurs at all or, if it does, to what degree. However, there is some logic in suggesting that it must be precisely those aspects of the primary relationship that are current and unresolved, that also get taken out of the family and projected into a therapeutic relationship. The child, like the adult, albeit unconsciously, senses that this is a chance to try yet again for a different outcome. In the author's experience, this is, in fact, what happens.

Sandler et al. (1975), in their study report, defined four categories, or four levels, of transference. The first level is the so-called character transference, one's global defensive style; the second is transference predominantly of current object relationships; the third and fourth levels are characterized by the transference of past object relations experiences, and transference neurosis, respectively. They acknowledged that transference of predominanty current relationships may also include manifestations of revivals of past object relationships. Character transferences are useful as indicators of individual and family defensive modes, and the understanding of transferences of current relationships is essential for integrating individual therapy with family therapy. Thus it is these two types of transference that are referred to in this chapter. The point to be made is that in collateral therapy we have the potential for the transference to the therapist of a relationship problem that is current in the family, and both—that is, the actual family and the transference—are there to be worked with. Given this, one has to ask oneself within which of these should the crucial work be done? The author feels strongly that the individual child has a right to private, separate therapy in which to explore his or her relationship problems. Equally, when at all possible, the child and the parents and/or siblings should have the chance to work these shared problems out in the current relationship. An approach taking back into the family therapy sessions the transferences to adolescent ward staff of the adolescent in-patient has drawn attention to some of these issues (Muir & Lewis, 1974).

The following case study illustrates the role and use of the transference in the collateral therapy of an individual child and her family and clarifies the importance of redirecting transference-derived insights back into the family sphere and allowing time for working through.

Case study: NICOLA

Nicola, 11½ years old, was the third child of a mother who died two months after her birth. During her pregnancy with Nicola her mother was noticed to be jaundiced, and this was put down to the pregnancy, but following the birth of Nicola she was investigated for jaundice and found to have abdominal cancer. She died from brain secondaries two months after Nicola's birth.

Nicola was placed in a special-care nursery at 4 weeks, and she was returned to her family after her mother had died. However, her father found he could not cope, and so Nicola was fostered out until she was 16 months old. During this time she was regularly visited by her father, and, in the last four months of fostering (from 1 year to 16 months), she was also visited by the person who became her new stepmother. Nicola surprised her parents by showing no separation problems and by adjusting easily when she was returned to the family after Mr and Mrs X married. Her reconstructed family at this time consisted of Mr and Mrs X, Michael, aged 9 years, Jenny, 7 years, and Nicola, 16 months. Nicola apparently bonded well to Mrs X and has maintained a good relationship with her ever since. Her younger brother, Derek, the only child of the second marriage, was born when Nicola was 3½ years old; she was reported to be 'delighted' and spent a lot of time with him. At 4½ years she went to kindergarten, and although she achieved bladder control at 18 months (two months after being returned to her family), she started wetting at this time. She showed considerable anxiety about going to kindergarten. Her entry to school was easier, and she was reported to be happy there, achieving within the average range, although she was said to show poor concentration. Her enuresis had continued and on referral was described by the urologist who examined her as an 'incredibly difficult problem of bedwetting' with no organic cause.

Nicola was referred primarily for help with her night-time enuresis; her stepmother also reported that Nicola was unhappy, and both parents complained about her babyish behaviour and the fighting between her and her elder sister, Jenny, now 17 years old. They came asking for hypnosis for Nicola so she could 'get back' to the dramatic events of her early life.

The assessment process involved a family assessment and two viewed[1] individual assessments of Nicola in the playroom. The family presented at that time as an apparently well-functioning but inhibited group who appeared to cope using denial, isolation, and avoidance. In her individual sessions Nicola was appeasing, compliant, and inhibited; she evidenced low self-esteem and tended to deny any worries or concerns. Her use of a game called 'SOS' and her need to deny her palpably sad affect in the final assessment session were seen as cries for help and evidence of increased distress in the context of being handed over to another therapist.[2] Although she had been dry during the assessment sessions, she began to wet her bed every night between the last individual assessment session and the final family assessment and contract-setting session. It was formulated that Nicola's enuresis might have its source in early separation and loss. Her use of denial and avoidance were seen to preclude more direct and effective ways of coping with her affective issues. The maintenance of her enuresis in an apparently coping, reconstructed family context was considered to reflect a lack of family resolution of issues connected to those early losses and adjustments. Thus it was decided that they should be offered some weekly non-intensive individual psychotherapy sessions for Nicola and regular collateral family therapy for the family. The author had viewed the individual sessions and offered to take Nicola and her family on in the ongoing therapeutic work.

The first time the author met the family was at the contract-setting session, which was attended by the author and the male psychiatric consultant who had assessed the case, Nicola, her stepmother, and her younger brother. Her father was out of town for several weeks; her older sister, Jenny, was reportedly working for her examinations, and Nicola's older brother, Michael, had left home and was working on a farm in the country and so could not attend the family sessions. In this session our initial formulation was presented to the family and our suggestions were discussed. It was agreed that Nicola would be seen weekly and her family would be seen regularly, but less frequently.

In her early individual sessions, Nicola said everything was fine at school and in her family, but did add that Jenny was 'a bit mean' and would not let her into her bedroom. She did not think she had any problems except 'I would like to stop wetting my bed'. Her play continued to be controlled and inhibited and consisted mainly of setting up competitive guessing games, which she made sure she won. These early sessions allowed time to think about the initial formulation and to add some further constructs to it. Nicola's birth and earliest development occurred in the context of loss by death, psychological unavailability, and separation. She was toilet-trained during the time she had been separated from her foster mother and was bonding to her new stepmother. Katan (1946) found a relationship between enuresis and separation from a loved one who has completed the toilet training. It would seem possible that toilet training that occurs in the context of a loss might also only be tenuously mastered. Certainly Nicola's next major separation (entry to kindergarten) appeared to precipitate her enuretic problem. Her entry to kindergarten also meant giving up her stepmother to her brother. Katan (1946) found that the development of enuresis could sometimes be related to the birth of a sibling, especially of the opposite sex. Nicola had shown no apparent jealousy towards her younger brother, but her first break from her stepmother meant that she was leaving her exclusively to her brother in her absence, and this may have contributed to her regressive symptomatology. Her competing or fighting with her therapist indirectly through game playing while maintaining a compliant and appeasing relationship could be seen as age-appropriate but also evidenced her difficulty with direct and open expression of what she might perceive to be unacceptable affects or impulses. Given that these ideas might offer some explanation for the development of her symptoms, the important question was, why was it being maintained?—in other words, what purpose was it serving in the family?

The transference provided some clues. Her stepmother had said, and Nicola herself in her early sessions affirmed, that she did not want to talk to the doctor who assessed her. She said she was afraid of him and that she much preferred a woman; she added that it was easier for her to talk to a woman than to a man. It was clear, however, that she was also finding it difficult to talk or play with her female therapist. Her therapist was not unaware that her dual role as therapist for both Nicola and her family was an ambiguous one and that concerns about confidentiality might be contributing to Nicola's difficulty, despite that issue having been carefully clarified for her. However, the predominant anxiety seemed to be family-related; Nicola did not have 'permission' to talk, and thus her difficulty was more a reflection of some of her concerns about her rights and place within her family. Something was happening (or not happening) in this family that was making it difficult for Nicola to give up her regressive symptoms and achieve a comfortable latency at this critical time of approaching adolescence.

The family members answered this question each in their own way in our next family session, which included Nicola's parents, Nicola, Derek (8 years), and Jenny (17 years). The therapist had insisted firmly that despite Jenny's examinations her presence was necessary in this session. She attended very reluctantly. Both parents suggested that Jenny's and Nicola's excessive fighting was due to Nicola's irritating, intrusive behaviour. Dad made it clear he could only too easily understand how Jenny felt. Jenny, agreeing with him, said that she only needed to look at her father and he would turn and chastise Nicola. It was clear that there was a strong alliance between Jenny and her father. Mr X said he understood how irritating Nicola could be because he found her babyish behaviour annoying himself; he said that she did silly things and asked irritating questions, always at the wrong time. He added that when she was not being like a 4-year-old she was trying to butt in on adult conversations. 'She doesn't act her age', and everyone agreed that she did not seem to know her place. Mrs X was a mediator and a buffer between Nicola and the rest of the family, and their seating reflected that. Derek tried, sometimes successfully, to engage Nicola in some clowning. He frequently tried to extricate the family from the serious nature of the discussion by this clowning, and when that failed he yawned and announced that he was bored. Mr X gazed distantly out of the window, but he had by this time acknowledged that his and Jenny's alliance against Nicola was a significant problem.

Following this session, Nicola talked for the first time in her individual sessions about her place in the family. She talked of feeling left out and picked on; she had permission to do so because her family had already talked about it. These feelings were most strongly related to her father and Jenny. The therapist and Nicola puzzled together over her 'irritating questions'. Nicola said she was trying hard but she just could not seem to get it right; she did not know how to talk to her Dad, or how to ask him questions. She said she could ask her stepmother questions and that she had talked with her about her birth mother. It became clear that most of what she knew about her birth mother she had learned from her stepmother. The therapist wondered aloud, 'What is the big question behind all these irritating questions; what is it that Nicola wants most of all to ask

her Dad?' Nicola paused briefly, then said, 'How did he feel
when my mother died?' The therapist agreed that this was a
pretty important question, which needed to be asked. There was
a great deal of discussion between Nicola and her therapist
about how she was going to be able to ask her father that question. Nicola was afraid he would be angry, and she wanted the
therapist's help. It was planned to bring it up at the next family
session. Nicola then wanted to know how the therapist would
help her ask this question. She was told that the therapist would
explain to the family that one of the reasons Nicola did not
know her place in the family was that she did not yet feel she
had a place. She was trying to find out where she fitted, but she
was having some trouble getting it right. It would also be
explained that it was hard for her Dad (and Jenny) to help her
because she reminded him (them) of the loss of her mother,
which was very sad. The therapist would suggest that sometimes people cope with sad feelings by getting angry and irrita-
ble, and that that might be a reason why Nicola found herself
being an irritating nuisance. Since Nicola's irritating questioning was the most difficult for Dad, it would be important to
understand what it was Nicola wanted to know from her Dad.
At that point Nicola would ask her question.

It happened pretty much the way it had been planned, and
Nicola asked her question in a rush. Her father did not seem to
hear at first. He looked stunned, and Nicola was crying; so was
Mrs X, who started to comfort Nicola. The therapist reminded
Mrs X that she was good at comforting and being with Nicola,
that she had always done it well, but that Mr X needed some
help to get closer to Nicola and comfort her himself. It was suggested that they change places. Mrs X appeared to understand
and she seemed relieved. Mr X moved his chair closer to Nicola;
he was crying, and he was trying to talk to her. Nicola put her
head on his shoulder, but his arms remained at his side. Mrs X
obviously had something to say, but she did not speak, so the
therapist asked her what she wanted to say. She turned to her
husband and said, 'Put your arms around her'. She said to the
therapist, 'It's so hard for him, he's not one to show his feelings.
I know how to get what I need from him; Nicola doesn't.' However, he had done his best, and his arms, hands clenched, finally
rested across Nicola's shoulders and back. He told Nicola why he

had had to give her up for 16 months, that he had wanted to keep her but he could not cope, and he had got her back as soon as he could. He added, 'I feel the way you feel'. Derek had long since stopped trying to turn the session into a joke and was crying with his parents and Nicola. He said he understood now why we were all meeting. Jenny was not there (she had refused to come because she said it was Nicola's problem and had nothing to do with her), so it was suggested they get out a family album and share some memories with Jenny. It was then that Mr X announced that all the photos had been destroyed. When it was agreed that this was a pity, he said, 'There might be one or two somewhere'. The therapist made it clear that she expected them to have found some photos and looked at them together before the next family session.

In the play-room in the intervening week, Nicola said she wondered why the therapist had chosen to see her and why Dr B, the psychiatric consultant who had assessed her, had not chosen to continue seeing her. She wanted to know if there had been any men viewing her sessions. She said, when asked, that she did have some feelings about Dr B passing her over to another person. Her therapist suggested that she seemed to have some questions about why a man would not want her and why a man had handed her over to a woman. It was suggested that those feelings and questions must be very like some of the feelings and questions she had about her place in the family; that it must seem to her that her father had not wanted to be involved with her and had handed her over to her stepmother. Nicola agreed and added that she's worried about not pleasing Dr B just as she feared not pleasing her father. In a later session she announced that she had not wet her bed for two weeks. She said that she thought she was getting on better with her father, but that he had not yet produced any photographs. The issue of termination of her therapy was raised by Nicola at this time, and she said she wanted to see how the next family session went before deciding how much longer she would need to come to her own therapy.

In the next family session Mr X agreed with Nicola's impression that everything had been going well. He said he had not managed to find any photographs, however. He said he was surprised because he had thought there would be one or two lying around. Mrs X then said that it was she who had wanted a 'clean sweep' and had asked for the photographs to be destroyed. She said that it had been hard for her to come in to the family in place of Nicola's mother. She said that she could not have coped with feeling that she had to compete with her predecessor. She had doubted that she could take her place. Mr X said that he, too, had thought it was better to bury the past and to look forward, not back. He paused and added that he could now see that one cannot always do it that way. It was agreed by all that feelings do not disappear as easily as photographs. The therapist wondered aloud about those photographs and whether it was too hard a task for Mr X to manage to find them. He cut in quickly saying he was sure his first wife's mother had some. The session finished with an agreement that Mr X would have finished the task of getting the photographs and spending some time with Nicola and Jenny looking at them before the next family meeting. His suggestion that he and Nicola come together to report on the success of the venture was seen as an important statement about the change in their relationship and his ownership of responsibility for and interest in her.

In the playroom, Nicola next surprised her therapist with a photograph of her mother. She talked animatedly about how Dad had arranged it, and how she had chosen one out of three photographs her grandmother had sent. She said, 'I look a lot like her, don't you think?' In her play she symbolically described the therapeutic process by drawing a maze and tracing paths back to the beginning. She told me, 'I had no trouble deciding that I only need three more sessions because things are going so well'. After some careful exploration of what she meant by that, it was agreed that she would have three terminating sessions. Nicola used her three final sessions to indulge herself in some really uninhibited sensual play with sand, clay, and water. Oral and anal themes were interpreted in terms of her hungry questioning and her now acknowledged wish sometimes to be like a messy little baby.

The final session, with Nicola and her father together, was reassuring. In general there was less denial and avoidance. Nicola obviously felt she had a secure place in the family; Mr X said he was very seldom irritated with her now, and that they were talking together more. When the therapist asked if Mrs X had found that the family work on mourning her predecessor had undermined her place in the family, Mr X said, 'If anything, it is strengthened', and he added that that was because they were now able to talk about it more openly. Nicola had not had a wet bed for five weeks, and this was without being woken to go to the toilet or using an alarm (all of these measures had been adopted earlier in efforts to solve the bedwetting problem), and often after she had had a drink late at night before going to bed.

It is true that Nicola's underlying internalized conflicts were not fully understood by either her therapist or herself. It was not possible to arrive at an individual intrapsychic formulation that could have added a fuller understanding of the sources of symptom choice. Any interpretative work was ego-based and related to her relationships within her reconstructed family. Only in interpreting her questions about being handed over was her original handing over by her birth mother, her father, and her foster mother raised, and then it was only alluded to and not directly discussed. This was because immediately felt and expressed affects were in relation to those currently in the family. It would have taken a much longer contract of individual work to achieve immediacy of affect in relation to any previous abandonments. It is questionable that it was even necessary or relevant. It may be that at some time in the future Nicola will decide herself to go into therapy in order to deal with any unfinished business. It was her decision to finish with the resolution of conflicts between her and her family and within her family and with the giving up of her symptom.

The question about what purpose Nicola's symptomatic behaviour was serving in the family was in some way answered. Her family coped with their difficulty about owning and working through their anger and grief by denial and avoidance. Nicola's presence, however, was a chronic irritating reminder. She had a place in the family as an irritating nuisance and providing a source of irritation and anger for her father and Jenny, who could thus avoid feeling sad. Her stepmother's (originally denied) anxieties about her own place in the family compounded the need for family denial of the importance of the loss of the first Mrs X. The current Mrs X was able to cope with her own anxieties by projective identification into and with Nicola. Nicola, who had difficulties with feeling sure of her place in the family and in particular with Mr X, mirrored perfectly her step-mother's anxieties. It was in fact only after some work had been accomplished in this area that Mrs X was able to own up to her doubts about being able to find *her* place in the family. For Nicola, who had already been handed over several times and who continued to feel unsure that she had a place in the family, perhaps it was better to have a place as an irritating nuisance rather than to risk having no place at all.

Muir (1975) stated that

> The more interpretive work can broaden into the group properties of the family of origin the better. The more the patient's defences, inhibitions and distortions can be understood and re-experienced in the light of the group properties dimension, and the more the particular family myths of the patient are clarified, the more clearly his own need to perpetuate symptom or character activities can be seen as complementary to a family need. [p. 14]

The work with Nicola and her family took place over a six-month period. It is difficult to predict what might have happened if Nicola had been seen in individual psychotherapy alone. One could assume that it would have taken longer, and it is possible that her core grief at losing her place with her birth mother, her family, and later her foster mother may have been worked through. If the family only had been seen, Nicola's diffidence, her fear of displeasing her father, and her inhibition and denial may have prevented her from confronting her father with her important question, 'How did you feel when my mother died?', because implicit in that question was the all-important question, 'How did you feel *about me* when my mother died?' It was this implied question that her father in fact answered for her in the family session. It was a frightening thing for Nicola to approach her father with that, and she needed to have a neutral confidante and ally with whom to work through her anxiety in advance, and in whom she could trust a sharing of the task of confronting him. She needed her own private individual time to work on these, her own private individual anxieties.

She also needed to know and feel what she was not supposed to know and feel (Bowlby, 1979), and in order for that to happen her family had to know and feel what they were avoiding knowing and feeling. It was essential that they shared the experience because unless all are able to integrate it may be difficult or impossible for any one individual to do so.

Nicola understood this. When she was asked in her last session what had been for her the most important part of the therapy, she answered, 'The day we all cried together'.

NOTES

1. The clinic where this work was done is part of a teaching hospital. The one-way screen is used frequently for teaching group supervision and peer review purposes.

2. This prospect was discussed in her last assessment session as part of the possible plan for ongoing management of the case.

PART TWO

THE PSYCHOTHERAPY
OF INFANCY

Over the last two decades or so we have seen a very considerable renewal of interest and attention, with a more empathic approach, to the birth, quality of life, and potential difficulties of the newborn and the young infant. In terms of the therapeutic aspects, some major work has been instituted in the United States, where, for example, such terms as 'infant psychiatry' and 'infant mental health' have become accepted in the field of child care. The first of these is linked with the name of Eveoleen Rexford (Rexford, Sandler, & Shapiro, 1976) and the second with the clinical study of infants' well-being as practised by Selma Fraiberg (1980) and her colleagues in the Child Development Project established in 1965 at the University of Michigan Medical School.

Similarly, the early work of John Bowlby (1965) and James Robertson (1953), as also the more recent work of J. H. Kennell and M. H. Klaus (1971), have provided an important impetus and support for a great deal of therapeutic and preventive endeavour instituted in maternity and paediatric wards and in Special Care Baby Units by medical, nursing, social work, and psychotherapy staffs (Szur et al., 1981; Bender & Swan-Parente, 1983).

In referring to the psychotherapy of infancy, one would have in mind, in terms of chronological age, a period ranging from birth to somewhere between 3 and 5 years, though in qualitative terms it is defined rather by Winnicott's description of infancy as 'referring to a phase in which the infant depends on maternal care that is based on empathy rather than on what is or could be verbally expressed' (Winnicott, 1965, p. 40).

On occasions when direct help for the child is indicated in addition to counselling for the parents, it has been found possible to engage with infants, even within their first year, who are able to respond to and make use of their own individual sessions. (In this, as in most work with children, the parental support for therapy will, of course, be an important factor.) In chapter eight Genevieve Haag presents a report of such long-term but rewarding work.

A valued background to much of this work has been the study of Infant Observation, as initiated and developed by Esther Bick (1964; see also Miller et al., 1989). This consists essentially in observing the growth and development of an infant within the everyday home and family setting, beginning from the early weeks and continuing for a year or two. Although Infant Observation began as an aspect of the training of child psychotherapists, the richness and depth revealed through these detailed and relatively unstructured observations have since attracted widespread interest and engagement from other professionals concerned with children and families, such as doctors, teachers, social workers, psychoanalysts, and family therapists.

Among those whose work contributed greatly to a deeper understanding of infant experience and the development of psychotherapeutic approaches that could offer help to both infant and parent in times of special stress or apparent impasse, Martha

Harris brought to this field a special depth of understanding and sensitivity. Perhaps a brief reference to two particular pieces from her published work may serve to illustrate something of these aspects.

In a 'therapeutic consultation' with two parents and their 22-month-old infant, reported in an early paper (Harris & Carr, 1966), Martha Harris' sensitivity to the little boy's communications, together with her implicit respect and encouragement for the parents to 'follow their perceptions, and to use their latent resources without increasing their feelings of helplessness, dependence, and failure', offers us an important theme and an influence that might inform our work in many other contexts.

A more recent paper, 'Some Notes on Maternal Containment in "Good Enough Mothering"'(1975), is concerned with early mother–infant interaction in terms of the 'pre-requisite for mental growth of a primary maternal object who can be an adequate container for the infant's personality, the "good enough mother" about whom Winnicott (1965b) has written'. Continuing with this theme, she describes the concept of the 'container' formulated by Bion (1962) in terms of 'the infant's need for a mother who will receive the evacuation of his distress, consider it and respond appropriately', thus giving the infant 'an experience of being understood as well as comforted.'

Further, there is the aspect of the 'primal containing or "skin" function', as formulated by Esther Bick (1968) in terms of the mother 'holding the parts of the [infant's] personality together', with her holding arms and through the qualities of her emotional understanding and responsiveness to the child's communications and needs.

Martha Harris considered it likely that failure to introject a primary object able to contain and provide a basis for the integration of the personality might presage a degree of pathology. Drawing here on the work of Meltzer (Meltzer et al., 1975), she added that this might present in varying forms and degrees, 'from the extremes of autism and functional mental defect, to the less obviously pathological or stunted states of shallowness and superficiality, of inability or reluctance to give deep emotional commitment' (Harris, 1975).

Characteristically, she concludes that it also seems likely 'that areas and states of non-containment, of two-dimensionality and mindlessness exist in the development of every infant and are therefore in us all'.

[R.S.]

CHAPTER FIVE

Brief therapeutic work with parents of infants

Isca Salzberger Wittenberg

This section begins with the beginning of the life-cycle. The first encounters are with a young couple who are awaiting the birth of their first child but are burdened with many fears and anxieties. In a second case a mother is helped to find her way out of a state of severe post-natal depression. The third series of interviews is with a young family who are being torn apart as they struggle to cope with a tragic loss. Although in each of the cases no more than a few interviews were given, yet the therapist was able to interpret in some depth, and the changes that were revealed over the time were profound and moving.

[R.S.]

When a few years ago the Tavistock Clinic set up a Brief Counselling Service for parents of children under five, I was very interested to participate in this new venture. I particularly welcomed the opportunity of seeing parents during the pregnancy and in the first year of their baby's life.

Previous experience of brief work had convinced me that at critical points of transition in a person's life even a few interviews can be useful. The new situation often produces an inner turbulence and may drive the individual urgently to address previously undigested anxieties. To be able to talk about their worries and fears, to be listened to by someone who can bear to stay with psychic pain and help them to think about their feelings in depth, may give clients some understanding of the nature of their problem. In some cases this may lead to a realization that more ongoing help is required, but often the insight gained and the experience of being understood is enough to enable clients to manage their lives more constructively and in some instances even to undo a block in their development. This latter outcome is only likely to occur when the problem is limited to a specific area of personality and has come to the fore through some recently experienced stress.

Having a baby is a most disturbing as well as a very exciting event. New parents in particular are undergoing major life changes. Up to this moment they have been a two-some, but now they need to make space for a third person. This new entrant into the couple's life radically alters the nature of their relationship, requiring them not only to care for each other as partners, but to be jointly responsible for the baby they have created. A mother is likely to harbour some fears about the kind of baby inside her, of what it might do to her body, as well as worrying whether she can provide a good enough environment for its growth. In the last few months, the burden of carrying the baby, anxieties about the birth, and the responsibilities facing her may weigh heavily. After the baby is born, the wonder and joy at having produced a live baby have to be matched with the realities of the ongoing strain of looking after a physically and emotionally demanding little one. Not only is the actual work of taking care of a vulnerable young infant physically taxing, but the baby's communication of his/her terrors of helplessness, of falling apart, of struggling to survive will put to the test the parents' capacities to be in touch with, tolerate, and attend to such extreme primitive anxieties with sympathetic understanding. In each partner the nature of their relationships to their own father and mother and siblings as well as their infantile anxieties will be evoked. What they have internalized on the basis of their own experience of having been babies, children, and in their parents' care will deeply affect the way they perceive the new baby, how they interpret its behaviour, and the way they deal with it.

While the mother is likely to be the main care-taker, the father, too, is called upon to take on a new role, helping with the baby and supporting his wife with his understanding, thus parenting the mother. In addition, he will have to cope both with the jealousy that may be evoked by the closeness of the nursing couple and with envy of the mother's ability to feed the baby. All these upheavals, external and internal, while causing temporary distress, may also lead to a spurt of emotional growth and deep satisfaction for one or both parents. If the burden becomes too great, however, and the anxieties aroused too unbearable, temporary or even more long-term breakdown may ensue. Alternatively, past unhelpful defensive patterns of dealing with feared emotions may become re-inforced, to the detriment of the parent–child relationship.

The study of infants, which includes detailed observation of babies within their own families for a period of some two years, has made us aware of the intricate interplay between the mental states of infant, mother, and father. One learns at first hand about the most primitive anxieties and the defences against them, observes how adjustments and maladjustments come about, watches character in the making. The responsiveness of mothers and fathers plays a vital role in laying the foundation for the children's emotional growth, the structuring of their personalities, and the specific vulnerabilities that they may be subject to throughout life. But the baby's endowment also plays an important part. Moreover, a responsive baby may help to pull the mother out of a depressed state, while a 'difficult-to-satisfy' infant may undermine a mother's confidence in her ability to care for her baby and may precipitate a vicious cycle of persecutory behaviour between them. Infant observation also helps one to study one's own feeling responses to the triad of baby, mother, and father. We need to become aware of the strength and nature of the emotions evoked in us in order to empathize with parents and infants and not to allow prejudices and judgemental attitudes to interfere in our professional work.

The following are likely to be some of the chief hazards:

1. *Over-identification with the baby.* There is a tendency to identify with the infantile wish never to be frustrated, to have a perfect mother. This attitude tends to show itself in being impatient when the mother is at first clumsy in her feeding or keeps the baby waiting for a feed, expecting her to provide instant relief, be constantly available, infinitely patient, never tired, never having needs of her own. There is an assumption that all distress in the baby is due to inadequate mothering and could therefore be avoided.

2. *Jealousy of the baby* is often less obvious but probably always present to some degree. We all harbour an infantile wish to be nursed, fed, carried about, given exclusive love and attention, and we may therefore feel jealous of the baby, noticing only the satisfactions rather than the distresses that are part and parcel of being an infant. Sometimes this leads to the view that the baby is being indulged too much—for instance, that the mother feeds him too long, or should not let him go to sleep at the breast.

3. *Competitiveness with the mother* has its roots in childhood rivalry with our own mothers and the wish to have babies of our own. It shows itself in a judgemental attitude towards the way the mother and father handle the infant and in unfounded doubts about the parents' capacity to be good caretakers. We tend too readily to be critical and need to be aware of an inclination to step in and rescue the baby (which is only seldom necessary). We may feel inclined to give advice rather than being supportive and understanding of the difficulties of parenting a baby twenty-four hours a day.

It is essential to be aware of such tendencies in ourselves when we engage in counselling parents. There are a number of ways of setting about this task. My own approach is based on insights gained from psychoanalytic work. I attempt to get in touch with and understand the parents' feelings, their unconscious phantasies, and the nature of the anxieties that interfere with their ability to care for the baby in the way that their more adult selves would wish to do. The work is intense and emotionally demanding. It requires of the client an availability and awareness of feelings in depth and the capacity to reflect upon them anew. The therapist needs the experience of ongoing psychoanalytic work in order to be able to discern quickly the nature of the underlying anxiety and to have the conviction to face it fully and unflinchingly with the client. In some cases we may have to weigh up whether the baby is in any physical danger, but more often it is the emotional development that is at stake. I am convinced that we can best help the baby by the help we offer to the infantile aspects of mother and father, thus setting a model for them of being interested in thinking about and containing infantile feelings.

The following examples will illustrate some of the stresses experienced by parents and the way I found of working with them. I have of course changed the names and not revealed any personal data that could enable any person, other than the clients themselves, to identify the individuals discussed.

From boyhood to fatherhood

Mr A was referred by his doctor because he had recently suffered severe panic attacks. He told me that a month previously, when setting off on a long journey, he had become breathless and felt pains across his chest. He was terrified, sure that he was very ill, and had gone home. A few days later he managed to board the train but felt awful while away from his wife. Extensive physical examinations revealed no abnormality.

When I asked whether anything special had happened around the date of the onset of the symptom, he replied that he was going to redecorate the flat and prepare it for the arrival of their first baby, which was due in two months' time. He quickly went on to say that he had been told that he would shortly be promoted to replace the retiring manager of the department of his firm. He added that he was not an emotional type and did not as a rule worry much. When I encouraged him to tell me about his family, he told me first that his mother had been unhappy since moving out of town; she often complained on the telephone, saying how miserable she was. Mr A felt he should have advised his parents not to leave London. When I said that he seemed to feel responsible for his mother's unhappiness, as if it were up to him to make decisions about where his Mum and Dad should live, he exclaimed: 'Did you say my father was dead? He is alive.' When I wondered what made him mis-hear what I had said, he replied that his father had had a serious heart attack some eighteen months previously. I commented on the similarity between the symptoms of a heart attack and those Mr A had experienced at the railway station. Mr A commented cheerfully that his father was much better now, and he himself was fitter since going to relaxation classes. I noted that although this was no doubt helpful, he seemed to reassure himself quickly rather than wish to explore what might be the underlying reasons for feeling so much stress. I said that I had gathered that he was going to take on more responsiblity on two fronts, at home as well as at work; perhaps that felt like stepping into the shoes of his father just as at his job he was taking over the boss's place. Mr A now told me that the baby had not been planned; his wife had wanted it, but he was not at all sure he was ready yet. He had thought that they would wait for some years, until the flat was sorted out. He passed lightly over the fact that his wife had had a serious kidney problem, reassuring me that there was really nothing to worry about, and quickly returned to talking about his work. I pointed out that he seemed to find it easier to talk about his job, as if running away from the very worrying situation with his wife, which was perhaps too frightening to think about. I added that he seemed to be faced suddenly with a great deal of worry and responsibility: his wife in bad health and expecting a baby, his father suffering from a life-threatening disease, an unhappy mother. He said 'Well, I've made light of it all, I've actually not thought about it. I am always surprised when my wife or mother gets upset and worried.' I said he seemed to try to put such frightening thoughts away but that then they caught up with him, as they did at the railway station. I thought he experienced the demands of all these needy relatives inside him as if they were attacking his body. He might perhaps also feel that it is easier to be the ill one than the one who has to take care of others. Mr A now returned to the theme of his ageing parents and mentioned his childhood memories of a sick and needy grandmother who had lived with them. He was an only child and very close to his mother. His father, he commented, was uncommunicative about feelings but good with his hands, making and repairing things in the house. He wished he could ask his father's advice about how to redecorate and fit out the kitchen. I said that perhaps he wished he had learnt from his father how to be the head of the family, to look after wife and child, to be a grown-up man, and that he was talking as if it were too late to do so now. Fighting tears, he exclaimed: 'Well, my father might die at any moment.' When I commented on his distress, he began to cry, saying he had never been close to his father. I said he seemed to regret this deeply, also wishing perhaps to tell his father before it was too late that he admired his creative and reparative abilities. Mr A's head was bent, and he was nodding and crying. He said he was going to see his parents that weekend and would speak to his father. He said the interview had been very helpful. I asked whether he would like to come again on his own or bring his wife, and we agreed that he would discuss the matter with her.

They came together for the second interview. What emerged in this session was Mrs A's anxiety about her husband's state of mind and his inability to be supportive to her. While obviously carrying a burden of anxiety and depression, she, too, was inclined to dismiss her worry about the future. They clearly cared a great deal for each other but were so worried about upsetting one another that they were unable to voice their anger, complaints, and worries. This lack of communication had resulted in a rather unproductive and unsatifying relationship.

Third interview

They reported that when they had gone out to enjoy themselves at the weekend, Mr A's chest symptoms had reappeared. He thought it was because he felt guilty at going out when the repair work in the flat was still left undone. I said perhaps he felt that he was escaping from a task that was essential. I added that I had in mind not only the flat, but also the neglected, unattended state of their marriage, which left both of them depressed and anxious, unable to enjoy life together and to look forward to having a baby. Mrs A cried as she told me how helpless she felt in the face of her husband's panic attacks and depression. She also felt very hurt that nothing she did made life seem worthwhile for him; he was not even excited about the coming baby. Mr A said he had thought that their marriage would be more along conventional lines, 'where I earn the money and you do everything else'. This made Mrs A reply, 'Your Mum always did *everything* for you'. He agreed, saying he had been spoilt: 'It was great, mother did absolutely everything, I did not have a thing to worry about—it was like having a hotel room at home.' I commented that perhaps now this also made him feel guilty, linking this to his worry about the state of his home. I wondered whether the redecoration of the flat was such a terrible burden to him because it was experienced in his mind as having to restore his mother who, because of the way he had used her, was felt to be in a worn-out, messed-up state. At this Mr A burst into tears, and when he recovered, he exclaimed: 'Where was I, why have I never felt anything like this before?—Oh, I wish I had! What did I do with my life up to now, why have I taken everything for granted? It's now so hard to do something about it!' Mrs A stroked her husband's hand, saying, 'There have been happy times, you know'. At this he turned angrily towards her and burst out: 'Don't, it is good to cry and to feel like this, I've never done it till now!' At the end of their interview Mrs A spoke about her difficulty in distinguishing between asking her husband to help her and actually pushing him too much in a controlling way.

Because of the imminent birth of the baby, I saw the couple only once more, and they seemed then to be able to communicate a little more openly with each other. Nevertheless, I was so worried about them that I got in touch some time after the birth of the baby. The mother reported that they were coping far better than they had expected. She thought that they would want to contact me some time again in the future.

Comment

In spite of Mr A's attempts to run away from emotional problems, there was clearly also a wish to explore them. Otherwise he would not have agreed to his doctor's suggestion that he seek counselling, nor been so responsive to my interventions. I could not but feel sorry at his being so suddenly faced with multiple new responsibilities, a reality for which he was ill prepared. The realization that he had remained a baby in relation to his mother and his wife, had not faced his rivalry with his father, and therefore had not learnt to identify with his adult masculine capacities, left him at the mercy of feeling persecuted by feelings of guilt and impotent to repair the situation. Fate had now forced him to make a choice between opting out by physical and mental breakdown or else facing reality, the guilt about his exploitation of his mother and wife and the denigration of his father. To take responsibility was felt to be an overwhelming task, as for him it meant not only repairing the present external situation but making up for all the neglect in the past. Clarification, naming the real source of his anxieties, had enabled Mr A to become painfully in touch with his feelings. But this also provided relief. For what had seemed a threat to his life became a realization of his greed, his ingratitude, and his misuse of his objects. It also lifted the unconscious burden of guilt that he had carried for a long time, and this made it possible to think that there were ways of being reparative in the present without having to be omnipotent.

It may be considered that this young man was confronted in too abrupt a way by me, but I think it was important to get to the root of his persecutory anxiety quickly in order to relieve intolerable pressure. This is especially important in brief work. I was guided in this by my countertransference, and I had also noticed that there was in this man an impressive determination to get in touch with his feelings and not shrink from painful truth. The fact that I treated him as someone able to face difficulties, unlike his wife and mother in the past, enabled him to draw on his strength and to display his masculine abilities. I think it is interesting to note that in the first interview the appreciation of his father began to emerge, while in the later sessions the relationship to his mother became the focus of attention. He felt driven to re-examine and to repair the relationship to both parents as he himself entered into parenthood.

I do not usually follow up clients who have attended the counselling service. The fact that I did so in this case is an indication of the degree of worry about physical and mental health that the family carried and that had been projected into me.

Unresolved mourning:
Making space for a new baby

The general practitioner wrote as follows:

> I would be grateful if you would send this family an appointment. Betty and Mike, both in their early 20s, have been together for some years now and seemed to manage very well after the birth of their first baby, Ricky. He, however, had a serious illness involving many months of in-patient treatment and died aged 17 months. Betty was heavily pregnant with Christine at the time and she was born six weeks after Ricky's death. Initially they seemed to be coping well with both grief and the arrival of the new baby, but it has become apparent that the stress has become enormous and neither of them is coping. One of the main problems is that Mike, who tends to be quite buttoned up, has become very destructive, which made Betty recently briefly leave home. She herself is very angry at the events surrounding Ricky's death and Mike's bad behaviour. I am afraid they are having a great deal of trouble containing all these bad feelings within their relationship. I am also worried how this might affect the new

baby, who is 7 months old now. They have come to me asking for professional help. I hope you will be able to do something for them.

I saw the couple within a few days, just before Christmas. They were half an hour late arriving. He was blonde with a round, soft baby-face, wore two earrings in his left ear, and looked very depressed. She was dark-haired and pretty, and she had dark rings under her eyes and an angry, withdrawn expression. They sat down on opposite sides of the room. I said that I had heard from their doctor that there had been difficulties in their relationship since their older child's death. They both stated emphatically that it had nothing to do with Ricky's death. They had quarrelled a lot of times before, and Betty had twice left Mike. They did add, however, that recently they argued 'about every silly little thing'. I commented that they seemed troubled by this, but the fact that they had come together indicated that they were both interested in doing something about their relationship.

I wondered why they had come late and learnt that they had had a 'tiff' on the way to the Clinic. Betty was angry that Mike had crossed over to the other side of the road. She had taken this to mean that he did not want to come, especially as last night he had told her not to worry. Mike said firmly that there was never any question of his not keeping the appointment at the Clinic. I said they were showing me how easily they misunderstood each other at present, and it also indicated Betty's doubts about Mike. Mike said he got violent sometimes and hit her. Asked what made him feel angry, he replied that Betty did not listen to him or want to understand him. Betty said, 'but when I ask you what the matter is, you just sit there and don't answer'. I said they were telling me that the communication between them had broken down, and each of them appeared to feel hurt and rejected by the other.

Betty said Mike had been wonderful with Ricky. When I wondered whether Ricky had been a bond between them, which was now broken, both denied this. Betty said she had left Mike when she was six months pregnant with Ricky; but they got together again because, when they were close, they had a wonderful relationship. Now, however, it was worse than ever before. I could sense a great deal of anger in the room and therefore ventured to say that perhaps they were angry with each other because they had not been able to keep Ricky alive. From this point onwards Ricky was at the centre of our conversation. Mike said he was very angry with the hospital, and he reported various examples of mistakes that had been made. He added that Ricky was a wonderful child, a marvellous chap, he was so proud of him. Christine, Betty said, was nice, but ordinary—Ricky was special. She asked whether I would like to see photographs. She produced a picture of Ricky, showing a charming, smiling little blonde, blue-eyed fellow, crawling in his cot. Christine was dark-haired, a fat and rather pudding-like baby with a solemn expression. I commented on Ricky's friendly smile, and Mike said that was how he was all the time, always cheerful and full of fun in spite of all he had to go through.

In telling me about Ricky, Mike became quite animated, while Betty showed little emotion. I spoke about Mike's pride in his son and then asked about his illness. They said he seemed fine when he was born but when they were planning to leave the hospital, the doctor informed them that Ricky had aplastic anaemia and would need blood transfusions every six weeks. He was all right for some months, then not so well, but he always recovered again after transfusions. During his second year he began to have bouts of illness, but much of the time they still thought he would be all right. When he was 15 months old, a specialist told them that they had to be prepared for the likelihood that Ricky had no more than two to four months to live. He was put on chemotherapy—and there followed descriptions of the mistakes they thought had been made by the nurses and doctors. I asked whether they were blaming the hospital for Ricky's death. Mike replied: 'I can't help wondering. After they moved Ricky to another room, he just went down, and after 6 days he gave up.' Betty said, 'All this time I was pregnant. The new baby was to be a "bone marrow" for Ricky, but he didn't wait for it.' I asked whether they felt disappointed and perhaps angry with Ricky for giving up the struggle when they were trying everything to keep him alive. Mike agreed, saying, 'Why, when he fought so hard, did he have to die just then'. I said they must have felt utterly helpless and as if someone must be to blame for this tragedy. Betty said that his illness was thought to be hereditary. If so, it would be on her side, but in fact all the males in her family were all right—Ricky had a rare disease. I said I thought the feelings of anger and blame seemed to have got into their relationship and made it hard for them to talk to each other. 'At first', Betty said, 'we were inseparable—we met a lot of single parents and separated couples at the hospital; some left their partners because of the illness—*we* were regarded as the ideal couple'. The doctor at the hospital had been worried that Betty might reject the new baby and told Mike to look after her, but in fact Betty had taken to her and it was Mike who was not interested in Christine. I said perhaps it felt to him to be disloyal to his son to love the new baby. Turning to Betty, I said she seemed to find some comfort in having a healthy baby that flourished, while Mike had lost both a son who was like him and the closeness with her and so felt left out and angry. I asked Mike about his work. He had taken a course in plumbing but had given it up half-way through—he regretted that now. He had had a job, lost it, and then he had wanted to spend all his time with Ricky. He would like to get back to work now, it had given him satisfaction in the past. I said the absence of work added to his feelings of helplessness and doubts about being able to be constructive. I ended the interview by saying I hoped they would find time to talk to each other, as they had done today. They eagerly agreed to come again two weeks later, just after New Year.

Second interview

I hardly recognized Betty, she looked so much better, with her fresh complexion and pretty make-up. Mike also looked more cheerful. They reported that they had had a very good Christmas. Mike said he had felt so much lighter when he walked out of my room after the interview last time, it was as if a heavy burden had been taken off him. Things had been so stuck between Betty and himself, but ever since our meeting they had gone on talking to each other. When he felt hurt he told Betty what it was that he felt hurt, or angry about. Betty agreed that their relationship had much improved. Mike, she thought, had been more caring, but she was still not sure of him. Mike said: 'I am doing all the talking, it is all one-sided.' I commented that it seemed to be Betty's not being sure about him that made him feel uncertain that she loved him. Betty said he was constantly asking to be reassured, even when she felt that things were going well between them. She admitted that she was rude to him sometimes and called him 'stupid', but she did not really mean it.

Mike said that much of the time he could not get through to Betty. I noted his vulnerability to feeling unloved and unwanted and remembered that they had told me that Betty's mother helped out with the baby while he was not in touch with his family. It emerged that he had lost his father in childhood and had never felt close to his mother since then—'she never listened'. I pointed out that he seemed to have quite a history of feeling not listened to and that this might make him very sensitive to Betty's non-availability. At this, Betty added: 'He wants me to be his Mum much of the time, but I have got the baby to look after.' I said this might leave Mike feeing rather excluded, especially after being already so hurt by losing a son. Mike exclaimed, 'I feel such a failure, with no work and the baby dying'. I said that all that might make him particularly dependent on Betty's approval. At this Betty looked across warmly at him, as if this was a new insight for her. Mike visibly brightened up. He reported that he had gone out to look for work. I said that having a job was a very important way of feeling needed and useful. While Betty had the advantage of being reassured of being productive by being able to feed the baby, he had less opportunity to prove to himself that he had the capacity to be constructive.

We talked a little about Christine. Mike said he was enjoying her more now, although Ricky was always present in their minds. He said that they did lots of things together now, like decorating the flat, while before he had spent almost all day watching television, and so Betty and he had really not communicated—she was always busy with the baby. I said it seemed that, while everything appeared to have come to a dead end with Ricky's death, they now felt that their first child was still a part of themselves, and they could, therefore, invest in the present, in their home and their new baby. They said that Christine was a very different baby, much quieter than Ricky; but they both commented that she was repaying them with smiles these days—'she has come more to life since we have been less pre-occupied and given her more attention and love.'

Betty mentioned that she could be more open with Mike because she was less frightened of him. I said I remembered that Mike mentioned that he used to hit her. He said he had not done so recently, he did not let himself get into such a state. 'I have come to realize that it is better to talk rather than to act on one's feelings', he added thoughtfully. Betty said that he became violent under the influence of drink, and she was always worried when he went out to the pub; even if he had had only a couple of drinks, she felt tense, and he reacted to that. He thought the drinking had started two years ago. I said that sounded as if that was at the time they learnt about Ricky's illness, and, like watching TV, drinking was a way of escaping from worry and painful feelings. When he said that drinking make him feel more alive, I added that it was to counteract the dead feelings inside him.

They again stressed how enormously things had changed for the better and that they really felt close to one another, and for the first time really interested in Christine. I commented that they seemed to have done a great deal of work together and wondered whether they might wish to carry on by themselves rather than continue our contact. I added that if they wanted to have further appointments at some future date, they could of course get in touch with me again. I hoped that they would do so if their relationship deteriorated, or they were worried about the baby. They agreed that they wanted to see how they managed on their own. They both warmly shook my hand, and Mike gave me a big wink and smiled as he went out of the room.

Comment

This was a very moving encounter. I felt that Mike and Betty cared deeply for each other. It needed only a minimum of help to enable them to look at how the anger and depression about their child's death had got into the way of their supporting one another. I was particularly impressed by the father's responsiveness to being given a chance to be understood. This made it possible for him to talk to his wife instead of bottling up his feelings and putting his despair and hurt into destructive action. He seemed to be the main carrier of despair. By projecting her feelings into him, Betty had been freed to take care of the new baby; yet she had done so at the expense of cutting herself off from her feelings and from her husband. Christine's rather deadpan expression suggested an absence of an alive interchange with mother and father. By working at the unresolved feelings of mourning for the dead child, the parents were enabled to be in touch with their loving feelings for each other and to invest them in their new baby. I could have seen the couple for a longer period but judged that it was important not to interfere in what seemed to be a close working relationship.

Post-natal depression

When Mrs D rang the Counselling Service, saying that she wished to consult someone about difficulties over her baby's birth, our sensitive secretary gained the impression that she was severely depressed and therefore arranged for her to come to see me a few days later.

First interview

A pleasant-looking woman, Mrs D immediately delved into the terrifying birth experience with Debbie. She cried throughout the interview, drying her tears with the many tissues she had brought with her. She had not expected the birth to be difficult. Contractions had been normal, but then the baby became 'stuck'. Neither the epidural nor the anaesthetic worked, and she was in severe pain. Eventually the baby was extracted by suction, and 'it all felt like being tortured'. When I commented

that it sounded a very frightening experience, she nodded agreement. She had talked with many friends, who had passed it off
as 'just a difficult birth', not understanding how dreadful it had
been. She lost a great deal of blood, was severely bruised, and
required extensive stitching. The following morning she was
asked to get up but fainted on the way to the bathroom. Everyone had told her that she was brave and strong, yet 'I was in the
most terrible pain and feeling dreadful'. I said she must have
been very shocked and have thought that nobody understood
how awful she felt. Perhaps she might be afraid that I, too,
would simply be reassuring instead of appreciating what a
frightening experience she had had and that she was still feeling dreadful. I added that it sounded as if she had thought that
she was dying. Mrs D began crying more copiously now, saying
that she still suffered from the consequences of the birth. The
episiotomy had left her not only very sore but so damaged internally that she had had to undergo a laser operation recently.
She had not been able to have intercourse because it was too
painful. Her husband and she were close and she had missed the
sexual relationship. She said that it was all so dreadful, they
had not in any way had a normal life since Debbie's birth. I
commented that Debbie's arrival seemed to have disrupted
everything.

Mrs D said her husband and his family, with whom they were
staying, adored the baby and could not understand why she
found Debbie so difficult. She herself could hardly bear to be
with her. She found the baby demanding and could not stand
her crying. I said she might feel that it was she that needed
looking after. She agreed, saying that for weeks and months she
thought, 'there is this bundle that I am supposed to nurse, feed,
and clean up, and I feel I cannot. I just want to turn away and do
nothing.' I said it seemed that she could not provide for the baby
when she felt her own needs, especially her emotional needs,
were not attended to. I also wondered how angry she might be
with the baby whose birth had caused her so much pain and
disrupted her relationship with her husband. She replied, 'I
know it is irrational, but I blame the baby for all this and I don't
trust myself to be alone with her'. I said it sounded as if she
were afraid she might hurt the baby. Mrs D cried for some min-

utes. She said sometimes she felt that she could not go on any more, but until now nobody had understood how she felt. Everyone had been trying to be nice, telling her how well she was doing, but that had not helped. Her husband was kind, and he was wonderful with the baby. She was glad to be out of the home much of the day and liked her work in an accountancy firm. Debbie was looked after by a minder who was good with her and had only one other child to attend to. I said she seemed to feel that this was safer for the baby and herself. Mrs D said that every time she looked at the baby she went over and over the birth experience in her mind. She added that it was good to be able to talk to me. She reiterated that she did not feel that anyone had listened to her before like this and understood how dreadful it had all been and how awful she still felt.

She asked whether she could come again soon, and we fixed another appointment four days after the initial one. I ended by saying that I thought it might be helpful to try to find times when she and the baby were more at peace, so that they could meet on some basis of pleasure, instead of distress, which was such a reminder of what agony had been involved in her birth.

Second interview

Mrs D looked a little brighter and said she was relieved to be able to come. There was one thing in particular that I had said that had been important to her. Every time she thought about the birth, she now remembered that I had said that she had thought that she would die. This summed up just how she had felt, and it was a comfort that somebody had recognized this. She had been able to look at the baby more and feel less angry, although the thoughts about the birth still went on and on in her mind. She then told me how resentful she had been last Christmas, when nearly all the presents she received had been for the baby. I said that even before the baby was born she had been afraid that the baby was robbing her of what had been hers before. I asked about her family and learnt that she had a sister who was married and had two children. I wondered whether Debbie was felt to be more like a sister than a baby of her own—a rival baby who had robbed her of her mother's attention. I also referred to the fact that it was going to be Christmas now and perhaps she felt that I was giving presents and attention to a child of my own rather than more of my time to her. She replied that she thought this Christmas might be a bit better than the last. I suggested that maybe when her needs and her painful experiences were given attention here, she was able to give more of herself to the baby. She told me that they were planning to buy a house of their own and hoped to move the following month.

Third interview

Mrs D reported that, although she was still crying when she came to see me, she was doing so much less at home. What emerged in this session was primarily that Mrs D had been very efficient and successful in her work and had thought of herself as a 'superwoman'. It became clear that the birth had disrupted this notion of herself as so capable and in control. I said that the delivery had thrown her back into a state of feeling helplessly dependent on others, like a small child. She seemed also to feel that these others had inflicted the pain and suffering on her on purpose, like torturers.

Fourth interview

Mrs D reported that she felt much better. They had moved, and she felt very pleased to be in her own home rather than staying at her in-laws'. She now had more space and freedom. Debbie was crawling up and down the corridor. I commented that there seemed to be a feeling of more space for both of them, that she and the baby could be near, yet not too close to each other. Mrs D talked of her love of gardening and hoped that Debbie might enjoy sharing this activity with her. She sounded altogether more hopeful. I agreed to Mrs D's wish that the fifth and last interview should take place after Debbie's birthday, a day she was dreading.

Fifth interview

Mrs D immediately started crying but said she had not done so for some time. It was good to have a home of their own, the sexual relationship with her husband had returned to normal, and she was enjoying Debbie. She mentioned that the baby was becoming very independent, was developing well, and had begun to sleep through the night. Mrs D looked proud as she told me that everyone finds her delightful. The baby minder had commented that Debbie seemed so much better these days. She was no longer restless and fretful. Mrs D thought this might relate to her feeling less upset and more at ease with the baby. I said the move and the birthday were quite a big event, marking the fact that they had all survived this very difficult first year. She seemed to have begun to enjoy her family. She said her husband had been thinking about another addition to the family, but she was in no hurry to have another baby. It was nice, though, to see Debbie settling down to toys, and she liked playing with her. I asked about the birthday, and Mrs D said it had all gone very well, and a good time had been had by everyone. They had invited friends, and Mrs D had made a big birthday cake.

Then she started to cry as she told me that she had been terribly upset by a dream she had had the night after Debbie's birthday. In the dream, she had seen the baby sitting inside the gas oven they had recently acquired. The baby was trapped and screaming, but she had just stood by looking on and did nothing. Mrs D cried heartrendingly, saying she was still terribly upset about the dream—it was so awful. I said what felt awful was that the dream showed her murderous feelings towards the baby, allowing it to be tortured. I thought the birthday had once more aroused her anger at the terrible birth experience. I reminded her that at one point we had talked about Debbie feeling like a baby sister. Perhaps the birthday had brought up childhood feelings about her mother's baby who was to stew and never get out of the stomach to have any life so that it should not rob Mrs D of her mother's attention. Maybe she felt that such hidden early feelings were the reason for her having such a punishing labour when she had thought that the baby might kill her. I recognized that she was feeling dreadful and very miserable about such murderous phantasies. I thought that alongside such thoughts she also felt very sorry for the baby, who was trapped inside and whom she had not been able to help to get out. This too must have made her feel helpless at the time of her birth. I thought that she was able to deal better with her feelings during the day-time and that these thoughts had now become contained within a dream.

Perhaps, as this was our last meeting, she might also feel angry with me, as if I were a mother who now replaced her with the next baby. Mrs D gathered herself together and told me the interviews had been extremely important to her. 'I don't know what would have happened if I had not had this opportunity to come and talk to you', she said; 'I feel I might have hurt the baby', and after a pause she added, 'or committed suicide'. We talked about whether it was appropriate for this to be the last time we met. Having given it some thought, Mrs D said she felt it was. We agreed that if she continued to be worried, she would contact me. I also suggested that when she became pregnant again, this might well be a time when she would wish to have further help. Mrs D asked me to write to her new doctor. She wanted me to explain about the birth and about her depression. She wished the doctor to know that she had been to the Counselling Service and that if she got depressed again this was the kind of help she wanted, rather than to be sent off to a psychiatric hospital or treated with anti-depressant drugs.

Comment

We see that Mrs D's experience of giving birth to a baby not only was felt as an attack on her body, but shattered the omnipotent image she had of herself as a 'superwoman'. This resulted in a life-and-death struggle between the strict internal voice, which demanded that she be perfect, and the rage with her child who had forced her to confront her vulnerability and her negative feelings about mother's babies. It was hard for me to decide during the course of the fifth interview whether it was safe for this to be our last meeting. But I trusted Mrs D neither to act on her feelings nor to push them out of her mind, but to

seek further help if necessary. I think it is important to remember that uncertainty about what has been achieved and worry
about the future are always present and are integral elements of
the burden of anxiety carried in brief counselling work. It is
essential that enough trust has developed during the course of
the intervention for the client to feel that one is truly interested
and concerned and therefore available to be contacted again
when needed.

Summary

I hope that the examples presented here in a brief form convey
something of the variety of problems parents brought and the
kind of interaction that took place between us. The comments
show some of my reflections at the time of seeing the parents
and subsequently.

I have found working with parents of infants to be deeply
moving and rewarding. One becomes aware of how prone parents are to feeling inadequate, helpless, persecuted, enraged,
depressed, and guilty. When there is no one to unburden themselves to, these emotions escalate, and anxiety quickly becomes
overwhelming. It seems therefore important to provide a readily
available counselling service, where parents can talk over their
difficulties without being given reassurance, offered facile solutions, or infantilized by an expert. I think the clients I saw
experienced me as someone genuinely interested in helping
them to understand themselves as well as their babies, someone
who respected their adult strivings to be good parents while
helping them to examine the more infantile and destructive feelings that interfered with their task.

I set out with no rigid technique in mind and found myself
working a little differently with every case. My experience of
psychoanalytic work helped me to be able to listen, to encourage
the exploration of the roots of the current anxiety, to stay with
psychic pain, and to believe in the emotional strength derived
from facing the truth. It always seemed to me that I was
doing very little, and I was astounded at the dramatic improve-

ment that often resulted. Of course, many questions remain unanswered, and the degree of long-term benefit the client derived is uncertain. Yet I have no doubt that in many instances a dynamic shift did in fact occur. In speculating about the reason for this, I would suggest that the clients were locked into an unhelpful pattern of relating, feeling persecuted and being persecuting. Conversations with me opened up a new channel of communication between destructive and loving aspects of themselves, between infant and adult selves, and this led to a better understanding between husband and wife, between parent and baby. As a result, hope was restored, and a benign circle of interaction emerged, which produced satisfaction and in turn increased the parents' confidence in their capacity to look after their babies and help them develop.

It seems to me appropriate to work briefly with parents so as not to encourage dependency and to avoid the danger of disturbing the new intimate relationship developing between parents and their offspring. On the other hand it may be important to offer on-going help where the parent has little internal containment or external support. Long-term help is likely to be essential where destructive feelings towards the infant dominate, and this may be the case if the parent has had a deprived childhood or been abused. There is another group of parents who, while they may be helped in their relationship with their baby, may indicate their need for therapy for a wider range of problems and can be encouraged to refer themselves to the appropriate agency. The parents I have worked with on a brief basis, although they experienced anger and at times hatred towards each other or their babies, showed great concern and were primarily worried lest their negative feelings would take over. While it may be wise to be cautious about what may be expected from a few interviews, I suspect there are many parents who could use such an opportunity to develop their own resources to understand themselves in their struggle to find a better relationship with their babies and thus lay a sounder basis for their emotional growth. It is a privilege to be allowed to play a small part in such a process, and it provides those of us who work in this field with a deep sense of joy.

CHAPTER SIX

Infants' sleep problems

Dilys Daws

We move here into the area of a General Medical Practice, where the child psychotherapist joins in the work of the Baby Clinic in seeing families who bring worries other than purely medical ones about their children. It has proved possible to enable them to resolve these difficulties, often within the space of a few interviews, and the chapter examines the theories and the technique involved.

[R.S.]

Psychoanalytically based brief work

Sleep problems appear to loom large for many present-day parents. These problems are presented urgently and over-whelmingly. Families often negotiate a referral by repre-senting themselves as being 'at the end of their tether'.

Reprinted by permission from D. Daws, *Through the Night: Helping Parents and Sleepless Infants* (London: Free Association Books, 1989).

I work one half-day a week in the Baby Clinic of a General Medical Practice and see families about problems of babies' or small children's development. The most pressing of these are often sleep problems, and these need to be seen quickly. I have found that as few as one or two consultations may allow a change in the parents' approach to the baby, which breaks a deadlock between them. For me, as a psychoanalytically trained child psychotherapist, this work is a departure from longer-term intensive work, and I am here beginning to examine the principles underlying it.

The technique that I use in this work is to combine a structured questioning about the details of the baby's timetable with a free-ranging enquiry into memories of the pregnancy and birth, and of the parents' relationship with each other and with their own parents.

The parents I see have usually been offered much advice already and often feel that they have 'tried everything'. What I give them in the first place is simple: a *free-floating attention*. As they tell their story, *unconscious threads* draw together, and connections emerge. Because I do not at once offer solutions, they are less likely to react negativistically. They are left able to free-associate and to perceive me as interested, receptive, and capable of holding on to a great deal of information. In this setting it is striking how economically parents can convey much focussed information. It seems as though all ordinary parents have a 'story' to tell about their baby, which is as dramatic and moving as any work of literature. What is also communicated, and confirmed by my interest, is the uniqueness of each baby and its family.

As this story unfolds, themes emerge about the nature of their relationships. For instance, the meaning of not sleeping may change with the age of the child. But underlying it at every stage seems always to be some aspect of the problem of *separation and individuation* between mother and baby, with feeding and weaning problems closely related.

Separation problems

Simplistically speaking, the problem for a mother in getting a
baby to sleep is the basic act of putting the baby down—that is,
of separating herself from the baby and the baby from her.

Joyce McDougall (1974) describes how a baby needs to come
to terms with the loss of the breast–mother 'and create psychic
objects that will compensate for his loss'. His capacity to do this
will be circumscribed by his parents' unconscious fears and
desires. Through over-identification parents tend to spare their
children 'the inevitable confrontation with reality. The anxieties
to which this primal separation gives rise are usually qualified
by terms such as annihilation and disintegration.'

This quotation conjures up powerful images of psychic processes. The consultations in which parents relate the details of
their confused nights of wakings and feedings are a live illustration of the disintegration to which Joyce McDougall refers. The
fragmented experience starts to come together while listening to
these details and making a more integrated pattern of them,
within my own mind in the first place.

One extreme example illustrated this: The mother of Barnaby, aged 4 years, and Clare, aged 6 months, had consulted
many doctors, homeopathic practitioners, and so on, about many
different complaints in herself and her children. She came in
great distress about both children's sleeping problems. She
talked non-stop about her many attempts to get help for this
multitude of complaints and her confusion about what to attend
to first. There was no dialogue between us, and ten minutes
before the end of the session I stopped her to point out that she
was leaving no time for me to talk.

I then said that I had had two thoughts while she was talking. One was that it was very difficult to bring up children. The
second was that she had consulted many professionals and that
they had all got it wrong for her. The mother was very taken by
this. Because I offered no advice, I was in no danger of getting it
wrong myself! More seriously, I had recognized that, full as she
was of her many conflicting anxieties, she had no space to let in
yet another opinion. The following week she brought her husband, and both told me, very painfully, of their own difficult

childhoods: I remarked that as well as leaving them unsure of their individual ability as parents, their different childhood experiences had given them conflicting ideas of how to be parents; they had reinforced these with the contradictory ideas that they sought and elicited from the many professionals they had consulted.

Thinking about this enabled both to be more effective with their older child. Barnaby's alarming temper tantrums went within the following week, and his sleep problems improved slightly. Their attention turned to the baby, Clare, who was waking frequently during the night and needing to be breast-fed by mother. They repeatedly asked, 'Should we leave her to cry?'

I described how there seemed to be no idea of any middle way between going in every time or abandoning her totally. They then asked if it would make her feel insecure and damage her if she was left for a while. I said perhaps we could turn the question around and think about how insecure it would make Clare feel if she thought that they had to come in every time she called out—that they could not trust her to manage for a while on her own, and that they could not trust their love and care for her to carry on for a while from the last feed. The parents knew that this reversal of mine was not superficial and 'gimmicky'— that I had been moved by their accounts of their own childhood insecurity and that I knew they felt damaged by it. While seriously keeping in mind the dangers of insecurity, I was able to suggest that Clare's position was not the same as theirs— with two loving parents safely at hand, her need was to experience herself as separate from them.

The problem for these parents, as for many others, is in feeling that what they have given the baby is good enough. Health visitors and doctors all know of the mothers who wonder whether their milk is 'good'. Such a mother may find it hard to let a baby know clearly that she believes he has had enough food and care and can manage on his own in the night.

Sometimes difficult birth experiences keep on getting in the way of a mother's picture of herself and her baby. Matt was nearly two and not yet weaned; his mother was embarrassed by this but could not let go of him. In the first session she cried as she told me about his birth. She had prepared herself well, but

when the time came it was all unexpected, rapid, violent. She spent ten days in hospital and began to recover. On the last night the hospital offered to baby-sit, and she went out to dinner with her husband. She came back and found her baby apparently neglected: crying, hungry, in need of a nappy change. She felt she should never have left him and that this experience must have damaged him permanently. Since then he had had problems in getting to sleep except when held at the breast, fed, and allowed to go to sleep from there. He had never been able to lie in his cot and fall asleep on his own.

We talked about how the first 'letting go', his birth, had gone so wrong and that she could not trust herself to let go of him without doing him some damage. There seemed to be an assumption that bad experiences were the only significant ones, as though Matt's mother felt that all the good experiences when his needs had been met must be obliterated by any bad ones and, further, that any letting go or separation were the same as bad experiences. We talked about how Matt might be able to enjoy a feed, let go of her and she of him, and then lie in his cot, savouring the memory of his feed and digesting the experience along with the milk. We noted that emotional as well as physical growth comes through these experiences. His father had always been an enjoyable part of the bedtime routine but had then handed Matt over to mother. His mother now sometimes entrusted his father with putting him into his cot.

She left a bottle of milk and biscuits within reach and offered herself less quickly to Matt in the night—the breast-feeding soon faded away, and Matt stopped waking up in the night. His mother then thought of the milk and biscuits as being too much a direct substitute for her breasts—she felt he would become someone always relying on food for comfort. She replaced the bottle with a musical toy, which Matt loved and played to himself as he lay in the cot going to sleep and when he woke up in the morning. She made the leap herself, and presumably therefore enabled her son to do the same—of creating a symbol instead of a direct substitute for herself.

Over the weeks the mother's relationship with her husband improved—two years of Matt's wakefulness had left little time for parental intercourse. She relaxed her tendency to

exclude him from aspects of caring for Matt, through her idea that only the breast could send the baby to sleep. She became able to let the father help her with the weaning, and when Matthew was weaned, his father could be an equal partner in caring for his son.

The musical box served somewhat belatedly for Matt as McDougall's psychic object or Winnicott's (1971) more widely known transitional object. It often feels as if what I am doing for mothers is offering them a temporary transitional object through the medium of words. Thinking together about their position with the baby, then putting into words what I feel is going on enables them to hold on to these words when they go back to their baby and renegotiate their relationship in the following nights. The words contain the combined thoughts of the mother and myself about the transition from one state to another.

McDougall quotes the works of Fain and Kreisler (1970) on babies suffering from serious psychosomatic disturbances in the first months of life. One important group is comprised of infants who are only able to sleep if rocked continually in their mothers' arms and otherwise suffer from almost total insomnia.

> Fain's studies suggest that these mothers have partially failed in their function as a protective shield against exciting stimuli, because they have overexercised this function. Instead of developing a primitive form of psychic activity akin to dreaming, which permits most babies to sleep peacefully after feeding, these babies require the mother herself to be the guardian of sleep. The author links this breakdown of the capacity to recreate a good internal state of being into symbolic form to an allied failure to develop autoerotic activity. Fain's observations lead him to the conclusion that these babies do not have a *mère satisfaisante* [satisfying mother] but a *mère calmante* [tranquillizing mother]. The mother, because of her own problems, cannot permit her baby to create a primary identification which will enable him to sleep without continual contact with her.

McDougall also suggests that in Fain's observations the mothers are 'performing an *addictive* function. The baby comes

to need the mother as an addict needs his drug, i.e. total dependence on an external object to deal with situations which should be handled by self-regulatory psychological means.'

Dreams and dreaming

It is appropriate when thinking about sleep problems as being in part separation problems to be led on by Fain to thinking of *dreaming* as part of the attainment of psychic individuality. Frances Tustin (1972) also writes of the stage where

> identification with a mother who can bear the pains of bodily separateness begins to take place. . . . Thus the capacity for representations and the use of skills develop. Dreams begin to take the place of random discharges and bodily movements. Innate forms begin to be transformed into thoughts and fantasies. The psyche as we know it begins. The child becomes psychologically viable and continent.

Palombo's recent work on dreams is exciting. In *Dreaming and Memory* (1978), he states that 'the dream itself—and not merely the interpretation of the dream—plays a positive, integrating role in normal emotional development'. Palombo seems to illuminate what may be crucially happening in dreams. He convincingly suggests that dreaming plays a central function in assimilating memories of the day into settled long-term memory. Thus if dreaming is insufficient or interrupted, the consequences are very serious for child and adult alike—they are left with a jumble of unassimilated experiences.

Perhaps what goes on in my consultations with parents is somewhat akin to this dream-work. Parents nearly always come in a distressed state with a confused mass of information about the baby's behaviour through day and night. All this is set in the framework of relationships and emotions. I think that an integrative process comparable to that of the dream is set in motion by my listening and *putting it in place in my mind to begin with*. I think that this helps the mother to start to 'dream

it over' for the baby, which then leaves the baby freer to follow
its own dreaming.

Luke, aged 6 months, and his mother illustrate this well. Luke's mother came to see me in a panic about having to wean him in two months' time because she was going back to work. She was feeding him constantly, night and day. We looked at how her grief at the coming separation, which felt like a forced one to her, had left her unable to discriminate between when Luke needed her and her breast and when he needed to be away from her. He fed often and was often sick. She muttered that her milk was poisoning him. I asked about her own upbringing, and she told me about her mother's uncertainties in her marriage and in her sense of herself as a mother. Her sense that she and her milk might be really 'bad' for Luke and her anxiety over the parting to come were both interfering with her ability to see how he was really using her. Luke meanwhile played in my room, bringing toys to his mouth and then blowing bubbles and uttering little 'talking' sounds. I showed the mother how the use of his mouth and the pleasures he could get from it were developing and that the beginning of speech included the use of his mouth to communicate at a distance from her, not just clamped onto the breast.

The following week she came back to say that Luke had slept right through the previous night. At first she could not remember whether anything different had happened that day—then she recollected that she had stayed out with him in his pram as long as possible and had kept moving. She had fed him once in the morning and once at night. As she talked, Luke pulled himself up and bit at the straps of his pram. His mother said she had just realized he had a tooth when he had bitten her breast. We speculated that by not being allowed at the breast on and off all day Luke had calmed down from a continual state of excited arousal. He was free to use his toys and experiment with his aggressive feelings without worrying about hurting his mother. His sense of self could develop both emotionally and cognitively. Similarly, mother was free to own more of her feelings towards her baby—it occurred to her that the separation to come had masked her natural feelings of *not* wanting to be with her baby all the time. I asked mother if she had had any dreams about all this. She laughed and said, 'I don't get to sleep for long enough to dream'. Then she recalled a dream a week previously, just after Luke's christening. In the dream she was wearing a white dress with buttons down the front. One button was open, and the baby's godfather had done it up for her. The economy of this dream is quite startling: the allusions to this mother beginning to button herself up against breast feeding, and the associations to sexual feelings and a wedding bring together the themes of our work. She had begun to speculate that her extreme closeness to Luke had caused her to feel more distant from her husband. She was starting to think about whether a more appropriate space between her and Luke would enable her marriage to come back to life. The white dress perhaps alluded to a new 'wedding' with her husband. The christening, a ceremony of recognizing Luke as an individual, was well timed for this family.

This dream was like a going-over in her mind, a commentary, on all these issues. It seemed to have set her free for the partial weaning process later in the week. Luke, in turn, was set free to sleep and have his own dreams.

Palombo also suggests that

Parents are in reality the original 'interpreters' of dreams. The repeatedly reassuring presence of his mother or her substitute after the experience of an awakening dream is a crucial element in any infant's learning to distinguish between his inner and outer worlds. . . . The child just beginning to talk brings his awakening dreams to his parents both for reassurance and to take advantage of their ability to translate his strange experience into words. . . . The parents' failure to supply what is needed at this point may have a serious effect on the later accessibility to the child of his early memories and of fantasy material in general.

Joanna's mother (Daws, 1985) showed me how hard it can be in reality to be an interpreter for a child's dream. Joanna, aged 12 months, would cry out during a nightmare; when her mother went in to her, she was rejected—that is, she was treated as a part of the nightmare. Joanna slept badly; she had many of these nightmares and frequent temper tantrums during the day.

Joanna's mother vividly described feeling that her baby saw her as a 'witch' in the night.

It seemed appropriate to go quite explicitly through a simple Kleinian version of child development and talk about the child's difficulty in managing her own aggressive and destructive impulses, and her need to project these into her mother. This mother was interested intellectually but also responded instinctively. The sleep difficulties had started at six weeks, after a brief period when father had to go away. We connected the sleep difficulties with mother's own panic at this separation and her resentment with father for not being there to support her. After ten months of bad nights, Joanna slept through the night for two weeks. After that there were some broken nights, but the relationship between mother and daughter changed dramatically from mutual fury to a loving, teasing one. By understanding the nature of her baby's fears in the night the mother was better able to respond to them. The baby now had the experience of being understood and was comforted by this understanding. She no longer needed to wake repeatedly to seek it.

Containing a baby's anxiety is difficult just because it so easily connects with parents' own anxieties. There are often real external causes for anxiety—birth difficulties, as with Luke's mother, or fears perhaps that a baby will die during the night. This kind of fear is based on grim reality; everyone has heard of such tragic events. Talking through these fears and experiences makes them more manageable. When the mother meets the baby's anxiety in the night it no longer connects with her own infinite dread, and she can respond to it appropriately. It seems as though my work involves directly containing the mother's anxiety so that she can go back to the baby and contain it for the baby.

Oedipal implications of sleep problems

Most parents know how compelling the force of a baby's anxieties can be. In oedipal situations—that is, where the reason for not sleeping seems to be an anxiety about the parents being together and excluding the child—parents often find they have slipped into some way of allowing their child to dominate their time together without ever having intended it to happen. Either the child always seems to be in bed between them, or, just as detrimental to a marriage, intruding into their evening together. Helping parents to see the advantage for the child itself of their having a flourishing marital relationship can support them in confronting the child's jealousy.

Often small children suffer from nightmares, and we might speculate that the strength of their emotions causes these. The book, *Where the Wild Things Are,* by Maurice Sendak (1970) can have an amazingly therapeutic effect on children in the grip of these feelings. Max, the hero of this book, makes so much mischief that his mother calls him a 'wild thing' after he says to her, 'I'll eat you up', and is sent to bed without his supper. In bed he dreams that he goes to where the wild things are, tames the monsters, and becomes their king. After a year of this he becomes lonely and goes home to 'where someone loved him best of all'.

What seems to work in this story for a small child is the acknowledgement of the wild feelings inside himself, making friends with them and overcoming them within himself, and getting back to a loving relationship with his mother. Having this book to read to them may often help children to manage their nightmares, as also may patient listening by parents to children recounting the content of these dreams. The parents' task is in helping children to deal with the force of these—the actual having of the nightmare may be a useful form of self-awareness for the child about the fierceness of his own emotions.

The father's role can often take the form of supporting the mother in not letting babies and small children exploit their mothering. He can help the mother to feel that she has given the baby what is reasonable during the day, and that nothing more is owing to the baby. Single parents are vulnerable if they have no one to support them in this way. Working mothers may have similar difficulties. They and their babies may actually need more time together to become reunited after the day's separation, but this may merge into a guilty reluctance to face the baby's feelings about being put down.

A crucial problem for parents is in dealing with a baby's anger in the night while feeling their own anger at not being allowed to rest and sleep. Many parents are justifiably afraid of battering their baby in the night. The fear of going too far may stop them from being reasonably firm. Expressing anger within bounds may be as much a relief to the baby as to the parents. Babies who go on crying in the night undermine parents' belief in the quality of their parenting and undermine their judgement.

Looking at sleep problems makes us aware of the complexity of the emotions involved in being a parent. We see the subtlety of the process by which mothers and babies move from their early closeness to seeing themselves as two separate beings. Sleep difficulties punctuate uncertainties at every stage. We see how receptivity to the needs of babies, understanding of their fears, and spontaneous offering of comfort need to be tempered with a gradual setting of limits. Understanding of a baby's fears enables a parent to contain those fears; the baby gradually learns to manage them himself. A parent does not need to take on the baby's fears as though they are his own.

In this work the connections I make with relationships and parents' own early experience hinge directly on thoughts about immediate practical solutions. I tend to suggest solutions less than do some of my colleagues (e.g. Douglas & Richman, 1984), though I always have in mind the many devices and practices that help a child to sleep better, and I am much informed by what other parents have told me works for them. There are of course many real difficulties in families' life situations and also temperamental differences that can lead to children's sleep problems, and varied ways in which parents can approach them (Daws, 1985). Solutions are as much the province of parents as of myself: my task is to restore their ability to think effectively so that they can provide the answer for their child.

This work is psychoanalytically based, although it is usually very brief. By this I mean the approach of taking in and reflecting on what parents tell me so that an understanding and integrative process that begins in my mind can then take over in theirs. Many of these parents have had difficult relationships with their own parents or been deprived to some degree. In several cases their own mothers had died before the baby was born. They had not had confirmation of themselves as a mother from their own mothers. This brief work can only touch on such experiences, but making the connection does seem to enable parents to differentiate themselves better from their children. Just as there is a drive towards development and integration in young children, so does there seem to be a similar integrative thrust in parental capacity with many people even while carrying personal difficulties inside them. I do not usually say much to the parents about their use of me. On the contrary, I tend to take it for granted that I perform for them the same sort of parental function as Palombo describes parents as doing when they 'interpret' their children's dreams. This parental function is a combined one that contains both 'maternal' receptive and 'paternal' limit-setting aspects. I look together with parents at their baby, acknowledging the baby's uniqueness, and hence help them stand outside fixed ways of thinking and reacting. Although some of the success of this work derives from experience gained through seeing many families with sleep problems, it cannot be done in a routine way—the impact of each family's stress and bewilderment must be received afresh each time.

The night before starting to write on sleep problems, I dreamt that *I* had a baby who was waking and feeding repeatedly in the night. I was confused and despairing of how to sort it out. This baby obviously represents in part the sleepless inner-city London babies that I have thought about. What is also illustrated is the integrative process that a DREAM carries out (together with the hidden wish-fulfilment!), which allowed me to translate my jumbled thoughts and experiences to some extent into the structure of my written accounts on this subject. As one appreciative parent said, 'It worked like a dream'.

CHAPTER SEVEN

Joint psychotherapy with mother and child

Helene Dubinsky

In contrast to the two previous chapters, the two cases described here require longer-term intensive work. Both mother and child are seen jointly as patients, and the therapist finds a way of interpreting that enables each of them to hear something that can offer an insight into themselves. At the same time it is clear that they are also discovering new possibilities for understanding and for communicating with each other.

[R.S.]

Many parents of children who are referred for psychotherapy recount tales of misery or persecution that they experienced when the child was an infant. Frequently the mother had been depressed and felt unable to soothe the baby. One has a glimpse of the mother's hurt and of how a sense of mutual rejection and disillusionment can set in between mother and baby.

A new mother beset by anxieties about whether she can keep her baby alive or can respond adequately to its needs easily loses touch with her identity as a coping adult. She herself may need mothering and holding to enable her to contain these overwhelming feelings.

A professional observer listening to the mother's anxieties and noting her fragility and depression, as well as the baby's own difficulties in responding to her, may enable the new mother to be in touch both with her own and with the baby's distress and thus to contain them and to allow for a new growth in their relationship. In this way, what Genevieve Haag has called 'normal maternal interpretation'—by which she means the mother's natural ability to understand her child—may be set in motion. Often, however, the call for help only comes at a time when the child is already much older and professional therapeutic help is needed.

I have found that joint psychotherapy with mother and child is helpful in certain cases where a good relationship failed to develop in the early years and where it seems important to attend to this before thinking of the child's own personal difficulties. This often seems to be the case where the mother was depressed during the child's infancy. Joint work with mother and child or parents and child can also be valuable in cases where one or both parents are in such massive projective identification with the child that either the child will not separate or the therapy may be sabotaged because of the mother's great need for a vehicle for the projection of the unwanted parts of herself.

This chapter describes work with two children, aged 4 and 5, respectively, whom I saw jointly with their mothers for short-term psychotherapy.

Mrs H and Sammy

Sammy, aged 4, was referred to a Child Guidance Clinic by the local nursery. He screamed uncontrollably whenever he was brought to the nursery. All efforts to enable him to separate from his mother failed, and they ceased attending.

The family was known to the clinic, as two years' previously his older sister, Mandy, then aged 12, had been referred for school refusal. At that time a colleague and I had offered some family sessions as well as an individual assessment for Mandy. The father was said to be unable to attend because of his work commitments, so we had several sessions with various combinations of the six children in the family.

The mother, looking frail and shy, was ostensibly co-operative but left an impression of a highly intelligent and powerful woman, with much hostility beneath her shy smile. She described a deprived childhood: she had felt unloved by her mother and acutely afraid of her aloof father. She had been school-phobic and in adolescence had ceased to attend school at all. At the time of the family meetings, Sammy was two, and throughout the sessions he sat so motionless beside his mother that we had become concerned about him. Mandy, after a prolonged individual assessment, returned to school, and the family meetings were interrupted by the mother's seventh pregnancy.

When re-referred, Sammy presented a very worrying picture. He seemed to have stopped developing since the birth of his baby sister and to have lost the few words he had used constantly to his mother, and he was gripped by intense panic attacks when anyone outside the family came to the house. Completely shut in his own world, with no interest in play or anything around him, he communicated only by gestures or an occasional single word to express what he wanted. His mother said that he liked dancing and swaying to music. Both he and his baby sister were sleeping in the parental bed.

My colleague and I made a few home visits, as Mrs H said that the baby was too small to come all the way to the clinic by bus. Following these visits, I offered to see Mrs H and Sammy on a regular basis once a week at the clinic. We met for over a year: Mrs H, Sammy, and Rebecca, the baby. Often there was another child present who had come to give Mrs H some help with the journey to the clinic. Then there was a sister, Jessica, who wanted to attend the meetings because, the mother explained, she had become very frightened of a naughty little girl and did not want to go to school. She attended the meetings for a number of weeks, drawing very quietly, and then went back to school.

For months Sammy was like a terrified little creature in the room, clinging to his mother as if in panic, persecuted by my voice and my eyes. He would hide behind his mother's chair when she encouraged him to look inside his box, sobbing and screaming, 'No, No, I don't want, I don't want!' These were the only words for many months. Meanwhile Rebecca, a baby with very delicate features but who was nevertheless a most determined, precocious little infant with no fears, explored the room, sometimes sitting looking at me with searching eyes and at other times looking very satisfied and playing with Sammy's toys. When Mrs H was breast-feeding Rebecca, Sammy leant against the other breast, ignoring Rebecca with a closed, stubborn expression on his face. Sometimes—and this was most worrying—Sammy burst into crazy laughter from behind the chair.

These sessions became very important to Mrs H. As we worked together, she became more in touch with the troubled child within herself. Although there was so strong an infantile thrust as to keep the very ill, frightened, and controlling part of herself in Sammy, now as an adult she felt guilty and wanted to help Sammy break out of his delusional world. She brought her dreams to sessions, and it was very striking how Sammy would stop crying, turn around, and 'listen' to his mother's dreams, as if listening to some music. At times I was able to talk about a witchlike creature, often present in mother's dreams, and to link this also with Sammy's terror of me, in a way that seemed to make deep sense to Mrs H and to which Sammy seemed to listen. Then, just for a brief moment, while the 'persecutors had hidden their faces', there was peace in the room and a space where feelings could be thought about. And as the sessions went on, there were more of these short moments of peace and contact.

There was an important session when Sammy had come back in his former state of terror, and his mother explained how frightened he had been by the storm and thunder the previous night, and by a lorry in the street that morning on their way to the clinic. Sammy was shouting and squatting like a terrified animal behind his mother's chair, but among all the shouts we heard him say clearly, 'I'm frightened!' Following that session, however, he soon became able to stay for a short while on his own in the nursery. Not long after this I had a telephone call from the nursery teacher. She told me that Mrs H was a changed woman, helping Sammy in a gentle and firm way to be on his own for a couple of hours, and also helping teachers with the other children.

After regular meetings ceased, Mrs H came to see me on a number of occasions. At times she appeared very depressed, being consumed and overwhelmed by the wish to be pregnant again, a wish opposed by her doctor and by her husband. At times she was in touch with the fact that her constant wish for a new baby expressed a deep need to counteract her unbearable feelings of inner loneliness. I have not seen the mother recently, but I think that one may hear from her again.

Sammy is now at a normal infant school, where he plays and joins in the activities and apparently can use some language. There has certainly been some progress, but I think this is very precarious and that it is likely that he will be in need of individual help in the future.

Hemesh and his mother

This case was still in treatment at the time of writing.

Hemesh, 5 years old, was referred to the clinic for a second opinion. He suffered from severe retardation—his vocabulary consisted of only a few words, and even these were difficult to understand owing to a severe stutter. His mother had great difficulty in controlling his behaviour. At school he was 'all over the place', incapable of concentrating, and hitting out at children, although not considered unmanageable. There was also a query as to whether his retardation might be due to brain damage, as he had been ill at birth. At times he dribbled profusely.

As there had been an early traumatic separation, I decided to see the whole family together for assessment, but I was told that the father could not take time off work.

Mrs N is a young Indian woman in her late twenties, with a round, appealing face that conveys depression except when she smiles and it becomes full of light. Both mother and Hemesh are short and a bit plump, but whereas Mrs N is slow in her movements, Hemesh bounces like a rubber ball, quick in his unpredictable and sudden changes of behaviour.

During the assessment, Mrs N spoke mainly of her difficulties with Hemesh, saying that he never listened to her and had severe tantrums, when he would hurl things around. She could not take him to friends or to shops because he behaved so badly and created scenes, demanding things he could not have. He would not go to sleep unless his mother was in the room. The main complaint, repeatedly expressed, was that he was not like any other child.

Mrs N told me that Hemesh had been born prematurely, and she had had to spend the last month of the pregnancy in bed since the baby was not gaining enough weight. At birth he had weighed 3½ lbs and was in an incubator for a month. He was given a dummy to pacify him but then cried constantly when the dummy fell out. Later he sucked his thumb.

Until about the age of 2, Hemesh had cried day and night, never sleeping more than an hour at a stretch. His mother had stopped breast-feeding at 2 months because she did not have enough milk, and he was hungry all the time. He would suck for a short while at the breast (or, later, bottle) then fall asleep at the breast, only to wake up a few moments later, crying, to be fed again. He was sick after most of his feeds.

About herself, Mrs N told me that she had come to England when she was 21 and had lived with relations while taking a secretarial course at college. She had stopped work when she married. Her husband worked long hours because they own their own house and have to pay off the mortgage. He has one job during the week and another one on Saturdays. She said that they have a happy marriage and that they had not wanted another child after Hemesh. Her eyes filled with tears when talking of her mother, who had died two years previously. In these interviews I thought Mrs N was very depressed and had a deep sense of worthlessness because she thought she had failed as a mother and had given birth to a little boy who was 'half human and half monster', so unlike the children of her friends, and she felt deeply ashamed of herself. Often I, too, was made to feel that way in our meetings—inadequate and unable to help.

In the assessment I was somewhat overwhelmed by Hemesh's frenzy, the rapid succession of his activities, and his states of mind—one moment of play, then some spoiling attack, followed by seeming persecuted and frightened. Mrs N responded to Hemesh's behaviour in a helpless, nagging, moaning kind of way. But I felt in Hemesh and in his mother a capacity for warmth, and from the second meeting noticed that while most of the time Hemesh appeared oblivious of anything I said to him, he was, in fact, taking notice when I spoke to him and would suddenly respond with a brief, mischievous look at me. I offered to see them both for short-term therapy, having in mind to explore their relationship.

In the first sessions the pattern was very similar to that of the assessment. Hemesh would run ahead to the room and first sit in his mother's chair with a mischievous grin on his face, but soon it was as if a storm had taken us over. He would scribble something quickly on a piece of paper—often a face that I thought was himself. The next moment the face would be covered with black or red dots, and soon he would be scribbling everywhere in the room. Mrs N, who sat very tense and unhappy, would say, 'take your coat off, Hemesh', 'Don't do that, Hemesh—be a good boy', but when the scribbling got out of hand one of us had to grab Hemesh to stop him. I remember feeling uneasy in that situation, wondering how persecuting he might find it, having two 'nagging Mums' after him. Only his obvious satisfaction in being back each week reassured me. At times his wild random outbursts were short-lived, as he would be checked by his own anxiety about getting his hands dirty and would suddenly stop, look anxiously at his hands, and moan in a little baby voice to his mother, 'dirty'.

From time to time Hemesh said a word, but usually I needed mother's explanation as his accent and stutter made it difficult to understand. My great difficulty was finding a way to talk to both of them, so, instead, I would speak to Hemesh, commenting to mother about what was going on. But often she would be sitting looking somewhat aloof, passive, and depressed. I experi-

enced then feelings of helplessness and inadequacy stirring in
me which I think were mother's and being communicated to me
through the mood she was projecting. During a lull I would
speak directly to her, asking how things had been during the
week between Hemesh and herself.

Some five weeks after starting therapy there was a session
that brought hope to me and I think to all three of us. They had
smiled when I met them in the waiting room, and Mrs N's
expression seemed less depressed than usual. Hemesh indicated
his wish to take a garage that he was playing with from the
waiting room into the therapy room. There he placed the garage
on the table and his cars inside it—lifting the gate and shutting
it again, taking cars in and out, making car noises. He seemed
happy and appeared to be concentrating on the game. I commented on his pleasure, perhaps because the cars had found a
safe garage/home now. He said 'Yes'. He had a long look inside
his box, then turned round and stared fixedly at his mother, who
giggled nervously under his glance.

I said that perhaps there was now a place here where their
feelings could find a home, and I spoke to mother of a time when
Hemesh had been in an incubator and they were separated; how
the feelings of that time long ago still needed a place, a home
where they could be thought about. Mrs N's eyes filled with
tears.

Meanwhile Hemesh had dropped his car deliberately under
the table and went furtively under it to get the car out. I commented on his secretiveness—this time to both of them. He
banged his head against the table coming out, then went back to
his absorbed play with the garage.

After my usual question about how the week had been, Mrs N
talked with some animation—they had played together with
Lego, and she had told Hemesh stories. Hemesh had talked
about school, then asked how his mother had learnt singing
when she was a child, and whether she had sung the same
(English) songs as he did now. She had explained that when she
was a little girl she sang Indian songs and learnt them from
sitting and listening to other people singing. I commented that
Hemesh seemed to show a great interest in mother's mind and
in how one learns about things. A little later, when Hemesh was

shutting his garage, he said, 'prison'. Then he took up a felt pen and began scribbling very quickly over the garage, until suddenly he stopped short, saying 'Oh!' very worriedly as he showed his hands to his mother. Then he went across to the sink, turned on the tap, and began soaping his hands under the running water.

I commented on the nice garage suddenly turning into a horrible prison from which there is no escape. Hemesh then became very frightened and angrily attacked the door with the black pen, saying 'pooh'. This response seemed to confirm my comment and to reveal further related anxieties.

Recalling Hemesh's earlier fixed staring at his mother, together with the activities that followed, it seemed to me that he experienced a feeling of being able to get right inside his mother and having her all to himself, and similarly of getting inside every corner of my room; but that he then became frightened of being attacked by other 'babies inside Mummy', or by other 'pooey, nasty children' inside my room. I said something along these lines, and Hemesh went on washing his hands for some time while Mrs N, sitting with her back to the sink, turned around from time to time, uneasy, worried, saying 'Mind, Hemesh', in a plaintive voice.

There was a silence. Suddenly Hemesh turned around and, looking at his mother and at me, said very clearly the first whole sentence I had heard him say in the room: 'What are you thinking about?' Mrs N was amazed; in fact, we were both quite startled, and Mrs N burst out giggling.

Later Hemesh indicated that he had finished washing and dried his hands with mother's help. Suddenly he threw the towel into the basin then looked at me, grinning mischievously. He quickly grabbed the pen and excitedly scribbled all over the table and floor, then tried to grab the telephone next to me. I held him; he was laughing and went a bit limp, seeming to like my holding him. Addressing both Hemesh and his mother, I commented on his distrust of me, which he had shown by the spoiling attacks on myself and my towel, which might lead to further distrust and consequent loneliness. This, I thought, was expressed in his mind as a question of whether the towel, the room, or my attention were available only to him or to others also, and whether despite his attacks I would still be able to hold him. Hemesh took the scissors and excitedly tried to cut anything he could find—first the towel, then the furniture. I stopped him. Going around the room, he noticed some old bits of plasticine and chalk behind the blackboard and asked me what it was. I explained, showing him that some was plasticine and some was chalk. He looked with great interest and quietened down. The rest of the session was spent peacefully sorting out, with my help, bits of chalk dropped on the floor from the bits of plasticine, which he put in the garage with the cars. When it was time to stop, he began running somewhat wildly all over the room.

Discussion of the session
in terms of the relationship
between Mother and Hemesh

Mrs N is a timid, fragile, and vulnerable woman, conforming in a somewhat adhesive way to social expectations, who needs a great deal of reassurance about her worth and ability as a mother. The separation and anxiety consequent on Hemesh requiring to remain in an incubator for some time had evidently undermined her confidence in her mothering capacities. It seems probable that the early stresses affected both Hemesh's digestive system and also the development of a secure bond between himself and his mother. As a result she found herself not with the gentle baby she had longed for, but instead with a demanding, sickly child who seemed 'half human, half monster'. Further, her own fragility inhibited her development as a firm, confident mother, so that she begged, giggled, and cajoled more like an older sibling than a parent.

When Hemesh mentions the 'prison', one wonders whether this image may be an unconscious reflection of his experience of the cold, inhospitable incubator. It is also possible that the frequent violent vomiting reported to have followed greedy feeding had left him with deep-seated feelings of emptiness and a despair of ever experiencing satisfaction. A similar pattern of greed and rejection seemed present in his imperative demands when shopping. Hemesh constantly nagged for one toy or another but when finally given this, never looked at it again.

This session, when Hemesh brought the garage into the room, was also the first session in which he played in a quiet, absorbed manner. The garage seemed to represent the beginning of an experience of the session as providing a safe containing space in which to develop the relationship with his mother—safe, as long as one can get in and out. Perhaps it also told about his new experience of having been able to talk, to have access to his mother.

When he follows his car secretly under the table, we may think that part of the time he phantasizes that he is living inside his maternal object. This intrusiveness is, however, followed by claustrophobic anxieties expressed in his sudden terror that the garage has become a prison. This would illustrate the oscillation between the phantasied inside of the object as a containing place and the negative phantasy that it is a trap. This distinction is developed by Meltzer (1982), who distinguishes between projective identification into a container that receives the projections and helps to sort out confusions, and a claustrum that is the inside of an object that has been penetrated by intrusive identification.

These sequences, and others in the session, illustrate how Hemesh has now found a state of mind in which he oscillates between the fears of the claustrum and the safety of the container. Prior to this we may see him as having been 'trapped' in the phantasy of the claustrum. The persecutory nature of such a phantasy was indicated by the fierce destruction of the drawings of his face, which he covered with red and black spots.

It seems to me that in this session there emerges for the first time a stronger longing to get out of this state in which he experiences himself either as the attacker of the breast and rival babies or as the victim of their murderous faecal attacks. I felt there was a more urgent wish to be in touch with a strong containing image (of breast-and-nipple, mother-and-father).

I thought that the space provided by the psychotherapy had begun to give mother and Hemesh a container that was enabling them to talk, although still perceived by both as a precarious one, with rivals and persecutors lurking in every corner.

It was in this session that mother recounted that Hemesh had asked her how she had learnt the songs she sang. This represented something very important in his mental development—an interest in some mysterious qualities inside mother's mind. She had replied, 'I sat and listened'. This seemed to have been a real exchange between them, a demonstration that both had begun to listen to one another. Later on, when there was a long silence during the session and Hemesh asked 'What are you thinking about?' he was again, I thought, giving expression to his new awareness that he and his mother each have a space inside, a mind capable of thinking. At this point there is evidence that both mother and child have developed greater tolerance of separateness, with a consequent sense of individual identity, though there remains a need for this to achieve greater security and stability.

Conclusion

In the two cases described above I decided to see mother and child together for short-term psychotherapy. With Mrs H, I felt that this joint psychotherapy was necessary for a while; I did not think that the mother would have allowed the child to go outside her orbit, as she was in massive projective identification with him. Indeed, I think that for her the little boy was the receptacle for a very ill and stubborn child part of herself, determined to cling to and control the (internal) mother, in the same way that in her adolescence she herself had clung to her own mother, becoming a school refuser. She did not have access, therefore, to sufficient adult maternal capacity to manage the child. In Sammy there was an equally strong determination to cling to a psychotic delusion that he was the baby, the only one, living inside mother. I felt that only by seeing them together would there be room allowed for talking and thinking about separateness.

With Mrs N and Hemesh, the situation was almost the opposite, as there had never been a bonding between them, and I feared that offering her individual psychotherapy and separating them too quickly might reinforce Mrs N's desperate feeling that she had never been a mother to Hemesh.

In describing work with a mother and her child together in joint sessions, I have attempted to show the ways in which I shared with the mother my observations of the child's behaviour and its possible meanings. Referring to some experiences and feelings that may be shared by both mother and child in terms such as, for instance, 'the feeling seems to be that . . .' and referring to transference only in a tangential way does, I have found, generally increase the mother's capacity to notice and understand infantile levels of feeling in herself, too.

The hope is that this shared containing experience may enable the mother and child to relate better to one another and to the long-lost baby in themselves.

CHAPTER EIGHT

Some reflections on body ego development through psychotherapeutic work with an infant

Genevieve Haag

In this chapter the author observes and explores in depth the many links that may be discovered between developments in the emotional and psychic spheres and the way that these may be related to shifts in the development of mobility and physical functioning. The theme is illustrated and discussed in the description of an infant who, at the beginning of his second year, was observed to be seriously inhibited in mobility and responsiveness. Mme Haag began engaging the child at this time in a psychotherapeutic endeavour that proved rewarding in both aspects.

[R.S.]

This study, with a somewhat longer theoretical discussion, was presented at the Third World Congress on Infant Psychiatry and Allied Disciplines, Stockholm, 3–7 August 1986, and published in France in *Neuropsychiatrie de l'enfance et de l'adolescence* (1988), 36(1), 1–8. David Alcorn and Daphne Nash Briggs kindly assisted with the translation.

135

I n normally healthy babies the development of primary identifications and the genesis of primary love-objects will fit in
so smoothly and naturally with the processes of their motor
development, pre-conditioned by neurophysical maturation, that
we may not take note of the essential articulations involved.
Nevertheless, the use of the term 'psycho-motor' has now been
established for some decades, and it is clear that we are currently aware of the links existing between these three processes.
In cases that manifest serious pathology of personality development, especially when accompanied by tonic and motor disturbances, attention will naturally be focussed on exploring these
articulations.

The following pages present some brief descriptions of activities observed in a normal healthy infant. These may then be
looked at as a background to observations of another infant
whose serious inhibition of movement and 'psychogenic hyper-
tonicity' appeared to be linked to a major disturbance in the constitution of his body image or 'body ego'. Specific evidences of
this disturbance were apparent in the lack of any hand and
mouth co-ordination, difficulties in making eye contact in con-
cordance with back contact, and failure to organize space
'behind' him. Serious disturbance of the awareness of spatial
dimensionality seems to be a corollary of disturbance of the body
image.

Observational and clinical material

Some familiar and relevant observational data

In utero, especially at the end of gestation, the most important
contact surface is the back, which fits closely against one or
other of the curves of the distended uterine cavity. Many
authors (Schilder, 1950; Spitz, 1965) emphasize the importance
of skin sensitivity in the newborn, and we can observe in some
recordings of deliveries that the baby cried until an open hand
or a cloth was applied to his back, even when he was well placed
in a ventral position on the mother's abdomen (CPPA video
library, Sucy-en-Brie). This may be an expression of the new-

born's wish for back contact, though it could also simply be due to the exposure of large areas of naked skin as the normal birth processes 'strip' away the aequeous contact and amnion. It is in fact a commonplace observation that stripping babies to the skin in the first weeks of life, up to about the age of 2 months, will provoke crying, clutching, or trembling.

During the first phase of the Moro reflex, which occurs when a sudden change in the environment provokes an abrupt abduction of the infant's outstretched arms, we note that this brings the whole surface of his back onto a supporting surface. A. Szanto (1981) regards this seeking for maximal contact of the dorsal surface to be a means of regaining a feeling of safety when some sudden disturbance has created an impression of falling—of being unheld—whether in postural or emotional terms. I fully agree with this formulation. It is also perhaps a search for that fundamental sensation of back contact experienced within the period of prenatal security. Moro himself linked the second phase (hugging gesture) to clinging reflexes. These two phases would therefore relate to the effects of gravity and the bodily anxieties of falling which, as E. Bick (personal communication) pointed out, play an important part in the trauma of birth.

During the establishment of the earliest relationships of the newborn infant we must take note of the static helplessness of both trunk and nape of the neck, and the degree to which these are continuously given support by the hands, arms, lap, and other supporting surfaces of the mother, as, for example, when the baby is being bathed or changed. These are such simple activities, so much taken for granted, that we do not even give them a thought. It is only when one observes a baby who is failing to thrive and, though able to sit and stand, nevertheless resists giving up the position of lying flat in his cot, or perhaps just drags his back along the floor, that one becomes aware of the potential significance of early back contact.

Let us look for a moment at a healthy baby of six weeks with his mother after a bottle-feed. She holds him upright against her shoulder for a moment, his back well supported, allowing him to bring up wind, then lays him down for a moment with his back flat on her knees, his feet against her tummy. He pushes with his feet—and we may note in passing the equal importance of this contact with the soles of the feet. His eyes are focussed on her face, and as she talks to him he accompanies her with movements of his mouth. I would like to emphasize this association of back contact with eye contact and the accompanying sounds that carry their emotional messages, to which the interrelation of mouth and teat is added during a feed.

From the age of 2½–3 months onwards, one may quite often see babies who, while lying on their tummies and sucking at something, also place their hands on the nape of the neck, thus reproducing this element of back contact within an 'auto-erotic' context.

In a creche unit, when babies between the ages of 4 to 8 months are on the carpet, it is well known that the best way to calm any expressions of distress that may arise is to take the baby 'into the lap', with back firmly against one's body. Some babies will lift their heads after a moment to check one's face and will then more or less adjust to a strange face, but the initial calming effect seems in fact to be through this back contact. A little later on, at times of waiting or of confusion, some babies will seek back contact against a wall. One 10-month old little girl who observed someone beginning to feed another baby showed signs of being almost overcome by feelings of frustration and rivalry. She then crawled away on all fours to sit well 'backed up' and near the nurse (C.C.P.A. Video Library, Sucy-en-Brie).

Clinical material

Observation of Bruno

This little boy, about 12 months old, had caused concern because he would neither sit nor stand and did not move about at all in space. Recently, however, when placed in a sitting position, he had managed to remain sitting fairly well without support. But he was then a prisoner of that position and could not change it, except by allowing himself to fall abruptly onto his side. He had just begun to roll over onto one side, his only displacement in space. He did not crawl and could not bear being placed on his tummy, and he would scream then as though in very great discomfort. I noticed that he made no hand-and-mouth connections but frequently engaged in a barely visible sucking movement deep in his throat (hidden auto-sensuality, cf. F. Tustin, 1980). His hands would be held clutching his vest or a little flannel, which, at best, he could just convey to the edge of his mouth. Though he did not refuse eye contact, his gaze had little life in it, was rather unchanging, and had a curious tendency to 'escape' towards a corner of the ceiling, especially when one attempted to make contact with him on the changing table while he was lying on his back.

At mealtimes he appeared completely absorbed by the food; he never looked people in the face, nor seemed concerned to seek back contact. When sitting on the ground, he held his legs very stiff and his body rigid, without any lateral mobility. Space behind him seemed non-existent or perhaps terrifying. He would gaze into space before him, sometimes rocking his body back and forth a little, as though to 'launch forward', but remained firmly seated on the ground. He would then start to make rumbling noises with his lips, as if imitating a car. On several occasions I thought that being unable to move himself, he was more or less hallucinating being inside a moving car.

In my first observations I was able to establish that it was 'lateral' contact, together with firm verbal containment, that gradually succeeded in loosening him up and giving him the desire for movement and the ability to bend his body forward, for example, or to allow himself to fall on his side. At the same time, finger and mouth contact, which he had discovered, or rediscovered, seemed to help him to roll over several times. He accepted some exchanges with a ball, but for several weeks could return it only with the back of his hand.

I therefore encouraged the staff to change the emphasis from motor stimulation, which in fact made him stiffen more, and to attempt instead to improve contact. However, they continued to try to make him walk while holding his hands, which did not work too badly as long as they were behind him. On one occasion, his mother placed him standing holding on to a chair, and I noticed him checking whether she was still just behind him, and if she was not he would start to grumble and express great uneasiness. However, three months after the beginning of this activity (at 15 months) he began, when sitting, to turn right around, as if looking for 'space behind'. This risked becoming a stereotyped gyration. He still did not move from the spot, neither forwards nor backwards. However, contact began to improve, and he was taking more interest in other children's activities, especially nursery games.

One day, when he was 16 months old, I was sitting on the floor in the creche unit and thought it might be a good moment to try the 'boat on water' game with him. In this, one tips the baby up backwards until he touches one's legs and feet. At first he seemed very frightened, but then after some insistence and much reassurance he allowed the game to go on and suddenly seemed to appreciate the contact of his back and especially the nape of the neck, with the curve between my feet and legs. He moved his head sideways very gently, as though savouring this sensation, while looking intensely into my eyes. When I saw him again several days later arriving in his mother's arms, he gave me a good look and placed his right hand on the nape of his neck. There seemed to be good communication, recalling the contact and sensations of the previous scene. Whether coincidence or not, it was during this period that he began to move around by sliding along on his bottom and 'rowing' with his legs. There was still a long time to wait before he would find real freedom of movement.

When he was about 18 months old, I was able to begin individual interpretative sessions. I shall present two fragments from sessions, one when he was 20 months old, the other later.

Session at 20 months

During this session, after trying mostly to stick and unstick flat objects for some time, at one point he picked up two little interlocking blocks and tried to join them. He allowed me to help him a little, then separated them, pointedly turned his back on me,

and then again turned around towards me. Then he threw
behind him some toys that had been lying in front of him. Following this, he picked up a little cube, gave me a good look,
placed it between his eyes for a moment, pushed it gently up the
middle of his forehead, then back along the median line of his
head, laid it gently against the nape of his neck, and then let it
slide down his back. After a little pause he turned away and
scattered the toys lying behind him with large sweeping movements while making sounds of discontent. He repeated this
sequence twice, throwing aside all the toys lying behind him,
scattering them on both sides, until he turned back towards me.
It was as though he was showing that something which had initially been good had then 'travelled' from the eyes to the back, to
the space behind him in which it had suddenly been turned into
something bad, exploding all over the place.

It then became 'urgent' for him to draw his hair forward from
nape to forehead, showing that something remained attached,
namely his hair, though conveying with this (on the surface and
covering the forehead) the image of a 'façade', as if the inside,
confused with the space behind, had exploded.

His play in sessions now had to do with manipulating symbolic equivalents and centred around exploring hollows and
bumps. This alternated with sticking and unsticking and trying
to rediscover the right 'button' that might once again trigger the
experience of 'interpenetrating' eye contact, still a central problem for him.

The following is a fragment from a session at this time.

Bruno picked up a small red mug, put its convex base against
his mouth, blew, spat on it, seemed to mime expulsion, all the
while looking at me with a smile. He did the same with another
identical little mug. Then, a moment later, he turned it the
right way up and put it to his lips, exploring the inside with his
fingers and looking at me from time to time with pleasure. The
quality of his looking had at this stage clearly changed completely. I commented that one little mug was 'all shut, upside
down' and that he couldn't drink from it or spit into it. Then I
added, 'Oh! Now you have found another little mug with a space
inside.' I then made a link between this and my eyes, which he
had not seen for some days and which might have seemed

turned away and lost, but that he felt he could now enter into once more.

Quickly Bruno picked up a red toy casserole with its lid on. He was preoccupied mainly with the gap between lid and bowl, trying to open it from there (an unsticking manoeuvre), but he did not appear to see the large central knob, which would allow it to be manoeuvred easily. Even after this had been demonstrated to him, he returned to the gap, appearing to ignore the knob. I commented that it seemed as if the knob was to be like something that was lost to him, and like the little mug which he had been 'blowing and spitting out' from his mouth. He then picked up a fork, never taken up before until that moment, explored it a little, touched the prongs with his index finger, then put it between his legs and began twisting it between his fingers, as if crushing it.

I said that a fork, like teeth, can crush, so that it might seem better to crush it instead. He pushed the fork very gently towards me, with the tips of his fingers, leaning forward until he could make it half-disappear under my skirt, then leaned away to take it back, moving to and fro several times. Then coming closer as though emboldened and leaning towards me he made a gesture of scratching right down my breast with his fork. I talked about the baby who so much wanted to scratch at the closed and covered nipples as well as at closed eyes, and maybe this was how they then seemed to become 'lost' to him, like the lid-knob.

Bruno gave me back the fork. I pretended to eat. He took the fork again and 'fed' me. When I tried to approach his mouth to do the same, he drew back. I said that he was indeed frightened now of a nasty fork, which could seem like a baby's fingers that feel like scratching off a Mummy's buttons when he is very angry.

Bruno then went over to the glazed medicine cupboard, which he used like a mirror, and had a good look at himself and at me. This cupboard is near the window to which he tended to go before long vacations, but now the mirroring interested him too and perhaps also looking inside, like looking into eyes.

Returning to the toys, he renewed the game of passing them behind him, and I thought he sensed the end of the session coming. He took the little mugs and began to make them slide from top to bottom of the smooth vertical face of a large desk. It occurred to me that he might well be showing in his play then the absence of something firm and supportive—'solid buttons' to which he might attach or hoist himself into a standing position. (At present this is one of his persistent inhibitions.)

I associate this thought with what I think is the progressively 'verticalizing' function of the interpenetrating gaze. This may be illustrated by describing a lovely scene of the very gradual awakening of a 7-month-old baby observed by Dr Michel Haag and presented in supervision to Mrs Esther Bick.

Observation of Jeanne by Dr Michel Haag

Then she got up and held herself standing in front of this same side of her cot, against a wall covered in fabric. On this there were two little bumps to which Jeanne drew my attention, because, having noticed them by sight, she reached one with her right hand and the other with her left. I commented in reporting this that these two identical little bumps were on the same horizontal line, and at a distance from one another which more or less corresponded to the distance between Jeanne's outstretched arms, and that she was holding on to them. The report continued, 'This was the first time that I saw her vision guide her manual prehension in that way.'

Mrs Bick commented on how lovely it was when one can watch how the child can cope with things, one by one. 'I would say', she added, 'that a human being, so to speak, has begun to exist, with intelligence, thought, planning. And how gradually you half open your eyes, there is a bump, you can hold on to it, there is a finger, you can hold on to it, and as all this is collected together, you feel that you have a sufficient capacity to hold on without falling apart, that you can stand up and so on, and it is marvellous'. She agreed with the hypothesis that

---

This observation of an infant is an extract from *Observation of Jeanne,* privately published by Dr Michel Haag.

these two little bumps, which Jeanne had made the observer perceive as forming a structure, might perhaps represent for this infant the likeness of nipples on account of their appearance and their distance apart.

I would add my personal comment that the two little bumps represent a condensation of tactile contact: mouth–hands–nipples—linked with the mother's eyes that may be clung to during feeding.

[This kind of hypothesis comes into the infant observer's mind not as a ready-made theoretical construct, but through sharing in the baby's experience. Scenes like the game with the breasts (ibid., Vol. 1, p. 30) make a lasting impression on the observer.] Mrs Bick replied, 'Yes', and I would add that to notice all that requires an observer like yourself, someone who can pay attention to the smallest of details and link them together, that's when there is discovery'.

Confirmation and demonstration of the verticalizing function of the gaze, associated with back contact or, more precisely, with the feeling of the axis of the spinal column, can be observed in Bruno. When he had completely mastered the process of getting up, he then stood up, held a pencil very upright before his eyes, gave me a good look, and went to put his back very straight up against the wall, and another time also in a corner of the playroom.

Let us return now to the session with Bruno described earlier. We see that we are involved there in a more complex formulation, which now includes elements of oral conflict. (Indeed, he began to feed himself very soon after that session.) Following on the work with the 'button', he felt able to explore and shelter in a 'niche' under the table, to disappear and reappear, and to take a lot of pleasure in games of hide and seek. He wandered about more and more, sitting and standing, but did not achieve complete mastery of and flexibility in changing position until the age of 2½.

He was becoming rather irascible and ferociously competitive, which increased in proportion to the continuing improvement in contact, and as I sensed him to be increasingly individuating himself. From time to time during sessions he would come up

close for a little back contact against my body. Sometimes, after
a tantrum, he would need to recall with me the history of the
connection between the contact with his back and eye contact.
Thus at 2 years 4 months, during a session disturbed by an
intrusion, he scattered his toys about in a tantrum but then followed this by gently letting himself fall onto his side from a
sitting position, then gently rocked onto his back with his hand
resting on the nape of his neck—all the while looking into my
eyes, in the fixed and clinging manner of earlier days. I said
that he had at last recovered the good Mme Haag 'of the back
and head', after having been so upset and angry that it had felt
as if he had thrown away—lost everything. After a minute or
two he got up and at the end of the session wanted to take a
little sponge ball—the first time that he had wanted to take a
soft object away with him.

Shortly after this demonstration of his capacity to recover
this 'background object', I noted another change. He had had a
habit of biting the knuckle of his right index finger during the
most violent tantrums, which I interpreted as biting the nasty
Mme Haag side. Now during several sessions he would come
close and lean his right side against me when he felt annoyed
and put this same finger in his mouth, without biting and perhaps even sucking it, though I could not see clearly because he
would then be partly hidden. Following this, he would get up,
apparently calmed. These sequences confirmed my findings
(Haag, 1985a) on the identifications related to left and right
sides of the physical self. Bruno was making clear to me that
having one's side 'dissolved' into the 'Mummy side' appears at a
later stage than having one's back 'dissolved' in the 'back object'.

Some formulations and theoretical questions

The thinking of James Grotstein (1981), encountered at the time
I was working with Bruno—the young child discussed above—
has close connections with my own studies, as, for example, in
the following quotation from his writings:

> I first became aware of the Background Object in phantasies
> of patients with psychotic and narcissistic disorders, in which

there was a common experience that their backing seemed to disappear or that they had nothing behind them, no backbone, et cetera.

I completely agree with his definition of the Background Object as the 'personification of the cement that guarantees the cohesion of individual identity', though I have found less convincing certain further defining aspects that he has outlined.

How, then, would one understand Bruno's material in terms of back contact linking with interpenetrating eye contact? If we think about how we relate to babies, clearly we alternate between holding them from behind and holding them in front of us, face-to-face, on the look-out for those first moments of eye contact and smiling. We may therefore hypothesize that the baby has something approaching a very early object relationship specifically in visual terms and concomitant with identification with the background object.

I should like now to consider how this 'background object' connects with the theme of the two halves of the body. In Bruno's material one sees that in the transference relationship it seemed to precede the possibility of working on the theme of the 'Mummy side'. We have reason to believe that back contact, as described, ingrained in pre-natal and immediate post-natal life and secondarily combined with the interplay of eye contact, precedes co-ordinated articulation between the two lateral halves of the body, which undoubtedly pre-supposes the myelinization of the commissures at around the age of 3 months. Like the interaction of mouth and nipple, this back contact may then secondarily become one of the 'median' elements of union between these two sides (Haag, 1985a).

Cleopatra Athanassiou (1986) has carried out some extremely interesting work with babies which broadly supports my hypotheses here and has also put forward some theoretical considerations about symmetrical and asymmetrical linking and their impact on adhesive and projective identification. In a baby observation of Gerald (who was less disturbed than Bruno), she described a child who had already acquired an asymmetrical structure and was able to put objects inside other ones, yet at the beginning of his first session, in a moment of panic, he ran to press his back against a wall, gazing out with terror as if into 'nothingness', until she saw such a change in his mood that she commented, 'Thus the various parts of the self could . . . pass from a state of total dispersion to a state of connectedness by simple contact along a magic wall'.

Didier Anzieu's (1989) concepts on looking and its relation to integration of the image of the background object mirror my own thinking on this issue. Further, in reference to Freud's comments on the body ego and touch, Anzieu adds,

> Compared to the other sensory dimensions, touch has a distinctive characteristic which not merely places it at the origins of the mind, but in fact implies that it is continually providing the mind with what we could call either a mental backdrop, the background onto which psychic representations are projected, or a containing envelope which enables the mental apparatus to possess such representations.

Conclusion

I have tried to show that there is a very early level of body ego organization that can have some impact on postural tonicity, general motor activity, and the structuring of space, taking as an example the case of a young boy who had considerable difficulty in this sphere. I suggest that such problems exist even where developmental troubles are less pronounced, and the question is how best to uncover and deal with such handicaps in the first year of life. Answering that question may well be of great help to the kind of patient described by Dr Grotstein (1981), where psychotic and narcissistic nuclei underlie borderline or severely neurotic personalities. In terms of technique and of ways of approaching such severely disturbed children, the important thing is to discover what kind of splitting the child has set up, and thereby what he feels is most persecutory or threatening for his fragile experience of living.

PART THREE

PATIENTS TREATED
IN ADOLESCENCE

W e now turn to thinking about the processes of adolescence, looking at some social and historical issues as
well as at the particular experience of contemporary
young people. The need to plan clinical services that can take a
proper account of their sense of separateness and struggle for
independence from their families (as well as attachments, however ambivalent) is stressed. One can observe how some of the
needs, battles, and conflicts of infancy may re-emerge, though in
newly powerful forms, in response to growing demands, internally and externally, during the latter years of latency and on
into early adolescence and beyond.

[R.S.]

CHAPTER NINE

Thinking about adolescence

Rolene Szur

In *As You Like It,* Shakespeare (1599) presents two young women who escape from an 'imprisoning' parental environment to find a world more to their own liking and discover independence and sexuality within the natural order of the Forest of Arden, with joy, uncertainty, and laughter.

In *The Awkward Age,* Henry James (1899) describes a nineteenth-century history of subtle parental exploitation and social pressures that gradually lead on to the 'imprisonment' of two sensitive and dependent young women within bleak and arid marriages.

Contemporary images of adolescents sometimes seem to be coloured with expectations not unlike those that accompanied the arrival of atomic energy. It is as if they represented an explosive force that, while it might generate some light and heat, was equally likely to shatter 'the world as we know it'. This has stimulated a considerable psychoanalytic literature, some of which is explored in the following pages.

We may begin by noting the concept of developmental lines as defined by Anna Freud (1965) in terms of a progress from dependency to emotional self-reliance and adult object relationships. The first stage she saw as a 'biological unity between the

151

mother–infant couple, with the mother's narcissism extending to the child, and the child including the mother in his internal narcissistic' milieu (Hoffer, 1952).

It was as a seventh stage that the 'pre-adolescent prelude' to the 'adolescent revolt' would be reached, i.e. 'a return to early attitudes and behaviour, especially of the part-object, need-fulfilling, and ambivalent type'. Typically this would then be followed by Stage 8, viz. 'the adolescent struggle around denying, reversing, loosening and shedding the tie to infantile objects, defending against pre-genitality, and finally establishing genital supremacy with libidinal cathexis transferred to objects of the opposite sex, outside the family'.

Anna Freud warned that analysis of adolescents presents particular problems:

> Since the child's immature ego is insecurely balanced between the pressures from within and without he feels more threatened by analysis than the adult, and his defences are kept up more rigidly. This refers to the whole of childhood but is felt with special intensity at the beginning of adolescence. To ward off the oncoming adolescent increase in drive activity, the adolescent normally strengthens his defences and, with it, his resistance to analysis. [A. Freud, 1966]

She refers also (ibid., p. 60) to adolescent and pre-adolescent regression from 'object cathexis' to 'love for his own person' leading to a narcissistic object choice, an idealized self with whom he identifies. 'Adolescent partnerships formed on these grounds,' she comments, 'are frequently accepted as true pre-stages of homosexuality' but are more significant as pointers to regression than as predictors of the individual's future sexual role.

We might think again here, however, about the importance of the supportive friendship between Rosalind and Celia and their shared journey to the Forest of Arden, a journey that will free them from the tyranny of a paternal figure who has decreed banishment or death for Rosalind, the bolder, more 'masculine' partner of the pair. It also proves to be a journey in which the young women attain independence while discovering their individual strengths and weaknesses over time. As the story unfolds, we find Rosalind taking on the garments, role of, and some identification with a man. We also see her caught up in a tragi-comic enactment of the dual aspects of her personality until, one might say, she is able to 'marry' them within herself and to be married to Orlando. (A common assumption that Rosalind's—like Portia's—masculine presentations of them selves are related simply to the absence of female performers ignores the importance of their roles in demonstrating the presence of 'masculine strengths' in both these women.)

Clinical experience of work with adolescents does indeed make clear the importance of close supportive friendships in the processes of growth towards independence and maturity. These passages present views of the adolescent development and struggle principally in terms of individual relationships and internal experiences.

Another dimension of this struggle, as a societal event, was presented by Robert Gosling (1975) who, writing in a foreword to a book on adolescence, commented, 'Everybody's head is set spinning by adolescence, the adolescent himself, and his elders and youngers alike'. 'But', he continues, 'beyond the arena of the family, what lies there? What is the alternative society, not only to the family as it is, but to large-scale established society as well?' What lies there in fact may be powerful established institutions on the one hand and newly emerging and challenging social groupings on the other. Governments may be seen to be 'never up to their tasks' and always working on outmoded assumptions.

This may well be the way in which the 'governors' within the family may also be viewed. Indeed, within this present century major technological changes alone, precipitating major social changes, both directly and indirectly, may well be felt as being outside the moral or personal experience and competencies of parental generations.

'Perhaps', Gosling suggests, 'the most pervasive influence on the adolescent . . . is the projection on to him of hopes for the future'. The revival of such lost hopefulness and the memories of idealized visions that have faded may well add some burdens onto young teenage shoulders which confuse, alienate, or overwhelm the sense of individual identity.

Certainly facing up to differences and conflicts between the generations, including rivalries and feelings of envy on both sides, would allow for healthier forms of struggle and promote development. This can be the time when the adolescent has to struggle with almost claustrophobic anxieties of being either caught in a projective identification with a static image of Father inside a 'Father's world', or trapped—perhaps 'drowning'— inside Mother in an emotionally engulfing soft and fluid world. The urge to be free of this can have positive aspects; it may also have the quality of having to 'break free' in a way that is experienced as forceful like the act of birth, and indeed may give the adolescent a triumphant sense that he or she is their own sole 'progenitor'. The degree to which adolescents often 're-make', re-construct, their own physical selves, as if creating a species new-born on the planet, and similarly the gangs in which they can feel that their attachment is one that they have chosen to make, with chosen gang-mothers, sisters, brothers, has a similar quality. Where there is a delinquent element, it seems reminiscent of the Mafia as 'the Family'.

Donald Meltzer (1967, pp. 46–97) views the gang as representing typically a response to the crisis of puberty with its 'upsurge of genitality' and the expectations of responsibility. The defining qualities of the gang are seen to be the intensity of the splitting processes that impose a pattern 'in which parts of the self are projected and the group is drawn together' in a very 'unstable but passionate way through the workings of mutual projective identification.' This would be in contrast to the latency child, who has a 'strong tendency to act out his relations to internal parents and siblings, these latter also being parts of the self, by forming groups' that mirror the patterns of family and social hierarchies in a more stable way.

The distinctions between clubs, gangs, and families, at times illuminating, can, however, sometimes seem to be relatively superficial and fluctuating. Meltzer (1986) refers to families that slip into a 'narcissistic state of gang formation' when the parental figures are 'strongly impelled by negative identifications' with their own parents.

In writing of narcissistic relationships, Victoria Hamilton (1982) comments that these often reveal a history in which there has been for the Narcissus 'an exclusive and possessive relationship with one parent, usually the mother, and an excluding or remote relationship with the other'. She considers the 'teenage love affair' to be characteristically one that may 'reproduce many features of the early relationship between infant and mother'. (This is in terms of the early synchronicity of mother–infant relationships as emerging in adolescence with qualities not dissimilar to those reflected in the story of Echo and Narcissus.) 'However', she adds, 'the adolescent unlike the infant has the capacity to distance himself from his parents. He knows that departure from home is imminent and essential. Acute anxieties and ambivalence over this future event often interfere with his capacities to *think about* detachment.' He may act out instead, truanting and tricking, or 'seek the supernatural, which he wrongly conceives to be a place.'

We may see the obverse and complementary side of these narcissistic individual and group relationships in the fierce rivalries, intolerance, and aggressive exploits that may take place either individually, within a socially 'shifting semi-cruel world of adolescence' as described by F. Scott Fitzgerald in the 1920s, or between rival groups of football supporters 'hitting the headlines' in the 1980s. Further, it seems sadly possible that when rape and especially such incidents as group rape occur, girls are being attacked as representing a rival and alien group as well as objects of sexual conquest.

The formation of groups within the larger society may operate at levels of splitting that have the function of idealizing the 'in-group' and projecting all the negative features into the 'out-group'. This can occur at any age level, but may be particularly characteristic of adolescence, as an aspect of the emphasis on the assertion of a strong and positive identity of one's own.

Attachment to the in-group then entails hostility to the out-group. Currently this might be seen in the tensions that develop between 'teenagers' and 'oldies', between native British citizens and immigrants, between 'blacks' and 'whites'.

Chapter eleven describes a study of both matching and cross-cultural work with adolescents belonging to varying minority groups. The positive and negative features that emerge from this study seem heartening in their revelation of the degree to which the essentials of experience have shared roots, and this can in itself be an important discovery for the child—and a confirmation for the therapist. It may be the kind of discovery that is conveyed by James Berry (1979) in these lines from his poem, 'Revelation':

Unexpected this arrival,
this face white, not black
like yours, and you come to know
his works, his thoughts, his pains
and pleasures. You see his
home within walls. He has
no wings or receding horizons. . . .

And you are surprised you can
sort out mountains of words.
You are surprised you
can wonder together, who really
is the governor of boundaries.

I would like to add, though, that there have in my own experience certainly been some cases where I have thought that the children might have gained something extra from a therapist whose cultural experience had been closer to their own. Child psychotherapy as a discipline developed in response to a recognition of the need for psychoanalytic help to be available to the community as a whole, and it does seem important therefore that this should be matched by a professional presence that reflects the whole community.

L. K. Thomas, in an unpublished paper entitled 'Inner and outer world: The place of psychoanalytical psychotherapy in a multi-cultural world', makes a strong plea on this issue; though it would also surely be sad if there were to be a pressure towards 'segregation' in the field of psychoanalysis, which has a long tradition of recognizing and understanding the universality at the heart of all human experience.

Turning now to follow the developmental process of adolescence as an individual experience, we see this beginning with the onset of puberty and the biological changes accompanied by the growing image of an adult self developing within the child. The difficulties of this period of the life-cycle are often stressed—especially, perhaps, in contemporary Western societies (see Erikson, 1950; Hoxter, 1964; Rayner, 1971. In traditional Zulu culture, for example, the 'transition from childhood to adulthood' would be marked first before puberty with an 'ear-piercing ceremony', celebrating the children's increased status—and preparation for 'opening their ears' to new knowledge and responsibilities—followed not long after by the puberty ceremonies. Such occasions would be shared by others of the same age, themselves playing an important part, amounting, in a puberty ceremony, to taking 'virtual control over the whole procedure' [Krige, 1936]. Such events would seem well designed for a safe promotion of age-group initiative, together with social cohesiveness.) Powerful hormonal forces and physical changes can bring a sense of insecurity and sudden mood swings, exciting aggression as well as sexuality. The ways in which individual young people are able to respond to these new experiences and to emerge from the internal developmental tasks in an integrated way will have a major effect on their ability to cope with external and social demands in their moves towards greater independence and autonomy.

The adolescent process is generally considered as proceeding through three phases, though these will of course vary considerably from one individual to another. Early adolescence, beginning at about 11 and continuing to around 15, often an especially stressful and explosive period, may prove to be a time when the struggle for an autonomous sense of the self is expressed or experienced as rejecting and hostile by both generations. Some parents may be able to be relatively tolerant of this, seeing it as a re-appearance of the 2-year-old's self-assertiveness; for others it may be seen as the re-emergence of an innate personal negativism.

Volatility may exacerbate the difficulties, as parents can feel that they have been misled or let down when they are suddenly confronted with some erratic change of mood. This is described by Hyatt Williams (1975) as the parents 'never quite knowing with whom they are dealing from moment to moment', 'philosopher', 'clamouring baby', or 'delinquent'.

A strong undercurrent precipitating adolescent children's turning away from their parents is related to 'sexual desires and conflicts connected with the parents, which are gaining in strength' at this time (Klein, 1937). Concurrently, general feelings of rivalry towards parents are likely to be stimulated now that they may more realistically feel themselves to be a potential challenge. At the same time parents (and other adults) may themselves be contributing to this. They may experience difficulties in enabling children to become adult, consciously or unconsciously seeing them as threatening their own authority and status.

In the middle phase of the adolescent progress, towards the age of about 18, there is likely to be a continuing endeavour to feel at ease with a new and changing physical self, with sexual and social identifications, and with the shifts taking place within the internal parental images and phantasies. Sometimes all this can feel like a risky and lonely process and may be a time for reaching out for narcissistic relationships. It may also be a time when figures of 'gurus', pop-stars, sometimes political leaders or admired teachers may appear to excite powerful attachments. Melanie Klein (1937) related this to 'the process of separating hatred from love' at a time when establishing separateness from the parents may involve very negative feelings towards them and may carry echoes of anxiety and confusion belonging to early infantile experience.

The need 'to preserve goodness and love within and without' then 'becomes all the more urgent'. Idealized figures may therefore be bringing some sense of security because of the feelings of 'love, admiration, and trust towards them', which in the unconscious mind may 'seem to confirm the existence of good parents and of a love relation to them' (Klein, 1937), thus assuaging feelings of anxiety, hostility, and guilt.

Although there are, of course, children who can maintain good relations with their parents even during these difficult times, some degree of conflict and confrontation is more generally part of the adolescent process, until hopefully a reduction of anxiety and guilt enable more integrated, accepting, and loving relationships to develop with increased maturity.

In late adolescence, after 18 and perhaps continuing into the early 20s, while one's place in the world is really that of a young adult, many of the uncertainties and anxieties of the earlier years may be far from resolved, and one may have begun to understand that in some ways there is a journey that is only just beginning. This is a period that Erikson (1968) refers to as 'more pre-adult than postadolescent' and the age when many of the patients who are referred have broken down, often following attempts at engaging in intimate relationships or competitive situations. But despite some similarities between certain adolescent episodes and neurotic or psychotic episodes, adolescence is not an affliction but a normative crisis, possibly with a high potential for growth. He suggests that our society seems to be 'in the process of incorporating psychiatric treatment as one of the few permissible moratoria for young people who otherwise would be crushed by standardisation and mechanization.' However, internal conflict and contradictions may make it hard for them '. . . to come to the therapeutic appointment and hard to leave it'.

The difficulties experienced by many adolescents in establishing themselves in an analytic relationship have been the subject of some study and attention over the years. Indeed, the recognition that it might be important to take into account certain features specific to the needs of adolescents was given practical acknowledgement when in 1960 Dugmore Hunter and others instituted a separate Adolescent Department at the Tavistock Clinic, and similarly with the establishment of the Brent Consultation Centre, staffed by psychiatrists and psychotherapists linked with the Hampstead Child Clinic, now the Anna Freud Centre (Novick, 1977).

An outline of the style and structure and certain of the conceptual approaches within the current work of this centre is contained in the account given in chapter ten by Rosalie Joffe of some of her own psychotherapeutic work with suicidal adolescents.

In recent years (1984), the London Youth Advisory Centre has set up a service where, in addition to psychotherapy, consultations and counselling are also available from medical staff where this may be especially appropriate, and a general information service on educational and other needs (Wilson, 1987).

The importance of re-designing services in order to respond to some special aspects of adolescent difficulties was addressed in a paper by R. Bird (1987, delivered at a conference entitled, 'Navigando in Acqua Tempestose'). In this he wrote that the

entry of an individual into the process of psychotherapeutic treatment involves the crossing of two major boundaries:

1. *Referral*　the movement of the individual from the outside world of the community into the specialized world of the clinic, usually feared and often unknown. 'When adolescents ask directly for help for themselves, then they are already on the way to crossing this first boundary'. When the request comes from adults, family, or professionals, it may be important to think about where the anxiety belongs and whether it has indeed been split off so that the young people are out of touch with their own proper anxieties and need some help in this respect.

2. *Assessment, or exploration.*　This is 'the movement across the internal or emotional boundary, from a position of experiencing oneself as the victim of symptoms or situations to a position of seeing oneself as a part of those symptoms or situations; of learning that they are intelligible and that through understanding one can influence the symptoms and the situations. [Bird, 1986]

'Adolescents will need help in crossing both these boundaries.' They may feel anxious and hesitant about coming, and it is important for them to have the sense of being given 'space' to come to their own decisions without pressures from adults.

In order to address these problems of motivation, and also having in mind the large number of referrals of young people who do not reach the clinic at all, the Adolescent Department has, over the last ten years or so, set up a special Intake Committee. This includes a senior psychiatrist, psychologist, social worker, and child psychotherapist who meet weekly to consider all requests and to explore resources in relation to these requests. Most importantly, however, they share their thinking on referrals that are from 'surrounding adults' in order to try to identify the location of the anxiety and to consider how it might be moved from the adults to the young people concerned in a way that might enable them to come to the clinic. One of the team members will later contact the referring adult by telephone in order to explore further and to discover whether the concern or anxiety is being felt by the young person, or if not, where the main distress is located. Surprisingly, many young people between 16 and 18 years of age have not even been asked whether they might like some help or how they would feel about attending the clinic. Following these preparatory explorations, the committee may consider further consultations with the referrers and offer family or individual therapy, or some combination of these possibilities.

The work with individual patients as described here illustrates the importance of regarding adolescence as a discrete phase in which both the individuality and the unique nature of the stage is important, as well as the element of transition between latency and adulthood. As mentioned earlier, adolescents are notoriously difficult to induct into analysis, so that procedures established in the Brent Consultation Service, and similarly those developed in the Tavistock Adolescent Department, are directed at facilitating this process for them.

An additional factor in working with adolescents may be the delicate issue of maintaining and respecting the confidentiality of the analytic relationship while recognizing the role of parental responsibility and support. This can be especially critical in situations where the adolescent may feel that independence from intense early attachments can only be won by massive rejection.

We tend to think of the later stages of adolescent development and entry into young adulthood as 'going out into the world', and to reflect on what kind of world they will find. In particular during periods of wide unemployment among young people it may be especially difficult to feel that there is no longer a place for you at home, nor one waiting for you 'out there'. The experience of working with a deprived boy in mid-adolescence described by Barbara Forryan (1988) conveys a painful image of this profound sense of 'homelessness'.

The boy, Tony, aged 14 and living in a children's home, began his psychotherapy by tearing up bits of paper and throwing them into the bin near the therapist. She comments that he was showing something of his feelings about himself—all bits and pieces, unwanted rubbish—but that maybe she might be able to receive these feelings and think about them, reflecting that 'a rubbish bin is an unflattering analogy for the mind of the therapist', but that collecting the rubbish in one place and providing a container did in itself seem to develop some value for Tony: the fact that his therapist remembered and thought about what he showed her in their sessions.

Living in the children's home had meant being given 'the new-boy treatment': being beaten up when he moved there, having his small possessions endlessly stolen from his 'unlockable locker', and hopelessly resigning himself to the experience that nothing could be done about all this. His therapist acknowledged the distress and pain that these events must mean for him, and she was also able to help him to be in touch with the extent to which he was projecting the bad destructive parts of himself into others. Some time later he asked why his mother had not kept him and tried to think about her with more understanding and compassion. The therapist comments that adolescents like Tony, who 'have no sense of themselves as a whole person' and feel a 'desperate need for some identity, may form an identification with a delinquent group'—'partly as a protection against experiencing themselves as dependent with no-one to depend on', 'submitting themselves to the mores of the delinquent group, which can only offer a very spurious pseudo-solution'.

For such emotionally homeless children, submitting themselves to the power of delinquent group cultures can seem to offer a hope, however false, of a safe and familiar haven from which to evacuate their terror, pain, and humiliation into the world of people 'out there'.

In sharp contrast to Tony and the world he lived in were the cases of two very gifted young people in very favourable circumstances, who 'seemed quite unable to enjoy their good fortune' (Harris, 1976). Both suffered long periods of depressive states and withdrawal, which in the girl were accompanied by anorexia. It seemed as if within their somewhat idealized 'worlds' and latency images of themselves they too had begun to feel shaken by an awareness of deep areas of destructiveness and envy directed towards their internal parental figures. A pervasive sense of acquiring gifts and goodness on false pretences now undermined the feeling of being rightfully and securely able to enjoy them.

Adolescence is often characterized as a time when the wilder phantasies of infancy and the potency of adulthood within the body and mind of one person may present the risk of an explosive internal alliance or, alternatively, of severe splitting and breakdown. However, the volatile transitional nature of this time may also offer moments of sensitivity when adolescents can respond positively to the prospect of finding some deeper understanding of their relationships with others.

A dream that may illustrate something of these processes was reported by a generally resistant and challenging adolescent girl shortly before the Christmas break. This had been preceded by a period of acting out. For two or three days prior to the dream she had complained that men in the streets, especially on her way to and from sessions, were calling to her in obscene or threatening ways. While acknowledging that there could be genuine cause for concern over this, I felt that the 'epidemic' quality of the encounters suggested an element of acting out. It seemed that what was being enacted was an identification with a phantasy of the therapist as the sexual mother deserting the baby and therefore in danger of attack from the anger and envy that were aroused. Interpretations along these lines were initially rejected with outrage and fury, but in the sessions that followed she began to acknowledge that her demeanour could have been provocative of envy and of sexual interest.

A few days later she brought a dream that the world was about to end because the earth was travelling out of orbit 'definitely not in the right place', and she had joined in some looting, taking a pair of very high-heeled red shoes from a woman, and a mohair dress (similar to the rug on the couch). Then she had wandered along a suburban street, feeling terribly deserted, as she listened to some men discussing the earth and its path in the sky.

The mood and contents of the dream indicated that at the deepest levels the separation was dreaded as if it meant the death of the nurturing mother. It contained also a recognition that she felt herself to be 'looting' from the analysis, not acknowledging its value or source. This led to a feeling that she was not entitled to and could not hold on to it. With the disappearance of the external figure, she would therefore have nothing enduring 'inside', no protective internal image. The atmosphere of sadness, and hint of guilt, that the looting that preceded the Earth's disappearance was also making it happen, brought a new tone of concern and grieving. It seemed that there had been a lessening of the 'splitting-off' processes by which she had previously been able to 'disown' her own feelings of deprivation, envy, and hostility by 'exporting' them into strangers, who then turned into frightening persecutors. This shift was borne out by much of the material during the following weeks, when she showed a new interest and concern over the exploitation and impoverishment of the Earth's resources, and distress about the baby seals who were dying because of the polluted water. The last day before the holiday she said she was beginning to feel that the analysis was doing her good, adding, however, that this made her afraid she was being brainwashed.

In exploring the adolescent process mainly in terms of a universal experience and, with a clinical focus, emphasizing principally the difficulties and the problems, it might seem that one is failing to acknowledge and value all the individuality and inventiveness, the adventure, challenge, and vitality that are equally a part of this process.

In the case descriptions presented in the following two chapters, however, some of these qualities do emerge. What also seems to be very important, perhaps especially for such periods of change, is the factor of hopefulness, and while clearly this is a sadly fragile strand for the group of patients described in chapter ten, some of the young people presented in chapter eleven do seem to have managed to hold on to this, despite difficult times.

Work with suicidal adolescents at a walk-in centre in Brent

Rosalie Joffe

While this chapter explores further the issues surrounding the significance of the setting as a factor in supporting the therapist's work and the patient's sense of containment, it also brings one sharply in touch with the extremes of confusion and despair that can overtake young people as they struggle to find a way out of conflict and inner loneliness. Rosalie Joffe's analysis of her work in this context provides many vital insights into the state of mind of these unhappy adolescents and helpful guidelines for those who hope to protect them while they are travelling on this dangerous road.

[R.S.]

This chapter is based on my own work at the Brent Consultation Centre and the freely drawn-upon rich collective fund of knowledge of my colleagues there. I propose,

---

An earlier version of this chapter was presented in 1982 at the Day Conference of the Brent Consultation Centre. The views expressed here are the author's own.

in the chapter, to refer briefly to the framework of this Walk-In Service for Adolescents and the technique of interviewing. This is followed by some general observations about suicide, first aid for workers in the field, and, lastly, clinical vignettes.

The setting in which I work is an old house in Brent, with four interview rooms, a waiting room, and a staff meeting room, on two floors. The administrative staff are located on the third floor.

The Walk-In Service is funded by the Education Department of the London Borough of Brent, who also fund psychotherapy for adolescents in the borough. There are research projects as well, which are, in the main, privately funded. Young people between the ages of 14 and 23 are encouraged to walk in or to telephone for an appointment. There is no waiting list. It has been our experience that almost all the adolescents who refer themselves in this way are too disturbed to be helped in short-term intervention. We see the client weekly or fortnightly four to ten times. It is understood by the client from the beginning that the aim of the interviews is to explore together and understand the problem and then to decide what help would be most beneficial. Should this help turn out to be psychotherapy, the adolescent knows that the therapist will be someone other than the interviewer—either a Brent Consultation colleague, if the client lives in the Borough of Brent, or, if not, someone in an outside agency.

All the interviewing staff are either analysts or child psychotherapists. They all work at the Centre part-time and meet once a week as a group. In working with suicidal adolescents, it is important to have a support group that can help to contain anxiety and contribute to the understanding of the transference and countertransference reactions that may be present and may be impeding the work. Further, the support group can be of help in building up a central shared body of knowledge about adolescent development and breakdown.

There has been much debate at the Brent Consultation Centre over the pros and cons of our policy of extended interviews. Opinions against such a policy have included the danger of the blurring of interview and therapeutic roles and techniques, including the encouragement of regression and development of the infantile transference neurosis, increasing the difficulty in transfer to a therapist, and the loss to therapy of the impetus for help afforded by the initial crisis. I find that with this careful preparation adolescents are less likely to refuse to transfer and to end their therapy prematurely. I have found this policy particularly relevant for suicidal young people. Although those who are self-referred are consciously seeking an alternative to killing themselves, they are also unconsciously driven to put into action their unconscious fantasies/conflicts and seek confirmation that their search for help is futile. They are only too ready to experience early transfer, or indeed an ending of an interview, as rejection and as a further reason for killing themselves. The extended period of interviewing allows one time to initiate an alliance to counteract the tendency to compulsive action.

I understand this work as a holding experience for the suicidal adolescent, during which I communicate my awareness of his affects—his hurt, rage, destructiveness, and fear of going mad or breaking down, and of his projections onto me. It is most important that within this context he should experience my ability to take seriously his suffering and his pathology, and that I will be able to bear whatever he communicates to me without retaliation.

While I use the transference to understand the pathology or dynamic processes and the client's inner world, I will not attempt to facilitate regression or the infantile transference neurosis. I will, however, verbalize the here-and-now transference, by which I mean what is happening between us, how he is experiencing and using me, and his defensive manoeuvres. At times I may link these verbalizations with the past, and I certainly make more use of linking with the outside world than I would in therapy. Transference interventions are determined by the aim of averting the danger of acting out by leaving, suicide, or other destructive actions, or to further the aim of promoting future therapeutic alliance with a future therapist. Observation of the countertransference, in the sense of monitoring the feelings evoked in oneself by the client, which belong to the client, is a useful tool in understanding the adolescent's transference. It is in this area that the support group at the Centre is most

important in helping to distinguish between our own unconscious defences against the immediacy of the adolescent transference and the projective identifications of the client. (For more
detailed information on the work of the Centre see Hurry, 1986,
and Laufer & Laufer, 1985.)

An overview of the suicidal adolescent

One can understand the period of adolescence as part of the normal developmental process between childhood and adulthood—a
mental process by which the adolescent comes to be his own person and to own his own body. He needs to become separate from
his primary objects and to integrate his relationship to the parents of infancy, childhood, and adolescence, and to peer groups,
followed by the establishment of a stable gender and sexual
identity. Adolescence is characterized by fluidity, by change, by
progressions and regressions, when the adolescent is unable to
resolve these tasks, when the adolescent feels—as happened
with one girl—that she cannot go forward into an adult female
life, nor, with her hated female mature body, return to childhood, resulting in an inner feeling of impasse. It is when this
fluidity is no longer possible that we refer to 'breakdown' or
'breakdown of the adolescent process'.

By extending this developmental concept, the image of one's
body has its roots in the very first experiences at the mother's
breast, which will in turn be influenced by the mother's relationship to her own body as a woman and mother. So the child
will relate to his or her body as lovable or hateful throughout
the developmental stages—oral, anal, and oedipal—all within
the parental two- or three-person relationships. With the onset
of puberty all this has to be renegotiated within the context of a
now mature body, which is capable of sexual intercourse, of
creating babies, and which has a new potential for violence.

I wish to define a suicide attempt as an action that contains
the possibility or the thought of death. The reality of death is
physical; the notion or thought of death, however, is a psychic

one. I illustrate what death meant psychically to three young people in my clinical section.

I believe that at the time of a suicide attempt adolescents are in an acute psychotic state—perhaps a transient one, or perhaps one of long duration. This is true despite the rational-sounding post hoc reasons they may give for the decision to die or denial that they meant to die. The ability to relate to outside events and people becomes distorted—as with an analytic patient who, because of her inner feeling about herself, projected her own 'madness' into her mother. Whether the suicide attempt is of the so-called minor 'cry-for-help' variety or of a more serious nature, I regard all suicide attempts as violence directed at the person's own body. There is great resistance on the part of the adolescent to accept the seriousness of his act, as there often is in parents and other helping professions involved. They seem to collude in ignoring the adolescent's own claim that he cannot continue with his life.

Adolescents who have made a suicide attempt unconsciously experience it as an attack on their internal objects or, as in the case of Jane, on their hated mothers' bodies, insofar as they are similar. The function of self-preservation seems to be lacking. The adolescent has split off the loving, care-taking part of himself that he should have taken over from his parents. Murderous impulses towards the self remain unchecked. Before the act of suicide there is another kind of killing; with the young people I have seen, it seems as though they have psychically killed off all the good, loving qualities in the internal representation of their mothers or fathers (or both) and in their inner representation of themselves or that self that related to the good-enough parents. They are left with the hated, harsh, criticizing parents in them and the hating, and hated, full-of-faults parts of themselves. All hope seems to be gone. There is only despair and anger, and the compulsion to rid themselves of these hated qualities. But psychic killing is not physical killing. The caring, positive qualities are not irrevocably lost or killed off. They are there to be found again and rekindled. It is our job to facilitate this.

Many of these young people desperately ward off hope. Hope contains within it the potential for failure and disappointment. Yet they do hope! They invite us to carry that hope for them—

even while they insist that it does not exist. We try to enable them to own it for themselves again.

It is a tricky path the worker needs to tread. Death can be seen as a punishment for sexual or violent feelings as well as the end of *their* suffering, but also as the fulfilment of an unconscious fantasy. They not only fear rejection and abandonment but seem to need to provoke it. Feelings of dependence on the worker can give hope and relieve anxiety. It may also be felt as a seduction towards their shameful wish for bodily care, now sexualized. The worker may soon become the persecutor, the recipient of the adolescent's projections, which formerly were experienced in relation to the parents. The interviews become a shameful secret; the analyst is held responsible for their shame and failure and can become the object to be attacked by suicide.

In the analysis of these young people, we have come to recognize danger signs such as their vulnerability to holidays and weekends, which confirm their unlovableness. We recognize such action substitutes for suicide as leaving the analyst before a holiday, extending the break, or threatening the continuation of therapy, or compulsions to change the structure of the analytic setup—for example, the need to change times, payment, and so on. We found that they began temporary sexual partnerships during holiday breaks.

I come now to the section I have referred to as 'First Aid for Therapists'. When I am trying to create a process of alliance where adolescents can take from me what I offer, I find it useful to remember five simple statements:

1. A suicidal act may, and often does, end a life. (A dead adolescent is dead.)

2. The adolescent's guilt and concern for the suffering his suicide will cause his parents often seems totally lacking.

3. If someone is determined to kill himself, I will be unable to prevent it; the secrecy of a suicidal plan increases its potency as a weapon to be used against our help.

4. The suicide attempt is always a sign of serious pathology; the suicide act takes place, I believe, during a transitory psychotic episode.

5. Whether or not the outcome, physically, is serious, a suicidal act is an attack on the person's own body.

1. A suicidal act can end a life

If we miss the opportunity to put the adolescent in touch with the part of him- or herself that wants to live, we may not get another chance. He or she may be dead. They arouse anxiety in us, and I think this is as it should be. While they are driven to disown it themselves or in their parents, we will need to keep for them their concern and, hopefully, to share it and eventually to give it into their own keeping.

Nor must we miss the opportunity to confront these people with the reality of death. Death can mean different things to adolescents, and they may be protecting themselves from its full realization. Many intend to kill themselves, yet they behave as though something of themselves will remain alive, or, unconsciously, they expect a rebirth. Some intend to destroy, knock out, or put something of themselves to sleep without the intention of killing themselves. The notion of death may symbolize many things. It is our task to uncover these fantasies, to spell out what death means in real terms, to remind them of their fear of death, to stand in the way of their denial of their wish for help, their wish to live.

2. About guilt

Many suicide attempts follow a row with the parents, and this may be used to trivialize the event. At such times these adolescents are filled with anger and hate, their self-loathing reinforced. Love and concern for themselves and their parents can now more easily be pushed aside. They see the parents as guilty; now it is they, not the adolescent, who are made responsible for the suicide attack on that child whose parents are seen as not being loving enough. It is this kind of projection of which we will find ourselves to be the subject in such therapeutic relationships. We need continuously to give the adolescents back their own guilt and responsibility for their attacks on themselves and on ourselves. They seem to want us to prove to them that we, too, like the parents, can be regarded as having nothing of value for them and may also be uncaring. Our own feelings of inadequacy may collude with this, and if we accept their projections and experience uselessness and guilt, we may be prevented from helping the adolescent to be in touch with his feelings of helplessness, futility, and failure.

Suicide is not only an attack on the adolescent himself, but on the people who are important to him at that time. Many adolescents have complained that their parents' obvious concern and love make it impossible for them to kill themselves. 'Why should I have to live for them?' is a common cry and contains the plea, 'Don't put me in touch with my guilt, don't make it more difficult for me to kill myself. Allow me to hate myself and my parents.' We must not be blinded to the unspoken plea, 'Help me to stop hating, save me from a world in which there is now no goodness inside or outside'.

3. The power of the suicide plan
(this is about omnipotence)

When adolescents feel unbearably out of control, vulnerable, and helpless, the idea of suicide gives them a sense of power over their own lives and a weapon to be used against others. It enables them to nurse a fantasy where it is the parent or therapist who is seen to be, and indeed is made to feel, impotent and helpless. Even in the midst of the adolescents' desperate search for help, for someone or some hope to hang onto, there would seem to be a paradoxical triumphant determination to prove themselves to be beyond help. Faced with the adolescents' omnipotence and our own feelings of being only human, anxious, insecure, and uncertain, defensively we may close our minds to the possibility of their suicide, or alternatively become as omnipotent as the adolescents in our determination to save them. I tell young suicidal people that if they have made up their minds to kill themselves, I know I will not be able to prevent it. I also always keep in the open my knowledge that they have a plan to kill themselves if all else fails. I hope my attitude to them demonstrates I can confront myself with—and contain—my own limitations and possible failure, with their death as the outcome. I try to keep them in touch with their problems and defensive omnipotence, with their need to reduce me to helplessness, to make me appear stupid. I do not enter into a power struggle with them. I spell out suicide as a weapon and how it may be used to attack me in the course of our meetings. Much of the usefulness of suicide as a weapon in the guilt and recrimination stakes is defused when it is no longer being used secretly.

4. Psychotic quality

It is not always easy to detect the psychotic quality from the adolescent's recall of the suicide attempt. This may be due to the post-hoc distortions that have been made because of the unbearably frightening nature of the experience. The adolescent naturally wishes to continue to avoid any awareness of the frightening nature of his state of mind at the time of a suicide attempt. The resistance to insight in these young people is an unconscious one and is linked with the need not to know, to destroy the fantasies that were driving them crazy.

These are often unconscious sexual, perverse, or incestuous fantasies, which are threatening to break through into consciousness. Immediately after an unsuccessful suicide attempt there is the likelihood of a repeat while the breakthrough of repressed fantasies is still operative.

Before a suicide attempt, there is often a driven quality in the adolescent. Despite the wish for help, for therapy, there is a compulsion to put an unconscious conflict into action through the suicide. The method of suicide may link with the content of the conflict. The adolescent will struggle against the emergence into consciousness of the underlying unconscious meaning of his suicide attempt. In a brief intervention one may not be able to interpret the unconscious motivation. One can, however, draw the adolescent into an alliance in the therapeutic process by showing him he is not choosing in freedom to kill himself but, rather, is compelled by forces he knows little of.

5. The attack on the body

It is not only the parents or their child who is attacked with a suicidal act—it is the actual body and mind at the time of the attempt. During adolescence sexual and aggressive feelings and conflicts are at their height. Attitudes to the childhood body are now further extended, to include the secondary sexual characteristics, the ability to produce a baby, to become a parent. The new attitude to the body will have been influenced by past experience of the parents' handling and caring for the infant and child's body, their attitude to it and its functions, to its maleness or femaleness. It is this body that may be attacked and hated, because it contains the adolescent's sexual identity, his conscious and unconscious sexual needs and fantasies, which the adolescent has not been able to integrate or come to terms with.

Adolescents may feel compelled to reject our help because of a fear of dependency. Dependency may be experienced as the wish for passive early childhood body-care, which in adolescence has become linked with sexual perversion and incest. They punish themselves by blaming and attacking their bodies. They may experience our offer of help as forcing them into dependence and may feel compelled to leave us instead of killing themselves.

Clinical section

Clinical example 1

The first and third adolescents described were seen by me at the Brent Walk-In Service. The second was seen by another interviewer and transferred to me for therapy once a week.

The first case is that of a young man of 18 who was sent to the Centre by his general practitioner because he had swallowed 40 aspirins at work, and a few days after his release from hospital 'he had walked into a truck'. He insisted that suicide was not, and had never been, in his mind. He continued to see me, he said, only because the doctor and I were so concerned. He said that I reminded him of his puzzlement at age 10, when his headmaster had given him rubbers, paper, and pencils after his mother's death, as though he had suddenly become poor materially. His mother had died of cancer after many years of illness when he was 10 years old.

The boy maintained that he was perfectly content with his life. His life, as far as I could ascertain, contained only externals and acquaintances with whom he had no emotional, loving, or angry relationship. He had not fulfilled his potential academically. He carried out a humdrum job for want of any desire or ambition. He had no plans for the future. This young man seemed totally out of touch with his affects. He had dealt with his sexuality and all adolescent tasks and problems in much the same way as he must have dealt with his feelings at the time of his mother's death. He paid highly for this with the impoverishment of his whole personality and life in order to maintain this smooth unruffled existence. He and his internal world seemed dead. Yet there was life in him: I saw it in his eyes. The repressed unconscious conflicts were alive: *they* made their presence known in the suicide attempts.

He came to the Centre clutching the letter from his doctor. While no muscle moved as he sat with me denying any need for him to be there, he continued to keep his appointments, and his eyes never left my face. The unblinking stare of his eyes did not make me in the least uncomfortable—they seemed to have a life of their own and to beseech me to ignore his words and to see only them. In *his* mind his father and stepmother were as uncaring and dead to him as he was to them and to his dead mother. I was able to confront him with his deadness as a way of coping with the rage and pain at losing his mother, his need to be as she was, dead—out of reach—to himself and to everybody. I was able to confront him with his present-day life, with his total aloneness and withdrawal from contact of a physical or mental kind with everyone. I think he came to accept responsibility for the urge to kill himself, to be dead. I arranged a joint meeting with his parents (father and stepmother), who *were* able, unlike him, to weep and express their deep concern, love, and fear for him. It was a most painful meeting for him; only his eyes seemed able to respond. I hoped he would no longer be able to treat them as dead, or again obliterate their concern and suffering in the face of his deadness and the wall he had built about him. He was unable to go further, but I hope that one day he will remember the hope there is for him in treatment, and that he will return. One might speculate that in his behaviour he was encapsulating both the dead, sick, unable-to-care mother inside him and relating to himself as the already dead son of a dead mother, with whom he was too angry to want to be alive.

Clinical example 2: Susan

The suicidal act may contain both the symbolic enactment of an unconscious masturbation fantasy and the attempt to destroy it finally in death. This struggle for both gratification and obliteration of the fantasy may undermine the adolescent's pursuit of understanding. This was seen in the treatment of a 19-year-old, Susan, who did not want therapy, yet accepted it. She was blonde, plump, and attractive and at times could look very seductive. She was sent to the Centre by her general practitioner because she was terrified of going out of the house away from her mother and was tortured by her thoughts about the two muggings she had experienced, followed shortly thereafter by a suicide attempt.

This young woman wanted help; she wanted to be freed from her fears. It was difficult, however, for her to commit herself to therapy and life because she needed to avoid at all costs the content of the unconscious fantasies, which were threatening to break through into consciousness. She sought to give up her sexuality and become a little sick girl, a victim for whom her mother would have to care. Susan insisted that she was ill only because she had been a mugging victim twice, and that she had made a suicide attempt only to escape her fears of being attacked again. She was perfectly happy to explore her suicide attack, but only as an attack on herself in order to make her mother sorry she had not been more sympathetic over the second mugging.

It was an uphill task to help this girl to see beyond the attacks, to be in touch with what was driving her crazy. She felt she was a born victim, through no fault of her own. Any attempt on my part to help her to see beyond the muggings, to understand and explore, was experienced by her as my being unsympathetic like her mother, as blaming her. Susan, too, would stare unblinking at me and refuse to be the one to begin to speak. *Her* stare however *did* make me feel uncomfortable! It seemed to say—well, do your worst. It seemed to dare me to lose patience with her like her mother, to give up on her. Her silence had the quality of unconsciously forcing me to take the initiative and responsibility, but if I did speak first it was experienced as an attack, as an intrusion into her. If I did not, she felt desolate. It contained also the unconscious longing for me to come in and find her, bring her out, and help her. With verbalization to her of these feelings Susan was able to relate to me how as a little child she used to pack her toy suitcase and run away from home to the bottom of the garden, where she would long for her mother to become anxious and come and find her. She related, very sadly, that her mother never even missed her, and that her mother's main aggression towards her family was to punish them by refusing to talk to them.

As a child and early adolescent she had been a 'terrible tomboy'—efficient at cricket and boxing, for example. She had an intense relationship with an older brother, who sadistically, amidst much excitement in both of them and fear in her, would attack her physically. The most exciting element of this interplay was for the brother to jump out at her and take her unawares. He was delinquent and a prototype for her future boyfriends.

Her other main impression of her childhood was of her wonderful mother, to whom she was a constant source of trouble through her extreme proneness to accidents.

The wish for the victim role, which helped Susan abdicate responsibility for her own excitement and aggression, became increasingly clear to me, as did her preoccupation with death. She showed liveliness only when she was recounting some accident to herself, or a near-catastrophe from the past. She was a

Catholic, and she used her religion to reinforce her own prohibitions against aggression and sexuality, which, she felt, were shared by her mother. Susan had never come to terms with being a woman, although she had several times made forays into heterosexuality—beginning relationships with unsuitable men but running for cover, back to her mother, when sex would have become unavoidable.

She eventually was enabled to tell me that she had been terrified that she had in some way provoked the two muggings, or even wished for them. She recounted how she had battled against unconsciousness during the actual muggings, yet seemed to long for the awful giving-in, which would also, she feared, terrifyingly have spelt death.

The two attacks evoked her incestuous sexual excitement experienced with her brother and contained in her unconscious masturbation fantasy.

For Susan, death, however, was not final. She half believed you could return after dying whenever the fancy took you and nursed a feeling of rejection and resentment that her dead grandfather and a much-loved pet had never returned to her.

Her relationship to her mother was complicated. She could sever the tie between them *only* in anger, or for short periods. Her mother's lack of sympathy towards Susan after the second attack, and over the earlier childhood accidents, was interpreted by her as her mother's blaming her for them, representing the secret interplay with her brother. She was constantly in a dilemma—on the one hand, to have and accept her sexuality (felt as wicked) and to leave/reject mother; or, on the other hand, to keep the good mother–daughter bond by ridding herself of her own badness and sexuality, which in turn made her become prone to hatred of the mother, who seemed to demand this. The night before her suicide attempt Susan had engineered a row with her mother. She was filled with anger against the mother who, she felt, blamed her for the attacks which Susan unconsciously experienced as sexual. Unconsciously she was angry with her mother who loved men: her father and her brothers. Yet while repudiating such feelings in Susan, her mother did nothing to protect her from her brother and the muggers. There was no loving internal caretaker left to protect her from the punitive hatred of her own sexuality. She was driven to destroy her sexual body, which caused such terrible conflicts, but in so doing she was unconsciously driven to do harm to herself and so experience once and for all time the orgasmic death she feared and was so excited by. She imagined herself as dead, watching her mother's terrible remorse.

Clinical example 3: Jane

An example of a symbolic plea to be saved in the face of a secret conscious resolve to die illustrates how 'killing' came to mean something other than death to one adolescent. This very ill young woman of 20, whom we will call Jane, came to the Centre because of her unreasonable jealousy in relation to her boyfriend, whom she imagined as having affairs with other women. She was also concerned about her hostility towards older women. Her mother had killed herself when Jane was 16, and this had followed a previous psychotic breakdown and hospitalization.

Jane spoke of her mother in an idealizing way. She had clearly displaced her critical and angry feelings for her mother onto other older women, such as teachers and aunts, whom she experienced as threatening, frightening, and highly critical of her. I believe that the current close heterosexual relationship had triggered off certain feelings of guilt and conflict in relation to her dead mother. Just before the mother had killed herself, Jane had fallen in love with a man and had been forbidden to speak to him by her mother.

Jane was beautiful and intelligent. She made her way by charm. She cultivated an 'as if' personality, reflecting back to people what at any given moment in time seemed expected of her. She experienced herself as shallow, empty, pretty. She treated me in a charming, seductive way, inviting me to smile with her at the 'silly ideas' that were driving her mad. She was driven to force me to have the same 'seeming' relationship with her as she had forced herself to have with her mother, in order to overlook the frightening and mad things her mother did and said. Jane had spent her life trying to run away from what was happening internally. She now obtained a job that necessitated travelling, which cut short our first contact.

She put out of her mind the horrifying, mad qualities of her mother in order to keep for herself an image of an ideal mother. It was clear that she was trying to make me into the bad mother in order to preserve this idealized internal one—and in this way to rid herself of the badness and madness she felt was in her. Leaving may, at times, be regarded as a symbolic killing off, which also contains the hoped-for rebirth somewhere else without the terrifying and hated thoughts, feelings, images, and fantasies influenced by the past. I hoped she would remember these insights when her running-away failed again.

She did, and she returned to see me four months later, much more desperate. Her condition was deteriorating; she could hardly hold herself together. Images and thoughts were breaking through into consciousness. She clearly hated her shallow, lying charm. She seemed to experience herself now as mad, even as the psychotic mother. She terrified herself one night by seeing her mother reflected in her image in the mirror. I learnt how the mother had terrified Jane the night before her suicide by coming into her room. (I suspect that Jane sensed a sexual attack.) Jane had fled to her father for help. The following night, Jane locked herself in—in retrospect, she now felt she knew it was going to happen. She had obliterated from her mind the terrifying aspects of her mother and her belief that her mother wanted her dead too, and her own guilt that she had done nothing to save her mother.

She had become terrified of death. She became confused. She felt unsafe walking in the road, in case a car killed her. Yet she had managed to obtain tablets with which to kill herself. She seemed driven to kill the mad mother in her *and* the false, 'as if' Jane. She had agreed to have treatment and to take sick-leave. However, she informed me she would do one more business trip, because she needed the money. It would take only a few days. She assured me she could convincingly put on her 'as if' face to see her through. She almost convinced me, until she gave me a small Easter egg to keep for her. Then I knew that she would make an attempt to kill herself. The Easter egg represented the baby part of herself that might have a chance to grow if the other two selves were killed—both the false 'as if' socially charming self and the mad dead mother self. I chose to understand this as her unspoken plea to protect her from herself. I had her admitted into hospital immediately. In hospital she refused to speak because she feared lest it might be with the 'voice' of the mad Jane that contained the dead mother, or of the 'I', which spoke for the 'false face' she could 'put on'. The untainted self communicated by writing, drawing, or painting— new-found skills—belonging solely to an emerging 'me' within herself.

Summary

All three adolescents were seen at the Brent Consultation Walk-In Centre when they were actively suicidal. Prior to recommending therapy for them, an endeavour was made, with varying degrees of success, to hold/contain and to put them in touch with the drivenness or compulsiveness of their behaviour, without necessarily understanding the content of the underlying conflicts.

The first young man could not commit himself to further exploration of his inner life but was confronted with his murderousness in the way he deadened his own inner life and that of his internal objects, and his attacks on his parents and his own body. Guilt and concern were rekindled.

I have extracted examples from Susan's therapy to illustrate something of the conflicts that underlay her drivenness to seek release from tension by action contained in attacks on her body. She came to understand something of the unbearable impasse she found herself in, caught between her progressive moves towards heterosexuality and the regressive incestuous pull to her mother.

Jane was different. She had not yet made a suicide attempt. I realized her defenses against psychotic anxiety were crumbling and that she might not be able to be held in the interview set-up until arrangements could be completed for her admission to a therapeutic ward. Thus the support of the General Practitioner was also enlisted. Although I represented the good mother rescuer she longed for, with whom she would find her true self, I also understood the less benign transference. I was also the mad mother who wanted her dead, who had to be lied to and circumvented in order for Jane's 'me' to survive. She felt compelled to triumph over me by killing off the false 'I' who was compliantly working with me.

CHAPTER ELEVEN

Work with
ethnic minorities

Gianna Williams

The theme of group identities and of intergroup differences and potential hostilities referred to in chapter nine here forms the focus for a study of these issues in individual relationships. Specifically, it explores within the context of a workshop how far and in what directions ethnic differences or similarities might be seen to affect the psychotherapeutic relationship. This exploratory small-scale research endeavour, focussed on a number of 'self-referring' teenagers, may not provide, nor claim to provide, universal answers. It does, however, offer some very rewarding, hopeful, and interesting developments.

[R.S.]

I wish to express my thanks to Ms Chriso Andreou and Mrs Alicefay Eichelberger for permission to quote from their material.

I n recent years an Ethnic Minorities Workshop was set up in the Adolescent Department of the Tavistock Clinic, with a view to exploring the potential effects of ethnic and cultural differences as a factor in the psychotherapeutic dialogue. Some members of the workshop felt that such differences were of relevance only during the assessment phase or within brief interventions and suggested therefore that if we wished to focus on cultural differences, discussion be limited to the presentation of work of this kind alone. They considered that once a patient had become engaged in treatment of a long-term nature, and if the work was well held in the transference, then the cultural differences would have receded. Other members, however, considered that cultural factors could remain relevant through many years in treatment, quoting from examples of their own clinical experience.

We decided, therefore, to alternate presentations of brief work with presentations of ongoing long-term therapy, and to explore these issues on the basis of detailed material. One of the issues that we were also able to explore was the relevance of cultural similarities or dissimilarities between patient and therapist.

This chapter refers to four adolescent cases presented in the workshop, including both brief intervention and long-term work. The first is an example of brief work, which I undertook with a West Indian adolescent aged 18.

Winston:
A brief intervention

Winston referred himself to the Young People's Counselling Service because he had very nearly been run over by a train as he was 'writing' graffiti in the Underground, and he kept having nightmares in which he woke up just before being run over. He also found it difficult to go to sleep.

He had gone to see his general practitioner, who had told him about the Young People's Counselling Service at the Tavistock, and, after much hesitation, he had telephoned.

In his first session he told me that he had taken three weeks before referring himself. He did not feel like going to see a 'shrink' and 'this place is right in the middle of Bunkin'. From previous contacts with 'Hip-Hop' adolescents, I knew that 'Bunkin' refers to a residential middle-class London and to its inhabitants.

I took up Winston's use of this word as a test of whether he was going to be understood by me and related it to his hesitation about referring himself. Was he going to meet a white Bunkin who 'wouldn't have a clue' about his culture? He asked me if I knew something about graffiti art, and I said that what mattered was the meaning graffiti art had for him. It cannot have the same meaning for all Hip Hops. I explained that I was hoping to get to know him a little during our four exploratory meetings (the Tavistock Young Peoples Consultation Service offers a maximum of four sessions to self-referring adolescents over the age of 16), and perhaps what I did not know, he could tell me. This suggestion seemed to please him, and he was then able to talk about the very frightening incident in the Underground and about his difficult nights.

I asked if he had been 'writing' for a long time in dangerous places. He said very proudly that he was one of the first to 'write' in every single station of the Victoria line. When you accomplish something of this sort, you become a 'king'. He had his tag (code name) on many bridges on the canal; that meant painting at night, lowering himself from a bridge with ropes. Didn't I know that where you paint—the more daring, the better—is at least as important for a graffiti artist as the quality of his work?

He said in a rather challenging tone that he knew the people in the crew that had written a piece right here at the Tavistock. He had not seen it, but that is a good crew. It must have been a good piece. He knows it was over the entrance porch, and it is not there any longer. They have 'buffed' it. (We had, in fact, kept a very colourful piece of graffiti that had appeared overnight above the entrance porch to the Tavistock for some months; only recently had it been 'buffed'.)

I asked Winston whether he would have felt better about coming to the Tavistock if he had found the graffiti piece was still there. He said that it would have made a difference if it were his piece; but standing comfortably on a porch is chicken-feed for him. 'You don't become a king if you don't face danger.' I asked whether, since the accident, he had returned to write in the Underground. 'You have got to', he said. 'If you don't face the danger again straightaway, you chicken out.'

It became apparent in this session and in the subsequent ones that the prospect of 'chickening out', of being laughed at by 'the others', was as bad a nightmare for Winston as the one of being run over by a train. He told me that there are two very different ways of writing: 'You can join a crew and the tags of all members figure in the piece, or you can go it alone. You get on a train with your rucksack (the spray cans rattle much less in a rucksack than in a bag) and get off at a station. You have practiced the piece at home and know the shape, the colours. You can act fast. And you know the time you have got in-between trains. The difficult stations are the ones in central London where there are people around even late at night. It is much easier to write in Bunkin stations. The more you have outdone others in these expeditions, the more they are going to laugh at you if you chicken out.' But it was getting really hard to keep at it since the scare and not sleeping at night. He was not going to get stoned with gangia to forget about it. He was not going to opt out like a Rasta; his brothers are Rasta. He was not going to have any of that.

I felt that we were homing in on something very specific to Winston and not dictated by the culture. I asked if he would tell me about his family, and he seemed as eager to talk about it as about the graffiti.

He is the eldest of three brothers—one still at school, the other, just one year younger than he, unemployed like him . . . well, he played in a steel drums band at night. His father had died of cancer when he was 13 years old. His father had also been a Rasta, like his brothers and like the rest of his large extended family.

He had been brought up a Rasta. His hair (now very short) had never been cut until he had it cut off when he was 14. His mother did not mind, because she stopped being a Rasta when his father died. She converted to another religion, 'where they don't treat women so badly'. He did not remember the name of it.

She works as an office cleaner at night. She goes out at six in the evening. In the morning, she sleeps. There are rows between his mother and brothers all the time because the mother's new religion says that it is a sin to smoke gangia and both his brothers smoke it heavily. He also did when he was a Rasta. Yes, even when he was little. Rastas call it the 'weed of wisdom'.

What happened when he was 14? He cut his hair, he said, and went into 'break-dancing' and 'body-popping' in Covent Garden. He did not want to be like his brothers. Nor like his father?— Nor like his father. So he became a Hip Hop at 14, and he was one of the best dancers. Then he broke an elbow when he was 17, and he stopped going to Covent Garden. You can't let people see you with an arm in plaster, can you? I asked whether he felt he would be laughed at.

'Sure you would.'

'Like you would if you chickened out of writing in the Underground? Would your brothers laugh at you?'

'They would be the first.'

'And would your mother laugh at you?'

He said with conviction that no, his mother would not laugh at him. She was happy when he got out of the Covent Garden possy, because she felt he was going to break more bones. And she would be happy if he got out of writing in the Underground, because she knows a woman whose son tripped on the rails when he was running away, and he was electrocuted. I said I thought he was also scared of being electrocuted, but he felt he could not give up being a king just for that. I thought he *was* scared and I was not laughing at him. I said it sounded as if he felt there were lots of enemies and no friends, but he did not talk about his mother as if she were an enemy.

'I just wish she stopped going on about the graffiti. She doesn't understand that's my life. Well, that and Hip-Hop music. That's what I live for.'

'And maybe die for? I don't mean the music. That is not going to kill you.'

He laughed, but then looked thoughtful. He said, after a very short silence, that he was going to bring me a song he had written, because he writes the words and makes the rapping and the music.

'All on your own again?'

'No, I play in a rapping group.'

'So you are in a possy.'

'Well, I don't hang much together with the others. We go to the pub sometimes.'

'And you haven't told anyone in the possy about your scare and your bad nights?'

'I told you, they would laugh.'

'Because of your having scary dreams? I expect a king is not supposed to have scary dreams. He can't be frightened of getting electrocuted.'

'I wouldn't be a king no longer, would I?'

In the next session, the third one, Winston brought me the last song he had written, and he said I could keep it:

When I was one I killed suckers with a gun
When I was two I drank special brew
When I was three I moved up to Super T
When I was four I had girlies by the score
When I was five I was kicking it live
When I was six I was full of tricks
When I was seven I sent girlies up to heaven
When I was eight I was in a state
When I was nine I took to crime
When I was ten I started all over again.

He recited it with the rapping rhythm, and he obviously wanted to impress me.

I felt I should help him come down from his high and made a point not to refer to the sexual theme until much later in the session and very tangentially so.

I said that the song did help me to get to know him better.

He looked at me in an interrogative way, as if to say, 'You don't take it seriously, do you?' I said I knew it couldn't be the truth, but there was probably some truth in it, and I thought he had brought it to me not just to show me how good he was at rapping, but because he knew that it would help me to know him better and I may be of more help if I did. He said he had slept better this last week. He had had no nightmares.

Had he done any writing?

Yes, on a bridge.

I did not comment on the change of location.

I said, looking at the song that he handed over to me, that I was very interested in what he imagined he could have done when he was one.

He laughed: 'I shot suckers with a gun.'

'I thought you told me your brother, whom you can't stand and don't want to be like, was born when you were one. I am not sure you were so happy when he was born.'

'I can't tell you, can I? How do I know how I felt when I was one?'

'I think it is possible you started disliking him from the beginning. You were still very little, and your mother had another baby. Maybe you felt life would be better without him.'

He looked surprised and said with a sort of mock bravado, 'I could have shot the sucker'.

'Well, not quite, but you might have felt like getting rid of him in one way or another. You still seem to feel that way about both your brothers.'

'Yaaah.'

'It doesn't mean you would really shoot them. There is a lot of difference between wishing to do something and doing it. I don't think you ever really took to crime either.'

'Well . . . not when I was 9.'

'What sort of crime?'

'I have never killed nobody, but you have got to be good at racking spraycans if you write graffitis. But (proudly) I have never been caught.'

'I am thinking you did get close enough to proper crime, if there is such a thing as proper crime.'

'What do you mean?'

'I mean killing another one of your mother's children. I mean Winston.'

He looked very thoughtful and said, 'I don't really want to kill myself'.

'I know a part of you is very scared that you might. It is the part that speaks when you sleep and you have nightmares about trains. But you are so frightened of being laughed at in a world of enemies. I don't think your mother sounds like an enemy, even if she goes on about the graffiti. Maybe she is the only person you trust a little because you know she doesn't want for you to break all your bones or kill yourself under a train.'

'She likes me a lot better than she likes my brothers.'

'Maybe when your father died, although you were only 13, you felt you were the closest to a man there was in the family. You were the eldest son, and you had to prove to your mother and to all the world that you were fit for the job. Your song is full of it.'

'Full of what?'

'Of tasks too big for your age, like drinking special brew when you were 2 and sending girls to heaven when you were 7. You know I don't take it literally. I just take it to mean that you might have felt you had to pretend you were a man before you were a man. A better man than your father. Being a Rasta was good enough for your brothers. Your mother wasn't a Rasta any longer, and maybe she would like you better than she liked your brothers if you stopped being a Rasta, too.'

'But I couldn't have stayed a Rasta because it would have meant sticking together with my brothers, and I hate everything they do.'

'You seem to find it difficult to stick together with anybody. You don't like belonging to a "writing crew", you go it alone. You said you don't hang about much with the "music possy". Like a very lonely only child.'

Winston seemed puzzled and interested in the possible link between his hostility towards his brothers and his perception of being surrounded by enemies in his peer group.

We spent the rest of this session and all of the following and last one talking about his lonely and rather desperate predicament.

He seemed to find relief in envisaging links and exploring the possible meaning of his way of life, and I felt he was able to put some trust in me, although I was a white Bunkin and although I could offer him only such a brief contact.

I had described the nature of our work as an attempt to 'draw a map', as different from 'starting a journey', and in the fourth session we discussed the possibility of his seeking more long-term help, which he seemed very eager to do. 'But perhaps later', he said.

It must be apparent from the foregoing material that the issue of culture, in particular an adolescent rather than an ethnic culture, loomed large at the beginning of my work with Winston. It might have been more difficult to establish contact with him had I been totally 'clueless' about Hip Hops or graffiti or the meaning of Bunkin. But I feel that this is rather marginal and can even represent an obstacle in the understanding of an individual patient if it fosters preconceptions and generalizations about the shared meaning of belonging to one of the typically West Indian group cultures.

In fact, one of the problems that needed attention in my work with Winston was his very idiosyncratic way of being a lonely Hip Hop, incapable of forming a meaningful contact with any 'brother', with any of his peers.

I do not feel that my being a white psychotherapist was as much of an issue for him as it is in some cases. It would probably have been much more relevant if he had remained identified with the often anti-white Rasta culture, rather than growing in opposition to it.

Probably, making an issue of colour felt to him too close to the hated values of his father and his brothers, a complex issue that we could only touch upon but certainly not work through in the space of four sessions. The reference to a white girl-friend ('just a fling'), which he made in the fourth session, would confirm this hypothesis.

He was also very little interested, I felt, in the type of Hip-Hop 'rapping' that is meant to convey a social message. The song he chose to bring to me was all about Winston, not about social injustice. One of the greatest injustices he seemed to talk about was the birth of his brothers. His need to be King, his daring graffiti—'writing'—seemed to be much more related to his personal history than to a defiance of society.

The detailed material reported above illustrates that, even within the space of a brief intervention, cultural issues became much less central as our work proceeded.

Milton:
Long-term work

Milton was a 14-year-old boy from the same culture as Winston, and his case was presented by Mrs E, an American psychotherapist from the South of the United States, with an accent clearly identifiable as belonging there.

Milton was referred to a child guidance clinic because of violence and painting graffiti in the school toilets. He had also developed very severe alopecia and had many bald patches when he started attending his sessions. He had had his hair very beautifully cut to cover the patches.

His mother had recently remarried, a very large, tall Rastafarian, who had converted her to his faith, but he was having considerable problems in the relationship with his two stepsons, who were both equally unwilling to convert to Rastafarianism. He opposed Milton's attendance at the clinic, where staff were all white. His mother was keen for him to attend and supported the treatment, in spite of her conversion.

Milton, who lived only a few minutes away from the clinic, had no difficulty in walking to sessions, although at first he was often late. Psychotherapy, on a once-weekly basis, began with a long series of sessions when he was silent most of the time. It became apparent that coming to treatment in order to please mother and defy stepfather was initially a significant and very undesirable component of his motivation. One of his first verbal communications was 'You know how Izo (step-father's name) calls this place and all people like you? He calls them Babylon.'

Although Milton, in his occasional communications, was very contemptuous and mocking of his stepfather, caricaturing his Rasta speech ('I and I sey so, I and I sey me caan believe it'), it soon became apparent that he himself had very mixed feelings about seeing a white therapist from the notoriously racist southern states of America. He seemed convinced this would be a clear indication of her being racist.

During the predominantly silent initial months of treatment his communications took place through striking graffiti drawings, often including a written message, undecipherable to his therapist.

Only very occasionally did he write in 'blockbusters' (explicit graffiti letters), and only later in treatment did he start deciphering his messages. The first was 'I am number one'. His specialities were 'wild star', 'bubble', and 'computer'—all very cryptic graffiti styles, especially the latter.

His dozens of graffiti drawings, although cryptic, seemed to convey clear messages: the wish to make it very difficult for his therapist to understand him and a statement of allegiance to the Hip-Hop group culture of graffiti—one very different from that of his stepfather.

Milton's alopecia, which had developed after his mother's marriage to a Rastafarian, suggested the presence of a psychosomatic symptom related to his step-father's belief in the Rastafarian creed, which holds that it is sinful to cut one's hair, and which attaches religious and political importance to the wearing of the long dreadlocks. Was the symptom an expression of attacks in phantasy on the potency of an external and internalized (Klein, 1946) father whose potency was being 'lost'? The issue was taken up principally in the transference, in terms of an attack on the therapist's clinical potency, and only tentatively related to step-father.

It may have been coincidence, but, to his great relief Milton's hair started growing again a few months after treatment started. The following is an excerpt from a session at about this time.

He sat down and started immediately on a graffiti piece. When he was about half-way through, I asked him what it said, and he answered, 'It says nothing yet'. Then he said, 'Well, it is a smile'. He had written what I now recognized to be an 's' and an 'm' and an 'i', followed by what looked like a hat. He said, yes, it was a hat, a conga hat. Was it part of the word? 'You ought to know, and if you don't know what it is then you'll just have to wait.'

The extent of the communication was much greater in this session as compared with previous ones. He signed this graffiti with a new tag (code name) and told Mrs E that up to then he had always signed his graffiti in the session with a fake one (PIKS for Portobello Intelligent Kids). Only other Hip Hops knew about his real tag. Now she also knew.

In a subsequent session, Milton even told her where she could find his graffiti and admire them if she ever travelled on the Central Line, now that she knew his real tag. The locations were nothing as daring as Winston's, and he always wrote in a crew, on the wall along the platform, not on the other side of the rails. He was not a loner, nor a potential king. He continued to paint graffiti in sessions, but they became more explicit. At times they departed largely from the graffiti style and included paintings very significantly related to his state of mind at that point in the therapy.

In a session close to a holiday break, for instance, when he was very resentful of his therapist going away with her 'white brats', he painted a figure representing himself with a head full of hair and very light skin, except for some brown marks on the side, holding a gun pointing at a clock. His therapist had been talking of his resentment about not being in control of her time. Following that session, she saw him half hiding behind a pillar on the platform opposite to hers in the Underground station close to the clinic, obviously monitoring her movements. Milton's transference gathered in intensity, and his possessiveness was clearly verbalized with very searching questions: 'Had she seen the Carnival from the balcony of her room?'—In other words, did she live at the clinic, as the Notting Hill carnival takes place at the week-end.

Once the alopecia had totally receded, he developed briefly a form of eczema, which produced white patches on his forehead. He had often been looking at the reflection of himself and his therapist in the window next to the table where he painted his graffiti and often had moved his eyes from his very brown arm to her very white arm also resting on the table. The interpretation that he might again be talking with his body, this time by whitening his skin with his eczema, was not perhaps so far-fetched, because the eczema gradually receded.

Milton's therapy lasted for over two years, and he was late at times, but he never missed a session, not even at the time he was busy hiding himself behind his cryptic graffiti and his suspicious silence.

There was initially a marked split in the transference, insofar as he challenged and steadily defied the therapist in her personal role—that is, in her attempts to penetrate behind the façade of the material, interpret, make sense and at the same time set limits, while the maternal transference soon developed into a possessive and passionate attachment, albeit coloured with ambivalence. At the time, when he presented Mrs E with his first 'SMILE', she felt very convinced that he was able to smile to Mummy, but not to Daddy.

Milton's suspicious attitude clung initially to the racial issue, which was certainly much more prominent in his case than in the case of Winston. He seemed to be saying that he would not put his trust in this Babylon woman who spoke with an accent that spelt racialism to him.

We discussed at length in the workshop how central to the initial difficulties this issue had been. Would Milton have found it easier to put his trust in his therapist from the start had he been treated by somebody from the same ethnic background? I think that this is doubtful. His mixed feelings for the mother by whom he felt betrayed because she had been swept off her feet by a new Daddy and had even converted to his faith were very central to his conflicts and would, I think, have found other avenues for expressing themselves in the transference relationship. This could not have been sunny from the start, if it were to mirror his painful mixed feelings for his maternal object (both internal and external). Gradually, over the two years, his therapy did help him to work through the smokescreen that he used as a protection against the pain of his jealousy.

Salvatore:
like with like

We now turn to two cases where the therapist and the patient have the same ethnic origins.

Salvatore is an Italian boy of Sicilian parentage, whom I saw twice a week for two and one-half years. He was 16 when he started treatment. In discussing this case, I shall focus only on those issues that are most relevant to the subject of this chapter.

Salvatore was referred to the clinic because of uncontrollable outbursts of violence, both at home and at school. His parents had emigrated to England from a small village in Sicily when his elder brother was 2 and his mother was pregnant with him. Two more boys and two girls were born in this country. The grandparents had joined the family when Salvatore was 5, and they all lived in rather cramped premises.

The language spoken at home was Sicilian dialect, which contains a number of words of Spanish and Arab origin and is quite different from Italian. The grandparents never learnt any English, and his mother, who had only worked in the kitchen of an Italian restaurant, had never learnt much of the language. His father was a bricklayer and was fluent in English, although he spoke with an extremely heavy accent. The issue of language loomed large from the beginning of treatment. Salvatore, who had recognized my first name as very obviously Italian, asked me, in English, whether I would want to speak Italian with him. I said I would stick to English, but if he ever wanted to say something in Italian he could, and I would probably understand.

Salvatore told me, very early in treatment, that he profoundly disliked attending the Italian Consulate Classes that his parents were forcing him to attend. He was meant to take an Italian O-level. Later on he told me that what he was supposed to learn in those classes was a third language, which had little to do with the dialect spoken at home. He disliked the Sicilian dialect and made it very clear that he felt himself to be British. He was born in England, he said, and could not see why his parents were so keen on Italy, a country that had forced them to emigrate because there was no work there for his father and they were nearly starving. As he was clearly growing up in very

marked opposition to his country of origin and perceived anything Italian as an imposition, he was not at all happy about my
possibly being Italian myself. He went through a very prolonged
period where he made fun of my accent and repeatedly said he
wished that if he had to come to the clinic at all, he could have
seen someone British like himself. After two or three months of
treatment where the transference was very negative, he devised
a compromise and decided that perhaps I was also born in England like him of Italian parents, hence my first name, but perhaps I was also British, and I must have married someone
British because of my surname. After a holiday in Italy where
he had visited uncles and aunts in the village of his parents'
origin, he spoke with extreme contempt about that savage place,
where there was only one television in the bar on the village
square, girls were being kept at home until the day of their
engagement, and they were considered prostitutes if they were
seen out with boys they were not engaged to, where all the families were too large because of the crazy idea of not using con-
traception. He was very contemptuous of the Catholic religion
and had refused to go to Mass on Sunday from the age of 13.

Salvatore asked whether I also had a large family, thought I
probably did, at least seven or eight children, then said perhaps
not, because an English husband 'wouldn't settle for that', perhaps I had married somebody British and civilized.

It became clear that I would have been perceived as all the
more civilized and acceptable, the fewer children I had, the
fewer patients I had other than Salvatore.

It was clear that he found it very difficult to forgive his
mother for having given birth to four children in very close
sequence after he was born. As this issue became more and more
gathered in his transference relationship to me, we were gradually able to look at his hatred of everything Italian as deeply
related to the question of large families and mothers with too
many children to look after. As our work proceeded, he became
less reluctant to attend Italian classes and actually passed his
Italian O-level. His relationship with his parents and his siblings also improved, and he became much less violent.

During the second year of treatment he occasionally used
some Sicilian dialect, obviously eager to discover whether I

would understand—which, fortunately, I did. I thought it was important for me to answer always in English, especially as my Italian would have been that 'third language' which belonged to the social class that had inflicted the need to emigrate on his parents.

He wondered how I had come to live in England; were my parents immigrants like his because they had nothing to eat in Italy? The fact that I understood Sicilian made him think I also originated from somewhere in southern Italy and had just done well for myself, and that is why I had such a cushy job.

It was probably, at least partly, in a vein of competition with me—'the successful second-generation immigrant'—in his mind that Salvatore decided to take some A-levels. This had seemed a very unlikely prospect when he had started treatment and seemed determined to leave school as soon as he could. He chose Italian as one of his A-levels, and he again attended an Italian Consulate class for children of immigrants, many of whom shared his mixed feelings about their family's country of origin.

The very perceptive classroom teacher suggested that as part of preparation for A-level the students could write a play about the experience of being a second-generation Italian immigrant.

Salvatore sometimes brought excerpts from this play to his sessions, and I felt he was trying to tell me something about the nature of his identifications. One dialogue he had written was between an Italian mother, speaking in Sicilian dialect, to her son, scolding him for going out with an English girl, saying they were 'all prostitutes', and that he should choose himself 'a nice girl from where you come from'. The boy answers that where he came from is Hounslow, and he has chosen for himself a nice girl from Hounslow.

As we discussed a possible meaning of this play and its connection with the transference relationship, he said that after all, I had an English surname, so I had seen better and married an Englishman; what was wrong with his having an English girl-friend? It is interesting that even though his girl-friend had an English surname, her maternal grandparents had emigrated from Sicily. This relationship did not last very long, and the next girl-friend was a second-generation Italian immigrant who spoke fluent Italian as well as her family's dialect. They had met at the no-longer-hated Italian classes.

The case of Salvatore highlights the crucial issue of the nature of identifications which a child from an ethnic minority takes up and which, for Salvatore, appeared initially to be based more on opposition to his culture of origin than on a positive identification with the country of adoption.

In this case I had the feeling that a marked split had taken place in the family. The parents and grandparents had evidently preserved a marked idealization of their native country, while in Salvatore one of the children, at least, carried the burden of resentment against that mother country which had starved and forced them to emigrate. For him there were also very personal features. His expressed contempt for the large Italian families no doubt reflected the difficulty for this extremely possessive boy of sharing his own mother.

I am sure that the issue of rivalry with the brothers would have emerged in the transference, whatever the nationality of Salvatore's therapist. It was perhaps just gathered more easily in his transference to me because of his perception of me as being possibly yet another Italian mother of many.

Melina

The case of Melina provides another example where 'like worked with like' in terms of ethnic origin, and where the issue of iden-tification and of the type of identification is very central. An 18-year-old Greek Cypriot girl, she was referred by her general practitioner because she suffered from a large number of symp-toms likely to be of psychosomatic origin: hyperventilation, dizziness, fainting spells. She had a sister one year younger and two younger brothers, all born in England.

The referral letter included the information that both parents were on medication: father for anxiety states, mother for a severe, long-standing depression. The latter had never worked, nor ever learned to speak English. Melina, a pale, pretty girl, came across in the initial presentations at the workshop as a leaf in the wind, with no firm grip on anything or anybody. She spoke with great ease with her therapist, herself a Greek Cypriot. In fact, Melina appeared to hold herself together by talking but put across a feeling of lacking deep conviction in anything she said. This included her references, very frequent from the beginning of treatment, to the Greek Cypriot culture.

It occurred to us that this might be, partly, a transference manifestation, as Melina recognized the name and surname of her therapist as Greek Cypriot.

Perhaps the references to the culture were a way of identifying with her in an adhesive way, the only type of identification she seemed to be capable of (Meltzer et al., 1975). She seemed to perceive her therapist as a mirror image of herself. For instance, she was sure she would meet her at a concert of a very sentimental and glossy Greek singer who was visiting London at the time.

Melina did not seem, initially, to be capable of any strong emotions—neither positive nor negative ones. This is not surprising in view of the lack of containment that she had probably experienced in her home environment (Bion, 1962). At the beginning of treatment, the very large number of psychosomatic symptoms suggested that what she could not experience as a state of mind was transformed into a state of the body.

One of the first occasions when she spoke with some intensity of feeling was when she told her therapist that she had received a birthday card from a Greek Cypriot boy she had known from her childhood. She had heard that his parents had arranged a *proxenia* (arranged marriage) for him without his consent. She had passed by the shop where he works, but had not had the courage to enter. When she received the birthday card, she had phoned him to thank him. He had told her about the *proxenia*, sounding very angry about it, and had said that he was too young to get married and was not going to let his parents force him. She seemed very happy about it.

She said she, herself, 'wouldn't want to get married, neither to him, nor to anyone else'. She was even frightened of a boy kissing her. But should she ever get married, she would want it to be through a *proxenia*. There seemed to be certain aspects of safety and protection in the culture of origin that appealed to

Melina because of her fear of sexuality: probably, at an earlier level, her fear of all close and intimate relationships (Bion, 1970). Her sister seemed to have completely opted out of the Greek Cypriot culture. She wore miniskirts, was engaged to an English boy of her choice, and seldom joined in family gatherings.

An excerpt from a session where Melina described the reception at her cousin's wedding might convey the very striking discrepancy in the identifications of these two sisters.

Melina took an envelope out of her handbag as soon as she sat down and said, 'Do you want to see the photos of the wedding?' Without waiting for me to reply, she took the photos out of the envelope and started handing them to me one by one, explaining who the people were at the ceremony, in Church, and at the hotel reception, pictures of the bride and groom dancing, pictures of a number of relatives. I noticed that her mother and father did not figure in any of the pictures.

There were many pictures of the 'bloumisma' (the bride and groom standing in the middle of the ballroom, relatives pinning five-, ten-, or fifty-pound notes on their clothes). She told me that they collected about £10,000. The wedding must have cost that much, but the parents are paying for it, so the couple is going to keep the money.

Her sister and her fiancé were at the wedding. 'Yes, they came', giving me a knowing look, and Tony (the fiancé) said, looking at all the money that was pinned on the couple, 'I like that—now I want a Greek wedding'. She was annoyed and told him that at the rate they were going now, not having been to see any of the family to introduce him to them, who did they think was going to come to their wedding? I tried to return to a subject we had repeatedly spoken about before— i.e., her resentment of her sister, who is now in a couple and makes her feel left out. I was even hoping I might get a chance for a transference interpretation. Melina interrupted me to say she does not care about that any more, she has got used to it; sometimes she feels her sister might just as well move out and not be there, she is hardly at home anyway. And would I believe it? As soon as the 'bloumisma' was over, they got up and went, and he (emphasizing the *he*) said, 'Thank God that's over. I hated the music, people speaking Greek, but the food was good.' They did not even wait to speak to people. She was sure no one would bother to go to their wedding. All right, his family would, but they are English, and 'You know what they are like, they will come, eat and drink and nothing else, they will not pin money'. Where is the money for the wedding going to come from, anyhow? Her father hasn't got £10,000.00 to spend on her sister.

I sat there listening, and I found my chance to interrupt her when she paused for breath. I said, 'Melina'. She did not hear. I said 'Melina' again, and she looked at me. . . .

This excerpt provides an example of Melina's torrential verbal communications and of her wish for her therapist just to listen and agree with her, as any Greek Cypriot girl with her heart in the right place would. She assumed that her therapist would disapprove of her sister and her fiancé, not think much of English weddings and English people, and would like all that she herself liked and dislike all she disliked.

It is interesting that, although very idealizing of Greek culture, Melina was very contemptuous of her Greek Cypriot parents. Her identification with the culture somehow bypassed the parents, who were not as involved in it as Salvatore's parents were in Italian culture. It must be remembered that Melina's parents suffered from depression and anxiety states, and this might be one of the reasons why they were unable to participate in family gatherings.

It was possible to get closer to something meaningful in the depths for Melina, adolescent in age but emotionally a great deal younger, when she started talking about her love for Greek food and, in particular, 'galaktoboureka', a special sweet that she was very fond of (*gala* in Greek means milk). She was sure that her therapist was very good at making galaktoboureka and that she liked it too. Her mother had never made it. She is no good at cooking anything. There was a great deal of feeling in this reference to the special sweet she loved from her early childhood, and she was much more reachable in the session when she spoke about it.

The marked idealization of the therapist as a source of good nourishment, a delicious *galaktoboureka* breast, probably facilitated by the therapist's ethnic origin, was, like all idealizations, based on a precarious split and on the expectation that the therapist would collude with the denigration, the necessary counterpart. Denigration of the mother who cannot provide good food, denigration of the British culture ('You know what they are like').

The dramatic reaction to a summer break, when Melina was able to experience the full impact of her therapist's absence, felt lost, dis-anchored, and full of rage at the abandonment, greatly contributed to lessen her idealization of the therapist and paved the way for a process of integration that has, since then, helped this paper-thin girl to enter into the realm of three-dimensionality and to tolerate the psychic pain engendered by mixed feelings.

Conclusion

Clearly, the few examples presented cannot provide a general answer to the question of the impingement of cultural factors on work with patients from ethnic minorities. It represented a relevant issue in some cases more than in others. In all cases, to disregard this and not to attempt to make emotional sense of it as obviously one of the factors permeating the material and the quality of the transference relationship would have been a hindrance to the work.

Surveying greater numbers of workshop cases, however, does not necessarily clarify the issues, as the picture becomes yet more complex and the number of variables greater. We found, for example, in cases where 'like worked with like', that the advantages needed to be considered together with disadvantages, chiefly of an 'us-and-them' element emerging in the transference. We were also confronted with the difficulties of 'non-like' therapists needing time to familiarize themselves with 'foreign' sets of values that informed a patient's way of life and neither could nor should be dismissed therefore, nor reduced to 'pathological manifestations'. To quote Freud (1909b), 'When we cannot understand something, we fall back on abuse'.

It seems very important to me to guard against the risk of doing so. This is something that applies to differences in ethnic origins but is not confined to them. There are, after all, uncountable areas of foreignness that confront us when we try to understand, in depth, another human being.

'Killing the time'

PART FOUR

SPECIAL AREAS OF WORK

As we continue to extend the applications of psychotherapy, we are increasingly drawn to work with those who have experienced external traumas in addition to the universal psychic trauma. The universal traumas arise from the losses and changes of normal development, especially those which are experienced as threats to narcissism and omnipotence, closely linking with the traumas and conflicts stemming from inner wishes and fears, the perverse, sadistic and envious desires. Freud (1940) wrote . . . 'In these circumstances instinctual demands from within, no less than excitations from the external world, operate as "traumas", particularly if they are met half-way by certain innate dispositions. . . . No human individual is spared such traumatic experiences; none escapes the repressions to which they give rise.'

As child psychotherapists we have striven to acknowledge and integrate such traumas in ourselves and have used the transference experiences of personal analysis to struggle with the residual immature and psychotic parts which continued to regard such matters as too full of fright and conflict to be countenanced and integrated. The strength which we have gained by re-living these universal forms of trauma enables us to support and require our neurotic, or potentially neurotic . . . patients to face and experience similar events. With some justification we think that if we can do it we may be able to help others to do likewise.

Yet we may feel guilty and inadequate when our patients have been exposed to trauma way beyond our own experience; external traumas such as extremes of deprivation, the traumas of physical abuse or sexual abuse, murder or incest in the family, or the trauma of physical disabilities which often entail the risk of death and the repeated frights and assaults of surgical interventions from infancy onwards and which entail perhaps some long term or permanent losses in terms of human fulfilment.

As we continue to extend the applications of psychotherapy we cannot know in advance what we may discover or what may be possible or impossible to achieve, so it is worth trying new fields, so long as we can bear with our uncertainties and watch and learn from every step of the way.

[Shirley Hoxter, 1986]

Physical and mental
disability and disorder

CHAPTER TWELVE

The triple burden

Francis Dale

This account of psychoanalytic psychotherapy with two children suffering from congenital physical handicaps reveals a number of emotional and psychosocial problems that may confront such children. It describes how they were able to be helped to overcome these 'emotional disabilities' and to develop healthier self-images that could meet the demands and challenges of the outside world.

[R.S.]

Children born with physical handicaps suffer a terrible burden. They are 'different'—often noticeably so—from their peers, with consequent impairment to the establishment of a healthy self-image. Frequently less mobile and

This is a slightly revised and abridged version of an earlier paper, 'The Body as Bondage: Work with Two Children with Physical Handicap', *Journal of Child Psychotherapy*, Vol. 9, No. 1 (1983), pp. 33–45. Reprinted by permission.

unable to join in normal physical pursuits, they often suffer from chronic pain, both from the disability itself, as well as from corrective surgery.

The two children discussed in this chapter both suffered in all these ways. In addition, the mother of the younger boy— David—while suffering on her son's behalf, had also to cope with being a single parent and having come from a very damaging family background of her own.

The story of these two boys is a painful and distressing one, but also hopeful because both children began therapy sufficiently early in their development to help repair some of the psychic damage incurred and to limit some of the more serious long-term consequences associated with their handicaps.

In both boys the actual physical damage to the body had been more or less corrected before or during therapy. However, the damage that had been wrought 'internally' on the psychic structure and on the way these children perceived and felt about themselves remained in need of attention. The main task of therapy has been to form an alliance with the less damaged parts of the personality in order to work through the experience of being damaged so that the 'internal self' could be freed from the bondage of the handicap and the psychic and emotional consequences arising from it.

Case material

David

David was born with club feet that had to be strapped up in restrictive adhesive plasters when he was just 2 days old. The regular changing of these plasters—as well as other surgical interventions—caused enormous distress and suffering to both David and his mother. At one stage he was taken into care for a while when his mother, no longer able to cope with his screaming tantrums and awesomely destructive behaviour, broke down. At this time David was referred for therapy.

He was 4 years, 3 months old when he began treatment, and on our first meeting I was struck by his vitality and charm and his close resemblance to the character 'Just William'. He has a small but sturdy body, and it was only when he walked (with a peculiar rolling gait) that I noticed his physical disability. From his very first session, David showed, in spite of an apparently tough outer shell, how much the inner child had been damaged by these 'attacks' on his person at a time when he did not have the capacity to understand what was being done to him, and how he needed to have someone with whom he could share his concern about a part of himself that was felt to be very vulnerable and fragile. In the early sessions, this vulnerability showed in his play with some toy animals. Whenever he could not get an animal to stand, he would become very agitated and say that it 'spoilt his game' or that it had 'broken its leg'. On one occasion he held up a duck, said it could not walk because it had broken legs, and placed it in the back of a toy ambulance. It seemed that he was telling me about a baby part of himself that was felt to be broken and damaged like the duck, and perhaps of a time when he could not walk and had to be carried.

As therapy progressed, David's play and fantasy came to revolve more and more openly around his physical disability. Soon after missing two sessions because his mother had had to go into hospital with delayed concussion after a fall, he was very subdued and wanted continual reassurance that the 'feeding Mummy' had not been irreparably damaged; he wanted me to give him 'food and drinks', be a 'milkman Daddy' and make a 'tent' for him to climb into. Following this episode, he wanted me to help him make a 'three-wheely' from plasticine. Into it he placed four figures: a 'man to drive it', a lady figure, and two little figures, which he called 'boy and sister'. This had followed David asking me to 'make crying noises for Mummy and baby' and his putting a tiny plastic baby inside my mouth, saying, 'keep him there'. The 'three-wheely' car seemed to stand for some kind of safe 'container/ambulance' (perhaps also standing for him in that it had one wheel missing and was not complete), in which the injured Mummy and baby could be cared for by Daddy driver. This was confirmed to some extent when David pulled off the feet of the boy and sister figures, saying, 'They don't have legs', and also that a 'three-wheely' is for 'when people can't walk'. Putting the 'baby' into my mouth seemed more ambivalent—as if he was not certain whether I stood for a protective Daddy who kept baby safe inside, or for a monster Daddy who bites the baby for his greedy attacks on Mummy, which make her ill.

During the week David could allow himself to be in touch with his baby feelings and for me to be the feeding mother or protective father; but by the weekend the thought of being an 'outside baby' was often more than he could bear. During one Friday session he retorted angrily when I referred to the 'shut-out baby', saying, 'I'm a big boy—why you call me a baby?' and then was full of accusations and recriminations about my abandoning him at weekends. He scribbled on the couch with a red felt pen, saying, 'baby's bleeding', followed by 'Mummy said "go and pick baby up" ', showing how he experienced the weekend as a psychic wound—as an equivalent experience to having broken, bleeding legs again—and how he felt I just dropped him and did not hold him. This feeling of abandonment was clearly expressed at the end of another Friday session, when I had related his wanting to throw water over me to his showing me how the good feeding experience turns bad when he gets shut out at the weekends. David looked very sad and said in a pathetic voice, 'Mummy gone shopping, no-one to look after me'.

Just before the summer holiday, when it became apparent that David would again have to have corrective surgery on his feet, which were getting worse, the feelings and fantasies regarding his legs became expressed in a much more intense and immediate way. He began cutting at my knees with a plastic knife, stamping on my feet, and throwing felt-tips at my legs, saying they were 'bullets in my knees' needing to put the pain into me. He also showed how unsafe and unheld he felt by trying to break his drawer (which he used as a cot) by throwing it at me; and how he felt that the good 'milk' from the taps had turned into an angry bottom mess by turning the tap on full-blast trying to flood the room.

It is likely that one of the fears uppermost in David's mind was lest his attacks might actually make me ill or cause me to send him away, as had happened when he was taken into care. Thus, when he asked me on different occasions if he could 'step on my toe' or 'what would happen if he threw a bin of water over me', or, when he had thrown it, if I had 'been killed', he was showing how thin the boundary between fantasy and reality was for him. The fact that I did survive his attacks and that therapy continued must have gone a long way towards enabling him to overcome his intense anxiety and feelings of persecution. He began to share his concern about his legs more openly, asking me, 'Do you want to see my legs?' and then standing on the twisted outside edge of his foot, saying, 'It hurts when like this' and talking about the 'boy who is cut and bleeding and needs stitches'. I became a protective figure again, whose job it was to look after mother and baby.

Even when first mention was made of the summer break, David only referred briefly to me as a more punitive figure, 'Policemen don't like people—they take them away', before continuing with the theme of my helping to take care of the 'lady and boy in ambulance who are hurt'.

With the summer break only two weeks off, David began to regress again. As if demonstrating physically how strong the link was between breaks in therapy and his earlier experience of being a 'shut-out baby' in hospital with broken legs, his feet became so twisted under him that I found it painful to watch him walk. He started speaking in a baby voice, wanting me to read to him or to give him 'ice-cream', as well as showing his jealousy and rivalry with my 'other babies' by repeatedly wanting to act out the story of 'Goldilocks and the Three Bears'. It seemed as if David was identifying with Goldilocks as the baby who would be shut out of the family when I would be on holiday with my imagined family, and who wanted to steal inside the Mummy and take over all the good things from the other babies, leaving them with all the mess and spoiled food.

That David experienced the break as my pushing him out of the safety of being an 'inside baby' was touchingly illustrated in the penultimate session, when he anxiously asked if I could 'put baby kangaroo back in pouch', and in the final session, as I carried him back to the waiting room, 'Am I little bear?' He also demonstrated how angry, hurt, and confused he felt regarding the frequent breaks in therapy when, following a week's absence because of his mother's illness, he suddenly said, 'Why you always on holiday? Where were you?—I didn't see you' and then kicked me. This demonstrated just how inadequate explanations can be where such important issues are at stake. On the level of external reality David 'knew' that he hadn't come because his mother had been ill. However, on the level of psychic reality this was an irrelevance. It was my job to see him, no matter what—reason did not come into it. David's final words in this encounter told me where my priorities should lie: 'You should go on holiday when I go.'

After David's operation, he came to me very readily but could not walk properly because of the plaster casts on his feet and had to be carried. He had brought some toys with him (two little girl figures and a baby figure) and began the session by making an attack on them. He wanted me to 'blindfold' them so that they could not see and then wanted me to make a 'fire' and put them on it. When I commented that he seemed to want to burn the babies he thought I had been seeing when he was in hospital, he replied 'yes, burn the babies'. However, his burning attacks on my other 'analytical' babies soon became reintrojected to show how devastated he felt inside. He had piled more and more dolls and then his car onto the fire, until it was toppling, and then he said, 'This is funny isn't it? All dead. Put baby in ambulance. Baby dead. I'm dead.'

Soon after this incident, David's mother took an overdose and was admitted into hospital. Somehow David did not collapse. In spite of feeling at some level that his angry attacks on me—as the bad clinic Mummy who did not feed him and shut him out into the cold—had been responsible, he was able to explore with me his guilt and even attempt to restore the damaged object. I had to be 'a policeman who arrested him' and then he became a monster from whom I had to hide (presumably to protect me from his monster attacks). David did express anxiety regarding his mother, but in a constructive way; he gave me 'medicine', and I had to pretend to drink it and say 'ugh', following which he asked if it was 'Mummy'. When I commented that he was afraid that I might be the Mummy who had been ill from the bad medicine, he looked sad and said 'Mummy not well—hit her head. You be doctor and make her better.' Here David seemed to need me to differentiate for him between his real mother who was ill and me as the internal mother who had survived—as well as his hope that I could be a good Daddy doctor and make his mother better again with 'good' medicine.

This session touched me more deeply than any other because, for perhaps the first time, David trusted me enough to be able to surrender himself completely to his baby feelings: his pain, his confusion, his vulnerability, and his dependence. He again showed how frustrated he felt about the long intervals between sessions by telling me I was 'dead and had to do what he said' and by tying me up. He squeezed water from his bottle into my shoes and hit me with keys, saying they were knives, demonstrating how he needed to put his pain into me, and how he experienced the keys that shut him out of the room as the knives that cut him. He wanted to be carried to the sink and for me to fill his 'bottle' with 'lots of milk from the tap'. I took this up as David wanting me to be like a Mummy who always had lots of milk for him. From this point, he began to regress and become like a baby. I had to carry him and 'feed' him while he made grunting baby noises. When the bottle became empty, I had to fill it for him, and when the 'teat' fell off, I had to retrieve it. At the end of the session, with the bottle still clenched in his mouth, he indicated that I was to carry him to the waiting room, and only there was I allowed to retrieve it.

Given all the traumas at home and the frequent unplanned disruptions in therapy, I think it is remarkable that David could manage so successfully to contain all the anxiety and uncertainty and for enough trust and hope to have survived to enable him to preserve me and the relationship intact. Undoubtedly many factors played a part, but the link between the removal of the plaster casts and his regression to being a baby seems to me to be a most crucial one. The removal of the plaster casts was significant for two reasons: they acted as support and protection for David's feet, but they also hid the result of the operation. With the taking off of the plasters, both David's anxiety regarding his feet—and to some extent his need to defend himself against it—and the protection the plasters provided against further hurt was removed. Once the casts were off, David had 'visible' evidence that his legs were better, and the feeling that the operation was really a punishment was diminished. It was as if he now had proof that the plasters had acted

as a cradle for his feet—as a protective skin or shell that facilitated the healing process, rather than being left with the uncertainty that they might be a disguise to hide what terrible things
had been done to him. In the context of this relief he could turn
again, trustfully, to the protection and holding provided by the
therapeutic situation.

Malcolm

The second case concerns a boy who came into once-weekly
therapy when he was 15½ years old. Malcolm was referred because of 'difficulties in coping with life'. He had told his doctor
that for the past two years he had been 'preoccupied with
thoughts of life and the workings of the mind' and was unable at
times to distinguish between reality and fantasy. When pressed
to expand on his worries, he could only repeat that he could see
'one mind looking at another mind'.

In subsequent meetings between Malcolm, his parents, and
the clinic psychiatrist, it emerged that Malcolm had suffered as
a child from asymetry—a congenital deformity of the body in
which the skeletal tissues on one side of the body grow at a
different rate from those on the other—and he had been in hospital for nearly a year when he was 7 years old to have the
thigh-bone in his left leg lengthened. Both he and his parents
were quick to deny that this had anything to do with his 'problem'.

During this meeting Malcolm expressed various anxieties. He
was, he said, very conscious that his body was different from
other people's, and he avoided situations where this might be
noticed. This meant that he never joined in with his peers in
gymnastics, games, or any competitive sports. He also expressed
a fear about being mad and said that he sometimes felt that he
was 'falling apart'. In addition, he mentioned that from an early
age he had wanted to be a girl, and how he 'envied girls' and had
always wanted to play with them at school.

I found Malcolm to be a slightly built boy with girlish features, looking younger than his 15 years. The left-sided asym-
metry was mainly noticeable in his face, in which the left eye

and left side were slightly smaller than those on the right. His left arm and hand were also noticeably smaller. He was holding himself in a very rigid and tense posture, and he had a guarded and defensive look on his face. The image that immediately came to mind was that of a hermit crab caught out of its shell, feeling naked and defenceless and trying to hold itself together by muscular tension. (I later came to feel that this image was a very appropriate metaphor for understanding the particular vulnerability of children like David and Malcolm.) After the first few meetings it became clear that while on one level he was co-operating in asking for help and coming to see me, on another he was desperately fending me off. The following extract from an early session is fairly typical of the confused and convoluted way his thinking blocked any attempts at understanding.

Malcolm began by saying that he had these troubles. I wondered if he could tell me about them.

He replied that he just couldn't stop thinking about world problems.

Were there any in particular that bothered him?

No. He just felt that he had 'this problem', which he always had to think about and that thinking about it stopped him from concentrating.

I again wondered if he could try and tell me a little more about this problem. He responded by saying that there were times when he could be distracted by something that interested him, but then he would realize that he hadn't been thinking about 'his problem' and wouldn't be able to remember anything, and his mind would go blank and he could panic.

After several sessions like this one, my mind was becoming blank. I was confused, could not think clearly, I was losing track of what was going on in the session and becoming increasingly frustrated. What I failed to realize at the time was how much I may have been experiencing something like Malcolm's confused state of mind. It also had the effect of powerfully attacking my capacity to think.

When I was able to point out how his thinking capacity was being used in a very destructive way in order to prevent understanding and not to promote it, the underlying cause of his present difficulties—his catastrophic experience in hospital as a child—began to emerge. Little by little we were able to build up a picture of what it had been like for Malcolm to be taken away from family, friends, school—a familiar environment—and subjected to various traumatic surgical procedures, to have to lie on his back in traction for a whole year. It became very clear in therapy that he had experienced the ministrations of the doctors and nurses not as helpful, but as an assault or invasion on his person in which he was a passive and defenceless victim at the mercy of cruel and sadistic persecutors. This, coupled with the humiliation he had felt at having to be fed, bathed, and toileted for so long a period, meant that his relationship to me as 'some sort of doctor' (he repeatedly and mistakenly referred to me as a psychiatrist) was full of ambivalent feelings. On the one hand he wanted, and needed, to come to see me, but on the other the very fact that he still needed help made him feel belittled and humiliated all over again. He defended himself against these feelings by being very contemptuous and dismissive of me. He was only coming to me out of 'curiosity' or 'because his parents' wanted him to. As for me, I was just doing a 'nine-to-five job', had a 'cushy number', nice family, no worries, long holidays, and so on.

That he was relating to me as a bad, uncaring therapist whom he wanted to punish was shown in the following way: for some months he had been missing sessions without letting me know in advance that he could not come. This put me to considerable inconvenience, since he was my last patient of the day and I made a special twelve-mile trip to an outlying clinic just to see him. During the particular session in question he began by complaining about the 'formality' of my seeing him according to a 'timetable' (he had been early, and I had made him wait), and how it was 'too medical'. I replied that he seemed to be relating to me as a rigid 'medical' Mummy who only worked according to a timetable and that perhaps he was being reminded of the family of the hospital, where he could only see his mother at certain times. He then remembered being in hospital on Christmas day and watching from a window as his parents loaded up their car with presents that he had no room for and driving away. I commented that when I 'went away' he felt that I was like a parent taking all the 'good things' with me and leaving him feeling empty and abandoned. This feeling was so unbearable he had to put it into me, to leave me feeling rejected and abandoned by not turning up for his session, when I had driven all the way to see him. (Malcolm had commented earlier that the distance to the clinic from London, my home, was the same as his parents had had to travel when they visited him in hospital.)

Following this session and in the run-up to the Christmas holiday Malcolm began to acknowledge more positive feelings in the transference. He commented that it 'felt safe' here and that he felt 'more at home'—even taking off his jacket to 'get the full benefit of the fire'. (It was snowing outside, and I had switched on the electric heater.) With the break one week off, he also remembered how terrified and panic-stricken he had felt once after his mother had gone home after a hospital visit: 'I lay in bed screaming and screaming, until the nurses phoned my mother and told her to come over and stay in the hospital.' For Malcolm, his life had become a continuous nightmare from which there was no awakening. He would often say to me, 'If only I could forget, it would be all right'.

Some indications of how he experienced his predicament at an unconscious level can be seen from an association that followed my commenting on his avoiding any situations in which he might feel exposed or vulnerable. He spoke with great feeling of an incident in his garden, when a fledgling bird had fallen out of its nest while the parent bird flew around and around, frantically calling for it. He had gone to fetch some milk for it, but on returning saw that his dog had found the baby bird and gobbled it up. Clearly this incident can also be seen as an allegorical expression of his own experience, in which he (the fledgling) had been forcibly removed from home (pushed out of the nest) and swallowed up in the hospital system (been eaten by the dog). Whether or not the dog also stood for his own sado-masochism, which took a perverse pleasure in preventing the rescue of the fledgling part of himself, is more uncertain (although he did mention that it was *his* dog and that after swallowing the bird it had come to him wagging its tail).

As therapy progressed, Malcolm began to get in touch, on a more conscious level, with the damaged child he was still carrying inside, so that he became increasingly able to relate to people and situations in the here and now and less in terms of his earlier experiences. This was particularly important in relation to school and his attitude towards people in authority. When Malcolm had returned to school from hospital—having missed a year of schooling—he also had to contend with being in a class a year below his old one, as well as being virtually immobile for the first six months in a plaster cast that came up to his waist. It was particularly painful for him to recall how humiliated he had felt at being pushed to and from school in a pram every day by his mother and to have had to be helped to go to the toilet. As a defence against both real and imagined 'attacks' on his self-image (at school he had been taunted with being a spastic and a cripple), he cultivated a particularly biting form of sarcasm, which he used to good effect, becoming expert at uncovering and exposing the weak spots in others. When he came to see how his sarcasm drove people away and how destructive it was—both for him and for others—he began to show some remorse. More importantly, he began to appreciate how much his parents had suffered on his behalf and how much he had made *them* suffer: 'I didn't want them to forget what had happened to me. . . . They really must have thought I was an ungrateful little bastard.' From delighting in others' misfortunes—because then 'someone else' would be worse off than he—he began to develop the capacity for empathy—as, for example, when he tried to feed the fledgling. More recently, on going to hospital for a check-up on his leg, he had seen a crippled girl who was 'really' paralysed, and he was able to comment on how he had 'once been like that' (the implication being that he no longer physically or psychically experienced himself as such a cripple). He felt 'safer inside' and hence less vulnerable on the 'outside'. I felt that it was a major step for him when he could say that his mother knew him better than anyone else, that she seemed to know what he was thinking—'almost as if she had been in hospital as well'—and adding that there were two people he could not fool: me and his mother. It was both an admission of gratitude and a sign that the trust and confidence that had been shattered by his experience during and after his hospital admission had begun to be resurrected.

Discussion

It is difficult, if not impossible, to enter fully into the pain and suffering of children like David and Malcolm and to experience the true depth of their despair, anguish, and terror. But without at least trying to do this, we cannot begin to understand their predicament, let alone try to help them. It is here that I feel that an understanding of the psychic and symbolic nature of the skin as a boundary or container is essential, both for our understanding and for the treatment of such children.

If it is true that in the early stages of development the skin functions as a boundary or container, not just for the body but for the emerging personality as well, then any traumatic injury to the body may also be experienced as damaging to one's internalized objects and their capacity to protect the integrity of the self from attack or, even worse, from disintegration. We can see an illustration of this in Malcolm's statement that he sometimes felt as though he were 'falling apart': as if he had experienced the operation as an attack, not merely on his body, but on his personality as a whole, the very core of his being. Falling apart means literally 'not being held together'. Malcolm learned to 'hold himself together' by using his thinking to censor or ward off any thoughts that might relate to his 'problem'. His intellectual capacity had come to be his 'shell' or protective membrane, which 'filtered out' from his conscious awareness any dangerous ideas or feelings that might threaten his precarious stability. If he relaxed his mental tension even for a moment, there would be a blank or void, and he would feel overwhelmed by an experience of panic and internal collapse. Here he seemed to be expressing his fear about an internal space that had no containing object to stop him from falling apart, no 'skin' to hold him together. Terror of falling into a void, an 'inner nothingness' from which there is no escape and no hope, is movingly portrayed in the lines from 'Samson Agonistes' in which Milton expresses overwhelming despair and hopelessness about the loss of his sight:

> O dark, dark, dark, amid the blaze of noon,
> Irrecoverably dark, total Eclipse
> Without all hope of day.

In addition to the terror of an internal void, there is the terror of separation, and, indeed, these seem to be intimately bound together. The picture of Malcolm lying alone in hospital screaming and screaming until his mother came, or of the parent bird searching frantically for its offspring that had fallen out of the nest, convey this better than words can.

I believe that the role of the therapist who works with children who have suffered from such catastrophic experiences must be first and foremost to provide a safe setting, like a 'first' psychic skin or a shell. Within this previously intolerable experiences can be re-examined, re-experienced, and, hopefully, after having been modified and transformed by the analytic experience, reintrojected in a more acceptable form. In both David's and Malcolm's case there are many similarities in the way in which the therapeutic relationship was used as a kind of transitional shell or skin where the inner process of healing could take place. The image that immediately comes to mind is that of the hermit crab that has to find a substitute skin or shell in order to protect its vulnerable parts from attack. If it is to grow and develop, it *must* give up its old shell, which has become too small and inhibiting, and find a larger one. It is precisely at this time, when it is 'between shells', that it is at its most defenceless. For David and Malcolm, the 'in-between times', when they felt most exposed and vulnerable, were almost invariably connected with breaks in therapy. Malcolm's lack of a containing 'skin' was very clearly indicated in the last session before one Christmas break, when he talked of needing a new leather jacket because he was suffering from the cold, and on another occasion before a summer break, when he complained that he had hardly been able to get out of bed to come and see me and had just wanted to 'crawl back into his shell'. Here we can see quite clearly how he experienced the coming separation as the psychically equivalent experience of being without a shell. With David, the lack of a containing skin was similarly experienced as a need to 'get back inside', to be the 'baby kangaroo inside Mummy's pouch'. In David's case, the experience was most intimately bound up with the original trauma to his body. In this connection, I remember David running into the therapy room after a break and shutting the door on me. He adamantly refused to let me in, until I had allowed him to 'shut the door on my legs'. This shows, I think, how being shut out of me as the therapist Mummy over the break was for him the same as having broken, bleeding legs all over again.

I would now like to turn to the ways in which Malcolm and David attempted to defend themselves against the pain and confusion. Both experienced the damage to their bodies as an attack or punishment. Malcolm in particular felt himself to be the helpless victim of a terrible injustice. He repeatedly asked the question 'Why me?' and believed that he must have something very bad inside for such a thing to have happened to him. He would often comment that he could not understand how anyone could like him because he was 'so horrible'. David expressed the same sort of feeling of having something bad or dangerous inside and often pretended to be a monster or tiger, which I would have to 'punish' or 'lock up in a cage'. The fear of having something 'bad' or monstrous inside sometimes appeared to be enacted externally. Both coped with their pain and fear by projecting it outside into others, as David 'cutting' my legs just before his operation and putting 'bullets' in my knees, while Malcolm put his rejection into me by not turning up for his sessions.

Another way of coping was by developing a 'second skin'. Like the hermit crab without a shell, they were both desperate to find some sort of protective covering. For David, this was a protective shell of toughness. He rarely if ever cried, even when he was in considerable pain from his legs, and he always had to prove his toughness. With Malcolm, it was through the perverted use of his thinking capacity, which made people avoid any sort of confrontation with him. His 'shell' was a razor-sharp mind, ever alert for possible dangers and attacks. He often commented to me that no one ever got the better of him in an argument. I think it is true to say that as a result of his physical infirmity and enforced immobility, he was driven into adopting a passive verbal type of defence and into an identification with girls. Because of his distorted body image and physical disability, he could not develop his own concept of maleness through accepted channels of physical competition and rivalry, and so he temporarily gave up his identity as a boy.

It seems to me that one of the most important factors in understanding and helping children with this particular problem of being both physically and psychically damaged is to be aware of how crucial it is for them to find someone who can experience the pain with them, who is not destroyed or turned bad by their attacks, who does not retaliate, and who does not reject them. The therapist, then, has to act as a focus for the projections and, later, the introjections that are the necessary preconditions for any real change to take place. When this internal transformation takes place, the children can then become free of the bondage to their bodies, in much the same way as the butterfly emerges from the chrysalis (its transitional shell) to leave the caterpillar behind forever. For Malcolm and David, therapy seemed to help by providing—in the therapeutic relationship—an opportunity to experience and to introject a less rigid and inhibiting skin or shell within which the process of healing and growth could take place, so that they could finally be released from their own images of their handicap.

CHAPTER THIRTEEN

Psychoanalytical psychotherapy with the severely, profoundly, and multiply handicapped

Valerie Sinason

An extension of a psychoanalytical psychotherapeutic approach to the field of mental and multiple handicap has begun to offer significant contributions in this area. The history of psychoanalytic involvement in work with mental disability is described, and the nature of 'secondary handicap' is examined, distinguishing between mild secondary handicap and what the author defines as 'opportunist' handicap. The understanding of the experiences of the children whose histories are revealed and the insight into their inner struggles, fears, and frustrations sheds new light on a dark area and raises new questions.

[R.S.]

Acknowledgements to *Psychoanalytic Psychotherapy*, for permission to print large extracts from my paper, 'Secondary Mental Handicap and Its Relationship to Trauma' (*Psychoanalytic Psychotherapy, Vol 2*: pp. 131–154), of which this is an extended version of one of the two case discussions; to the Tavistock Clinic for supporting the mental handicap work; to Jon Stokes, Sheila Bichard, S. S. Segal, Anne Alvarez, Frances Tustin, Susanna Isaacs-Elmhirst, and Michael Sinason for continued assistance and insight.

225

I ndividual psychoanalytical psychotherapy with the mildly and severely handicapped (though not the profoundly multiply handicapped, to whom we have only recently started to offer help) has been a scarce but valuable treatment ever since psychoanalysis began. In 1901 Freud formulated the theory of secondary gain that could be derived from an illness, and which is the central factor in what is now referred to as secondary handicap (1901b). He later described 'somatic compliance'—the way in which bodily ills with their organic base become fixed with a 'psychical coating', a particular emotional investment (1905e). Thirty years after Freud formulated the gains that could come from illness, L. Chidester and K. Menninger (1936), two psychiatrists/psychoanalysts, were trying to promote advances in this field by stating that 'mental handicap has long been looked upon as an organic condition, therapeutically hopeless, and probably for this reason few psychoanalysts have attempted to apply their methods to the study of retarded children'. However, despite the interest of leading psychoanalysts, and psychiatrists, including Melanie Klein (1931) and Pierce Clark (1933), the conviction that emotional disturbance was caused by handicap was too widespread to alter.

The work of Canadian psychiatrists/psychoanalysts in the 1960s, nearly thirty years later, clearly documents the increase in the Intelligence Quotients and improvements in the quality of life that followed therapy (Scott Clifford, 1963; Sarwer-Foner, 1963), but that, too, did not ripple far. In 1966 I. Phillips pointed out that the unavailability of psychotherapeutic services was still due to a misconception that behavioural or emotional problems were a function of mental retardation. Even with the aid of new psychoanalytical theories on thinking (Bion, 1967), applications to this client group were minute. In 1977 Heaton-Ward noted how few conferences on mental handicap considered mental illness, whilst Gulatieri (1979) commented that 'even in the training of professionals who work with mentally handicapped clients there is a tendency to focus on disorders of cognitive development to the exclusion of emotional and social behaviour'. The work of Frances Tustin (1972, 1981) provided further inspiration and understanding of learning difficulties for those working with autism and mental handicap. She specified how cognitive defects could be acquired and how the autistic state could be a reaction to traumatic awareness of separateness. Theoretically, autism and handicap can spring from similar relationships to trauma. In terms of conceptualization, however, the two groups are largely separate.

At this moment in time, partly because of ideas of normalization, there has been wider interest both in psychoanalysis itself and in its application. Perhaps, too, workers in the field of mental handicap know from long experience and experimentation when behaviour therapy helps and when it does not. Also, the small number of psychoanalysts and psychoanalytical psychotherapists now working in this area have the benefit of past and present psychoanalytical theory that, despite ambivalence, has woven its way into cultural understanding.

The growth of the Tavistock Clinic Mental Handicap Psychotherapy and Psychology Research Workshop since it was first founded by psychologist and psychoanalyst Neville Symington eight years ago has been considerable. In the last five years in which it has been co-convened by Mr Jon Stokes, an Adult Department psychologist and psychotherapist, and myself, and now by educational psychologist Mrs Sheila Bichard and myself, the monthly open multi-disciplinary meetings and the introduction of ten-week termly courses on psychotherapy and mental handicap have proved highly successful.

These developments are part of the historical change we are going through. As a result of our social progress and the fact that we offer education to all, we can now feel free to consider the emotional aspects of handicap. We have the luxury of viewing the multiply handicapped at a point when they are considered 'educable' (Segal, 1967), a term hard won through centuries of work by psychiatric and educational pioneers.

Clinical and social issues

What, then, can we offer colleagues? First, and most basically, the conviction that all human beings have an inner world as well as an outer one—an unconscious as well as a conscious mind—and that therefore those with a handicap need just as much access to psychotherapy as others. We therefore disagree with A. Reid (1982) when he comments: 'The scope for individual therapy is limited. Such patients do not have the intellectual resources to benefit from in-depth psychotherapy.' As Jon Stokes (1987) has aptly expressed it, 'we find it useful to distinguish between *cognitive intelligence* and *emotional intelligence*'. In other words, however crippled someone's external functional intelligence might be, there can still be intact the richness of emotional structure and capacity. To reach this, guilt must be dealt with—the guilt of the patient for his handicap, and the guilt of the worker for being normal.

The Tavistock workshop was first called the 'subnormality' workshop. Now it is called 'mental handicap'. No other professional area has gone through such speedy name changes. Right now there are terms like 'special needs', 'exceptional children', 'print-impaired', 'learning difficulties'. No new word can take away from the painful issue of *difference*. The experience of *not* being handicapped, of being normal, evokes great guilt. We might agree with the concept that we are all handicapped, and it is only a matter of degree (Segal, 1967). However, the experience is not the same. The normal can slowly cope with the narcissistic injuries that life provides, with the failure of the adolescent wish to be Bardot, Newman, Einstein, Beethoven; the normal can reduce their horizons to realistic levels. However, those whose horizons are organically or internally attacked and reduced—what happens to them if they become more aware of differences?

Opening your eyes to admitting that you look, sound, walk, talk, move, or think differently from others takes great reserves of courage, honesty, and toleration of envy. It can be easier to behave like the village idiot and make everyone laugh than to expose the unbearable discrepancy between normal and not normal.

Primary and secondary handicap

In handicap there may be organic or traumatic damage that affects the person concerned. However, as I have mentioned earlier, there is also the particular use that the person makes of this. 'Handicap is the actual physical effect of the disease, injury or genetic pattern on the body of the person concerned . . . disability is the effect of that handicap on the life, heart and soul of the person concerned' (Sisters against Disability, 1985).

This distinction between primary and secondary handicap dispenses with the older view expressed by Doll (1953) that there was a difference between true subnormality and the 'pseudo-mentally-deficient' whose intelligence is blocked by background and emotions. Similarly dispensed with is the idea that the 'true' handicapped patient has a condition only caused by brain damage. Researchers (Segal, 1971; Shaffer, 1977) find no difference in learning difficulty between brain-damaged or non-brain-damaged children. Although nearly all children with an IQ below 50 (Crome, 1960) have organic brain damage and are more susceptible to psychiatric disorder (Rutter, Shaffer, & Shepherd, 1970), researchers (Corbett et al., 1975) are very aware that this cannot be the only factor and that the reason for the extra vulnerability is open to question. In showing facts like these psychiatry has offered a space for psychoanalytical psychotherapy to explore the reasons.

Freeman (1970) points out that emotional disorders in the adolescent with cerebral palsy are frequent but not directly related to brain damage. Goldstein (1948) in discussing the 'catastrophic rages', the temper outbursts often attributed to brain damage, considers that they may be due to a number of factors, such as over-protection from the usual consequences of bad behaviour, the imposition of painful, unwelcome procedures, or excessive and unreasonable environmental pressures.

The difficulties in defining handicap due to organic damage as distinct from secondary handicap are reflected in the multiaxial classification of child psychiatric disorders. Rutter, Shaffer, and Shepherd (1975) make it clear that there is no consensus as to the degree of behavioural disturbance that can be expected as part of mental retardation, and that is why the IQ is given at its current level.

This uncertainty is reflected both in the lack of confidence in the IQ and in the way it is used. Castell et al. (1963) found the average IQ of severely handicapped subnormal patients to be as high as 60. An explanation for the high figure is that Section 33 of the 1959 Mental Health Act made it easier to detain compulsorily in hospital adults thought to be severely rather than mildly handicapped. 'This may sometimes lead to the abilities of individuals thought to be in need of hospital care and control to be underestimated.' At the same time that the IQ is being used in a confusing way, its meaning is most open to question. Dr V. Gibb in research in Lewisham (personal communication, 1986) has found Down's syndrome patients with IQs of 70 and over, as has C. Cunningham (personal communication, 1982). Before this it was thought that there was a lower genetic IQ ceiling. She, among other researchers, as well as psychoanalytical psychotherapists, is also arguing for the distinctions between emotional and performance intelligence to be recognized.

Underlying the questioning of the IQ is also the widespread knowledge of secondary handicap: the attacking of intact skills and intelligence as a way of coping with the original handicap. Wright (1968), for example, has found that one-fifth of mute children often developed mutism as a reaction to an underlying speech or language handicap. As well as being aware that stereotyped behaviour and language come into this category among the mentally handicapped, other workers have pinpointed the parallel processes with the physically handicapped. Dorothy Burlingham (1963) comments that the auto-erotic movements of blind children are referred to as 'blindisms'. Joan Bicknell (1983) has pointed out that the whole network around the handicapped is often equally involved in fighting insight to keep the handicapped individual in his secondary 'sick' role.

The Office of Health Economics (1973) describes mental ability as the product of three factors: 'inherited constitution, modification or injuries caused by pre- or postnatal injury or disease and conditioning and training of the intellect.' Friedrich and Boriskin (1976) have pointed out that 'within the population of maltreated children the handicapped are over-represented'. We are therefore looking in some cases of mental and multiple handicap at severely deprived individuals who have received poor parenting or even abuse.

Three types of secondary handicap

There seem to be three main groups where secondary handicap plays a part in the difficulties of the individual, even though there is an overlap between the groups. The first is mild secondary handicap, in those who have compliantly exacerbated their original handicap to keep the outer world happy with them. Second, there is opportunist handicap, by which I mean that added to the original handicap and linked to it there is severe personality maldevelopment. Envy of normality, hatred of the parents who created the handicap, hatred of the sexuality involved, inability or refusal to mourn the healthy self that is lost—all these factors merge and amalgamate with the handicap. John Donne expresses this most beautifully: 'Diseases themselves hold consultations and conspire how they may multiply and join with one another and exalt one another's force.'

We are all aware of the way in which children's or adults' minor or major ailments can be used to 'carry' emotional states, but fortunately these are usually of short duration. When environment, constitution, and original handicap are themselves severely debilitating, it takes greater courage and toleration of envy than the normal to avoid opportunist handicap. In the words of Daniel Defoe, 'Give me not poverty, lest I steal'. This group is probably the largest, and it is because their presence has been so accurately detected that workers are prepared to struggle with the moves to half-way hostels and sheltered housing. Workers *know* that these clients have more intelligence than they are willing to show. Nearly all referrals in this category include the comment, 'ESN—More intelligence than he/she will show, except when off-guard'.

Handicap as a defence against trauma

Another group is the one where handicap is in the service of the self to protect it from unbearable memory of trauma, of a breakdown in the protective shield (Freud, 1920g).

I have now seen several children and adults in whose case sexual abuse was the cause of the handicap and where those patients regained their intelligence and memory once they were able to disclose it (Sinason, 1986, 1988).

A boy of 10, who had organic brain damage in the form of cerebral palsy, had a secondary handicap that protected him from the memory of both primary organic damage and environmental damage.

Case material: Barry

This boy, whom I shall call Barry, was the second child born to working-class parents whose marriage was already in difficulties owing to the birth of a daughter who was born with a physical handicap. Depression over the serious illness of the daughter meant that Barry was seen as a perfect, quiet baby. Only a routine clinic visit picked up his cerebral palsy.

At the time his father left home, when he was 3 years old, Barry's attacks on himself were so dangerous that he was admitted to hospital. His father had behaved violently to his mother prior to their break-up, and there was some worry that Barry might have been hurt as well as having witnessed violence. Each time he left hospital, his attacks on himself recurred. Behaviour therapy merely changed the part of his body he attacked. At 5 he was admitted to a residential home for severely multiply handicapped children, but at 7 his violence was so great, both to himself through head banging and to staff through biting, that there was fear of what would happen when he was older and stronger.

Clinical material

In the waiting room, a slumped, twisted, ferocious-looking boy was jammed between his mother and a key worker. I could not see his face. When I introduced myself, his legs went into an amazing forceful action, as if they had a life of their own. Realizing I would not be safe on my own with him, I asked his mother and worker to bring him to my room and to stay with us. He grunted and screamed all the way to the room, but once inside he moved into a foetal position and then said clearly and distinctly the word, 'shy'. All three adults felt very touched. His mother said he had never said the word 'shy' before; she did not even know he knew it. Barry started ferociously banging his head. The sound really hurt, but I restrained his mother from moving to hold his hands.

I started talking, saying how he had said he was 'shy' and that was not surprising, as I was a stranger to him. He did not know me. His fist stopped in mid-air. I carried on speaking, saying he was telling all of us that he knew his Mum and key worker and all the people at the children's home. He was used to seeing lots of people. But he did not know me. His hand flopped onto his lap, and I was at peace, knowing that meaning was there and I was at work.

I then explained why he was coming; how people were worrying about him hurting his head and that they felt he was sad. I explained he would come to this room a few times, and that there were toys on the table. The moment I mentioned toys, he ferociously banged his head. When I said he was worried at being in this new room with toys, he stopped banging. Other features of this first session were that he banged his head whenever there was a sound from outside the room. Alternatively, he would curl up and close his eyes, like a baby. When I said there were five minutes left, he moved the vestigial fingers of his deformed hand and hid them under his head. I wondered aloud whether he was showing me his struggling handicapped hand now it was time to go, and maybe there was a struggle with the Barry who had powerful legs and could run and a handicapped Barry. When it was time, he kicked the table at me with great force.

At the second meeting he did not utter a word but fell asleep, only to stir to bang his head whenever the wind blew or there were footsteps. At one time when there was a loud noise he fell into a newborn falling reflex. I wondered here whether the tiredness was because of all the energy that went into maintaining an unborn state, where no other life existed.

It took me until the third session to tell Barry that I did not feel ready to see him on my own until I felt I could protect him and me from his violence. I thought we must be connecting more for him to allow me to have that thought and utter it and for him not to bang his head when I said it. Fifteen minutes before the end of the session he fell asleep.

During the fourth session a major change occurred. For the first time, with his head twisted away from me, Barry held up both his hands to show me not just the difference between his handicapped and non-handicapped hand, but also the secondary handicap he had inflicted by his own banging. He held up that hand in a way that only I could see it. There was a huge swelling on each knuckle, with a red bruise at the tip of each. I was aware of the thought that he had made two breasts, that maybe he was attacking his mother in fury at the handicapped body he had been endowed with, but also adding to his body at the same time. I did not feel I could make such a comment in front of his mother and worker. As that was the first private thought I had had, I felt the time must therefore be right for me to see him on his own. What I said was that he was showing me how angry he was about being handicapped and that when he banged his head he also made his knuckles larger. I then said, feeling terrified and daring, that I would see him on his own the next week, but his mother and worker would bring and collect him. As usual, he fell asleep 15 minutes before the end of the session.

The fifth session was the first on his own. It was also crucial, as it would determine whether therapy was possible. After the usual banging and kicking, he was put on the chair by his mother and worker, who then left quickly, looking relieved and apprehensive at the same time. Barry was in his usual foetal position. It was only in this session that I became aware that he always curled up with the normal side of his face showing and his handicapped side hidden. Gritting my teeth, I wondered this aloud. For a moment I sat in terror. To my amazement, he suddenly sat up bolt upright and faced me. He looked proud and furious. I felt overwhelmed.

The feelings he evoked in me at that moment made me realize with terrible clarity that the twisted postures he took up were a terrible self-made caricature of his original handicap, so he could not be seen as he truly was. I was filled with images from subnormality hospitals and all the twisted movements and guttural speaking that I had previously taken as inevitable consequences of retardation. I found myself wondering about that. I said he was now able to show me how he really was and that he was less handicapped than he made himself look, perhaps as protection. Barry fell asleep at his usual time 15 minutes before the end of the session, and this time I was able to comment to him that he knew the time was coming to an end and he wanted to be asleep. He would spit quietly and wake up when I spoke. I was also struck by the unborn state he seemed to remain in, where living tired him so enormously. The Home staff said he spent long hours sleeping as well as catnapping. Right at the end I asked him if he wanted to continue seeing me. There was no reply. I asked him to raise a finger if he wanted to carry on seeing me. He raised a finger and has continued coming for six years to date, with only two absences for colds, both on the last session before a holiday.

There was a big change in Barry over the next few weeks. In the waiting room he could be seen sitting upright or standing hugging his mother. Several therapists told me their patients were mentioning this boy in the waiting room who used to look terrible but was really nice-looking. The Home commented that he was calm for the rest of the day after coming to see me and for the next day. We were agreed that the next important stage would be for me to take him to and from the therapy room. After two months I did this, feeling extremely frightened the first time. However, he managed then and ever since, apart from a regression following the death of his sister. The triumph Barry and I felt at both of us managing the fear of his violence was visible in the proud way he hugged his mother and worker on his arrival back for the first few months of going alone with me. His mother even said, 'Well done, you brave boy'.

The next major change occurred after one year of once-weekly therapy. I was suddenly aware that when Barry banged his head, he was making enormous spitting noises and sound effects, but in fact he was miming banging his head. When I said he was not hurting his thoughts so much, he was thinking more about what I said, he lifted his hand to show me that the bumps had subsided. I told the Home staff about my observation, and they then realized that it was true in their environment too.

After eighteen months Barry stopped falling asleep, and I realized how sleeping must have been a protection for all the exhaustion he felt at being in the world, trying to control all the noises and actions around him. When I gave a comment he did not like, he would mime a head-bang and then mime sleeping and then open his eyes and say, 'Shut up', one of the few words ('Piss off', 'Shut up', 'Your chair', 'My chair') he ever said to me. He was losing his secondary handicaps, his defences against meaning, and he felt very mixed up and exposed about it. It was at this point that he suddenly burst into a terrible caricature of handicapped singing 'Old McDonald had a farm'. He was singing in the guttural voice I had often felt was intrinsically linked with handicap, just as I had felt previously the twisted postures were. But there was something in the meaning he was conveying that made me say, with great terror, that maybe he felt there was room here for the animal noises and feelings in him; but maybe, too, he wanted to see if I was an idiot who thought that this was his real singing voice. He looked at me in a startled but proud way, whispered 'Old McDonald had a farm' in a normal voice that just conveyed a slight slur of brain damage, and then started to cry terribly and deeply.

This pitiful crying was a strong feature for the next six months, and it is difficult to put into words. It is not crying that is asking for a word or a hug. It is a weeping to do with a terrible sense of aloneness and the reality of that. Neville Symington (personal communication, 1984) has commented that weeping comes when there is a breakthrough with this kind of patient, and it represents a real awareness of all the meaning that has been lost in the years up to that moment as well as the aloneness of handicap. His mother and worker were very distressed to see the weeping state Barry was in. They were worried therapy might be too cruel for him. I felt worried at the pain he was in, and when he desperately wept, saying, 'See Mummy, go now', I had to struggle not to give in. We both managed to keep him in the room in this stage.

After this, the crying stopped, and Barry became more affectionate and responsive. He stopped injuring himself. However, he was still violent to staff and was more dangerous because previously he just had to be put into a chair and he would fall asleep. Now he would stand up again immediately and attack, as he did not mind physical changes so much. There was some attempt to masturbate as a new defence and self-comfort, but this stopped very soon. He understood the meaning of it too well. He was no longer startled by external noises and slept the ordinary amount of a boy of his age. After two years, there was a session in which, in the silence, my stomach gurgled loudly. 'Your tummy?' he asked. I said yes, it was my tummy. He giggled. I said he knew the sound was inside my tummy. He nodded. It started raining. 'Rain outside', he commented. There was a startled pause. A telephone rang next-door. Barry put a hand to his ear. 'Outside the room', he pronounced. From that moment there was an extra degree of hope and aliveness in the session; Barry had differentiated between inside and outside and had achieved a 'psychological birth' (Mahler et al., 1975).

Shortly after this I bought a soft toy, a puppy, for the therapy room, as Barry always gave me a Xmas card with a dog on it and because he had not touched the other toys. On the first occasion that he saw it, having been told several weeks in advance of its arrival, he held it to him and hugged it with his back to me, not uttering a single word or sound during the whole session. He has never managed to touch it since, only to look at it wistfully. When I commented on his fear of getting close to me, to the dog and the toys, his fear that he will be violent, he said, 'Stupid'. He knows the meaning of the word 'stupid' because he knows that that is not what he really is. After this he started whispering to the blanket, the chair, and the dog, so softly I could not hear. It felt as if there was a transitional talking space he had made, linked to the transitional object of the puppy. At the Home the staff commented that he had spent a lot of time talking to all the objects in his room. He was then able to spend an hour on his own with his mother each week, but his violence continued to be a problem, with staff needing stitches for bites and treatment for violent kicks.

When his sister died, Barry had been in therapy for three years. There was a temporary return of his head-banging. He returned also to his painful weeping, and after a period there followed sessions of absolute silence. On one occasion I realized with a shock that my mind had wandered away from him and commented that he wanted to be good and dead like his sister, the 'perfect' baby so I could be preoccupied with other things, just as he had been a quiet baby when he was little because his parents were preoccupied with his sister and their breaking-up marriage. While we were looking at these issues, Barry held out his hand to me. As I reached for it, he looked at the untouched dog and then said, 'Arm hurts', and cried. He kicked the toy mother and father dolls lying on the floor from his earlier throw. It had taken three years to move through the secondary handicap to the trauma of his organic handicap, his hurt arm, and his family life. The hurt arm seemed to be symbolic both of his organic primary handicap and the traumatic violence of his early home life. After six years, Barry can warn when he is feeling violent; he can maintain relationships and ask about changes in the staff shifts. With me, however, he is largely mute. At each new blow the environment offers, he returns to banging his head but stops once the situation changes; I feel he will always find life a painful experience, but he is now able to gain more from what his caring home can offer.

Discussion

Barry's mother speaks to him loudly and affectionately and slowly. He speaks to her, outside the therapy room, in a fast but stereotyped way. 'Alright?' he will ask her, as she often asks him. I think that question carries a knowledge that the speaker himself is not alright, but the listener will not bear this and will need to be appeased for being in the presence of a handicapped child. There is also a class factor involved in the linguistic code of address. Bernstein (1965) has postulated a restricted code for working-class communication, and 'Alright' is very much a working-class version of 'How are you?'. Although the latter form of address may be token in its wish to have a response, it does not restrict the answer by including how the other person should be, which 'Alright?' does. Simply by refusing to say 'Yes', the therapist is removing some of the other leaves of mild secondary handicap and making it clear that it is possible to have room for sad and angry feelings.

Barry's mother would ask me, 'Is he alright?' Barry was not spoken of as an individual, but as a shadowy representation of the not-properly-mourned healthy twin of himself he should have been. When I commented on how he had grown after the last holidays, his mother sadly said, 'Yes, *he would have been so tall*'. Her real speech was for the other Barry, the healthy one who never lived or died and has not been put to rest. The perpetual not-being-addressed is, I feel, a repetition of earlier nonreciprocal experiences; of being born in difficulties at the wrong time. Maude Mannoni (1967) sees in this indirect talking both the murder wish of the parent and/or the unconscious desire that the child stay ill. If Barry continues to use words and to experience his feelings and to make closer relationships instead of acting them out, the issue will arise of whether he can be placed with his mother. His mother does not want him. Slowly, he moves to face that old, yet new, trauma.

When Neville Symington's patient Harry (1981) was able to show and acknowledge his greater internal intelligence, he cried, 'I am capable of more than everyone thinks I am, but there is tomorrow and Sunday and Monday'. This means not just the strain of holding up the new experience of integration and intelligence without attacking it for a few days, but, I feel, the meaning of the future without handicap as a defence. The fear of the murder wish of the parent has to be faced and goes back even to prenatal experience. Pierce Clark (1933) felt that excessive sleeping and foetal postures of handicapped patients represented a return to the foetal stage to be enveloped in primary narcissism to avoid the damage to come. Symington (1981) felt that the patient's fantasy that he had been injured in the womb (via the creation of his handicap) was possibly based on reality.

Winnicott (1949) feels that birth trauma due to brain changes or the anaesthetic administered to the mother prove significant.

Barry has moved from sleeping and self-attacking. Now he faces me, struggling with his words and with a longing and fear of symbolizing.

Conclusions on trauma

Barry was born to depressed parents. He witnessed and probably experienced extreme violence as a toddler, and from the age of 4 he has lived apart from his mother. His IQ is in the severe handicap range (40), and he has the environmental determinants of handicap (Rutter et al., 1970) and trauma. Freud defined as traumatic 'any excitations from outside which are powerful enough to break through the protective shield. Such an event as an external trauma is bound to provoke a disturbance on a large scale in the functioning of the organism's energy and to set in motion every possible defensive measure' (1920g, p. 29). Barry exhausted and deadened himself, translating longings and communications into silence or blows to his head, the seat of his thoughts, to cushion his terribly impinged-upon world. He would also try to manage the helplessness inherent in trauma (Winnicott, 1949) by his violent attacks on those about him.

An opportunist aspect to this defence against a terrible memory was his physical appearance, his stupid smile, his posture and speech. In 'banging' his thoughts, he was also allowing all means of communication to deteriorate. Where there is trauma underlying opportunist handicap, there is further work to be done. Goldschmidt (1986) writes, 'the patient must re-experience the traumatic situation bit by bit not in the presence of an object which assumes the function of a shield against stimuli'. He quotes Hayman (1957) on the need for a protecting figure. For Barry, maintaining a physical distance from him during the first few months meant I was protecting him and myself from his violence.

Whilst it is known that handicapped children are over-represented in child physical abuse cases (Friedrich & Boriskin,

1976), there is a question as to whether this is due to lack of attachment and bonding at the start (Blacher & Meyers, 1983), something that certainly afflicted Barry and his mother. Barry's difficulty in speaking and his years of silence with me become easier to understand when we consider Maude Mannoni's comment (1967), 'When we are dealing with a child caught in the death-wishes of his parents, it is their words first of all which must be unravelled'. Barry, with his first gift of the word 'shy', was making sure his words were attended to. In considering the meaning of words in the relationship between the retarded patient and the therapist as connected with a gift, Mannoni adds, 'We have given back to himself the child walled in by terror and petrified in non-communication so that in his turn he may belong to the world' (p. 224). Sometimes it feels as if Barry does not speak because he so concretely experiences his new good words as gifts that he wants to keep them for his mother and fears using them up.

Goldschmidt (1986) expresses most succinctly the stage that has to be passed through first after trauma, and the stage Barry is in now. I am thinking of the way Barry will now say 'Hullo', or 'Time to go', quite clearly *after* his session has ended. In talking of a traumatized patient, Goldschmidt states, 'His great helplessness was something he could only show me at the end of his session—more precisely *after* the end, so I could no longer talk to him about it. It was as if he experienced therapy or myself as an electric cable with which on the one hand he did indeed want to come into contact in order to be brought alive but which he on the other hand must not really touch as it might kill him.

For the moment Barry yearns for contact, although it feels killing; and he speaks into a transitional space words that I cannot properly hear. As Canetti (1983) says, 'sometimes one says one's best and most important things to just anybody, one need not be ashamed for one does not always speak to ears, the words want to be said just in order to exist'. But the wish for words to exist has only developed through the satisfaction obtained from being with a therapist who could bear the meaning of non-verbal as well as occasional verbal communication. To speak directly to ears, to the healthy, seeing, hearing witness of emotional, sexual, or organic violation, is to face not only all the secondary and opportunist handicaps that have followed, but the event itself and the lack of protection from the parent. Also, there is the injunction from the parent to *not know* (Bowlby, 1979b). In addition to the widespread early fear of mother as life-giver and death-dealer, there is an extra traumatic ingredient if there is a real wish, verbalized or not, for a handicapped child to die.

Markova et al. (1984) were surprised by their research findings that although children with haemophilia were less proficient, took less care, and were more excited when handling sharp tools than the control children, their mothers did not correct their children when they used a knife incompetently and carelessly. I wonder whether the mothers were possibly unconsciously conveying death wishes by their lack of protection.

Even more deeply, then, the defence against trauma that has to be faced for growth to ensue is psychosis. For using the obliteration of the mind, cutting off the sight or hearing, sleeping, or becoming a robot, spending a vegetable life in subnormality hospitals, is not a sane solution. It does not work. Thoughts would reawaken, no matter how much Barry tried to beat them out of his head. The ghost of meaning still haunted him. Mentally handicapped can, indeed, mean mentally ill (Spensley, 1985).

When Barry angrily called me 'stupid', he was showing he knew that word, not because it had been said to him and he was parroting it back, but because very deeply he knew the meaning of the word. Stupid originally meant numbed with grief. Barry and other handicapped children and adults are in some aspects of themselves numbed with grief, but they can only so precisely know the meaning of the word and follow its laws of speech, facial expression, and cut-off eyes and ears and feelings and thinking if somewhere else they are not stupid. In Pasteur's profound death-bed words, 'Bernard is right, the pathogen is nothing; the terrain is everything'.

CHAPTER FOURTEEN

What autism is
and what autism is not

Frances Tustin

The title of this chapter brings a hopeful note of clarity into a situation which, as the author comments, is one that has been overshadowed with confusion and doubts—about definitions, diagnosis, methods of treatment, and potentialities for change. In exploring and comparing a number of approaches and in tracing the history of Mrs Tustin's own discoveries and insights, this study contributes a new breadth and illumination into the nature of the condition.

[R.S.]

The author's experience with autism

Mrs Tustin has worked intensively with autistic children for thirty years. After qualifying as a Child Psychotherapist at the Tavistock Clinic, she worked for one year in the Putnam Children's Center in the United States. At that time, the Center was a research and treatment unit for what they called 'atypical children'. Here, she looked after autistic children in their own homes, as well as working as a psychotherapist in the unit. She was also generously allowed to read the full notes of all the children who had been seen at the Centre since its inception ten years earlier. On her return to England, she treated autistic children in private practice who were referred to her by Dr Mildred Creak. Later, she went to work with Dr Creak at Great Ormond Street Children's Hospital, where she treated only autistic children. For ten years she was also closely associated with the Institute of Childhood Neuropsychiatry of Rome University, which had a research and treatment psychotherapy unit devoted to the care and treatment of psychotic children under 5 years of age. On retirement, she has supervised the psychotherapeutic treatment of autistic patients with visitors from England and abroad.

Too often and for too long we have stood outside and regarded him (the autistic child) with increasing theoretical bewilderment as his behaviour continued to transgress the laws of orthodox psychopathology. Our only hope at present is to get inside him and look out at the world through his eyes.

[James Anthony, *An Experimental Approach to the Psychopathology of Childhood Autism*, 1958]

The 'theoretical bewilderment' to which James Anthony referred as long ago as 1958 still hampers precise diagnosis of autism. For example, as recently as 1986, the Polish professor of psychiatry Andrzej Gardziel wrote: 'Several diagnostic scales are in use . . . some children diagnosed as autistic according to one scale may be excluded by another (Gardziel, 1986). This confusion and uncertainty about diagnosis would seem to be due to the emphasis that psychiatric modes of classification place on external descriptive features. In my experience, the difficulty in diagnosis largely disappears when we get behind the external phenomena and study the underlying reactions that have given rise to the external features of the disorder. Becoming aware of these underlying reactions brings unifying order to the diverse and seemingly unrelated external characteristics of autistic psychopathology.

But before embarking on describing psychotherapeutic findings, let me gather together what has been written so far about the diagnosis of childhood autism from an external point of view.

SECTION I

External descriptive diagnostic features

It would seem appropriate to begin with Leo Kanner's pioneering paper in which he descriptively differentiated the syndrome he called *early infantile autism* from inherent mental defect (Kanner, 1943).

Here is his description of Paul, aged 5 years:

> There was on his side, no affective tie to people. He behaved as if people as such did not matter or even exist. It made no difference whether one spoke to him in a friendly or a harsh way. He never looked at people's faces. When he had any dealings with persons at all, he treated them, or rather parts of them, as if they were objects.

He also writes:

> Every one of the children, upon entering the office, immediately went after blocks, toys, or other objects, without paying the least attention to the persons present. It would be wrong to say that they were not aware of the presence of persons. But the people, so long as they left the child alone, figured in about the same manner as did the desk, the bookshelf, or the filing cabinet. Comings and goings, even of the mother, did not seem to register. [Kanner, 1943]

At the time of its publication, and since then, Kanner's paper has aroused a great deal of interest. However, we have come to realize that the syndrome that Kanner described is very rare. One estimate is that its incidence is about 4 in every 10,000 children, its onset being before a child is 2½ years old. But it is rarely diagnosed then. The parents of autistic children tell sad stories of going from one professional to another before the child's condition was recognized. Thus, it would seem to be important to alert health visitors and other health professionals to the danger signal of a mother and baby who do not seem to be in touch with each other.

This brings me to *the* most outstanding feature of autistic children, which is their lack of normal social relations. In his 1976 paper, Dr Rutter, who is a leading authority on the symptomatology of autism, described such children's absence of eye-to-eye gaze and the way in which they did not assume the normal anticipatory gesture when picked up ('body-moulding', as Margaret Mahler has called it). He described how they did not turn to their parents for comfort and how they approached strangers as readily as those whom they knew well. He described how they did not play co-operatively and appeared oblivious of the feelings and interests of others.

From humane experimental work with autistic children, Peter Hobson (1986), a co-worker with Rutter, has demonstrated such children's lack of empathy. Working in the same way as Hobson, Uta Frith (1985) of the Medical Research Council has demonstrated their lack of imagination. I have found these two findings very helpful for understanding clear-cut autistic children. They are specific to them.

Rutter (1979) has described three symptoms as cardinal for the diagnosis of autistic children. The first is the failure to develop social relationships. The next is language retardation, some children being mute and others being echolalic, often with confusion in the use of personal pronouns such as 'I' and 'You'. The third symptom described by Rutter is their ritualistic and compulsive behaviour associated with stereotyped movements and gestures.

Writing from the same behaviourist standpoint as Rutter, Bernard Rimland (1964) has described in detail the external features of childhood autism and, in addition, has differentiated it from childhood schizophrenia.

Taking a wider perspective than both Rutter and Rimland, George Victor (1986)[1] has also distinguished childhood autism from childhood schizophrenia. He analysed a wide diversity of material from laboratory experiments with animals to parent's biographies of their autistic children. In Chapter 2, he outlines the following symptoms:

Rituals. He says these usually have the function of maintaining self-control and of keeping the environment from changing; autistic children's rituals are more bizarre than those of schizophrenic children and are clung to with more tenacity.

Isolation. He describes autistic children's aloneness, their detachment and their withdrawal.

Sensation. Victor describes such children's peripheral vision, their seeming deafness, and their oblivion to nearby events but tuning-in to distant ones.

Sex. He describes autistic children's wild excitements resembling seizures or orgasms; these children are hypersexual and very sensual.

Movement. He describes how they may roll their head, grind their teeth, and blink and grimace.

Sleep. He says that sleeping difficulties are common.

Miscellaneous symptoms. He describes autistic children's indifference to possessions and how they are upset by things that are broken or incomplete; he describes their panic after a slight change and their indifference to big changes.

Symptoms occurring in infancy. He also describes the way in which, both as infants and later on, they are content to be left alone for hours.

Arising from his work in the United States of America as head of a day unit for psychotic children and writing as a psychotherapeutic psychiatrist, Robert Olin (1975) distinguished the autistic from the schizophrenic child and also from the organically retarded child. He particularly compares their feelings of identity. Of the autistic child he writes:

> The autistic child's identity problem is one of feeling so small and insignificant that he hardly exists. So he defends against feelings of non-existence by using all his strength and ability to try to be a shell of indestructible power.

Such a child may feel that he *becomes* a car, a light switch, a pavement, or a record player. He becomes equated with 'things', instead of *identifying* with living human beings. Comparing the autistic with the schizophrenic child, Olin goes on to say:

> A schizophrenic child, on the other hand, feels that his identity is very scattered and diffused—like mist in the air. . . . His personality is like a broken dish or a handful of sand that has been thrown into the wind.

Olin continues:

> He [the schizophrenic child] fragments and confuses in the most ingenious manners. For example, his words frequently make no sense to the observer. Suddenly, however the observer discovers that there is a sort of secret message in what is being said and done.

By comparison, the undoubted autistic child is mute or echolalic.

Olin comments on another difference between the two types of psychopathology, in that hallucinations are usually a feature of the schizophrenic child, but not of the autistic child, although they may occur in treatment when the autistic child is recovering.

Olin illustrates the difficulties in differentiating between autistic and schizophrenic children when external descriptive features alone are used, when he writes as follows:

> Like the autistic child, the schizophrenic child may not be cuddly. He resists learning. He has difficulty in mixing with other children.

Later, in the same vein, Olin continues:

Some schizophrenic children have histories which are similar to those of autistic children.

Later, I shall show that going behind the external symptoms enables us to recognize those children who are unmistakeably autistic. But before I do this, I need to correct certain common misapprehensions about such children.

Corrections to misconceptions

The mistaken idea that *all* autistic children have been unloved as infants has led to an over-emphasis on environmental causes, as well as to over-indulgent forms of psychotherapy that were unsuitable for remedying the autistic condition. The notion that the autistic child had not been loved as an infant was first promulgated by Leo Kanner, who wrote of the mothers of such children as being 'cold' and 'intellectual'. Also, Dibs, the autistic child described by Virginia Axline (1966) was obviously unloved and unwanted. But this has not been the case with *all* autistic children. For example, the autistic children I have worked with had mothers who had been depressed when the child was a young baby, but they had wanted the baby and had not been unloving, although their attention probably left much to be desired because of their depression.

Apropos the notion of the mothers of autistic children being unloving, Helen Baker, a child psychologist in a Child and Adolescent Unit in Australia, writes as follows:

As a Child Psychologist, who has worked with autistic children and their parents over a period of twelve years, I have found absolutely no relationship between the existence of the condition and the lack of love shown by the parents. In fact, some of the most caring parents I have met are those who happen to have autistic children. [personal communication, 1988]

It seems to me that a variety of nature–nurture interactions can lead to autism.

Another popular misconception that needs to be corrected is that *all* autistic children are brain-damaged. As with their being unloved, just because some of these children are brain-damaged, it does not mean that *all* of them are.

Brain damage

Professor Adriano Giannotti and Dr Giulianna de Astis, who work in the research and psychotherapy unit of the Institute of Childhood Neuropsychiatry of Rome University and whose autistic patients are all initially investigated in the well-equipped Metabolic and Organic Unit of that institute, have written as follows:

> The fact that some of these features of autism are occasionally accompanied by minimal cerebral lesions makes it necessary to investigate an important problem. Many of the cases we have observed and treated with some success had been diagnosed as mental retardation, or even cerebropathy, with the consequence that any possibility for normal psychic development had been ruled out. Our experience in this matter has shown that electroencephalographically revealed cerebral alterations tend to disappear with psychotherapeutic treatment; thus we do not believe that these lesions should be given excessive importance for psychotherapeutic purposes. Cases in which the autistic condition is related to serious cerebropathic alterations . . . have been excluded from our experience. [Giannotti & de Astis, 1978]

In my own clinical work, which now spans thirty years, I only took those autistic children into psychotherapeutic treatment who had been found to have no brain damage that could be detected by the investigative methods that were available at the time. It is from these children, whose autism seemed likely to be predominantly psychogenic in origin, that the psychodynamic diagnostic findings in the next section are drawn.

SECTION II

Psychoanalytic diagnostic findings

Melanie Klein

At a time when the orthodox psychiatric view was that only adults could be psychotic, Melanie Klein was a pioneer in the recognition and treatment of psychosis in children. She did not, however, distinguish between childhood autism and childhood schizophrenia. Dick, about whom she wrote in her 1930 paper, 'The importance of symbol formation in the development of the ego', was obviously a child whom we would now diagnose as autistic, but Kanner did not publish his paper about 'Early infantile autism' until 1943—that is, 14 years after the publication of Melanie Klein's paper. Mrs Klein realized that Dick was different from the other psychotic children she had seen, but after much agonizing about this, she diagnosed that he was suffering from *dementia praecox*, as schizophrenia was then called. In her busy working life, she did not have the time to correct her diagnosis of Dick in the light of Kanner's findings.

Margaret Mahler

Working at about the same time as Melanie Klein but living in the United States, Margaret Mahler had many opportunities for personal discussions with Leo Kanner, and so she absorbed his findings into her theories. Mahler devoted the major part of her working life to the recognition and study of childhood psychosis from the background of classical Freudian psychoanalytic theories, which she extended. Hers is a developmental hypothesis in that she postulated that the earliest stage of infancy was a normal autistic one, in which she says: '. . . need satisfaction belongs to [the infant's] own autistic orbit (1968, p. 8). At this early stage, she thought that the infant had no awareness of the outside world. Mahler saw childhood autism as being the result of traumatic disturbance in this normal autistic stage of early infancy.

She went on to postulate that at around 3 months of age, the normal infant develops a dim awareness of bodily separateness from the mother and the outside world. Mahler used the biological concept of *symbiosis* to designate the mutually beneficial interdependence that developed between mother and baby in this normal symbiotic stage. She saw what she called *symbiotic psychosis* as being the result of disturbance in the normal symbiotic stage. If we use Bender's hypothesis (1956) that childhood schizophrenia can only be diagnosed after 5 years of age, *symbiotic psychosis* would seem to be a pre-schizophrenic condition.

Mahler's is a neat hypothesis. Not wanting to be without a theoretical framework, I turned to and used Mahler's theories in my first two books, *Autism and Childhood Psychosis* (1972) and *Autistic States in Children* (1981). But, like Melanie Klein, Margaret Mahler had been hampered by not having certain later findings at her disposal. These were the findings of such infant observers as Brazelton (1970), Colin Trevarthen (1979), Tom Bower (1977a), and Daniel Stern (1986). These findings cast doubt on the validity of a normal primary autistic stage. They indicate, as Melanie Klein had always asserted, that from the word 'go' the newly born infant has a flickering and fluctuating awareness of separateness from the mother and is alert to taking in experiences from the outside world. The hypotheses of both Mahler and Klein concerning normal infantile development have suffered from being drawn from pathological states. This was the case with Mahler's primary autistic stage and, in my view, with Klein's paranoid–schizoid position as being part of normal infantile development.

In *Autistic Barriers in Neurotic Patients* (Tustin, 1986) I corrected my use of the notion of normal primary autism. In this chapter I want to correct the confusion caused in my earlier book, *Autistic States in Children* (Tustin, 1981), by my not making a clear distinction between childhood autism and childhood schizophrenia. However, before giving my most recent formulations and their relevance to a differential psychodynamic diagnosis of childhood autism, I must mention the work of Donald Meltzer and his collaborators. In their book, *Explorations of Autism* (1975), they described their psychotherapeutic work with certain children who, in Meltzer's words, '. . . fall into the general category of *Early Infantile Autism,* but in various stages of evolution' (p. 3). Thus, they described children who had emerged or were emerging from the autistic condition, but who were not still autistic. They were not concerned with distinguishing autism from other types of childhood psychosis.

Meltzer implied, as I also think, that the nature of the child had played a decisive part in the autistic outcome. However, his work has taken him in a different direction from my own in that he has been drawn into exploring autistic children's aesthetic capacities. This is understandable since, as they emerge from autism, these shy, refined, sensitive children are almost invariably either artistic or musical or have a facility with words. They seem to have what is popularly called an 'artistic temperament'. Their hypersensitivity means that, for them, the conflict between destruction and creation is particularly intense.

As a practicing child psychotherapist, I have been concerned to sort out which children seemed likely to benefit from the treatment I provided, and also to pinpoint the understandings that had brought about progressive changes in these patients. I found that so far as I was concerned, the tight encapsulated autistic children were a simpler treatment proposition than the diffused and scattered schizophrenic-type children.

Let me now describe the psychodynamic diagnostic feature that, when occurring in a massive and total way, is specific and unique to autistic children. Becoming aware of this underlying feature enables us to see how the bewildering array of disparate external features described in Section I have arisen. It provides us with a simple hypothesis that makes sense of that complexity.

Differentiating the underlying feature specific to autism

The underlying diagnostic feature that is specific to autism stems from the fact that all human beings, like other animals, have an inbuilt disposition to seek shelter from frightening experiences. Thus, relatively normal infants will seek refuge within the shelter of the mother's arms (or those of a similarly well-known person) or hide beneath the mother's skirts. In normal development, the mother and other people are increasingly perceived as separate individuals. In psychosis this is not so. Schizophrenic-type infants *blur* the fact of their bodily separateness from the mother, whereas autistic children *shut it out* almost completely.

Schizophrenic-type children

Schizophrenic-type children seek refuge from frightening things, both internal and external, by cultivating the illusion that part of their body is still attached to the mother's body and that they are identical with her. As well as blurring the fact of their bodily separateness, this gives them an insecure sense of identity. Mother and child are like a pair of siamese twins or a pair of semi-detached houses (as a patient of Daphne Nash Briggs described this pathologically 'symbiotic' situation). Meltzer (Meltzer et al., 1975) has called it *adhesive identification*. Other workers have used the term *imitative fusion* (Gaddini, 1969).

Another schizophrenic mode of seeking refuge is by the illusion of breaking into and entering the mother's body and that of other people. W. R. Bion (1962) has shown us that this is an exaggeration of normal processes that Melanie Klein called *projective identification*. These processes seem to arise from the inbuilt capacity for empathy. (Schizophrenic-type children have too much empathy; autistic children have too little. Schizophrenic-type children are too open; autistic children are too closed.) Meltzer has called it *intrusive identification*. This gives schizophrenic-type children a shaky sense of identity, but it is dependent upon that of other people. I call them *confusional entangled* children, because their own sense of identity and their awareness of that of other people is entangled and confused. However, since there is a dim sense of separateness, some confused psychological development can take place, even if it is unregulated, bizarre, and distorted.

This is in great contrast to the encapsulated *autistic* child, in whom psychological development has almost completely stopped, although there are a few autistic children whose cognitive development may go along a narrow line with an obsessional interest in one thing—for example, spiders or beetles—about which a great deal of information will be collected. These children are perseverators. This shuts out unpleasant things in the outside world. The connection of autism with obsessionality is clear.

Also, in contrast to the feeding difficulties of the autistic infant, schizophrenically inclined infants are almost always reported as being unrestrained 'greedy feeders'. Mothers say such things as, 'It was as if he could never get enough', 'He never wanted the feed to come to an end'. This is different from the exuberant feeding of a normal healthy baby, who usually takes his feed, finishes, burps, and probably falls asleep.

Let me now differentiate the mode of protection that is particular and unique to the clear-cut autistic child. Schizophrenic-type children use a ready-made form of protection; they are wrapped up in other people's bodies, which support them, and thus they are overly dependent on other people. By contrast, autistic children originate their own protective covering. They are wrapped up in their own hard bodily sensations. I refer to this as *autogenerated encapsulation*. In contrast with the schizophrenic-type child, autistic children are unduly self-sufficient and ignore their dependence on others.

Auto-generated encapsulation

A hard, shell-like encapsulation is the psycho-dynamic differential diagnostic feature of autistic children. As Kanner realized, such children do not distinguish between alive people and inanimate objects; they treat them both in the same way. Thus, by pressing against a hard wall or against the hard part of a person as an inanimate object, or by turning their hard backs on people, they engender sensations of being hard and impenetrable—sensations being of pre-eminent importance to such children, although their excessive concentration on certain sensations causes them to be unaware of sensations with more normal objective relevance. For example, such children are unaware of being hurt if they fall down.

These children carry hard objects around with them, with which they feel *equated*. This is not identification; they have taken over the hardness of the object to become *equated* with it. It is difficult to find words that carry the essence of these elemental experiences and conceptualize these unconceptualized objects. These 'objects' are not differentiated from the subject's own body and are not used in terms of their objective function, but in terms of the hard sensations they engender. After I had suggested the terms *autistic objects* or *sensation objects* (Tustin, 1980, 1981), I found that Winnicott had been aware of them and, in his picturesque way, had suggested the paradoxical term, *subjective objects* (1958).

Many of these children develop hard, muscular bodies, as described by Esther Bick (1968). When picked up, they feel hard and unyielding. They are tense children who live in a sensation-dominated world of hard and soft sensations. These extremes of hard and soft sensations distract the child's attention away from the sensations that are appropriate to the situations of everyday life, which they share with other human beings. This means that they develop idiosyncratic mannerisms in order to engender protective sensations. These mannerisms seem meaningless to the ordinary observer. The attention of autistic children is so distracted by these auto-generated sensations that they appear to be deaf, or even blind. This idiosyncratic protective use of hard autistic objects prevents the use of objects in a normal play way. Without play and a normal sensation life, mental development is not stimulated (Tustin, 1988).

The oblivion of autistic children to shared realities is also increased by the engendering of sensation-dominated subjective shapes. These are anaesthetizing and tranquillizing. I have called them *autistic shapes* or *sensation shapes* (Tustin, 1984, 1986). These are random formless shapes that are not related to the shapes of actual objects. Thus, they are unclassified and unshared shapes. They are whorls of autogenerated sensations that deaden awareness, so that the lack of attention to shared realities arising from their use of subjective autistic objects is maintained and reinforced. An unthinkable traumatic infantile experience is shut away. Paradoxically, these sensation-engen-

dered shapes numb awareness of normal sensations. This numb-
ness is characteristic of autistic children.

In normal development, the association of shapes with appropriate objects leads to percept and concept formation. This association is the foundation of cognitive development. Thus, the
autistic child's excessive preoccupation with subjective sensation
objects and shapes prevents cognitive development, so that
autistic children appear to be mentally defective.

The massive and exclusive use of the auto-generated encapsulation is *the* distinguishing feature of autism. It is a particular
mode of sheltering, but a pathological one because it almost
completely halts psychological development. It is associated
with elemental phenomena on the borderline of the physiological and the psychological. It is a combination of psycho-reflex,
neuro-mental, and psycho-chemical reactions.

Autistic encapsulation serves a useful purpose as a refuge
from unbearable, seemingly life-threatening experiences. Thus,
I feel very concerned when I hear of people talking about
'removing the autism', 'curing the autism', or 'breaking through
the autism'. I have seen or heard of autistic children who have
been treated by people holding these views, who have become
distressingly hyperactive. Hyperactivity is not a feature of an
autistic child unless the autism has been interfered with by
people who do not understand its function. Other children
treated by methods that do not respect the autism have had
their extreme vulnerability exposed without having been given
sufficient opportunity to develop other more progressive modes
of protection. These more progressive modes can only develop if
a form of treatment is used in which the *infantile transference* is
understood and the children are given the opportunity to
re-experience the early infantile dramas that led to the autistic
encapsulated mode of sheltering.

Although autistic children look so ethereal, they are in fact
extremely dominating and powerful. They have developed an
adaptation that is extremely effective for shutting out the outside world. Unfortunately, this has prevented other adaptations
from developing. Sometimes I have had clinical material presented to me as being that of an autistic child. I was able to

show the presenter that the child was not autistic because the patient had not had the constitutional strength that is needed to generate the hard encapsulation that is specific to autistic modes of protection.

At other times, clinical material has been presented to me as indicating autism because the children had been distressed by holes or broken things. Several other types of patients—such as mentally defective or schizophrenic children—can be pre-occupied by these things, but only autistic children protect themselves from such things by a massive and exclusive use of auto-generated encapsulation.

The protective reaction of autism
used amongst other protective reactions

However, other than autistic patients may make a limited use of autistic encapsulation. For them, this is one means, amongst others, for taking refuge from unbearable experiences. But it is not the only one. For example, schizophrenic-type children who make a predominant use of projective, intrusive, and adhesive identification may have a capsule of autism. This is also often the case with blind or deaf children. In this encapsulated part, *sensation equations* predominate. There is no identification, even of an insecure kind. The subjective phenomena of *sensation objects* and *sensation shapes* protect the child's most vulnerable part. In this part, they completely shut out any awareness of separateness, as also the tantrum of panic and rage occasioned by this frustration, although in other parts there is a dim aware-ness of their bodily separateness from the mother and the out-side world.

Hanna Segal (1975) has described a schizophrenic adult patient who was so equated with his violin that he could not play to an audience, because he felt that he would be masturbat-ing in public. Obviously, as Segal points out, the violin did not *symbolize* his body, he felt that he had *become* his violin. For this reason, Segal has called it a *symbolic equation*. This seems to be a more sophisticated form of the body-centred autistic objects used by autistic children. Like these objects, the violin was not used in terms of its objective function.

As the auto-generated encapsulation of autistic children is modified and as they become dimly aware of their own aliveness and their separateness from other people, they begin to make a normal use of projective identification as a means of protection, as well as continuing to make a residual use of the sensation equations that generate autistic encapsulation. This use of several protective modes explains Dr Olin's puzzling observation that 'Early in life, some children appear autistic. Later, they appear schizophrenic. Or, some psychotic children develop, initially, a schizophrenia which later becomes autism.' In these children, there has obviously been a fluctuation from one mode of protection to another. Also, many neurotic patients, and even relatively normal people, have a hidden capsule of autism (S. Klein, 1980; Tustin, 1986). It seems likely that a capsule of autism may lie at the base of manic-depressive disorders, since all the autistic children I have treated, as they emerged from autism, were emotionally labile to a marked degree. An autistic capsule also seems to contribute to the terror-stricken inhibitions in phobic illnesses.

My present views on autism

It will have become clear that I no longer follow Margaret Mahler in seeing autism as a normal primary developmental stage. I now reserve the term *autism* for an adaptive response that partakes of the nature of an automatic reflex reaction to situations of unbearable awareness of bodily separateness from the mother. It seems to be a protective reaction that is specific to hyper-sensitivity and ultra-vulnerability. As we have seen, it can be used totally or partially.

As I said earlier, I have not found the majority of the mothers of these children to have been unloving. Some workers confuse autistic children with grossly deprived and neglected children who have been in and out of the care of the social work agencies.

They have often had other separations also, such as hospitalization. Such neglected children often show signs of autism, but
they also use other modes of protection. Autistic children are
different from them in that they are physically well cared for
and usually come from comfortable middle-class homes. It is also
rare for them to have been geographically separated from their
mothers.

Let me now gather together those factors that I have found to
be significant in the development of psychogenic autism. One
factor is that the mothers report that they were seriously
depressed either before or after the birth of this particular
baby—a birth that had often been long and protracted. Also, the
baby had had a history of feeding difficulties in earliest infancy.
I have also found that when they were carrying the baby, they
were in a particularly lonely-making situation. As H. S. Klein
(1987) has said: 'We are still somewhat in the dark about the
influence of intra-uterine experiences. . . . What is the effect of
the mother's mental state on her unborn child . . . is the child
sensitised to painful stimuli before birth?'

Sometimes the father had had to be away a great deal
because of his work, or for some reason he was not emotionally
available for the mother. Other mothers were not in the country
of their origin; some of them were a different nationality or
religion from their husband. Without being aware of it, the
mother seems to have resorted to the baby inside her body for
company and for solace. Thus, the birth of this baby may have
been difficult because, unconsciously, she did not want to lose
the baby from inside her body. When the baby was born, it left a
lonely, grief-stricken feeling inside her, which felt like a 'black
hole'. She became deeply depressed.

When he was 4 years old, as he began to recover, my first
autistic child patient, whom I have called John (Tustin, 1966,
1986, 1990), showed me that the traumatic experience that had
been shut out by the protective reaction of the autism was the
'black hole'. This was associated with grief, rage, and panic
about unbearable separateness from the mother's body. It would
seem that the mother would not be able to help him to bear this
frustrating experience, as it was too much like her own. John
brought home to me that to help these children, we have to go

right back to the beginning of life and to be in touch with the earliest of the baby's activities, that of sucking at the breast or bottle. In this early situation, babies have had very few interactions with the outside world, so inbuilt gestalts will play a major role. At first, it will not be the milk that is important to the baby, but the sensation of the nipple (or teat) in the mouth.

Mavis Gunther (1959)[2], who had much experience with helping mothers with the feeding of their newborn babies, writes about this when she cites 'the extraordinary apathy of a baby . . . if it is put to the breast but does not get the whole feeling in its mouth. If it has not got the right pattern of stimulus on its soft palate, tongue and oral cavity, it will stay apathetic.' Clinical material shows that such a baby feels helpless to replace what is felt to be missing. Such children feel they have lost—they know not what. They feel defective and mutilated. This means that they become very exacting, with a yearning for a completeness and perfection which is unattainable. Nothing is ever good enough. Parents (and therapists) struggle hard to meet their unrealistic demands. Insight into the origin of their perfectionism lifts a weight, both from these patients and from those who care for them. The function of the autogenerated encapsulation is to protect this seemingly wounded part. But this encapsulation does not heal the sense of being wounded, nor moderate the extreme sensitivity and vulnerability. It makes them worse, for these extreme states are shut away from the healing and toughening effects of human relationships. However, it seemed to be a life-saving precaution at the time.

In psychotherapy, as the autistic mode of protection begins to be given up, a hypersensitive, ultra-vulnerable wounded child emerges with a low tolerance for frustration. For such a child everything is magnified. As the capacity for play develops, as well as other aesthetic activities, these children can express these exaggerated states through these means, whilst beginning to take part in the shared ordinary events of everyday life. The autistic encapsulation had meant that their sensitivity was not used, nor was their vulnerability, which would have brought home to them their need for other people. We have to bring them down to earth whilst preserving but moderating their sensitive vulnerability.

Fortunately, in the type of psychotherapy that understands the use of the *infantile transference* we have a means of doing this. Through this, they can relive traumatic infantile situations in which they had had the illusion that they were being mutilated. They experience despair, rage, and terror that had been unbearable at that early time. As well as helping the children to bear these sensations, we help them to view these feelings, and the situations that provoked them, in a less exaggerated way. They begin to play and to develop a sense of humour. They see things in a more balanced way. It has been my experience that as they begin to react in a less extreme way, they are particularly joyful children. As they become aware of both 'me' and 'not-me', the *transitional object,* as described by Winnicott (1958), may come into play. Autistic objects completely shut out awareness of 'not-me' situations. Out-and-out autistic children do not even suck their thumbs; because they have to come through space to reach the mouth, they are experienced as 'not-me'. On the other hand, schizophrenic-type children are usually very addicted to sucking their thumbs, which they use as a primitive transitional object.

But not all infants who have depressed mothers and have feeding difficulties become autistic, although they may have other problems. I am convinced that there must be something in the genetic constitution or the intra-uterine experience of the autistic child that predisposes him (or her) to resort to autistic encapsulation as an exclusive mode of protection. A syndrome as rare as *early infantile autism* is likely to be the result of a rare combination of factors. We do not yet know all the factors that are involved. These children are still an enigma. But if we become clearer than we have been about what autism is and what it is not, we may be able to become clearer about the factors that are involved in its development.

Certainly, an interaction between mother and child is involved in the autistic outcome, but such children's genetic constitution, intra-uterine experiences, as well as the father's part in this sad story need to be taken into account. Another factor that is sometimes mentioned is that the mothers of autistic children seem to be whimsical and *precious* and to lack common sense. But as Salo Tischler (1979) so wisely said, the parents that we see in the consulting room are not necessarily behaving in the same way as they did when the child was first born. Since then, their feelings have been played upon by a very powerful child, who has been living in a strange, outlandish, rarified, extra-ordinary, exaggerated, auto-generated, sensation-dominated world. In a similar way, these children can have a powerful effect upon those who try to assess them. Thus, the mother can be assessed as being to blame for her child's condition, because the assessor is picking up the child's resentment towards the mother. Similarly an assessor who picks up the child's despair that his condition is irremediable may make dogmatic statements about *all* autistic children being untreatable.

Intensive psychotherapeutic work shows that neither parents nor child are involved in a blameworthy way in bringing about the autism. They have been caught in a web of inevitable reactions, for which they need our understanding and not our blame. A psychotherapeutic assessment that is concerned with tracing some of the threads of this web will give us a more precise understanding of an autistic child than a mere surface description of his peculiar characteristics. But this takes time and cannot always be done in one interview, although with experience one gets better at it. The understandings that we glean from such a preliminary investigation will assist us in helping the parents to be more in touch with their estranged child, as well as giving us clues about how to help this hypersensitive, ultravulnerable child who feels threatened with loss of existence. (Terror about loss of existence is different from the fear of dying that is characteristic of schizophrenic-type children. The fear of dying is associated with a sense of being alive. Autistic children are unaware that they are living human beings. Recovering autistic children have told me that when they first came to see me, they had felt like 'things'.)

Prognosis

In my own experience, which has been with autistic children who, as infants, had been cared for by a deeply depressed mother, the treatment outcome of the type of psychotherapy that used the *infantile transference* has been encouraging. All but one of the four out-and-out autistic patients who finished treatment (remember they are very rare) had been assessed as suffering from *early infantile autism* by Dr Mildred Creak, an international authority on the diagnosis of all forms of childhood psychosis. The one child who was not diagnosed by her was assessed as a Kanner syndrome child when he was 3 years old by Anni Bergman, Margaret Mahler's senior therapist. So there is no doubt that the children I treated successfully were autistic in the strict sense of the term. (I have seen six others who used marked autistic modes of protection, but who used symbiotic ones as well.) The four clear-cut autistic children, who were all seen in private practice, were under 6 years of age when they entered treatment. The first two autistic patients were seen four or five times a week, but as I became more experienced, the last two were seen twice a week. They all turned out to be intelligent and to have aesthetic gifts. At the end of treatment they appeared to be relatively normal and were doing the normal things for children of their age. They were sociable but a bit shy and hypersensitive. Two of them were slightly obsessional. I have heard about three of them who have all gone to university and have progressed normally. I am sure I should have heard from the parents of the other child if there had been any backsliding.

Professor Giannotti and Dr de Astis, in a special unit of Rome University devoted to the psychotherapy of psychotic children of under 5 years of age, made a rough-and-ready pilot survey in 1985 for their own purposes in order to assess the effect on the 39 psychotic children in their unit of the type of psychotherapy they were using. In the early days of the unit their psychotherapeutic technique had been influenced by my approach, but as the years have gone by it has been enriched by the growing body of experience of the workers in the unit. (Contact with this unit has also enlarged my own individual experience.) In this pilot survey the children were assessed on a five-point scale in terms of the reduction of their pathology. Since, at the outset of treatment, the children could do very little, it was possible to make such a quantitative assessment. This is not usually the case in psychotherapeutic work. Obviously, the children did not all start treatment at the same time. Some had been in treatment longer than others, the longest time being five years. The categories for the reduction of pathology that were used were social relations, stereotypes, age-related school capacity, and play capacity.

The results of this survey were encouraging to the workers in the unit in that, although some children had only just started treatment and others were in the middle of treatment, the average reduction of pathology up to the time of the statistical survey was 51.6% for the autistic children and 54.0% for the schizophrenic-type children. They had all made progress, but only one child in the survey, who had been the first to start treatment, had finished and so had 100% reduction in pathology. Obviously, the average percentages will increase as treatment continues. I have heard from the workers in the unit that improvement has continued to their satisfaction, but they have not yet made another statistical survey, since the one they made in 1985 gave them adequate confidence that the treatment methods they were using were sufficiently relevant to the needs of the psychotic children in the unit.

Conclusion

This chapter has sought to make a definitive differential distinction between what autism is and what autism is not. The view has been developed that autism is an auto-sensuous protection of an automatic reflex kind, which is indigenous in all of us but which can become over-used in such a massive and exclusive way that it constitutes a pathology. The massive and exclusive use of autogenerated encapsulation that has distracted attention away from unbearable traumatic infantile experiences has been found to be specific and unique to autistic children. This finding means that childhood autism can be diagnosed more certainly and more accurately than has previously been the case in the psychotherapeutic field. Such diagnostic assessment is not to enable us to pin and label patients like butterflies on to a board, but so that we can begin 'to look out at the world through their eyes', as James Anthony put it in the quotation at the head of this chapter. Effective psychotherapy with autistic children depends upon their being talked to by someone who has an inkling of the sort of world in which they 'live and move' and have their tenuous sense of 'being'.

NOTES

1. I wish to express my warm thanks to Bronwyn Hocking, who introduced me to George Victor's book and summarized Chapter 2.

2. I wish to thank Vivienne Wilmot for sending me Mavis Gunther's paper.

Deprivation and damage

As it became evident over the last two or three decades that physical abuse of children was more widespread than had previously been recognized (Creighton, 1978, 1987), so evidence was accumulating that this was true also of the sexual seduction or exploitation of children (Mrazek, Lynch, & Bentovim, 1981; Bentovim et al., 1988). The sad paradox is that children's vulnerability to sexual exploitation may lie not only in physical weakness and fear, but also because of their wish to be loved by and please their parents (Freud, 1909c), however confused the accompanying phantasies might be. For these reasons rejected and neglected children may be an especially vulnerable group, and the prematurely sexualized child may be in special danger of becoming the victim of further assaults, as if they bear an unconscious 'aura'. Others may experience themselves as so damaged physically and in their image of themselves as people that suicidal despair is not uncommon.

On a behavioural level Shengold (1967) suggested that children who suffer 'experiences involving over-stimulation', including being beaten often and severely or being exposed to repeated observation of intercourse or sexually seduced, were later driven to violent acting out. He viewed this as a repetitive attempt to discharge an excess of excitation or to find relief from over-whelming feelings of rage (and, one might add, fear). In certain instances this may be seen as precipitating activities that display something in the nature of a sado-masochistic addictive quality. These appeared to be present in the early sessions of the child who is the subject of chapter fifteen (a similar pattern was found to have reached psychotic proportions in the case of the 9-year-old daughter of a prostitute, who was referred to the in-patient unit of a department of psychological medicine).

Although 'emotional abuse' exists as a legal category, it is probably seldom cited on its own, though clearly it is present in all forms of child abuse.

One of the problems with cases of suspected abuse may often be the difficulties of recognizing and eliciting the evidence of its occurrence. Judith Trowell (1986) has described the procedures in which 'with colleagues' she saw 'the whole family, the children individually and in sibling groups and the professionals involved in the community', and her use of Mary Ainsworth's and Mary Main's Strange Situation Test for assessing attachment relationships in 1-year-olds and in older children.

Arnon Bentovim and the Child Sexual Abuse Team at Great Ormond Street Hospital (Bentovim et al., 1988) have developed a system of diagnostic interviews conducted with the whole family, and child psychotherapists have taken part in the work there and at the Tavistock Clinic, in the family interviews and in individual assessment or psychotherapy with the children.

Public attention in general tends to be concerned largely with legal and social work aspects of the problem, often with an emphatically punitive approach, sometimes directed towards the perpetrators, sometimes towards the professionals—social workers especially, and also paediatricians. Perhaps this is partly in the nature of a defence that might help to distance the most deeply distressing elements within the whole situation—the child's suffering, helplessness, and confusion. The work of encountering and attempting to heal the disturbances and damage suffered by two little girls, one of whom had been starved and the other sexually abused, is described in chapter sixteen.

[R.S.]

CHAPTER FIFTEEN

An account
of the psychotherapy
# of a sexually abused boy

Jonathan Bradley

In the psychotherapy of this victim of sexual abuse the young boy was able to express extremes of sado-masochistic and gender confusions—to a degree, however, that made the most severe attacks on the capacity for containment and for preservation of the setting. Eventually the child was able to find his way to some positive internal strength with which to support the therapeutic alliance. Although the sexual abuse of girls is more frequently reported, it has been emerging that victimization of young boys is far more common than is generally assumed to be the case.

[R.S.]

Background

Chris was referred to a Child Guidance Unit at the age of 4. At the time, his parents were concerned because he was about to start school and yet was living so much in a world of his own that he seemed oblivious to danger. This was

271

not their only worry: for some time Chris had been pushing pieces of plastic and cylindrical wooden bricks into his bottom in a compulsive manner. They had found that smacking him severely had not had much effect, except to make him more secretive. In spite of punishments, when given the opportunity, Chris would try to assault his baby brother (6 months old at the time of referral) in the same way that he assaulted himself.

When I met his parents to discuss the possibility of psychotherapy, I was forcibly struck by his mother's appearance. She wore very heavy make-up, giving a masklike look to her face. Her expression seemed frozen to one of cold indifference, and when she spoke her voice was without inflection. Yet, as Chris' father, talkative and friendly by contrast, acknowledged, it was only because of his wife's concern that they had finally come to Child Guidance. She herself described how two years previously, when Chris was 2½ years old, she had discovered semen in his anus whilst bathing him. She had made enquiries of the police and of the playgroup that Chris had started to attend. She had been told that there was insufficient medical evidence for prosecution, although a male playgroup leader had suddenly been dismissed. Later they learned that probably more than one child had been involved, and that Chris may well have been assaulted on more than one occasion. She had let herself be persuaded not to do any more about the matter, but some time after the assault Chris had started to assault himself with bricks. They had not come earlier because they had been ashamed.

The meeting gave Chris' mother, in particular, the opportunity to share much more than her concern about Chris having been sexually abused. Tears came, and she was able to describe what a terrible time she had had with Chris from the beginning. She and her husband were not British and had come to this country shortly before the birth of Chris, her first child. She spoke little English, felt totally disoriented, and missed her own mother terribly. She did not go to ante-natal classes and felt unprepared for the birth. Although she wanted to breastfeed, she had felt bombarded by a 'mouth that could never get enough milk', and she could not feed Chris enough because her nipples were so sore. When Chris was 6 weeks old, she had to stop breastfeeding, but he did not take well to the bottle. She could not read the packet instructions clearly and made mistakes when mixing quantities of milk. Her recollection was of his vomiting incessantly throughout the first six months of life. When he was 9 months old they had in desperation arranged for him to stay with his maternal grandmother, who lived abroad. He remained there for several months. There was another long separation at 2 years, when he was again sent to his grandmother's home. At that time Chris was suffering from inflammation of the tonsils, but a London doctor advised against an operation. Without consultation with the parents, however, the grandmother had arranged for a tonsillectomy, and this had been carried out whilst he was staying with her.

What would such a history of events have meant to Chris? Within the space of thirty months he had had several painful experiences associated with his mouth: the feeling that either he never had enough nourishment or that it made him vomit; and, in addition, he had his tonsils removed. Not only had there been two long separations from his mother, one at 9 months and the other at 2 years, but, soon after coming back to her, he had been sexually assaulted. The hope was that in intensive three-times-weekly psychotherapy he could begin to make sense of what had happened to him, at his own pace and in his own way.

Clinical material:
first impressions

Chris made a tremendous impact on me, and the impression I received inside the therapy room (in contrast to the quiet, still little boy with very appealing deep-brown eyes who had sat quietly in the waiting room) was of a boy who felt there was total chaos inside, and that he had to get rid of it. Given the choice of what to do in the room, he immediately started to play with the selection of animals, both wild and tame, which were in the tray of toys provided for him. It is impossible to convey the pace and elemental quality of these early sessions. Wild beasts and tame animals alike were let loose onto a 'table world' where 'small' was hunted and eaten up by 'large', to the accompaniment of a garbled commentary from Chris. In a very agitated way he told me about a world of 'much, much water', and 'big fires' that 'burnt the world to bits'. In this early play he made attempts to introduce signs of civilization in the form of a plasticine house, but in each session this was destroyed as soon as it was built, and lions and tigers quickly appeared to prowl in the ruins. It was a very powerful way of conveying the extent of the emotional destruction that had occurred during these terrible first years. Chris himself gave the impression of one not so much playing out but possessed by these powerful fantasies. They flooded from him at such a pace and in such a compelling way that I was faced with real difficulty: neither to become immersed (as Chris was) but to retain my own thoughts and perspective, nor to stand back so far as to lose emotional contact with the power of this fantasy world. In these early sessions, it was by being receptive to the primitive and disjointed level of the play and coping with the concomitant fear that nothing that was happening made sense to me that I made contact with him, and he was able to hear and respond to what I said. The quality of the emotional contact at these moments seemed to be that I was appreciating how he felt ransacked. He could, however, make no effort at description or differentiation other than at the level of being at the mercy of forces beyond his control, and which he felt took possession of his 'self' like the wild beasts took possession of the ruined house.

Towards the end of the first term more genuine play did emerge from the turmoil of the first two months. What Chris called the 'shark' (a quite realistic crocodile, in fact) and other wild animals made the sink their own place. At each session Chris would make it his first task to fill the sink to the brim with water. The temperature had to be just right and was tested by putting a plastic bottle (like a feeding bottle, but without a teat) into it. The activity had something of the quality of a meticulous mother preparing a bottle for her baby. However, the 'babies' were swimming lions and crocodiles, which would appear briefly above the surface of the water to 'feed' from the bottle and disappear again. Their diet was a carefully controlled one of hot and cold water, with an added ingredient of what was called 'poison—not-really'. Perhaps this added ingredient was some sign of 'trouble brewing', and certainly towards the end of term the animals sent more and more of what were called 'poison bubbles' to the surface, and Chris began to be more adventurous in his water-play: on one occasion there was a flooding of the floor that was so wild I had to intervene. As well as the development of 'poison', however, it became apparent that the animals, at least, were becoming increasingly attached to water, their natural medium. There was a particularly poignant ending to the final session before the first holiday:

A baby crocodile was put with the Mummy crocodile. Chris said that the Mummy was pleased to be with the baby, but sad at the baby going away. He then placed the baby crocodile in a beaker containing water and let it 'swim' a little. He then upended it, but slowly, so that the water trickled out. Finally the 'baby' was lying, without water, on the draining board. He seemed very sad and stood looking at the scene. He said without looking at me that the Mummy wasn't near the baby. There followed a silent and prolonged attack on my watch. For at least ten minutes, seemingly paying no attention to what I said, he went for my wrist, tugging at it, trying to pull at the watchstrap, hitting the glass, trying to bite it with his teeth. He left without a word.

In many ways it was an extraordinary term. I had encountered such mindlessness, particularly near the beginning of the term, that I wondered what manner of traumatic events might have produced it. It was certainly possible to surmise that the double assault referred to earlier might have led to such internal devastation. However, whilst there was much painful material about separations that were felt so acutely that they seemed like a separation from something needed for life (the crocodile without water), there was very little to suggest that abuse had taken place. In fact, I found myself wondering whether there had actually been a sexual assault. I did not realize just what would emerge under the impact of that first 'break'.

Clinical material:
confronted by abuse

After the holiday there was an extraordinary continuity of theme. At the beginning of the first session two crocodiles were introduced to the dry sink.

> They started talking about where the water had gone. One said: 'It's no use, there's none here.' What had gone wrong? The baby crocodile, in a persistent, piping voice, asked 'the Daddy' where he had been, and the Daddy, in a deeper voice, struggled to find a reply. Chris, perhaps reflecting on the plight of the crocodile, started to talk about my holiday, at pains to find an excuse for my absence, blaming it on people who closed the clinic and not on 'good Mr Bradley'. Whilst speaking, he was trying to fill the clear plastic drinking glass, put the gorilla in it upside down, and invert the glass onto the draining board so that the gorilla would appear surrounded by water. It was a trick he had carried out easily before the holiday, but now he could not get it to work. Nevertheless, I was taken aback at the despairing way he almost shouted, 'IT WONT WORK! IT WONT WORK! IT WONT WORK!' In the context it was not clear whether he was regretting the loss of something good that he felt could not be regained, or whether he was realizing the futility of keeping bad feelings out of the room. What *was* clear was the distress, and very quickly Chris started to put his feelings into frantic action. There followed a mad dash around the room, waving a large red felt-tip pen in one hand. He paused to pick up a brown crayon, which he bit in two and held in the other hand. He crawled under my chair, but then despite my efforts to acknowledge his intense feelings about what was felt to have broken down between us he started to run around the room again. He was very excited and, still grasping the pen and the crayon, he said that 'his willie was very big—it would go from the window and reach the door'. He took a pencil and felt-tip pen from his tray and put them near me, saying that he had to go away. 'People were travelling, they were flying into space, to another planet.' He made the sound of a space ship and exaggeratedly

made steps to signify stepping out at the other end. He became quieter and filled the beaker with water. The brown crayon was dropped into it, and then Chris, looking at me, drank from it, calling it 'a good drink'. He scrupulously cleared out the bits of crayon, putting them back into his tray. He then came very close to me, became conspiratorial, and whispered, 'Put the pencil up my bum'.

The extract, from which I have omitted interpretations in order to illustrate the relentless momentum of the activity, shows the devastating effect that the first break had had on Chris. He was affected at a level that he describes vividly in terms of animals deprived of water, their natural medium. There seemed to be an historical link to the abrupt separation from mother at 9 months, and again at 2 years. But it was not possible to make this kind of link in the context of the therapy for another four years! What was much more overwhelming in the room was the extent of his distress, which was not at all alleviated by the fact that we were now back together in the room, with a whole term ahead of us. Instead, this seemed to draw attention to the fact that there had been a holiday during which the 'water supply' so necessary for a crocodile's survival had dried up. The 'move to another planet', which occurred in this session, is best understood as a search for another 'place', or kind of relationship that, he hopes, will release him from the pain of dependence on this intermittent supply, which let the crocodile down so badly. Chris' actions during the session, such as crawling underneath my chair, drinking water with a brown crayon and calling it a 'good drink', as well as his asking for a pencil to be put into his anus, all point to the fact that a world of bottoms and anal intrusion is to be chosen as this more dependable place. Furthermore, by moving himself to his perverse planet, he seems to hope that he will no longer have to be passive but to be more in control of events.

Once this 'bottom planet' had been arrived at, preparations were made by Chris to stay there for a long time. I would like to describe this very difficult phase of the therapy, which persisted for slightly more than two years. I will describe how this 'bottom world' flourished in the room and the very difficult technical problems posed by this. Also I shall highlight some of the more important issues that had to be analysed in minute detail before this young boy could begin to free himself from the effects of the abuse.

The request for me to 'put the pencil up his bum' was an urgent one, and he seemed to be genuinely perplexed that I would not want to assault him. I was asked to do so on more than one occasion after the initial refusal, and one day, perhaps thinking that I was merely being inhibited by the sounds of other people working in the Clinic, he said: 'Go on, put the pencil in my bum; they won't hear. . . . You know you want to.' Similar 'invitations' were made when he needed to be accompanied to the toilet during sessions. It was when he began to realize that I would not be seduced in this way that more provocative attempts were made. He set out to seduce me with his bottom, and, within a very short time, had begun to take down his trousers during sessions. He started to hold not a pencil but a twelve-inch ruler to the entrance of his bottom. Facing away from me, he would gyrate in front of me, saying over and over, 'Put your willie in my bottom'. When frustrated thus far, he went even further by attempting to smear me with faeces or to attack me with his feet and hands.

Despite the difficulty of coping with his deeply disturbing material and with the physical attacks, it seemed important not to forbid him to undress in the room, nor even to assault himself, once I was sure he was not in danger of causing himself physical injury. This decision raised difficult issues, and I will return to these in greater detail. Briefly, however, a key factor in the decision *not* to intervene was the compulsive nature of Chris' behaviour. I knew from regular meetings with the psychiatric social worker who saw his parents weekly that Chris was still trying to push objects into his baby brother's bottom and had frequently been caught by his father with objects in his own bottom, even under his clothes. Veto and punishment therefore had not led to any lessening of these rape/rapist enactments, and it was difficult to see how they would change unless Chris developed internal control over the impulses. Nevertheless, the decision not to forbid this behaviour but to continue the task of interpretation was easier in theory than it proved in practice.

The difficulty was that Chris showed no reservations about what
he was doing. He was eager to come into sessions so that he
could take down his trousers and insert objects. It was frightening to see 'the symptom plucking up courage' as he began to be
preoccupied with his toys. Now, however, he was looking
through them with apparently only his bottom in mind. He
dreamily invented 'pseudo-technical' vocabulary to change the
name of objects just as he was changing their use. A bit of plastic was broken from a fence that had formerly been used in connection with toy animals. Henceforth it would be named
'findermeister', presumably some reference to the way it was
used 'to find' the faeces in his bottom. More and more objects
were renamed in similar ways as he became emboldened. He
became excited when he detected the 'scent' (for this is what it
seemed to him) of faeces. During this time my strongest feeling
was of helplessness. It seemed that no matter what I said, he
entered more deeply into the world of his perversion, for, more
and more, his perceptions, his imagination, his vocabulary, his
activity were being increasingly focussed on anal abuse.

Despite this, however, it was possible to observe what went
on and to keep thinking about the internal mechanism at the
root of the perversion. The most striking aspect of what was
going on in the room was that it was very difficult to believe
that I was working with a victim of sexual abuse. My feeling
was that I was the victim being abused and the one who had to
defend myself constantly from attack. At times it was only by
reflecting on the attack that I was being made to bear that I
could remain in touch with the Chris who did resent having
been made a victim of abuse and expressed this by making himself the aggressor instead of the helpless victim. Although this
wish to be the aggressor raised worrying questions about the
future, particularly if therapy should have to be ended prematurely, before it could be resolved, it was at least a relief,
within the context of therapy, to know that there was a part of
Chris that did reject the humiliation of being a victim. Much
more worrying were the moments when he invited penetration,
seeming strangely receptive to such thoughts and surprised that
I did not comply. These moments were very much in contrast to
those when I was being attacked directly. In these more 'reflec-

tive' moments he would take down his trousers and begin the ritual by choosing an implement. He would then 'produce' an erection by inserting an object. He rarely touched his penis, but, instead, with something like awe on his face, he would look from the object, such as a ruler, back to his penis, as if the intention were to achieve a straight line, and with his penis being seen as a continuation of the inserted ruler. When he had achieved the angle he wanted, there was clear enjoyment on his face, and it was then most of all that my words seemed such a feeble way of combating his absorption. Even when he did not actually have an object inside his bottom, there were times when he would be very preoccupied, lying face-down on the couch. It seemed at these moments as if no ideas or thoughts were possible that were not to do with being penetrated. Much later in the therapy—after five years, in fact—Chris talked about 'the man' (the rapist) having put an egg in his head, and one day it would hatch and he would be like King Kong and break down New York. The sentence conveys very dramatically the peculiar complexity of a situation where as well as identifying with the act of aggression, he is also the receptive one: the victim of rape as well as being the admirer of the big ruler.

Clinical material: moments of change

Occasionally Chris would seem troubled by what he was doing. I found that by recognizing such moments for what they were, and at the same time being very careful not to seem too enthusiastic about their appearance, it was possible for different kinds of behaviour to appear in the room. There was a particularly important week six months after therapy began.

He came in for the first session of the week and lay on the divan facing away from me, supporting his head on his hands. After this preoccupied beginning, he stood up and started to undo the belt of his trousers. It seemed as if yet again, as usual, he was about to go into his bottom, but then I noticed that his fingers were less adept than usual, and he was fumbling at the belt, not succeeding in opening the buckle. He looked at me, saying, 'only pretending', but continued to fumble at the belt. I spoke to that part of him which showed hesitancy, saying that it seemed as if his fingers weren't sure that they wanted to do that today. He stopped immediately and went to the sink, where he filled the plastic bottle three or four times as he gulped the water down. Suddenly he poured a bottleful on the floor. Very quickly I had to intervene as bottle and hand desperately flung water on the floor, making a flood. Even when I turned off the tap, he continued to spit on the floor. Later, when he had calmed a little, he returned to the sink and played with the animals, but this again broke down, and he held the filled bottle against his front, letting it pour onto the floor, as if peeing. Soon he took his trousers down and made his penis erect, but just as quickly pulled them up again. The rest of the session was spent between making a terrible mess in the room and preventing himself from pulling down his trousers.

The action in the room was so frantic that it was only afterwards that I was properly able to reflect on the importance of what had happened. I had seen Chris try to prevent the attack on his bottom by frantically turning to a feeding bottle, or 'feeding breast'. This in turn was denigrated by using it as if it were 'wee', but for the first time I had witnessed him fighting hard to express anger and helplessness more directly, instead of by turning away to an exciting and absorbing bottom place. There were at least incipient signs that the bottom was not as comfortable a place as it had been. And perhaps this sense of unease led, later in the week, to Chris being able to distance himself sufficiently from the assault and to represent to me for the first time his recollection of what had happened at the time of the sexual assault.

He came into the room in dreamy fashion. He played with the animals for a while, but then lost interest in them. He seemed to lose awareness of my presence and stood facing the wall, leaning against the 'working top'. In dreamlike fashion, speaking in an artificially adult voice, he said, 'Keep still, little boy, and I will give you something very nice in your bottom'. He wriggled his bottom as he spoke, but there was a smile on his face as if whatever he was reliving at that moment was something pleasurable. But I felt close to tears. It was as if I were experiencing the indignation at being so abused, which Chris didn't feel at that moment. Certainly the very detailed description of the man involved, including details of his build and facial characteristics, whilst seeming realistic, held no sense of pain. Indeed, there was pleasure at the recollection that the man used to give him sweets. Towards the end of the session, however, other feelings about the incident came into the room. At first these were expressed directly, at me, as he threatened to hit me and became provocative, saying that I wouldn't be able to defend myself if he hit me. Towards the end of the session he started to talk about the man again and said that he shouldn't have done what he did. Finally, at the end of the session, he said that if he saw him he would like to hit him in the face.

Clinical material:
building an alliance

It is striking to see how Chris' experience of the assault had become confused, and in particular how affectionate memories of how he would be given sweets by the man had, over the course of time, been made separate from anger towards the man about the assault. In the clinical material given above, affectionate memories of the sweets could be attributed directly towards the assaulter, but angry feelings about what had happened were expressed in the first instance against me and only then could they be directed towards 'the man'. It was the first indication that there were complex feelings about the assault: that there was anger at being abused and the wish to retaliate, as well as pleasurable memories. It was possible for the therapy room to become the place where the different strands of this complexity could be explored.

Often within the time of a single session there would be both frantic efforts to get gratification by abusing himself or trying to make me do so and also heroic efforts not to abuse himself or me. It was particularly difficult for Chris to find something else to do when he was trying to turn away from abuse, since all his inventiveness and imagination had been developed around 'the art and technique' of abuse. Although he had toys, paper, and plasticine, he did not seem to have any ideas about what to do with them, and this seemed to make the choice between 'abuse' and 'not abuse' a very stark one. As he became less comfortable about abusing himself, it began to seem as if there was a civil war inside, to which killing himself would be one solution. The pain, which was starkly present, seemed to be concerned with a growing realization that dreadful things had happened to him, and with the efforts to overcome the wish to go on perpetuating the assault. On several occasions, after stopping himself in the very act of taking down his trousers, he made dashes for the window to fling himself out. Elsewhere outside the sessions there were several 'accidental' falls, though fortunately nothing serious happened. The despair and also the impatience with me at not being able to free him from what he called 'the bad men' were conveyed dramatically.

He seemed incredibly weary at the battle not to pull down his trousers. He made a sword and dagger out of cardboard and felt-tip pens. He handed them to me 'to kill the bad men who come into the room'. Perhaps feeling that a remark I then made was not sufficiently to the point, he took them back to sharpen them! He then turned the pencil on himself, pricking himself with it, before I could stop him. Soon after, he went to the sink and poured hot water into the beaker, saying before drinking it—DOMESTOS! KILLS GERMS DEAD! He delivered the line as if proclaiming an advert and drank it at a single gulp. With that he slammed the beaker onto the draining board.

There certainly was pain conveyed in this play, but also, I think, a sense of achievement at being able to symbolize the conflict in this dramatic way. This seemed to encourage the search for play that was not only concerned with abuse. At first he used the geography of the room to help him. He would also climb up to the top window-ledge with animals and his plastic feeding bottle, as if it were some attempt to reach a place that could not be contaminated by the events that still continued to fill the rest of the room at other times. On this shelf very 'ordinary' contact between *tame* animals, such as horses and cows, took place. The play, interspersed by much drinking from the bottle, was nothing dramatic in itself. In fact, conversation was monosyllabic, and the scene itself consisted mainly of a small, dependent animal simply having a 'parent' or 'parents'. What gave a dramatic quality to these seemingly trite scenes is that they were the first genuine attempts, after 'rape' had entered the room, to explore a relationship between 'adult' and 'child' animals that was not based on abuse. I think tame animals were used in these scenes because they were felt to be safe, but there was also something aseptic or 'tame' about this early play, which took place in an attic of the mind where imagination had not yet been able to follow. His word for this place was 'heaven', but it did not have the enjoyment and imagination attached to it that was to be found in 'hell', which was the rest of the room. After a brief spell of play with the tame animals he would tire of them, or finish his drink. Sometimes they would be pushed down onto the floor, where their prompt fate would be to be eaten up or 'buggered'. The bottle, too, which had helped to sustain the play on the window-ledge, would be used to mess up the floor, and on one occasion the contrast between 'top' and 'bottom' was made absolutely clear as he undressed, held the filled bottle to his bottom, and said, 'have a drink, lovely bottom'.

In other ways, too, positive contact, painfully established on the top, would be demolished in the bottom part of the room, and increasingly a relationship with me that had been forged during a session would be broken down at the end. If I announced that it was nearly time to go, he would glance at the clock and say, 'Oh, it's bum time' and take down his trousers. Or, more frantically, faced with the 'nothingness' after the session, he would try to leave the room after putting a wooden brick next to his bottom, held in place by a paper towel, like a 'paper nappy'.

The crocodile came to be very important in this destructiveness, just as the crocodile play had been very important before the first holiday. There was an insight into this before a summer holiday.

At the beginning of the session I made a chart, giving details of the holiday. At first Chris was co-operative and carefully counted up to see how many sessions remained. Soon the mood changed. I 'became' Stupid Head, then Monkey Head, then I was offering him 'bum time'. He picked up a bottle and said he was going to make poison. I said that the poison was already being made and traced for him what had happened. He said loudly, 'It's an inside poison'. His face had a grin on it, and he seemed to like the idea, but his expression quickly changed, becoming wolfish. As I watched, he started to rotate his hips and then his stomach went into convulsions and his expression changed as he seemed to lose control of his stomach. I began to think that he might actually have lost control, but then he rammed the crocodile against his stomach. His stomach was vibrating, and this seemed to be passed onto the crocodile, which in turn started to vibrate. He flipped it away from him onto its back on the draining board, where it flipped and flopped like a landed fish. Chris' face looked quite triumphant as he grabbed hold of it and rammed its tail into the bottle, which had been intended for poison. The convulsions were allowed to pass down the crocodile into the water, and then the top of the bottle was screwed on. It was only then that he seemed able to think about what had happened, and he seemed genuinely to be in awe. I shall try to reproduce his comments—'Look at the power, its got power, hasn't it? It has got power power isn't it? hasn't it got power? It is power isn't it, isn't it full of power? Power isn't it? Hasn't it got power?'

The 'landing' of the crocodile seemed to be an attempt to look at the destructiveness associated with holidays, or separations. But unlike the scene between the two crocodiles at the time of the first holiday, there was an ability to look at the feelings engendered and eventually to get control of them. Towards the end of the session he showed that his mind was able to work on the problem by saying, 'We have thirteen sessions, then we miss six, then we start again'. The crocodile had got back into the bottle, and in the statement 'we start again' there seemed to be hope that there would be water on the return.

Discussion and summary

The material in this chapter has been drawn mainly from the first few years of intensive therapy, now nearing its end after eight years. It seemed that Chris had ceased to abuse himself outside the therapy room after the first year in therapy, but it was not until the third year that such behaviour eventually ceased in sessions, and it has not since reappeared. During the following years the focus of concern shifted from the experience of the actual abuse to an exploration of the many ways in which abuse and deprivation continue to affect development. I shall draw together some of the more important of these issues.

Oral material was very striking. As I mentioned, when the first break occurred there was a direct link between the baby crocodile, saying that the Mummy would miss the baby, and the attack on my watch. It seemed as if already there was uncertainty about the ability to keep the contact alive during the holiday, although surely he was attempting to do so by immersing the crocodile in water, its natural medium. This attempt failed, so that the departure to 'bottom-land' was driven by the conviction that the empty mouth can be substituted for by a filled bottom. Thus later in therapy the ends of sessions when a feeding contact was felt to be withdrawn were prepared for by the cylindrical object fixed in place by the paper 'nappy'. In this context the penis/object in the bottom may be seen as a nipple/mouth substitute, which persists as a particularly powerful perversion because it is felt to avoid the pain of separation. The long struggle, involving intense mental suffering, seemed related above all to undoing this artificial 'solution' to the pain of separation. The effect of the abuse was exacerbated by the fact that the assault had taken place so soon after a long separation from mother, with the added experience of the tonsillectomy. One may speculate that the sexual abuse by an adult while in his role as a carer and accompanied as it was by kindness and the gift of sweets seemed, perversely, to be experienced as an act of rescue from the bad experience associated with the mouth. It seemed that the initial discomfiture with 'bottom-land' was persecutory in nature. His attacks on me and remembered fragments from interpretations 'visited' him again in the form of nightmares and 'bad men' determined to kill him. He was so much in the grip of the perversion that it really did seem as if the loss of it would be like a death, since it had also drawn to itself many of his qualities and talents. This had made him fear that they had become so bound up with the perversion that they would not be able to survive outside its framework. Certainly there was something anaemic about his early efforts to establish play at the 'top' of the room. The exciting quality of the 'bottom' part of the room, with all its inventiveness of language and action, could only be combated by quantity. At the 'top', efforts to inject imagination and inventiveness into the play with the 'tame' animals were sustained by frequent drinks from the bottle of water, and it will be remembered that Chris turned to three or four bottles of water, drunk in quick succession, when attempting to fight against unbuckling his belt. The need for quantity was reminiscent of his mother's memory of the early feeding relationship, when she felt bombarded by a mouth that could never get enough milk. My experience was that the frantic attempt to consume large quantities of water left little or no space for attention to anything else. It seems as if one quality of the early feeding relationship was that preoccupation as to whether there would be enough milk to sustain life entered the relationship to such an extent that there was little space for other feelings to be contained, and, it seems, little space for 'reverie', such was the urgency at the level of survival. An extremely important part of the therapy, and one reason for its long duration, was the struggle for a maternal object that could prove resilient enough against virulent attack and later be sufficiently containing to allow an imaginative relationship to develop. The significance of the 'taming' of the crocodile was that the ability to sustain a relationship over a long separation was internalized, and it did lead to sustained attempts to bring imaginative qualities to bear on the relationship.

It can be seen how the abuse became tangled up with the effects of a very difficult infancy, but also profoundly affected his development. One important reason for his referral to the clinic was that soon after the abuse, Chris has started to abuse his baby brother and other children and to abuse them in the bottom, where he himself had been abused. This gives a clear picture of how the victim of abuse became the aggressor and made others bear the pain of sadistic intrusion. It will be remembered that because of the compulsive nature of the attacks I decided not to forbid Chris from undressing in the therapy room, nor even from attacking himself. In allowing this to take place, it was possible to analyse behaviour that otherwise would have continued to have a considerable impact at an instinctual level. Because of the potential for confusion in Chris' mind as to why he was not being forbidden to do things he would have been smacked for at home, it was very important to make it clear that I was not condoning the perverse activity that was being brought into the room, but that I was trying to understand why he did it. It was very important that the analysis of this behaviour took place within a framework strong enough to withstand virulent attack.

As therapy developed, identification with the violent aggression, and a sadistic wish to inflict pain on me and render me a helpless victim, all became worryingly clear. For a long time it was difficult not to have the foreboding that later Chris would pass from child abuse victim to adult abuser. However, identification as an active abuser, while alarming, did at least suggest the presence of anger at the abuse, even though this had to be pushed into others. A far greater cause for concern in many ways was the silent, almost reverential acceptance of the 'ruler' and the passivity that it entailed. Excitement had come to be associated with the act of being penetrated from behind, and there were clear signs that the sexual abuse would later have led to a sexuality of aggression either as perpetrator or subject of anal penetration.

Among many possible consequences of this identification was the effect on his intelligence. I have described the mindlessness of the first term, which tallies with his teacher's description of him as 'being in a world of his own, clearly unable to make academic progress, and of below-average intelligence'. It seems to me that a more recent report, which speaks of a lively ability and of flair, particularly in creative skills and group work that features discussion, illustrates how the ability to take in information and to make links between facts has developed considerably as the underlying suspicion about what 'taking in' and 'making links' entails has been analysed.

Some material from a session about five years after the beginning of therapy illustrates well some of the complex issues described here:

He came into the room, seeming diffident, and said that he wanted to tell me a story. He stood beside me and said that a bad man had captured a little girl. She screamed and screamed, but it was no good. Nobody heard her, and he carried her away to a special underground cave that he had got ready. At this point he drew the cave and described how there was plenty of food and water, so he didn't have to go to the shops. There was also a cooker, which would let smoke out at the surface in such a way that no one would guess that there was a cave there. The outside was also a swamp, so no one would find it by accident. The bad man knew a special path through the swamp, so he could come when he wanted. When he came he 'fucked' the girl in the bum. He used to like it when she cried and would tie her up when he went away so that she would be waiting when he came back. But a good man was looking for her. He didn't know exactly where she was hidden, but he managed to find a sewer that went near the cave. It was so stinky that he had to put a mask on, and then he had to crawl through the shit. He had another mask for the girl, and when he got into the cave he cut her free and put it on her so that she could crawl back through the sewer with him. After they had gone the man came back. He was very mad she had gone, but he couldn't do anything.

The story is a complex one—a condensed version of issues that had already emerged over five years and would continue to be worked through for years afterwards. The impact of the abuse is catastrophic for the sexuality of the victim. It is a 'girl' who is captured, and a girl, not a boy, who starts the long way back through the sewer, aided by the breathing space given by therapy. Of course the issue of sexual identity has been worked with directly, but do we know what the long-term consequences for sexual identity will be for a boy who had had to be the receiver of a penis? We are given a glimpse of why the perversity became entrenched in the description of the well-stocked underground cave where Chris could be part of a scene where he was at once the aggressor inflicting pain through anal penetration and also the helpless, passive little girl who could do nothing but wait. The journey back through the sewer, aided by nothing but a gas mask necessary for survival, is a tribute to the courage and endurance that this young boy has shown in tackling the effects of his very traumatic early years.

CHAPTER SIXTEEN

Psychotherapy with two children in local authority care

Julia, a neglected child, and a 4-year-old's view of sexual abuse

Margaret Hunter

The mental and emotional damage encountered in the two children about whom this chapter is written are painful examples of the kinds of harsh deprivation or mindless abuse that may bring children into care. Mrs Hunter's account of the history of her work with each of these small girls provides a vivid portrayal of the nature of the damage effected by the experience of such relationships. It also discovers the strengths with which each eventually finds in herself trust, understanding, and real concern.

[R.S.]

Breaking through to hope:
Julia and Susie

The two children about whom this chapter is written are two of the many who are neglected and abused by their families to the point where law intervenes and the Local Authority assumes parental rights over them. They become children 'in care' of the Local Authority. As workers in this field become more able to recognize and intervene in family situations of sexual abuse and extreme neglect, there is a growing need to address and help to mend the inner turmoil of these child victims. For we all now recognize that removing a 3-year-old from her father's prostitution of her, removing a starved 18-month-old from her parents' neglect, is only a first step towards safety and healing for these children. It is difficult but sometimes possible to support and guide abusing parents to better care for their children. Failing this, it is difficult but often possible to find new homes and better parents for these children. As workers in this field have long recognized, however, the children themselves often continue to have difficulty adapting to their happier circumstances, and too many of them will compulsively provoke in their new circumstances the rejection and the abuse of their early lives.

Child psychotherapy with these abused children gives us both understanding and insight into why this happens and can, as in the cases of Julia and Susie, offer a way out of these painful repetitions. In the Local Authority where I work we have come to recognize that some children have been so damaged by their past that their future development is at risk. In these cases social and residential workers find themselves planning a future for a child with strong reservations as to its success because the child involved is so aggressive or rejecting or unreachable. The problem that was in the family becomes lodged in the child itself and threatens to subvert all the external sources of help.

Julia was such a child. Rescued from a situation of life-endangering neglect to a caring home, Julia remained aloof and impervious to the attempts of her foster parents to make her 'at home' with them. She seemed incapable of emotion, of caring for those devoted to caring for her. When she was referred for psychotherapy at the age of 7, her social worker feared a breakdown of her foster-placement, with all the consequent pain, upheaval, and failure this would inflict on Julia, the foster parents, and all of those involved.

Susie, on the other hand, was referred for help as soon as she came into care, at the age of 3½ years. As a child exposed to sexual abuse who was to lose both parents because they were sentenced to imprisonment, it was already evident to the 'care team' that Susie would need special help to come to terms with her painful experiences.

Where a child psychotherapist is working within the Social Services, psychotherapy can be provided as part of the overall planning for a child, and the resources of the Local Authority can be utilized to support it. Both Julia and Susie attended sessions for over five years, Susie three times a week, Julia twice a week, and both therapies had planned terminations. Susie and Julia were brought to their sessions by social work assistants and residential staff, with a very low absence rate. Despite the trauma and pain that can be glimpsed in these two children's stories, my colleagues and I have felt the satisfaction of enabling them, by our group effort, to temper their pain with hope.

Julia:
'A frozen child'

Presenting problems

Julia was 7 years old when she was referred to me for help. The referral came from Julia's social worker in response to persistent difficulties her foster-parents of four years were experiencing with her.

Mr and Mrs Clark were very anxious about Julia's lack of development in their care. They found her stilted, aloof, unable to show emotion of any kind except for theatrical outbursts of noisy attention-seeking. She was difficult to control or to calm, talked a great deal in an agitated, often senseless way, and outside the home was often loud and rude to adults. Julia functioned poorly at school, being disruptive and inattentive. There was considerable doubt about her intellectual ability, for despite a pronounced reading ability, her comprehension was poor and she seemed to make little progress in her school work. At home the Clarks found her clinging and unable to play with her siblings, asking for constant reassurance during the simplest activities. When playing with her dolls, Julia always pulled their hair and played at drowning them.

But perhaps the most important facet of the foster-parents' difficulties with Julia was her lack of emotion in relation to them. Mrs Clark described Julia's self-conscious resolving, 'I must kiss Mummy good-night', which would then be carried out. But there was no show of spontaneous affection, no warmth to her, no coming for comfort or love. 'She isn't like the others', Mrs Clark grieved; 'you can't feel anything from her'.

Early history

Julia was the first child born to Mr and Mrs Evans, an educationally sub-normal (ESN) mother and a father described as having 'low intelligence'. Julia weighed 3lb 3oz at birth and was tube-fed for fourteen days. She was then bottle-fed, and there were constant feeding difficulties at home. She was admitted to hospital on four separate occasions in the first ten months of life for 'failure to thrive'. She gained weight in hospital. A baby sister, Anne, was born to the Evans's exactly one year after Julia's birth. Five-and-a-half weeks later an alarmed health visitor arranged an emergency hospital admission for Anne, who was severely dehydrated. Anne suffered kidney failure and died. The coroner's verdict was 'death due to natural causes'.

For the next five months a social worker and health visitor visited the home frequently. Julia had marked periods of weight loss, and there was no progress in her gaining weight. The home was described as dirty and chaotic, and Julia was frequently alone in her cot for long periods in a darkened upstairs room. There were allegations that Julia was being left alone in the house. Five months after the death of her infant sister, Julia was admitted to hospital in a comatose state. A 'place of safety' order was taken the same day, and care proceedings were instigated.

Despite her fragile body, baby Julia clung to life. With intensive nursing her weight was gradually restored, and she was received into care at a large children's home in the borough. At 18 months she was felt to be at a 6-month stage of development, sitting but neither walking or talking. Rapid physical progress was made over the ensuing months. She was walking just before the age of 2 years and talking in sentences at 2 years.

It was shortly before her third birthday that the Clarks had taken her into foster care, and she had seemed to adapt immediately and without upset to her new home.

'A baby too naughty to be seen'

The first few sessions introduced me to a lively, chattering 7-year-old who, despite her evident nervousness, soon took control of the room as if it were her rightful kingdom. I say 'the room' because there was something markedly wrong in her relation to my presence in the room. It is true that she talked, and yet her talk was constant, requiring no answer from me, and was less directed to me than it seemed to be addressed to an unseen audience she held in her mind. Many of my replies to her sank into an impenetrable blankness such that I did not know whether or not she had heard me. When she did answer or respond to my remarks, it very often was as if she had received the remarks from the room rather than from me. She did not look at me. Her eyes slid off me, she talked past me, through me. The effect of this was so powerful that I wrote after one session: 'One of us isn't here and sometimes I'm not sure if it's her or me.' It is difficult to give an impression of these early sessions. My notes are full of action, her abundant story-telling and play-acting of fantasy was rich and varied, and she threw herself into her parts with evident relish and energy. And yet the impression on me was chilling: something somewhere was dead.

I will quote at length from my notes of our sixth meeting. It was in this session that Julia clearly demonstrated her encapsulation in her infant self, deprived and starved, endlessly having to compensate in fantasy, or feel endlessly condemned to a life in a darkened room.

Session Notes

[Julia opens her box, prattling happily. The impression is of excitement to the point of distraction at being here, but no apparent response to me. She has not yet looked at me and seems to ignore my words.]

Julia: 'I'm going to play that game that I did last time. I told my Mum all about that game I played . . . [taking out family dolls] . . . good he's got his trousers back on . . . and here's the naughty Mummy. They're going to live in a new house because she's so horrible—that will be the new house . . . [opens the dolls' house]. I'll leave the roof off, to let more light in. This baby the Mummy's going to put it away. It's too naughty to be seen—it's got to go upstairs. Now where's the darkest corner?'

[Julia tries out various corners; none will satisfy. Finally she sits her on the roof beams.]

Mrs Hunter: 'This baby has to be in a dark corner?'

Julia: 'He can see everything from here . . .'

[She takes out the cot and another baby from her box.]

Julia: 'This baby doesn't want to see anyone. She's too naughty but the blanket is right over her face . . .'

[She fixes the cot bars so that one is on top of the baby beneath the blanket.]

Julia: '. . . Mrs Hill let me sit in the front of the car.'

I talk to her about her wish to 'sit in the front' with me, to not be shut out during breaks between our sessions: about her baby-self that she feels is excluded because she is 'too naughty to be seen' and wishes to be put on the roof-top, where she can see everything. I also talk about part of herself that wants to hide away from me, the baby-self that feels she is cut off from me by blankets and bars.

Julia: 'Yes. She'll look through the bars . . .' [said absently, as if to an inner voice].

Three weeks later Julia began to beg me for food in her session. She crawled on the floor, begging piteously and maintaining that she would starve unless I fed her. Although I was tempted to do so, I did not give her any food, feeling that it was important to empathize with her hunger but not interpret it materially: she was no longer starving physically but psychically, and this hunger can only be fed with understanding.

Snow White

In the subsequent two years of therapy, we were caught up in a flowing and ebbing tide: waves of torrential flooding, denigrating abuse poured out of her and into the room; and then, when I felt I could tolerate no more, small and sudden shows of affection and shy attempts to give me presents made the task suddenly worthwhile. A favourite occupation of hers was to pour cup after cup of water on the floor, laughing cruelly at the 'drowned babies' whom she crushed under her heels. Perhaps these were the rival babies drowning in their surfeit of milk from which she was so cruelly deprived.

On one memorable occasion for me Julia unrelentingly attacked, denigrated, and humiliated 'the babies', attacked the mother-doll's breasts with the sharp point of a pencil, and forced a sharp scissor between the mother-doll's legs. The babies were made to put their heads into the toilet to eat their food whilst she laughed and sneered at them. Instead of being able to interpret this, I had a sudden terrible realization that I was about to be sick. I had to forcibly distract myself by looking out of the window for a few moments. The feeling passed, and I was again able to talk with her about a mother who bears babies but does not feed them, who forces them to resort to a toilet for food, to their own waste products because the life-giving milk is withheld.

I detail these events because I think equally with the attempt to understand and interpret this child's fantasies has to be the ability to endure them. As is so vividly documented in *Psychotherapy with Severely Deprived Children*: 'an important function of the therapist seems to have been to experience and to bear and gradually reflect on intolerable anxieties on behalf of the patients. It is only after a considerable period of time that the patients are able to take back some of these feelings and begin to come to terms with them' (Boston & Szur, 1983).

When I have witnessed the growing capacity of Julia to modify her sadism and to allow her vulnerable, feared-to-be-unloveable baby-self emerge, I recognize that it is because I have somehow managed to both feel her pain and *not* to vomit it out.

Now Julia very often quietened at my words. Behind a chair or behind the sofa, she carefully built 'barriers' to keep me out. She pulled the curtains to darken the room and used a pillow with a rubber cover as an idealized love-object. She was at her most contemptuous of me when she masturbated on this pillow, burping and blowing raspberries whilst she told me, 'Aah, here's what I really, really, love'.

This made such a painfully graphic picture to me—this child alone in her cot, a rubber sheet—or was it her rubber pants—that she had to turn to in the darkening room? She had used her own body for comfort, burping to symbolically expel from her mouth the treacherous mother's milk. Despite my sympathy, these sessions were hard to bear. She was denigratory and attacking, she echoed back my words as I spoke, breaking my train of thought and preventing me from thinking. She made sudden sallies at me, spitting in my face or throwing a hard ball of plasticine at me.

Julia attempted over and over to reverse the situation to identify herself with the powerful, satiated mother, to be 'the queen', as she identifies this character. These are attempts to extricate herself from the unbearable pain and danger of being a helpless, starving child.

And so the theme of 'the queen' emerged and grew. One day Julia came into her session and looked into the mirror, chanting, 'Mirror mirror on the wall, who is the fairest of them all? Me, of course!' She vividly enacted the cruel stepmother's attempt to kill Snow White but told me: 'Only in this story she doesn't win, and Snow White is queen.' In subsequent sessions she makes herself a crown and strides up and down the room, ordering me to serve her and complaining—which causes us both sudden hilarity—at the 'poor service you get from servants these days!' She puts a small chair on top of her usual seat so that she is 'higher than me' in the room.

Now often entire sessions were spent with her rushing to her box, glaring at me suspiciously, and putting on her 'crown'. She adopted a loud, theatrical, overbearing personality, shouting over my words when I tried to speak to her, 'magicking' me silent with whispered incantations and gestures. She played out murders of evil despots and of good rulers and was haunted by ghosts, whom she triumphantly re-killed. Often I was reduced to an amazed audience as she left the room as triumphant and as bullying as she had entered it.

But at last another theme emerged—a game in which she desired my co-operation. 'I sit on this chair, my throne, with the crown on and you try to steal up behind me and get the crown. If you get it, then you can be the queen. But if I see you, you have to stop', she tells me. 'What is this game called?', I asked on one occasion. 'Oh, it's called "The Queen's Headache".'

And so I was able to talk to Julia about her suspiciousness of me, my 'queenliness' in making her come and go and her determination to master me, to reverse our roles as she saw them, to 'queen it' over me. And I could point to the 'headache' that such an attempt produced in her, her constant fear of my retaliation, a potentially endless rivalry between us. I was able to tell her about her cold 'Snow White' self, who felt cruelly betrayed by her mother and now by me and who wanted to rob and plunder from her mother/queen and become a queen herself. But the queen she becomes in fantasy is an evil one who is cruel, jealous, imperious because the child usurping the mother's position is angry, envious, and possessive, and these characteristics follow her into the fantasy.

Pinocchio

I am going to describe a series of events that took place two-and-a-half years after my initial encounter with Julia. These events brought together, in a cohesive form, what had been present in many threads woven in and out of our time together. These events summarize for me Julia's working-through of her desire to kill the mother/me and cut herself off from me or any mother.

This session followed shortly after the Christmas break. Julia had recapitulated, in the first few sessions after the break, her barrier-building games and had been particularly manic, somersaulting around the room and dancing on the table, ending several sessions with provocative scenes of masturbation. On this occasion, however, she entered quietly, with a sad, preoccupied air.

Session notes

[Julia gives me a gift of a painting—about a boy trapped inside a toothpaste factory, she tells me.]

Julia: 'I'm not going to build a barrier any more.'

[Julia sets up her 'game'. It opens with a mother and daughter arguing over homework. The mother insists, 'you must use your brain, dear'. The daughter does not want to, and she uses a computer. When the mother challenges the daughter, Julia, playing the part of the daughter, whips her to death with the plastic pillow cover.]

Julia: 'Whip! Whip! Whip! Now she's dead!' [She quickly munches on some crisps, which she has put out ready.] 'Hallo, Daddy! Mummy's dead!'

Julia [as Dad]: 'Is she, dear?'

Julia [as girl]: 'What do you want for tea, Daddy? Here's some crisps. Let's watch TV. You don't want to watch silly old sport, do you? Oh good! A cowboy film. Mmmm . . . mm!' [eating crisps and acting well-satisfied]. 'I think I'll go to bed now, Daddy, dear. Can I draw in bed?'

Daddy: 'Oh yes, dear'

Girl: 'My Daddy always lets me draw in bed.'

[She draws intently, and I ask 'what'.]

Julia: 'It's Pinocchio.'

Mrs Hunter: 'Pinocchio's father wanted him to use his brain.'

Julia: 'Yes, I know. But he didn't. He ran off to the land of fairgrounds.'

Mrs Hunter: Pinocchio also wanted to be a real boy, didn't he?'

Julia: 'Yes. He had to do something special—I forget what—to become a real boy in the end.'

Now I take up with Julia her wish in this game to be in the land of fairgrounds—i.e., doing whatever she wants to do. She kills her mother in this game, just like Pinocchio, who turned against a father who wished him to work.

Julia tries to ignore me but finds she 'cannot sleep' and adds a Jiminy Cricket character in her drawing. I talk about her feeling guilty: Jiminy Cricket is Pinocchio's conscience.

The session gains pace as she tries manically to have 'endless fun'.

She watches 'Jim'll Fix It' on 'television' and rounds on me in fury.

Julia: 'You see, Mrs Hunter, that's what I want—"Jim'll Fix It", not bloody Jiminy Cricket!'

If I recapitulate this session, I think the meaning of it unfolds like this: Julia comes in downcast and feeling trapped inside the angry barriers she has built against me. She is more and more finding herself in the lonely, darkened room of her infancy, less able to escape into distracting fantasy. She gives me a gift that communicates her trapped self and tells me she has resolved to not 'build barriers' any more. In the game she sets up, there is a dialogue between Julia as a daughter and her mother. It is interesting that the version of 'mother' that she focuses on is one who insists that Julia uses 'her brain and not a computer'. I think this is a reference to my thinking function as a therapist encouraging Julia to think and discouraging her from using an 'automated' self, since to think or to feel are both too hazardous to her. So she comes to a point where she wishes to 'kill the mother'—to cut herself off from a thinking, working mother–daughter relationship. Her panic at an oral level is quite clearly and concretely felt—to kill the mother is to starve, so she immediately fills her mouth with crisps, her own version of self-provided food.

Now she turns to a fantasy Daddy, who is indulgent and collusive and whom she can manipulate to share her indulgence in 'automated' pleasure—watching television. Yet when it comes to the night-time of her game, Julia does not sleep. She sits in bed and draws Pinocchio. The rest of the session—which I have much abridged here—is taken up by the importance of this Pinocchio association in Julia's mind. Pinocchio, the wooden boy, tried to cut himself off from a caring, thinking parent who wishes him to learn. Those who know the story will know that when Pinocchio has engineered a situation in which his father is falsely imprisoned, he returns to the house and gloats over his freedom and his enjoyment of his father's bed. It is at this point that 'Jiminy Cricket', the symbol of Pinocchio's conscience, visits him and warns him of his eventual downfall. That Julia identified herself with Pinocchio in this game is the certain sign of her feelings of guilt at 'killing the mother'. There is also the important theme of woodenness here. Julia has already told me in an earlier session, 'I want to become a REAL girl', so it is not stretching the analogy to find that the Pinocchio story is of very great significance to her. She tells me in this session: '[Pinocchio] had to do something special—I forget what—to become a real boy in the end.' What Pinocchio had to do in the story was to search for and find his father in order to become real. It is Pinocchio's dawning sense of concern for his father that sets him on a path to learning and becoming at last a 'real' boy. So, too, with Julia. She perceives me as the one who prevents her from being able to live in perpetual 'fairground land', and finally she rounds on me and accuses: 'that's what I want—"Jim'll Fix It" not bloody "Jiminy Cricket"!'. That is, she wants a collusive, magical, manic solution to her dilemma, not this dawning sense of conscience, caring, guilt—an amazingly clear example of the struggle to attain the depressive position.

Some time later, when this theme was still being played out, Julia again rounded on me with a sudden bitter intensity. She was in the throes of longing to be near me, driven back over and over again by sudden eruptions of hatred. She came towards me one day to show me her picture but suddenly stopped as if struck. She scribbled on a piece of paper and wordlessly handed it to me. It read 'I hate you'. As I talked about how she did, indeed, hate me the more she allowed herself to notice me, she announced, with her old theatrical skill: 'A trial! A trial! That's what we'll have!' And so it was that for four sessions she created a 'courtroom', drew up a list of charges, and prepared her 'case for the prosecution'. I was to be on trial for my life, charged with a varying and sometimes confused list of crimes. My major crime was felt to be 'being big, like a queen'. Subsidiary crimes were 'being angry in the court' and 'seeing other children'.

In this way this spirited little girl seriously considered her case against me. She had changed from that cold, unnoticing child who, entering my room three years previously, had made me feel I was not there, to this angry but composed plaintiff for justice. She was quite serious, and the day she pronounced me 'guilty' and sentenced me 'to death', she looked quite white and shaken. Now she prepared a weapon, a special weapon designed to kill me. It was made of a spoon with many sharp objects tied to it. I noted that this was a feeding-tool, a spoon, and talked quietly of her awful early feeding experiences and how she must have wished to visit back on Mummy that pain and grief and starvation. I had leave to talk a great deal in these sessions, for as a condemned prisoner she did not hide her sorrow at my fate. And so she could put off the hour of my execution no longer. She disappeared behind a cupboard door for several minutes. When she emerged, she was quiet and downcast. What was wrong, I asked. Falteringly she told me there was something about this weapon she had not realized '. . . It will, if I use it, break you into smithereens, it can really kill you . . . the only thing is—it also hurts the person who uses it.'

And so the weapon was put away, and Julia, the almost wooden girl, discovered love. For she could not kill the therapist she hated, without killing the therapist she loved. And by her cool calculations to rid herself of me, she discovered something inside herself that was bound to me, that would hurt with my hurt, that would feel destroyed at my destruction. So, like Pinocchio, she was on her way to becoming her 'real girl' at last.

Epilogue

Julia improved beyond recognition in her school work, allowing some of her imaginative and creative abilities to be harnessed to tasks outside her consuming fantasies. When she was 8½ years old, an educational assessment had found her to be of borderline ESN ability and suggested that an ESN(M) school would be appropriate. However, a year later, she tested well within the limits for normal schooling, and by age 13 she was considered 'well above average' by her teachers. Mr and Mrs Clark have noticed some changes in her: she has cried for the first time in the many years they have known her, and she expresses sorrow on some occasions when she has earned her foster-mother's anger. She is still a constant worry to them, however. She has days when she seems to be completely inaccessible to reason or restraint, and Mr and Mrs Clark are not convinced that she would really miss them if they were to relinquish their devoted but exhausting care of her.

There are still worries for Julia's future, but there are also grounds for great hope. For if this starved, neglected child could not finally bring herself to condemn the mother who starved her and shut her out, then neither has Julia condemned herself to a life in a dark and lonely room. There are many hazards awaiting her in her journey of reconciliation, but as long as she is searching, like Pinocchio, slowly but surely she is finding her way.

Susie:

A 4-year-old's view of sexual abuse

Unlike Julia, who took many months and years to rediscover her pain, Susie at just under 4 years was in the midst of her grief when she was referred for my help.

Susie and her older sister of 10 years had been taken into care suddenly, following a night raid on her home. The police found pornographic photographs of the older sister with a number of adult males. This child had been subjected to incest since her earliest days, prostituted by her parents, and subjected to any number of sexually abusive practices. The parents and several other men were subsequently brought to trial and imprisoned.

After three months in care it was clear that the older girl was beginning to use the relationships offered to her, and a certain amount of relief began to creep into her general attitude. Susie, however, was still considered an inaccessible child who veered from independent competence to sudden collapsed bouts of crying that could last literally for hours. Behind her volatile older sister, to whom she clung and whom she obeyed without question, she looked a tired and anxious little shadow. Whilst her sister made clear that Susie had played a peripheral role in the sexual scenes common in their home, Susie never talked of these. Care staff found her placatory and superficial.

Starting therapy

In the first sessions I found Susie very much as the care staff had presented her. Her approach to me was brittle, superficially friendly, and evidently uneasy. She flitted around my room from one thing to another, darting towards me and on my lap one moment and far away the next. I was struck by the extreme fearfulness of her manner as well as the over-closeness, for she watched me constantly. She was afraid of being shut in a room with me, and I compromised initially by leaving the door ajar.

Her fright was also such that I let her leave the first session after only fifteen minutes. More than a year later, suddenly recalling these events, she confided, 'I used to think you were going to take all your clothes off, but you don't do you?' This capacity of hers for frankness and the ability to perceive and take in my attitude towards her were two of her strongest attributes. They added up, in my mind, to a child who was essentially sound but who had had to tolerate extremely disturbing events from impaired parents.

In therapy, the first activity that Susie settled to was making babies out of playdough. Beds and covers swiftly followed, so that she had soon established a veritable nursery in my room. She fought over leaving these babies in my care, so that the issue was approached head-on: Could I be trusted to look after a baby? Swiftly the issues become more painful, and we were in charge of long lines of hurt animals who were lining up to be bandaged. I was constantly accused in these sessions of being careless or inadequate to the needs of these babies, and yet there was scarcely a session without also some magnanimity and forgiveness on her part.

One day, when I said I didn't understand something, she said to me sharply, 'yes you do—look, if my mother could understand this, you certainly could!' It was the only time she referred to her mother's disability and revealed her attitude towards it—she was bitterly but forgivingly aware of her mother's dullness. I began to be aware, too, that Susie had felt loved by her mother, and that there was an undamaged core of herself that was trusting and able. Her mother did sit wretchedly in confinement, sewing soft toys for her children and sending frequent letters written by others with the signs of her laborious attempts to write her children's names. She was completely illiterate.

Reception into care:
Susie's view

In the fifth week of our sessions Susie lined up not animals or babies, but a family, with another line of 'policemen' in front and 'doctors' behind. The family members were confusingly conveyed in different cars to various destinations by policemen that turned into doctors, all of whom acted with cold purposefulness and no explanation. I asked about the details of the scene in vain. Susie barked out monosyllabic answers: 'Policeman', 'Doctor', 'Over here', 'Get there'. Some figures were knocked over in the course of play, some fell off the table; these were coldly passed over and ignored. When I enquired, she looked at me sternly and rapped out, 'probably dead', and continued in fierce silence. Towards the end of the session she suddenly demanded the sellotape bandages thrown away in earlier sessions, tried to grab her 'babies' and run from the room. When I intervened in this, she adopted the opposite course of action. She spent the last minutes of the session holding onto the table and had to be dragged, sobbing, out of the room at the end.

In this way Susie conveyed to me the traumatic arrest of her family and their separation in police custody. (The parents were in fact taken to a different police station.) But she conveyed, even more forcefully, the experience of not understanding, of bewilderment and fright and unanswered questions: I am led to ask and wonder, I am treated with blank monosyllabic responses. The fallen figures in her play 'probably dead' represent a catastrophic loss, carelessly imposed.

Little wonder that at first she becomes the fiercely protective mother she had needed that night (demanding the bandages and her babies) or that she collapses and enacts again being torn sobbing away from me, as she was from her mother.

This theme of catastrophic loss entwines with a terrible bitterness very evident in Susie. More often, in these severely traumatized children, it is present to such an extent that it prevents any solace getting through to the child: these children are deeply cynical. I think it can be understood as the adults saying that they are acting in a child's best interest but being felt to really hurt and exploit them. So Susie often presented me with events that she claimed with adult-like authority 'wouldn't hurt' or dismissed in a blank manner my description of the hurt and pain of certain actions to her play people, laughing derisively and dismissing my concerns as unfounded—'it doesn't hurt!'—very much as some children are lured into the dentist's chair.

But the dentist can ultimately be believed to be doing some good if one can trust the judgement of grownups who are known and experienced as being adequate protectors of the child. When the child is actively exploited, lied to, used to service the adults for their own ends and not in her own interests, one can see how much more difficult the task of trust becomes. So Susie regarded her reception into care with embittered cynicism. It was not rescue, but further punishment in her eyes. Susie symbolized her experience of coming into care by cutting up a folded piece of paper. At first it looked as if she would produce a doily-like circle when the paper was opened out, but we were talking about a coming break, a separation from me, and then her separation from Mum and Dad. Her cutting became ever more vehement and misplaced, she muttered, 'and there goes a brother! and there goes a sister! now an arm! now a leg—see-saw, marjory-daw, Johnnie shall have a new master.'

My attempts to verbalize these events were impatiently dismissed, and she told me, 'Wait . . . wait', until I was silent. 'Now' she breathed and with a sound of a trumpet fanfare, 'Tarra!', began to open out the folded paper. 'Do you see what we've got?' The paper fell to pieces in her hands: 'It's a . . . bloody mess.' There was a long, infinitely sad pause in which I struggled to keep tears from my eyes.

In subsequent sessions Susie was particularly angry at any show of grief from me and laughed and taunted, 'What a pity! Fucking Wanker.' The accusation was, I think, that adults are felt to claim to be sorry but to act to produce hurt. Either the therapist is seen as a sadist or as an impotent or enfeebled protector. And one has to bear being very useless when it seems as if action, active protection, is called for. This is why it is important for me to work in concert with the social worker who can attend to the more active sorting-out arrangements for the child. As a therapist, one seeks to give the child an experience of bearing helplessness and despair, not fending them off by action. So one is witness to that sadness and bitterness wherein Susie describes her unprotected life and violent tearing-away from her mother as 'a bloody mess'. Echoing a theme I have heard from many children in care, where the children's home is portrayed as a dustbin for unwanted children, Susie once sang to me with saccarine sweetness on her sister's birthday, 'happy birthday in the gutter, happy birthday to you'.

As this child began to address her feelings of loss and to struggle with them, her view of her sexual abuse began to be revealed, and a core of bitter bewilderment and anger became the focus of many sessions for the next four years.

The trauma of sexual abuse

Every session, beginning in the second month, usually at the beginning of the session but also at any time during it when she remembered, Susie would pick up two figures and throw them behind the sofa. They were thrown separately to opposite ends of the sofa, and sometimes she would underline the point by throwing down a fence between them. These figures she named as the 'monster'—a King-Kong gorilla with arms wide out—and the 'ballet dancer'—a figure that stood on one leg, arms gracefully raised. This action, once accomplished, was always ignored—she rushed on to distract my attention with something else and refused to discuss or explore the action. When later I insisted on focussing on this, I did so against a barrage of interruptions and denials and her putting her hands over her ears and over my mouth.

Meanwhile, though, I was content to follow other parts of her communications, which brought less resistance and which were more urgent. In one early memorable session, Susie left me in no doubt of the sexual scenes she had witnessed and how they served to create bitter despair in her. This is a part of the eighteenth session:

'I am going to make pink', she announced. My tentative enquiries brought me no further information. She began to mix colours, test them on paper, clean her brush, remix. Clearly, 'making pink' was a very serious and difficult aim, and I silently watched as she began to be absorbed in this process. Having found a satisfactory pink, Susie now decided to paint her nails. Initially successful, this painting began to get messier, and her expression changed from pleasure to distaste and then to anger. She ripped at the paper and threw it on the floor. The pink nails, at first admirable, had become a contaminating mess to her. It seemed that the mess crept up upon her and that in her despair she was defiantly tempted to join in with it. She struggled greatly here and said aloud, 'it is going brown', as one distracted. I pointed out that there seemed to be two parts of her struggling to express themselves; pink, pretty Susie who wants to paint her nails pink like a grown-up lady, but this gets messed up, perhaps by a baby part of herself that feels in a mess, so that the pink goes poo-ey brown and she can't quite be that pretty pink grown-up she wishes so much to be.

She knocked the water over, more by accident than design, jumped up swiftly and laughed, cruelly taunting, 'I ain't gonna clear it up'.

I commented that she was feeling that the only way to win this struggle was to join in with the messing, despairing part of herself.

'Anyway, I don't want to go back.'

I query: 'Go back?'

'Here, I don't want to come back here no more.'

That ambiguous remark was full of the ambivalence of wanting to stay with me forever or to stay away forever. When I said to her that maybe she feared that I was now a messed-up, dirty therapist who could not help anyway, she looked anxiously at me. Taking a cloth, she started slowly to clear up the water.

'So you do feel that you can help to clear up a bit of the mess.'
'No, no, I don't . . .'

She looked at the cloth, now dirty from the water, and a look of stricken fear came into her face.

'The cloth has become dirty, and you are so afraid—you don't see how you can clean up this mess without getting messier . . .'

But her despair widened, and with a wild sweep of her out-flung arms everything on the table—paints, water, paper, toys, cloth, scissors—was swept onto the floor. We were both silent as the things thudded and rolled to their final destinations. The silence was so intense that I was aware of the drip-drip-drip of water from the table to the floor. She got up from the table, and her face was white as she pulled the armchair to the sink and, standing on it, she washed her hands at it. I said very quietly into this silence that she was pulling herself above this mess by saying that it did not belong to her—and it was me and my room. She looked with confirming distaste at me.

Then she crossed the room, kicking at the debris in despair. She was beside herself and seemed to have no place to go. She threw herself face down on the sofa. There was the sound of muffled crying. I started to speak softly, but she interrupted: 'Buzz off, you. Fuck off, you. Buzz off, you.' Softly now I tried to describe her pain and how sad and hopeless she felt, how the 'pretty pink' had ended up a mess. 'No, I don't. No. Fuck off, you.'

She began to sing loudly, 'Baa, baa, black sheep'—loudly and defiantly, her face hidden in the sofa. When she got to the line, 'three bags full', she sang, 'pee bags full, one for the master, one for the dame, one for the little girl who lives down the drain'.

I picked up this theme of pee getting everywhere, of a Susie who feels she's in a sewer, a bad, dirty place.

She began to push herself up and down on the sofa, her bottom in the air. I was unsure of what I was seeing and was silent. She did it more vigorously and splayed her legs. I said she was moving like someone having sexual intercourse. 'No' she sighed and got up. Then suddenly she thumped down on the floor and lay there wearily. Then dragging her body into position with tired weariness, she began to push her bottom up and down, legs splayed, pushing faster and faster and faster, frantically. It was the unmistakable position of a frantic, penetrating male. I spoke as much for my sake as for hers, describing her action, putting into words the savagery of what I was seeing.

At last the frantic little body stopped, and she sobbed exhaustedly on the floor. Silence fell. How long we stayed in this silence, I do not know. I was filled with horror, indignation, an anger that shook me. She looked so small, so frail, such a very lightweight elf of a child. Later I was helped to realize that I had felt many of the feelings that she must have experienced as a witness and participant to sexual intercourse in her home.

In this way Susie left me no doubt as to the nature of her trauma. It was sexual intercourse as a faecal mess that overtakes the wish to be a pretty pink-nailed grown-up. Susie takes two positions in the session—the exhausted little girl, who cannot cope with the herculean task of parenting herself, and, as a counterpoint, the driving, penetrating male. Sexual intercourse is seen to occupy a place of ruin and despair; it is a frenzied masturbatory activity in a context of hurt and hopelessness. There is also an element here of trying to inject life into something lifeless and dead, a sense perhaps of Susie trying vainly to resuscitate a dead, damaged object. I think she was, on some level, trying to revive a parent who had abandoned her and was internally felt as dead.

These abandoning parents appeared in so much of her material. She identified one aspect of them as 'a Mummy with no arms', which she made regularly out of the play dough I provided. A Mummy with no arms cannot hold or contain or control a child. This 'Mummy with no arms' first made her appearance when I failed to contain Susie in the sessions and allowed her to leave before the end of her time, or to not be forced into my room when she refused. Eventually I had to re-work this indecisiveness of mine and take responsibility for her staying in the room with me. The 'Mummy with no arms' lived in a house with no curtains or shutters, she told me once, complaining at their lack in my dolls' house. In this way she defined and began to communicate the lack of essential boundaries, the pain of seeing too much and not being confined to a protected, child's place in the home.

Another aspect of her mothering was put into 'the kind cow' who, Susie said, 'fed you with lovely, creamy milk'. But this feeding mother was also inactive and unprotective. One day Susie took all the smaller figures from her box, telling me they were boys and girls. The 'monster' ordered them in a deep zombie-like voice to balance in impossible positions. The cow was placed behind the children but seemed to have no role in the 'game', as Susie called it. Thinking of the posed photographs, I understood the fierce feelings with which she set out the game. 'What does the cow do?' I asked. 'Nothing', she answered blandly. 'They can't really notice she's there.' And at last a note of bitterness crept into her voice: 'She just does nothing.'

Session after session the children are now given 'trick rides' in a tip-up truck, until I make explicit her father's trickiness and his sexual 'games' with his children. Susie usually responds with silence, but in one session around this time she sings: 'There's a goat in a coat in my little bed, and there's not much room for me.'

So the monster that is excluded at the start of every session, is the 'goat', the trickster, the sexual father, hugely powerful and menacing; and the ballet dancer, it becomes clear, is the sexual mother, the one whose arms are occupied in a graceful pose, a mother with no arms for the children.

As Susie began to share these personae with me, she became more in touch with her unprotected baby self. The 'I can do anything and it doesn't hurt' Susie began to give way to expressions of fragility and pain. 'This little horse', she told me earnestly one day, 'is too little to ride on. If you did ride on it, its back would break.' Also, she told me a story that she referred to often in later sessions, about a baby lamb who, in full view of the cows grazing along the river bank, falls into the mire. 'Lassie' comes and saves the lamb, dragging her from the mud. 'She can't get the lamb all clean', she told me, 'but at last, only her little head'. So we began to clean Susie's head and to bring some semblance of hope and order from the mire into which she had fallen.

Some consequences of sexual abuse

The ballet dancer and the monster stood for the sexual parents who were fenced off from each other in prison, and the sad unprotected childhood that Susie suffered could be confided and shared and borne. But the consequences were deeper and harder to deal with.

For the first seven or eight months of Susie's therapy, the major task seemed to be to describe and discuss and to reevaluate the events that had happened to her. It was, in this way, largely a matter of external traumatic events. But more and more, as these things receded, so internal indentifications came to the fore.

If one goes back to that session where Susie acted out being a frantically sexual male, I had noted that there was here some element of revival—of trying to inject life into a dead object. And this, I think, became the crux of the matter for Susie—as I find it is for other sexually abused children—that the more they are abandoned, the more seductive and sexually placating they try to be. The part of Susie that is angry and critical of her sexual abuse is the strong part; it comes from the child who feels loved, who feels worth something, and who is able to criticize what is given to her because it does not compare well with the 'cow's creamy milk'. But the child whose mother has no arms seeks to seduce and placate and to get near the mother on any basis she can find, and this often means being like the sexually penetrating father.

Later, it is true, such a child looks back with bitter cynicism and complains that the cost of dependency was exploitation, but her fear of loss can be such—usually is such—that she invites exploitation over and over again, as the only way she knows to maintain contact.

So it began to be clear to me that after a break—at Easter, Christmas, the summer holidays—Susie was very seductive towards me, inviting me to see her pretty knickers, making a bed for me in the session, licking sticky lollipops, and suggestively fingering a yellow crayon that was 'Mummy's favourite colour'. She veered from seductive invitations to manic outbursts where she made 'slides'—dangerous exciting rides—for herself, which I was invited to join and I was assumed to enjoy watching. In this way Susie used excitement to keep her own loss and helplessness at bay and sought to seduce and control me by her sexual favours. It is this internal monster—tricky, sexually active, powerfully controlling—and this internal ballet dancer—superficial, seductive, sexually receptive—which is the long legacy of sexually abused children, and which takes so many careful hours of therapy to amend.

There was a time when Susie began to make what she called a 'double bed' on the floor of my room—actually, just blankets on the floor. The construction of the bed was always problematic, with much indecision and changing around and being unable to come to any resolution as to the way the covers went or where the pillows would be, and so on. Also, this 'making the bed' went on over several sessions—always towards the end of a session—and was never completed by the end. It seemed to be about two people who could sleep together with no physical contact, but who would talk to each other at night—and she showed me how they would prop themselves up on an elbow to do so. After some weeks she suddenly began this bedmaking with fresh vigour; she very intently laid out the covers and then, as if she needed a measure of whether the bed was long enough—she asked me, 'just lie down there a minute', and I did so. I think I had some half idea in the back of my mind that she would see by this that her worst fears were imaginary and that I was not about to be sexual with her. But—of course—she was beside herself with fright and spun around the room shouting, throwing covers and pillows in all directions, knocking over a cup of flour, which went everywhere, and the session ended in chaos. The following session, a collapsed and tearful Susie had to be dragged into the room. She sat far away, crying, trying to pull down her skirt over pitifully exposed legs. And I explained that I was wrong to lie down and what it had meant to her and her fear of my seducibility. Gradually, relief edged into her, and on we went.

Three and a half years later, Susie was still finding it difficult to come to terms with her feelings towards her father. Her play invariably portrayed families of mothers and children only, and there was often a conspiratorial air in her relation towards me and against the 'nasty monster' and sometimes the 'nasty boys'. This became very clear when she told me about the miraculous life cycle of the frog. Frogs swiftly became her 'favourite animal', and one day I understood why. Susie told me that tadpoles have two mothers to bring them up: 'There are no Daddy frogs.' When I demurred from this view, she pulled herself up indignantly. She had read the book four times, and it said that 'the Mummy frog and her "mate" made the babies!' Susie's 'mate' was her friend—how else does a cockney child use that word?

The more serious point of the story is that it demonstrates the long-term effect of Susie's early relationships: three and a half years on, she was still looking for a way around the necessity of fathers and their dangerous sexuality.

After five years, Susie added a father reluctantly but determinedly to her play family whilst we talked of her impending adoption. In a new family at last, only time will tell whether Susie can exchange the ballet dancer and the monster of her childhood for a real mother and a real father.

PART FIVE

THEORY AND RESEARCH

T his concluding section represents certain current lines of thinking on research within the field of psychoanalytic psychotherapy as a scientific discipline. It also explores new lines of thought in relation to our understanding of and approach to some aspects of clinical work.

In these ways, it is pursuing a tradition that began with Sigmund Freud and was renewed over the years by such notable figures as Anna Freud, Karl Menninger, Susan Isaacs, John Bowlby, and David Malan, among many others. It is probably true that all scientific discovery and judgement involve elements of intuitive insight and creative thinking, as does artistic endeavour. In the human sciences such insights must essentially play a greater part than in the physical sciences, and most patently so in relation to thought and emotionality. This can present certain specific problems of methodology and of ethics and requires new approaches and models for the purpose. Like medicine, which is often referred to as an art as well as a science, psychotherapy retains its human perspective, together with the scientific ideal, insofar as this might properly be defined as a constant endeavour to discover a little more of the truth and to understand it a little better.

In these, as in other chapters, discussions of theoretical developments that have influenced the extension and development of clinical understanding clarify the importance of mutual interaction between all these aspects of the work.

Here, as elsewhere in the book, evidence may be found of the ways in which differing theoretical standpoints may often contribute to one another, whether by clarifying particular distinctions and points of disagreement or by enriching areas of common agreement.

[R.S.]

318

CHAPTER SEVENTEEN

The splitting image:
a research perspective

Mary Boston

There has long been a split between academic and clinical psychology and between cognitive and affective aspects of development. However, some exciting recent research on infant development offers the prospect of healing the breach between these fields of study. These research findings, reviewed below, challenge some of the traditional theories and emphasize the need for openness to new ideas and theoretical formulations. Detailed observations made with video and film are found to link very closely with the infant observation studies designed by Esther Bick. (These are described in the Introduction to part two, 'The Psychotherapy of Infancy', and referred to by Genevieve Haag in chapter eight.) The author suggests that an emphasis in some recent child development research on the use of the imagination and of subjective experience, with more meaningful observational studies, could therefore offer possible models for developing new methods of research within the field of psychoanalytic psychotherapy.

[R.S.]

The particular difficulties of carrying out research in the human field has led to a long-standing split between the academic researcher and the clinician. The personality qualities required for exploring the depths of the inner world may well be different from those needed by the traditional researcher taking a more global and perhaps rigorously objective view.

Yet it seems important that the two approaches to phenomena of general interest in the human sciences and child care should complement and cross-fertilize each other, rather than proceed in parallel or at cross purposes. Unsatisfactory as the traditional medical model may seem when it comes to dealing with psychoanalytical observations, some ways of making clinical phenomena generally available for scientific scrutiny need to be developed. Stevenson (1986), quoting Tramontana and Sherrets (1983), suggests that clinicians ought to attempt research, even if it falls short of an ideal design.

The complications of evaluating psychoanalytic work lie not only in the difficulties of assessing inner change as well as symptom removal, but also in the realm of 'subjectivity' versus 'objectivity'. The fundamental basis for all research is good observation, but the utilization of the transference as the main therapeutic tool means that clinically observed phenomena occurring in the context of the relationship between patient and therapist are highly emotionally charged. The inevitable 'subjectivity' of this approach is not in keeping with traditional medical research models, though even in medicine there is a search for new research paradigms taking more account of the whole person. Porter (1986) suggests new methods and models are needed for evaluating processes in psychotherapy. There is a need for developing methods for describing psychodynamic changes in personality development and for the 'objective handling of subjective data', as Malan (1963) puts it.

The split between the 'objective' researcher and the 'subjective' clinician has also permeated academic psychology in its split image of development—the cognitive versus the affective: but in recent years, particularly in the field of child development, there seems to be a trend towards the healing of this split.

The recent research on infants puts increasing emphasis on the social context of development, and of observation, on the interaction between care-giver and developing infant, and also between subject and experimenter. The highlighting of minute details and sequences of infant behaviour, made possible by new recording techniques on film and video, has brought the findings of academic research much closer to the infant observations carried out by child psychotherapists (Bick, 1964). These latter observations, from which has developed the work described in the next section, had hitherto been considered 'too subjective', for they rely not only on looking at details of behaviour but in the capacity to identify introjectively with the baby, drawing on the experience of the child or infant within the observer. This kind of observation means using one's mind as a receptive instrument—a kind of human barometer, as it were, or, as Isca Wittenberg (1970) has put it, 'more like a radar screen than a searchlight'.

In this context, it is interesting to note the move in psychological research towards more meaningful observational studies, which take into account subjective as well as objective experience, as evidenced by the growth of 'health psychology'. Newson (1978) suggests that the language used by the detached scientific observer is not adequate to describe intersubjectively shared experience. He suggests that the participant observer point of view may reveal more meaningful responses. We must use the imagination in engaging the baby in a meaningful dialogue, stressing the historical dimension—the idiosyncratic strategies previously developed. This, of course, comes very close to our clinical concerns and methods. Emde and Sorce (1983) talk of using one's own emotions as a guide for understanding. Perhaps the 'counter transference' is being accorded some scientific respectability at last.

A bridge between the research and clinical approaches seems to require some acknowledgement of the scientific status of intuitive observation, if the interest in inner experience is not to be confined to art, literature, and therapy.

In our struggles to develop an appropriate methodology for psychoanalytic research, it is perhaps appropriate to review some of the recent work on child development, which illustrates how observations made from the varying viewpoints of workers in different disciplines can gradually come together to arrive at an increasingly coherent and generally accepted view of the developing infant—a view based on sound observation, but with due attention to meaning and subjective aspects. Kaye (1977) has talked about how the 'macro-analytic' approach can complement the microanalytic techniques, as the global picture revealed by the wide-angled lens needs filling in with the fine details provided by the zoom lens. This might be relevant not only in the developmental field, but in relation to the integration of different methods of research into therapy.

The recent research findings on infants illustrate the need for continual re-evaluation and re-formulation of the theoretical concepts that underpin our psychotherapeutic work.

There is, for example, no shortage of theories of child development, yet their integration with both clinical and experimental observations is, in most cases, patchy, to say the least. The theories, whether based on reconstructive or deductive evidence or on actual observations of babies and children, tend to acquire a life of their own and become increasingly impervious to further observations and evidence. This means that the careful observations of some of the pioneers of child development have become enshrined in theories, which may then tend to act as blinkers, obstructing the perception of new observations.

I have in mind the discrepancies between the developmental stages of the young infant as described by Gesell (1946)—incorporated now into widely accepted 'norms of development'—and Tom Bower's (1977b) observations of the sophisticated perceptual abilities of new-born infants and of much earlier co-ordination between sensory modalities. Bower, of course, and other recent researchers with new recording techniques and experimental methods, were able to observe new-born babies, never observed experimentally before. They also captured the moments of maximum responsiveness and had the babies propped up, rather than prone. There also seems some evidence that babies may have to re-learn, as it were, the co-ordination between senses as their motor abilities become more developed.

Nevertheless, the Gesell norms die hard, and the idea that infants cannot see or focus properly in the early weeks (refuted by all the recent researchers) is still very current in primary care circles.

Spitz (1965, 1983) is another pioneer whose classic observations of the emotional needs of young infants have contributed greatly to the increasingly humane care of infants. Nevertheless, his picture of the young baby, needing to be protected from external stimuli, leading a rather vegetative existence, unable to organize his perceptual field, has been challenged by the recent research, both on new-born babies and on the foetus. Obviously babies vary greatly in their degree of alertness, in general, and at different times, but the 'not fully born' or 'quasi dormant' 4-week-old described by Spitz does not accord with many psychoanalytic infant observations, nor with the research studies, nor, indeed, with the experience of many parents. Even the classic 6-weeks' smile has been challenged by Wolff (1963), who, when observing infants at home over prolonged periods, observed social smiling to occur as early as 3 weeks.

It is to be expected that observations made in different conditions and with different methods would vary, and these variations are themselves interesting areas for study. The problem is that observations such as those of Spitz, made in certain situations, have been used to underpin many psychoanalytic theories. Dan Stern, in his book, *The Interpersonal World of the Infant* (1985) suggests that the widespread theories of an initial period of undifferentiation or confusion, the stimulus barrier, or lack of distinction between inside and outside, self and object, do not accord with the facts. It is in the nature of theories that they do not easily accommodate new observations. Even relatively new books take the 'old' 'facts' for granted; for example,

We know that the infant has an ever changing field of perception in which there is no object constancy, such that when a piece of paper goes out of sight it 'ceases to exist'. An infant has tactile and olfactory sensations but they do not cohere. Memory is not developed enough for recognition of the object to occur. [Symington, 1986]

Are psychotherapists and clinicians now lagging behind the academic psychologists? Compare a professor of psychology, Rudolph Schafer:

> . . . our concept of what an infant is has changed markedly; we do not discuss him any more in such purely negative terms as the 'blooming, buzzing confusion' with which William James once characterized the baby's consciousness, nor do we see him merely as an assembly of reflexes or as random mass activity. We see him rather as a being with considerable powers to gather and process information from his surroundings even in the earliest weeks of life. [Schafer, 1974]

It looks as if, as Dan Stern suggests, we may have to throw out some of our traditional theories if the 'clinical infant' is to be brought closer to the 'observed infant'.

The research work has highlighted the importance of different sensory modalities, particularly the ears and eyes, which might lead us to rethink the central position of the mouth in psychoanalytic theory. Stern (1985) suggests that the 'feeding drama' is largely a creation of Western methods of spaced-out feeds, with hunger allowed to build up until satiation occurs, in contrast to so-called primitive methods of sucking every twenty minutes or so. Bowlby (1969) has emphasized that attachment is mediated in a number of different ways and does not just develop from the relationship to the breast.

The attribution of some sort of undifferentiated state to the baby in the early weeks does not seem to accord with the evidence of the sophisticated abilities of babies to perceive and respond to outside stimulus, from birth onwards, nor to the observations that babies respond quite differently to persons and to things (perhaps why they seemed uninterested in Gesell's rattles). Bowlby pointed out that the neonate seems biassed to react to stimuli emanating from people.

Techniques for monitoring the development of the foetus have revealed the baby, even before birth, to be a competent individual, able to perceive and respond to a variety of stimuli, particularly auditory ones. Musical preferences have been inferred from the foetus' varying responses to different sounds and music. A recent study, by Sandra Piontelli (1987), of babies observed regularly before and after birth, has revealed a remarkable continuity of behaviour from the fourteenth week of gestation onwards. Rapid-eye-movement sleep occurs to a greater degree in the new-born and in the foetus than in adults. This suggests the presence of some mental activity, dreaming or unconscious phantasy at a very early stage.

Work by Carpenter (1975), MacFarlane (1975), Sander (1976), and others suggests that very young babies, of a few days or weeks, have a capacity to distinguish between different caretakers, to tell mother from stranger, by various sensory modalities. Trevarthen (1985) claims to show clear discrimination of a stranger at 2 months, which is perhaps less surprising.

So what about the question of object constancy? Do objects really cease to exist for the baby when they are out of sight? Does it depend on what sort of object it is, as Newson (1974) suggests—object in the psychoanalytic sense, meaning a person, particularly the mother, or an object in the psychologist's sense, meaning a thing?

The idea that the baby does not have any sense of the continuing existence of any sort of object is, of course, based on the well-known experiments of Piaget (1953), in which babies of 6 to 8 months do not reach for a toy that is hidden, and at 10 months do not find it when it is moved (the so-called 'A not B' experiment). Does this mean 'out of sight out of mind', or that it no longer exists for them? A number of different workers have challenged Piaget's interpretations of these observations as well as of his other famous experiments. Freeman, Lloyd, and Sinha (1980) found that altering slightly the conditions of the object constancy experiment enormously affected the success rate of babies around 12 months old. Painting smiling faces on cup or screen improved the performance, whereas using upside-down ordinary cups and painting upside-down faces on them caused a marked deterioration. Encouraging the child to find the object also made a difference. Maybe babies are used to adults hiding away objects that they are *not* supposed to look for. In the experiments the babies seemed to be reacting to the social situation. They seemed anxious at upside-down cups, and we get a glimpse here of the emotional component of the response, which is not taken into account from the purely cognitive viewpoint. A further relevant observation by Trevarthen is that babies in general do not comply with instructions until the age of 9 months.

Bower claims to show that babies as young as 6 weeks show surprise, as measured by changes in heart beat, etc., when objects are made to disappear, as if they did have some expectation of their continued existence. They would also reach out to find a toy that has been made to disappear by the withdrawal of light.

The observation—well substantiated by infant observations carried out by Tavistock students of psychotherapy—that babies as young as 3 weeks may sometimes stop crying at the sound of mother's footsteps or preparations for a feed before mother comes into view, suggests to me at least the rudimentary beginnings of an image of the feed or the mother that is to come.

Piaget's well-known observations have become enshrined in much educational as well as clinical theory. Barbara Tizard and Martin Hughes (1984), in their fascinating study, *Young Children Learning,* point out that the emphasis on learning through doing which sprang from Piaget has led to much more emphasis on play in nursery and infant education than on language and conversation. There are numerous current challenges to the interpretations Piaget put on his observations and to the timing of the stages of development he outlined.

Margaret Donaldson (1978) has described some interesting versions of some of Piaget's other experiments. The Doll–Mountain experiment, where the child has to arrange the model mountains according to what could be seen from the doll's perspective, proves very difficult for children under 8 to do—they tend to represent their own point of view, and this has been taken as evidence of the young child's egocentricity. The child is thought not to be able to see something from the point of view of another. Martin Hughes (Donaldson, 1978) gave children an essentially similar task, in which the doll had to hide from a policeman, so he could not be seen, and then from two policemen, which means the consideration and co-ordination of two viewpoints; 90% of children between 3½ and 5 were then able to do the task correctly.

Similar results have been described with Piaget's conservation experiment. The introduction of a 'naughty teddy' who rearranges the things does seem to increase the likelihood of success at the task.

This suggests not only the importance of the task making sense to the child, but also alerts us to the possibility of the role of phantasy in the performance, usually neglected even in the social cognitive work. Susan Isaacs pointed out to Piaget a long time ago that children much younger than his 7- to 8-year-olds could understand causality, though they might resort to magical explanations when pressed or confused. Isaacs' (1930) careful observations of the social interactions and reasoning powers of young children seem only recently to have been discovered by developmental psychologists. Although she was one of the pioneers in making a bridge, perhaps it is because she became a psychoanalyst that her work became 'split off', as it were. Tizard and Hughes (1984) do acknowledge it, however, and give some very pertinent examples of 4-year-olds' reasoning ability. The discrepancies in the observations on children's reasoning powers suggest that modes of thought exist side by side, confirmed by commonly observed breakdowns in reasoning even in adults. The idea of development proceeding from stage to stage does not allow for the influence of conflict and emotion on achievement, nor the dynamic effect of past experience on the 'here and now', so important for clinical work.

It is in attempting to understand the subtle details of interactions in the consulting room that the therapist draws on his knowledge, from infant observation, of the importance of non-verbal communications and gestures. The recent studies of mother–infant and father–infant interaction are therefore of particular interest. A fascinating 'interactional synchrony' or 'dance' has been illustrated by both Trevarthen (1975) and Condon (1975), among others. Infants are observed to move synchronously with adult speech. This 'pre-speech' conversation is leading to some rethinking about theories of language development.

Brazelton's fascinating study of the importance of the mother's attention for the baby provides, in my view, the most compelling link between experimental and clinical work and also highlights the emotional component of the interaction (Brazelton et al., 1975).

Brazelton and co-workers filmed mother–infant pairs in natural interaction and demonstrated the fine degree of synchrony and mutual responsiveness between the two. Then, in an experimental intervention, the mothers were asked not to respond to their babies but to remain passive and non-reacting. The effect on the babies was dramatic.

> When she violates his expectancy for rhythmic interaction by presenting a still, unresponsive face to him, he becomes visibly concerned, his movements become jerky, he averts his face, then attempts to draw her into interaction. When repeated attempts fail, he finally withdraws into an attitude of helplessness, face averted, body curled up and motionless. If she returns to her usual interactive responses, he comes alive after an initial puzzled period, and returns to his rhythmic cyclical behaviour which has previously characterized their ongoing face-to-face interaction.

These observations clearly link with Esther Bick's (1968) clinical work on the importance of the mother's attention, acting, she suggests, as a kind of mental skin, holding parts of the baby's personality together, enabling fleeting states of integration, of what may well be disparate sensations and experiences, to take place. It links also with Winnicott's (1965) concepts of holding and the mother's adaptation to her baby. The functioning of attention may well account for some of the discrepancies in the various observations, as babies' performance may fluctuate considerably. The new experimental work captures the babies' attention and optimal response.

But the despair of the babies in these experiments, the complete collapse after only two or three minutes, bring to our attention the importance of the emotional response. It is this aspect that interests us as clinicians. What must it be like for the baby who has a chronically depressed and unresponsive mother?

The emotional responses of the children come through in a great deal of this work. Yet they are treated as peripheral by many of the researchers, whereas they are central to clinical investigation and to psychodynamic theories of development. As Urwin (1986) has stated, the split between cognition and emotion is still pervasive. The experiments on very young babies' powers of discrimination actually use the babies' emotional responses, such as surprise or distress, yet the emphasis is on what the infants 'know' or can do. If one thinks of the emotional significance for the baby of learning to manage a cup, one is not surprised to hear that it makes a difference to the object constancy experiment whether the cup is the right or wrong way up! Nevertheless, there is an increasing emphasis, in the more recent work, on emotional expressions as a language of infancy (Emde & Sorce, 1983).

Trevarthen (1985) brings cognition and affect together in stating that 'human knowledge is gained by empathic communication', in which neither cognition nor affect is dominant, but both go together. 'Basic empathy' is regarded as the first stage of development—part of a system of communication about a shared reality. Emotion is seen as regulating communication between persons, the infant showing a marked disposition to attend to others from the start of life, or even before, as babies learn their mother's voice before birth. Even 20-minute-old babies are able to imitate facial expressions, e.g. tongue protrusion; this is beautifully illustrated in a film by Marshall Klaus, *The Amazing Newborn.*

In an experiment on a 1-month-old's ability to distinguish mother from stranger, the baby became distressed, as did Brazelton's, when the mother had to speak to her in an expressionless voice, giving no eye contact. She looked away from mother's blank face. Later she made expulsive noises, as if dirtying her nappy. Carpenter (1975) also noted what she called 'purposeful non looking'. In the 'upside down cup' experiment mentioned earlier, some of the babies turned away, distressed. This avoidance reaction may be crucial to understanding the link between cognition and emotion and the central role of the parent or main caregiver in normal and pathological development. The mother's unresponsive face in this instance would seem unbearable to know about or look at, and the infant expels it (quite concretely). There would thus seem to be an intimate relationship between the emotional experience and the interactive dialogue described by the researchers. As Emde and Sorce (1983) put it, the emotional signalling between caregiver and baby—the pleasureable interaction—is important for development. Otherwise there is a 'turning-off' of the developmental process.

Wilfred Bion's theory of thinking places emotional experience as the first step in thinking processes (Bion, 1962). He suggests that an emotion has to be tolerated long enough to be thought about for development to occur. Emotional experience is then central for the development of thinking, symbolization, imagination, dreaming, and memory. But what *is* an emotional experience?

The baby is bombarded with a variety of raw sense data, not only after birth but before, for we now know that the foetus is by no means protected from all stimuli in the womb. The recent research suggests that the baby has a pre-disposition to organize his perceptual field in certain ways and to respond to particular configurations or patterns of stimuli. But what is the significance for the baby of the patterns he perceives? These innate preconceptions (e.g. of a nipple, eyes, face, or voice) need to come together with actual complementary experiences in the outside world (which is largely at first the mother or father). It is the aesthetic intensity of these realizations, Donald Meltzer (1986) suggests, that form the stuff of emotional experience and meaning. Some evidence for this formulation is found in the researchers' video records of the intense engagement between mother and baby—the early eye contact, the imitation of facial expressions, and the beauty of this early interaction when it is proceeding synchronously.

Where such emotional experience cannot be tolerated, because of too great intensity or pain (as perhaps temporarily with our experimental babies), it may have to be evaded or evacuated and then becomes unavailable for thought and further development. Bion (1962) links these kind of mental evacuations with meaningless talk, psychosomatic reactions, hallucinations, and mindless group behaviour (could the experimental babies' temporary non-looking, if the situation became repeated too much, become the gaze avoidance seen in autistic children?).

What enables the baby to hold on to the emotional experience, particularly if it is a distressing one? I think in the answer to this question there is a coming together of quite a number of clinical writers as well as researchers, even though their formulations may seem very different. There seems some agreement that there is something crucial for development in the mother's attentive responsiveness to the baby. This may be formulated, as with Newson's earlier attempt, as the mother's giving meaning to the baby's signals and more recently as empathic communication involving imitation and sharing of emotions or, as with Trevarthen, basic empathy, or, as with Brazelton, the early system of affective social interaction. To quote Stern, Barnett, and Spicker (1983), 'researchers, clinicians and theoreticians are in agreement about the central role of affect in development'. Psychoanalytic writers have always emphasized the emotional aspects of the parent–baby interaction, as for example in Winnicott's idea of 'emotional holding', and Bick's 'mental skin'. Bion's model is in terms of the mother's *containing* the baby's projections of undifferentiated feelings. She is then able to mentally digest them, so to speak, to make sense of them, and by her understanding response she enables the baby to have a meaningful emotional experience.

There is an increasing trend in recent psychotherapeutic work for the use of this model of 'containment' to describe the therapist's function in being receptive to the patient's projections, with emphasis on the feelings the therapist is made to have—the countertransference. The therapist needs to have what Bion calls 'maternal reverie'—to hold the patient's projections while pondering over them, tolerating the uncertainty of the meaning of quite concretely felt states of mind until the patient is able to take them back in a more understandable and modified form.

Satisfactory development, and likewise a satisfactory outcome for therapy, seem to require the internalization of this containing dialogue between mother or father and baby, between therapist and patient, with both its cognitive and emotional components. It is this internal feeling of containment that can provide a secure base of inner strength and confidence.

Bowlby's attachment theory is a notable attempt to integrate both the cognitive and the affective and the inner and outward manifestations of human social relations. His aim is to provide a scientific basis for therapy. Patterns of attachment behaviour in 1-year-olds, observed under standard conditions such as Ainsworth's strange situation test, are shown to have a predictive value and include detailed attention to emotional responses. These early patterns of attachment tend to persist and to contribute to the representational models or 'inner world maps' of the self in relation to parental figures—i.e., they become ingrained or internalized. The 'secure base' that the mother provides in these experiments, and which the therapist also provides for the patient in his internal explorations, Bowlby feels, is akin to Bion's concept of 'containment' and Winnicott's 'holding' (Bowlby, 1979a). Bowlby speaks of 'inner world maps', and from this point of view the drawing of a 7-year-old patient of mine (DRAWING 1) may be of interest (Boston, 1972).

DRAWING 1

This little boy lived in a children's home and came to see me for therapy, which involved a lengthy journey from another borough. He had quite an unusual interest in maps of all sorts, and one might see the change in the nature of his maps, as therapy proceeded, as indicating not only an increasing maturation but also as reflecting changes in the quality of his inner world and of his relationship to me.

DRAWING 1 is a map, done in the early stages of treatment, of his journey to see me. It is through wartime London, full of bombs, explosives, and confusion. He was, of course, born many years after the war, but it represented for him something that happened long ago in his life—the disasters and confusions of his infancy being re-experienced in relation to me. The treatment was very stormy at that time, the explosions occurring in the consulting room. His violent attacks and emotional outbursts seemed to be very concrete projections of painful feelings that he needed me to know by experience.

DRAWING 2 was done in the middle stage of treatment, at age around 8½. The war is over (he was, indeed, by then more manageable). It is less confused, but there are dangers. Fires keep breaking out, and fire engines are plentiful. There is some hope of putting out these fires.

DRAWING 3 is from a long series of 'garden suburbs', from the last period of treatment. He did this in lots of joined sections, of which I can only reproduce a part. The noticeable features of this series of maps was the availability of a variety of facilities—gardens, parks, church, town hall, police station, hospital, and even a psychotherapy department. These maps seemed to express a feeling of community concern, with an increased feeling of my concern for him, which manifested itself in a more secure and orderly 'inner world map'.

If an internalized helpful dialogue between mother–baby, therapist, and patient can promote healthy growth and development, what happens when there is a lack of such helpful interaction?

DRAWING 4, entitled, 'Mum and Babby', was done by a girl of 12, also living in a children's home (Boston & Szur, 1983). Among the many meanings we might see in this drawing, there is a striking image of a mother who neither holds the baby securely in her arms, nor, it would seem from the lack of eye contact, in her mind.

The lack of an internal *thinking* mother seems intimately connected with the marked learning difficulties shown by these deprived children. We came to the conclusion that this is their essential deprivation, and the introjection of a caring, thinking, feeling primary caregiver is part of the necessary equipment for cognitive *and* emotional development (Henry, 1983). Without this, there is an impairment of the capacity to take in, grasp, and hold on to thoughts, feelings, memories, and experience— the 'in one ear and out the other' kind of phenomenon. With this impairment go problems of identification, with taking inside good internal figures. Hence relationships tend to be superficial and conforming.

Of course these are extreme cases. One would expect there to be normal variations in the quality of the early interactional processes, which may influence development in more subtle ways. Some of the research workers are studying individual dif-

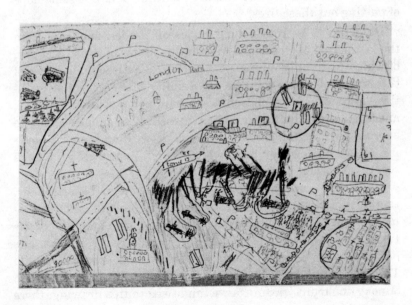

DRAWING 2

DRAWING 3

ferences in the early dialogue as well as more obvious asynchrony. Brazelton (1970, 1975), Field (Field et al., 1980), and others have tried to predict 'at risk' factors. Lynne Murray (1988) has studied depressed mothers' interactions with their babies. In fact, a whole new branch of therapeutic work, 'infant psychiatry', has sprung up, directly related to the developmental research.

Conclusion

I have dwelt at some length on the recent research on infants because of its importance from a number of viewpoints. (1) There are the beginnings of a theory of development, based on observational evidence, that accords with our clinical observations, which promise to provide a firm theoretical basis for our

DRAWING 4

MUM AND BABBY

work. (2) The research illustrates how work from different perspectives and disciplines can come together with more confidence in approaching the truth. This might encourage us to a multi-faceted approach to research in psychotherapy. (3) Emotional communication has now become a legitimate area for research. There is a hope that this may give those engrossed in clinical work the courage to look with research eyes at the emotional communications of their patients.

The first step might be the bringing together of clinical observations on similar types of cases so that some tentative generalizations or hypotheses can be formulated. This 'workshop' model is described by Margaret Rustin in chapter twenty.

A further step would be to develop such general experience into more specific hypotheses or research questions to be borne in mind when planning and reviewing clinical work. There is an urgent need for thinking about ways in which changes in personality organization and emotional state can be formulated and demonstrated. Tentative beginnings in developing such a methodology are in process at the Tavistock Clinic, where a long-term project on evaluating psychotherapy with in-care, fostered, and adopted children is in progress.

CHAPTER EIGHTEEN

The role of psychotherapy in the care of diabetes in childhood

George Moran and Peter Fonagy

The outcome investigation described here is, as far as we know, the first controlled study of the effectiveness of psychoanalytically based treatment modalities with child patients. The research model included an original design that combined complementary approaches. One of these consisted of the 'blind' monitoring of progress charts from a group of patients suffering from brittle diabetes in a hospital that included a Department of Child Psychotherapy. All received regular counselling and support. Their charts were compared also with developments in the case of one patient who was able to receive intensive psychoanalytical therapy and whose progress was monitored by a separate professional group. Cri-

We gratefully acknowledge the participation of Drs C. Brook, A. Kurtz, A. Bolton, C. Lament, and S. Marans on this project and the support of Professor A. J. Solnit, Dr P. Neubauer, the American Philanthropic Foundation, and the Special Trustees of the Middlesex Hospital.

teria for change included both physical and emotional factors, assessed separately and collated independently. Links between physical signs of change and independent assessments of emotional changes provide novel and encouraging evidence for the effectiveness of these methods in an area where a number of alternative methods of psychological treatment have shown far more equivocal results. A group of child patients with the same condition, whose local hospital was without similar psychotherapeutic facilities, was also monitored and could therefore constitute a control group.

[R.S.]

C riticisms of psychoanalytic work often include the assertion that its methods fall outside the sphere of accepted scientific investigation. It has been claimed, for example, that clinical evidence is contaminated by the effect of suggestion from the analyst on the patient under the influence of a strong positive transference (Grünbaum, 1984).

In this chapter, we describe two investigations that aim to test the effectiveness of psychoanalysis and psychotherapy in a systematic, verifiable way, permitting replications that nevertheless preserve the complexity of the psychoanalytic process (see Edelson, 1986; Moran & Fonagy, 1987).

Children with insulin-dependent diabetes require precisely regulated injections of insulin, timed in conjunction with their diet, in order to maintain the balance between carbohydrate intake and the insulin required to convert sugar into cell energy. To achieve this, it is necessary to monitor blood sugar level carefully, and the patient is considered to be in diabetic balance when the levels of blood glucose approximate to those within the normal, non-diabetic range.

A small group of such patients, often labelled brittle diabetics, have serious problems in controlling their blood sugar levels. Their lives are constantly disrupted by periods of hypoglycaemia and/or hyperglycaemia. (Tattersall, 1977, 1985). Admissions to hospital for treatment of life-threatening episodes of severe metabolic derangement are not uncommon in this group. Diabetologists have now reached the conclusion that the aetiology of brittle diabetes is based on psychological rather than organic factors (Schade et al., 1985).

The psychological mechanisms that precipitate these life-threatening disorders can be clarified in terms of a psychoanalytic model, which we hope to validate in the two studies reported here. Two fundamental premises underlie our model: (1) that psychological conflicts are causally related to fluctuations of blood glucose levels, and (2) that these fluctuations are caused by conscious and unconscious acts inconsistent with satisfactory regulation of the condition. Thus, we take the view that the major transgressions of the diabetic regime that underlie most cases of brittle diabetes are neurotic responses to anxiety and guilt arising from unconscious conflict.

On the basis of this model we recommend that interventions address preconscious sources of the child's anxieties, putting into words the conflicts that may underlie the diabetic mismanagement. Thus, for example, a diabetic child may unconsciously experience the symptoms of brittle diabetes as a punishment for unacceptable sexual or destructive wishes. Interpretation and insight into the conflictual unconscious wishes that have led to the self-punishment expressed in deliberately induced diabetic imbalance may bring relief to the child by freeing him from the neurotic need to disrupt diabetic balance.

The treatment study

In the first study we report, an in-patient treatment programme was set up on the basis of our experience with these patients to study the course of diabetic regulation.

The group of patients we studied consisted of nineteen children and adolescents diagnosed as suffering from brittle diabetes. They were under the care of the same consultant paediatrician. They had all had frequent episodes of hypoglycaemia and/or hyperglycaemia during the previous eighteen months and had been admitted to hospital for life-threatening diabetic imbalance at least twice during the previous year.

The paediatrician was attached to two hospitals, one of which could offer psychoanalytically informed psychotherapy as well as intensively monitored medical care. The eleven patients who had been admitted from this catchment area were designated as the treatment group. The remaining eight patients, who had been admitted to an outer London teaching hospital for stabilization of their diabetes following psychological assessment, were to be the comparison group. Psychotherapy was not available to them, but in terms of medical management their situation was identical.

A programme was designed with the object of offering treatment for the psychological disturbances underlying brittle diabetes. The methods we followed were based on 'the psychoanalytic proposition that disturbances of psychosexual development and/or object relations find indirect expression through behaviours which lead to chronic fluctuations of blood glucose concentration' (Moran & Fonagy, 1987; Fonagy, Moran, & Higgitt, 1989).

The eleven patients in the treatment group were on average a year older than those in the comparison group. Slightly more of them belonged to Social Classes I and II according to the Registrar General's (1975) classification. Neither of these differences reached statistical significance (see TABLE 1). Three of the children in the treatment group were below the third percentile in height.

Although the eight children in the comparison group received the appropriate medical care, the question of any psychological treatment was not raised with them.

Treatment

Each of the children was assessed at the time of intake both from a psychological and from an endocrinological viewpoint. On the basis of this information, psychodynamic hypotheses regarding the probable causes for their mismanagement of the diabetic regimen were formulated.

The information from which these formulations were constructed includes the child's age and developmental status, the

Table 1

Demographic and clinical features
of sample of 19 brittle diabetic children

	Treated group[1]	Comparison group[2]
percentage female	63.6	62.5
percentage of children in one-parent families	36.0	38.0
social class (percentage I & II)	45.5	37.5
age (years)	13.4	12.3
SD	(3.2)	(4.3)
range	(7–19)	(9–16)
age at onset (years)	6.9	6.1
SD	(2.5)	(3.9)
range	(2–10)	(1–11)
length of illness (years)	6.2	4.5
SD	(4.3)	(2.3)
range	(2–15)	(1–8)

[1]$n = 11.$
[2]$n = 8.$

age at onset of the disease, previous attitudes to diabetic management, educational progress, and developmental and social
histories including family characteristics and relationships.

The treatment recommendation called for psychotherapy
three or four times per week, on an in-patient basis, continuing
for a number of weeks or sometimes months. The extent of the
parents' participation in the treatment process depended on our
assessment of the degree of their involvement in the psychopathology, and in others on the age of the child. Staff members

were assigned to all but two of the parents in order to support them in understanding their child's problems and to assist them in thinking about ways in which they might unknowingly be contributing to these.

The mental health clinicians, physicians, and nurses involved with this project met regularly to discuss the management of the children on the ward. This aspect of the treatment in the integrated programme was seen as having a potentially supportive role for the progress of the psychotherapeutic work. For example, medical and nursing staff were encouraged to confront patients when they transgressed the diabetic regimen, but to avoid seeming to be critical or rejecting. The aim was to help the children recognize their need to be in the hospital to save them from their own destructive behaviour. Our expectation was that such confrontations would help strengthen the child's working alliance with the therapist, thus facilitating therapy.

Measures

The degree of each child's glycaemic control was assessed on the basis of repeated blood sugar measures and an assay of glycosylated haemoglobin concentration, which indicated the average blood glucose levels over the previous two to three months. [Two measures were used to assess diabetic control: (1) M-values (Schlichtkrull et al., 1965), an index of glycaemic control calculated from at least five blood sugar measures per day over six consecutive days; and (2) glycosylated haemoglobin (HbA_1) concentration, a single assay that reflects average blood glucose levels over the preceding two to three months. M-values and insulin dosage were compared on admission to hospital and discharge. HbA_1 levels were assessed on admission and at follow-up periods of three months and one year after the termination of treatment.]

These measures, together with insulin dosage, were noted at the time of admission and when the children had completed their stay in hospital. The children were reassessed at three months and at one year after discharge. Also upon discharge children were advised that if, at a later date, they found themselves in states of emotional distress similar to those they had learnt to recognize in therapy as likely to lead to their inducing states of hypoglycaemia or hyperglycaemia, then they should seek re-admission to hospital.

Results

The nurses' reports indicated that all of the eleven children in the treated group did induce diabetic imbalance by manipulating their diets: six increased their dose of insulin in order to induce hypoglycaemia, as well as the more frequently recorded omission of the insulin.

A comparison of HbA_1, values recorded on admission and at three months and one year following admission showed no changes in the comparison group, but a significant reduction for the treated group at three months and at one year (see TABLE 2).

TABLE 2

Mean HbA_1 values of brittle diabetic children and adolescents at time of admission and at follow-up periods

	Treated group[1]	Comparison group[2]
A. admission	14.3 (2.5)	12.9 (2.3)
B. three-month follow-up	11.1 (2.6)	12.8 (2.7)
C. one-year follow-up	11.5 (2.4)	12.7 (2.4)
t-test (A vs. B)	2.8*	0.1**
t-test (A vs. C)	2.5***	0.2**

*p < 0.02   **n.s.   ***p < 0.04
[1]n = 11. Standard deviations in parentheses.
[2]n = 8. Standard deviations in parenthesis.

The treatment group included three children with growth retardation. One boy, aged 7, was followed up over six years, and during this time his height increased from below the 3rd percentile to above the 35th percentile. Another boy, who was 12 on admission, did show some catch-up growth during the following three years, though he did not attain normal height. The girl, aged 12, also followed for three years, nearly returned to the percentile level she had reached at the time when her diabetes was first diagnosed. The mean M-values for these three children were reduced from an average of 91.7 on admission to 33 when discharged, and their mean HbA$_1$ levels were reduced from 13 to 9.

Discussion

This study provided evidence that a comparatively short-term programme that combined psychoanalytically oriented psychotherapeutic intervention with psychoanalytically informed ward management could achieve major and lasting effects on the blood glucose control of brittle diabetes in children and adolescents. It was also especially encouraging to find that the growth retardation of the three patients in the treated group could be reversed with the aid of psychological interventions.

However, we remained aware of the possibility that averaging data over a number of individual subjects in a psychotherapy research programme blurs the nature of the effect of the programme upon an individual child and thus could potentially provide misleading results (Gottman, 1973). In order therefore to evaluate more accurately the importance of insight in promoting a positive therapeutic advance, we decided to study in detail the concomitant variations of developments in psychotherapeutic insight and in diabetic control, as these could be observed in the study of a single case.

Single case study:
the relationship between blood glucose control
and variations in the themes of psychoanalysis

The process records of the treatment of a brittle-diabetic teenage girl over a period of three and a half years were studied together with a weekly index of the quality of diabetic balance during the same period.

Using a probabilistic framework, we predicted that improvements in her symptoms would occur in temporal association with developments in psychoanalytical insights. Psychoanalytic theory would require that conflict resolution could be seen to precede symptomatic improvement.

Diabetic control throughout was estimated on the basis of twice-daily urine testing. The content of the psychoanalysis was assessed by independent ratings of the analyst's weekly reports. During the course of the analysis the patient rarely talked of the results of tests for monitoring her diabetic balance. The analyst thus had only sporadic and inaccurate information concerning her diabetic control.

Time series analysis (Box & Jenkins, 1976) was used to examine the relationship between diabetic control and psychological conflict. This procedure permits the drawing of causal inferences by statistically describing the fluctuations, cycles, and trends of two processes: the psychoanalytic themes on the one hand and the measures of diabetic control on the other. If the two processes are uncorrelated, it is unlikely that they are causally connected. Concomitant variation, however, would imply causation if fluctuations in one process are predicted by fluctuations in another. In the latter case we may then legitimately make a relatively weak causal inference compared to the more robust causal inferences that may be made on the basis of experimental designs.

Case history

Diagnosed diabetic at age 8, Sally was referred for psychoanalysis at the age of 13 because of long-standing physical and emotional problems that had failed to respond to psychiatric and medical treatment over the previous five years. She was consciously and profoundly dissatisfied with being a girl and had a difficult and ambivalent relationship with her mother. One of her most prominent difficulties, her fear of attending school, preceded the onset of the diabetes by two years. Her anxieties were, however, aggravated by frequent admissions to hospital with hypoglycaemia and/or hyperglycaemia. In the five years preceding the analysis Sally was admitted to hospital, most often with diabetic ketoacidosis, between two and five times per year.

Sally was a highly intelligent (WISC–R full scale IQ = 130), resourceful girl who was in child psychoanalysis five times a week for three and a half years (A. Freud, 1965; Sandler, Kennedy, & Tyson, 1980). Analysis led to improvements both external and internal. Sally's school phobia completely disappeared. She received excellent examination results and was given the first job in graphic design for which she applied. Her fantasies and hobbies lost their previously masculine character, and she began to take pleasure in dressing in a feminine fashion. She developed adolescent crushes on young and older men. Her relationship with her mother became less fraught as they stopped sharing one another's worries and fears. Sally also began to take an active interest in working with young children. Whilst she had two to five admissions to hospital per year in the three years preceding the analysis, she had only one hospital admission during the three and a half years of analytic treatment and no admissions in the four-year follow-up period.

Content analysis and ratings of the treatment

The progress of Sally's analysis was detailed in weekly reports presented by her therapist and based on daily records written following every session. The weekly reports, of approximately 1,000 words, contained summaries of the major themes of the week, illustrations of the patient's difficulties and anxieties, the therapist's understanding and interpretation of these, and the patient's responses.

These 148 weekly reports were condensed within a clinical paper that was studied with a view to extracting the major analytical themes, defining these and judging their presence or absence in any particular weekly report over the course of the analysis. Although we succeeded in devising operational definitions for ten out of the eighteen clinical dimensions thus identified, crucial aspects of Sally's psychopathology and the analytic process defied our attempts at systematic definition and categorization. On the basis of this clinical report, we categorized five analytic themes to be part of the pathological structures (intrapsychic conflicts) underlying diabetic mismanagement. These concerned Sally's feeling unloved by her father, angry with him for his lack of responsiveness, and frustration of her wish to be loved, admired, and valued by him; rivalry with her mother for father's love and attention; ambivalence towards her, deriving from the experience of mother's psychiatric illness when she was 6; anxiety and guilt feelings over death wishes towards her parents and other family members who disappointed her; and, finally, conflicts concerning the threats associated with diabetes, both reality-based and as distorted by defensive processes.

A second set of analytic themes of comparable prominence in the treatment referred to material regarding Sally's symptoms. These included her imitation of boys and related fantasies, phobic anxiety in connection with attending school, her imagined or actual intention to punish herself, fantasies concerning a view of herself as being physically damaged, and manifestations of resistance to therapeutic progress in the analysis. Operational definitions were also formulated for each of the symptom categories to facilitate the rating of the presence or absence of each in weekly reports. To give an example, the generic definition given for phobic anxiety was 'specific fears identified during the analysis as conscious manifestations of anxiety deriving from unconscious conflict'. Such operational definitions of the ten symptoms and conflicts were categorized and illustrated in the instructions to raters.

Ratings of the weekly reports were then carried out by two independent raters—both child analysts—and the treating analyst on a five-point scale: 'Definitely present', 'Probably present', 'Possibly present', 'Probably absent', and 'Definitely not present'.

The correlations between the three raters were computed using Pearson's product–moment correlation coefficients. The inter-rater correlations were moderate to high, with more than 60% of correlations above 0.65. Three of the analytic themes (conflicts over murderous wishes, and the symptoms of a damaged self-representation and resistance to the analysis) had mean inter-rater coefficients of less than 0.6 and were excluded from further analysis. The average inter-rater correlations for the seven remaining themes ranged from 0.78 to 0.62, with a mean of 0.70.

Diabetic control was assessed in terms of weekly urine glucose content over the 148 weeks of Sally's analytic treatment and the two preceding years. In order to assess the quality of control for each of the 288 relevant weeks, fourteen tests per week (the specimen before breakfast and the evening meal for each day) were examined, and the percentage of tests showing less than 1% of glycosuria was computed (Ludvigsson, 1977). This yielded weekly averages of negative urine glucose tests ranging from 8 to 100%, with a standard deviation of 22.6%. To validate this index the correlation between all available random blood glucose measures taken at the hospital over the period of the psychoanalysis and the corresponding weekly index of glycosuria was computed, yielding a Pearson product–moment correlation of 0.84 ($df = 7, p < 0.005$).

Results

The association between diabetic control and the therapist's ratings of the seven reliable psychoanalytic themes was calculated, and 6 of the 7 correlations reached statistical significance. In order to examine further the nature of the relationship between urine glucose and the analytic themes noted above, lag correlation coefficients were computed between glycosuria and the ratings of psychoanalytic themes. For example, in looking at the dimension concerned with Sally's feeling unloved and in conflict about her anger with father, we wished to know whether the emergence of this material tended to precede improvements in diabetic control or, conversely, whether an improvement in diabetic control ushered in changes in the nature of the analytical material.

The detailed data on fluctuations in diabetic control and their correlation with analytic themes were then computed (after statistically eliminating trends, i.e. gradual shifts or drifts in the data). This revealed that the verbalization and interpretation of oedipal conflict in the psychoanalysis was associated with reduced glycosuria, i.e. an improvement in diabetic control, two to four weeks later. The related conflict concerning anger with father showed an alternative pattern, i.e. preceding the improvement by a week.

In contrast, however, two of the three symptoms showed a contrary relationship, in that following on improvements in diabetic control Sally experienced an exacerbation of phobic reactions and her tendency to punish and hurt herself deliberately.

Discussion

This study demonstrated that the working through of psychic conflict predicted an improvement in diabetic control. Sally's improvement over the course of the treatment both in terms of diabetic control and in other respects was heartening to her therapist, but these improvements were not the major foci of this investigation.

In view of the over-riding trend of improvement of blood glucose levels over the course of treatment, the long-term association between psychotherapeutic themes and diabetic control must be viewed with caution as a common underlying trend may account for their association. The association in the short-term, when common underlying trends were removed, is of far greater theoretical interest.

Grünbaum (1984) argues that symptomatic improvement in association with psychoanalytically derived insight may be totally accounted for by the intensification of the analyst's demand on the patient for improvement in association with self-understanding. Whilst it may be argued that the analyst unwittingly and consistently made such demands on Sally, it is very difficult to imagine how he could have made a consistent demand on Sally to improve blood glucose regulation in the absence of knowledge of her diabetic control. Yet relevant analytic material was found regularly to precede changes in glycosuria.

Furthermore, the temporal relationship of Sally's symptoms and glycosuria, although not initially predicted, is highly consistent with the psychoanalytic theory of neurosis and ill fits Grünbaum's model of the psychoanalytic process. Temporary improvements in Sally's diabetic control were regularly followed by an increase in other neurotic symptomatology. The increase in phobic avoidance and deliberate self-harm consequent upon improvement in diabetic control may be understood as a dynamically meaningful reaction, reflecting the patient's relative incapacity to tolerate states of well-being. We may assume that during certain phases of the analysis, particularly during its early years, good blood glucose control could only be achieved through temporary inhibitions, which exacerbated psychological conflict and led to a significant intensification of other psychological symptoms. A non-dynamic account of such a temporal association is difficult to formulate.

Conclusion

Our initial aim was to demonstrate that psychoanalytic data could be organized and examined in a way that is consistent with the canons of eliminative inductivism. We have been able to show that psychoanalytically informed insight-oriented therapeutic intervention can bring about improvements in a condition known to be resistant to alternative treatment interventions. The findings run counter to many current behavioural formulations of the determinants of diabetic control that stress specific skills or cognitive deficits in the aetiology of this disorder. The present findings underline the importance of focusing upon the personal meaning of diabetic mismanagement. Overall, the findings support our view of brittle diabetes as caused by the investment with unconscious emotional significance of some aspect of the disease and its medical treatment. Thus the disorder appears to be in no way qualitatively different from other neurotic conditions in which the hope of obtaining relief from anxiety and guilt may be seen as the principal motivation underlying symptom maintenance.

Blood glucose regulation in diabetic patients is useful for the systematic assessment of the efficacy of psychotherapeutic endeavours. Blood glucose control provides 'hard' suggestion-resistant measures of psychological status. Its clear link with behavioural problems offers an unusually precise indication of the extent to which a psychological procedure may succeed in bringing about a shift in habitual modes of responding, and, from this point of view, it could be recommended as a testing ground for the relative effectiveness of various forms of psychotherapeutic intervention. However, the rarity of the condition and the unique demands that diabetes places upon the child and his family call into question the generalizability of the findings to other psychological conditions. Nevertheless, we hope that we have provided a useful paradigm for research on the effectiveness of child psychoanalysis.

CHAPTER NINETEEN

Telling the child about adoption

Jill Hodges and Maria Berger

This is an application of research to the study of adopted children attending for psychoanalytic psychotherapy at the Anna Freud Centre. It discusses the question of when and how parents tell adopted children about their adoption and looks at this from the viewpoint of the meaning of the information for the inner world of the child at different developmental stages. The chapter draws on case material, on previous publications of the research group, and on a number of other psychoanalytic and non-psychoanalytic publications on the subject of disclosure of adoption.

[R.S.]

The question of when children should be told about their being adopted has been debated in the adoption literature for at least four decades, and we review below a spectrum of opinions. Our own interest arose when at the Anna Freud Centre we formed a study group on adopted children in psychoanalytic treatment. Our aim was to learn about the inner world of the adopted child; our basic data were the therapists' weekly reports containing a detailed ongoing account of the treatment process.

Discussion focussed on issues such as the adopted children's thoughts and fantasies about their adoption and biological parents; the way in which adoption impinged upon their sense of identity, self-representation, and self-esteem, and the effects upon their ego and superego development (Berger, 1979, 1980; Hodges, 1984, 1989; Hodges et al., 1985). However, a subject of a more practical nature kept recurring, especially on the occasions when we presented some of these findings for discussion outside the research group. This was the question of when to tell the child that he or she is adopted (Berger & Hodges, 1982).

Because of the changing patterns of adoption in recent years, this question applies for a decreasing proportion of adoptees— those adopted very young, whose knowledge of the adoption therefore must be gained after the event. The question itself however remains of concern to adoptive parents and to professional workers. Views fall within a continuum between two opposite positions: (1) the child should be told as early as possible, and (2) the child should be told as late as possible or not at all.

Telling as early as possible

'The safest rule is to start telling almost before he can understand what "adopted" means', writes Margaret Kornitzer (1976, p. 118). She explains: ' . . . a child who is old enough to know what it means is already old enough to be hurt by the information.' Another idea behind such early telling is that the child will not remember later any time when he did not know and will not be at the mercy of children or adults who did know.

She advises that telling be done in stages—in babyhood, using 'adoption' as a 'term of endearment' frequently, 'as a rhythm . . . with loving overtones' (p. 121). Next, at age 2 or 2½, the child is to be told stories about 'mothers and fathers who wanted a baby and never had one', then 'they heard about some babies who had no fathers and mothers, and chose one of them to come home with them and be their own forever and ever'. 'Very soon', the author anticipates, 'the child will be told or will guess with great pleasure, that the story is really about him'. In a 1980 version of a guide for adoptive parents, *Explaining Adoption,* the British Association of Adoption and Fostering Agencies follows similar lines, except on the 'chosen child' issue, which parents are advised 'not to overdo' and which by 1987 is no longer recommended at all. The guide suggests that from an early age the word 'adopted' is used in association with cuddles and endearments, so that although it will not be understood, it will carry positive meaning for the child.

In the United States a number of psychoanalytic writers have opposed very early disclosure of adoption information (Peller, 1961, 1963; Schechter, 1960; Wieder, 1977, 1978). Brodzinsky (1984) comments that 'Most adoption authorities', with the exception of the above, recommend early disclosure—at some point between 2 and 4 years of age—followed by periodic discussions and re-interpretation during childhood.

Knight (1941), one American psychoanalyst who favoured early disclosure, felt that the parents lived 'in continuous dread' lest the child might learn from outside sources, and perhaps without saying anything to the parents. He suggested telling the child 'as soon as he can comprehend' (p. 70). The child might think little of it and forget about it, but as he developed he should be told several more times, until he understood it. He advised: 'The first time the child is told, some time during the fourth year, depending on his intellectual comprehension, he should be told a story . . .' (p. 71). This is some two years later than suggested by Kornitzer.

Wieder (1978) was critical of early disclosure, stating 'In the adoptees I have studied, their development and relationships to the adoptive mothers were clinically indistinguishable from blood kin children up to the time they were told of their adoption. After the disclosure, the children's behaviour, thought contents, and relationships showed dramatic changes . . .' (p. 795).

He described (1977) these effects of disclosure at the age of 3 in the cases of three of his analytic patients, adopted soon after birth. However, we must note that Wieder's 'prototypical model'—the infant adopted soon after birth by an infertile couple ethnically similar to the biological mother—is now increasingly rare.

The main conclusions he presented were:

(1) The message of relinquishment, 'communicated at an age when fantasy and reality were not clearly demarcated . . . had endowed phase-specific fantasies of loss of object and of love with a sense of actuality' (1978, pp. 795–796). The result was overwhelming separation anxiety, including regression. He claims that 'far from forgetting', his patients 'were obsessed with the story and the fantasy distortions derived from it' (p. 796). He sees his clinical data as validating the assumption that early disclosure 'is traumatic and disruptive to the developing personality'.

(2) To tell the child between the ages of 2 and 3, at the height of the separation/individuation phase and of anal psychosexual development, that another mother and father made him but could not keep him, creates a confusion concerning the developing conceptualization of the term 'mother'. This undermines basic trust. Wieder says: 'The parents' dread that the child will hear becomes a "need to tell", which is projectively transformed into the "child's need to be told".' A toddler 'doesn't need to know he is adopted'—Wieder stresses—'he needs to know he belongs' . . . (p. 799).

One can see the force of his arguments, if one were to confine one's considerations to the 'prototype model'. However, a further observation should be added—viz., that the rationale in terms of 'parental dread' is based on a generalization. Parents differ as individuals and in class, religious, and cultural influences. While some may dread that their child will hear about his adoption from a third party and readily follow advice of early 'telling', others may dread much more the actual telling and keep deferring it. It is, indeed, to the latter group of parents that

Kornitzer's book and other adoption agency publications appear mainly to address themselves. 'Many adopters . . . wish that their child need never know, and shrink from the whole business of telling', Kornitzer says (1976, p. 115). *A Guide to Adoption Practice* (Advisory Council on Child Care, 1970) also discusses adopters' difficulties in telling the child. It points to their fears that the child will be upset, that he may love them less, may wish to trace his biological parents, etc.

For many parents the telling is an experience that undermines their wish to believe that the child is theirs. If both the toddler and his adoptive parents need to feel that they belong with each other, how does the use of the word 'adoption' as endearment fit in with this need? It seems that the idea behind it—i.e. that the child should grow up feeling that to be adopted is a nice thing—implies a kind of conditioning. It is conceivable that the child may connect the 'endearing' word with the story of adoption told him later. However, to our mind, whether he will feel as he grows older that his adoption is a happy thing will depend on many factors, and least of all on early childhood associations with the word 'adopted'.

It seems almost as though there is a wish that the child's early incomprehension should anaesthetize him against the element of pain that is part of the information and that this anaesthesia should persist and spare him pain when he does comprehend it. We would argue that some pain is inseparable from comprehending that one is adopted: this does not mean that one must assume it to be so intrinsically painful that one must try to prevent the child from knowing anything about it. Any child, as part of his development, must confront situations with an element of pain. The important thing is that these situations come about at such a time and in such a way that the child has adequate resources to deal with them; and we feel the same applies to knowing about adoption.

Brodzinsky (1984), reporting on the Rutgers adoption project in which approximately 300 adopted children and their mothers were interviewed, questions the widely accepted recommendation of early disclosure (usually between 2 and 4 years of age). However, he does not reject the policy per se, as in his view this does provide the basis for a trusting parent–child relation, relieves parents of 'the burden of deception', and minimizes the chance of the child being told in an unfriendly way or by someone other than a parent. It also allows parents to try out ways of handling the disclosure process before the child begins actively to ask questions.

He draws attention to the twin goals of adoption revelation—*telling*, the parents' task, and *understanding*, the child's task, one less often considered. The problem with early 'telling', from his point of view, is that pre-schoolers generally 'simply do not understand the adoption information presented to them', not because of any fault in the parents' presentation, but because of cognitive limitations at this stage of their development. More than half the twenty adopted 4- to 5-year-olds he studied either had no notion of adoption or fused the concepts of adoption and birth. By 6 or 7 years the majority of children made a clear differentiation between adoption and birth as alternative ways of entering a family and accepted that adoption was permanent, on the basis that 'my Mummy said so'. Among the forty children between the ages of 8 and 11, he found that children began to appreciate the uniqueness and some of the complications entailed by their adoptive status. He notes that for some of these children, 'the adoptive family relationship suddenly became tenuous' and 'much of the child's fantasy life now (became) centred on the biological parents' potential for reclaiming the child'. Only by early to middle adolescence did he find that in general children had achieved something approximating to the adult understanding of adoption as a legally based permanent arrangement.

Emotional, as well as cognitive, reasons may lead to a young child's inability to see himself as born to someone other than his mother. We know, too, that in the 8–11 age group where Brodzinsky found a number of children preoccupied with questions of the biological parents, many non-adopted children also have similar fantasies, which we know as the family romance (Freud, 1909c). We have discussed elsewhere (Hodges, 1984, 1989) how these fantasies can be seen as adoption 'theories', like infantile sexual theories, that address the mystery of the child's origins; also as ways of allowing the child self-representation as a wanted child, counteracting the narcissistic damage consequent on the knowledge that they were given up by the first parents.

Rationale for telling the child as late as possible

Wieder (1977, p. 801) feels that there is no 'best' time to tell and that the question should be 'When will be least traumatic?'

He mentions that many 'with tradition to back them up' question the need to tell at all. He refers to some views that latency is an appropriate phase, but he himself finds that ' . . . precise pinpointing of when structure, phase conflicts and cognitive development are optimal is difficult to generalise'. And he concludes, 'It appears that the longer the communication can be put off the better' (pp. 801–802). He believes that in adolescence adoptees should have access to their records, without, however, specifying when they should have been told about their adoption.

The most extreme view, well outside the mainstream of adoption thinking, is that, preferably, the child should never be told that he is adopted. This view is expressed by Ansfield (1971), whose main reason for not telling children is that 'the knowledge will hurt them' (p. 36). He thinks parents should have an option of telling or not, and that those who do want to tell form a small percentage of adoptive parents.

He suggests various precautions to safeguard the secret: telling as few people as possible, saying nothing to the adoption agency about intending not to tell the child, and other quite extreme measures. Though he concedes that older siblings must be informed, he advises that 3- to 5-year olds 'can be told the family is playing a game, and that no one is ever to know the secret, including the adopted child'. He acknowledges that this might be discovered but maintains that the 'later in life the child finds out he is adopted, the better equipped he is emotionally to handle it' (p. 45). Critical of insistence that the parents must tell the child, he notes a lack of research on the issue. Since the publication of Ansfield's book several such studies have been published; at least one (McWhinnie, 1967) had already appeared. There is now plenty of evidence that, in the words of the BAAF Guide for Adoptive Parents (Chenells, 1987), 'Adoption can't be kept a secret forever' (p. 5), and that not being told by the parents has detrimental effects on adoptees and their relationship with their parents.

The most convincing evidence, we think, is provided by research aimed at finding out what adopted people themselves think. Triseliotis (1973) interviewed seventy people who had asked the Register House in Edinburgh for information from their original birth entries. (In Scotland, since 1930, people over the age of 17 have been able to obtain this information; in the rest of the United Kingdom, since 1975, at age 18+). Of those interviewed, 60% wished to meet the birth parents; the rest wanted information about their backgrounds.

Over half this sample had not been told about their adoption by their parents but had found out from other sources. Triseliotis says 'The parents' reluctance to tell was resented and criticized. . . . Most adoptees failed to appreciate . . . the explanation that they were trying to protect them . . . viewed this kind of protection as misguided' (p. 36). This contradicts Ansfield's idea that parents should avoid hurting the child and therefore withhold the information from them.

Triseliotis states that the adoptees whom he interviewed 'were agreed that the child should be told by his own parents and on no account to be left to find out from outsiders or from documents' (p. 144). Most said they should be told when still children—somewhere between four and twelve. Some felt the ages between 4 and 8 were the most appropriate for telling. The studies of McWhinnie (1967) and Raynor (1980) also revealed that a vast majority of adopted adults felt emphatically that the source of the information should be the adoptive parents. McWhinnie concluded that children should be told before the age of 9, and that risks occur from the age of 5 onwards; Raynor notes that 'all too often' in her study those who learned after age 5 learned from someone other than a parent.

Other studies, based on counselling interviews with adoptees seeking access to their birth certificates in England (ABAFA, 1980a), report findings very similar to those of McWhinnie and

Triseliotis. The author of a West Midlands study, for instance, states that 'adoptees who found out about their adoption from sources other than their parents were conscious of the stunning effect of the disclosure at the time' (ibid., p. 13).

Thus one finding that emerges is that many people did discover they were adopted, although their parents had chosen not to tell them. A view like Ansfield's (1971) would strike us now as naive in its assumptions that a child can be kept from knowing, and that it is preferable to bring up an adopted child (and any siblings) in an atmosphere of prolonged secrecy concerning his or her origins rather than to tell them truthfully. The very fact that the child might sense something that is not talked about at home could risk creating both a distrust of parents and a feeling that knowing in general is dangerous, with possible consequent effects on learning. When the child does learn, as is probable, from other sources, there is now ample evidence of the 'stunning effect' of such a disclosure and the deleterious effect on the adoptees' feelings about the adoptive parents.

'Telling' in latency

Several analytic publications dealing with the issues of adoption express the view that the disclosure should not take place before latency. Marshall D. Schechter, Lili Peller, Miriam Williams, and others are all critical of the prevalent practice of early 'telling'.

Schechter (1960) discusses the high incidence of adopted children amongst his patients; he '. . . raises the question of the timing of the knowledge of adoption prior to the resolving of the oedipal phase', holding that knowledge of their adoptive status often coming at the time of the oedipal conflict 'can seem to prolong and actually prevent the resolution of this particular area of personality development' (p. 31). Based on material presented, he concludes that '. . . the immature ego cannot cope with the knowledge of the rejection by its original parents. . . . The child tends to react to this information by character change or symptom formation.'

Lili Peller (1961, 1963) is critical of telling the child between the ages of 2 and 4. Describing the young child's belief in the power of his wishes and his many misconceptions, she says: 'When he is told about adoption without having asked, the information may be either completely meaningless and hence quickly repressed or it conjures up these archaic fantasies and becomes entangled in them' (1961, p. 4).

These views might not be accepted by British workers in the field. Schechter's and Peller's views, for instance, are disputed by Raynor (1980). She surveyed 160 families of foster parents and adopters and found that 75% of the 105 parents of adoptees had told their children about their adoption before they started school, i.e. before the age of 5. According to Raynor's information from the parents, these children 'received the news with pride and pleasure or sometimes with indifference; it was only among the older children that parents had noticed any sign of shock or bitterness' (p. 94). Raynor concludes that telling before age 5 was least damaging, though many children did not understand the significance till later, and that the study supports Triseliotis' finding that 'those who found out late or came to know about their adoption from outside sources were the most hurt and upset' and also contradicts Schecter's and Peller's views.

Some reservations come to mind about these conclusions.

1. The people in the Triseliotis study who found out late did not, in many instances, find out until adolescence or young adulthood.

2. 'Early telling' in this study concerns an age-range that includes toddlers as well as school-starters. The experiences of children in the respective age groups would by no means be the same.

3. To be told after age 5 was, as Raynor points out, more often to be told by others or told 'in a far from ideal context' by parents. The vivid examples given by Raynor of damaging revelations indicate how extraordinarily rejecting some of these were. For instance, an 11-year-old caught stealing from his mother's purse was told about his adoption thus: 'I'm not your Mummy, Daddy is not your Daddy, and Sis is not your sister. We picked you out from a

lot of babies and now you let us down.' Whether the child was told before age 5 or not is hardly the salient problem here.

Issues of what to tell and how to tell

It is obvious that the question of 'when' cannot be treated in isolation from the content of what is revealed to the child and how it is revealed. This link is made poignantly clear by Triseliotis. Almost half of those adoptees interviewed by him, who were told by their parents, 'experienced it as negative and traumatic or as unfortunate. . . .' (1973, p. 29). This happened 'where the parents left it either very late to tell, or told him in a hostile way, or made belittling references to the adoptee's original background'.

By contrast, those interviewees who perceived the telling as positive experienced a feeling of 'well-being', of 'being special'. They were generally told earlier than the previous group. Their adoptive parents made little reference to their biological parents but conveyed 'a good image of them' (p. 31).

Two issues concerning the content of the information are discussed throughout the literature on adoption: (1) Whether or not to tell the child he has been 'chosen', and (2) whether, or how much, to tell the child about his biological parents.

The 'chosen child'

We have previously expressed our view that the 'chosen baby' approach is disingenuous (Berger, 1979). It certainly is at odds with the current situation, when the number of babies available for adoption is very small.

Several writers are critical of the 'chosen child' approach. Lillie Peller (1961) maintains that the term is either irrelevant or grossly misleading to the child, and is dishonest. Glenn (1974) is of the opinion that 'telling the child early, and repeatedly that he has been chosen by his parents . . . may lead the child to feel that he is special, an exception, and cause him to develop super-ego defects' (p. 417). Miriam Williams (reported by Schechter, 1967) thinks that to tell a child he is chosen 'only serves to deny the fact of abandonment by the biological mother' (p. 706).

Goodacre (1966) found that many adopters had rejected the 'chosen' approach, not only because it was inaccurate, but also because it was misleading. The Association of British Adoption and Fostering Agencies in the 1980 edition of their guide to adoptive parents suggests that they should not over-emphasize the idea of the child having been chosen lest he might come to fear that if he disappoints them they might send him back. In the further changed adoption climate of 1987, the 'chosen' issue has disappeared from the text.

Of course feeling precious does not have to be conveyed to the adopted child via stories of having been 'chosen'. However, the evidence quoted above indicates that adopted people have a profound need to feel special, particularly at the time when the facts of their adoption are being explained to them. The most painful and difficult question that confronts the adopted child is why he or she was given up (Hodges, 1984). Being told that she or he was 'chosen', 'special', etc. may temporarily help to shelve the question and assist in the construction of a self-representation as a wanted rather than an unwanted child (Brinich, 1980).

The biological parents

All studies based on surveys of adult adoptees that we have come across (and many autobiographical accounts) reveal a wish to have known more about their biological parents (Jaffe & Fanshel, 1970); McWhinnie, 1967; Triseliotis, 1973; ABAFA, 1980). How much should adopted people learn about this in childhood? Triseliotis' (1973) sample felt that 'background information should be gradually more available at a rate within the child's capacity to understand and absorb' (p. 41). In puberty and adolescence they had an 'intense desire and curiosity to know more about their origins' (Ibid.). Many parents, however, were reported to have revealed nothing more than the fact of their adoption. Ansfield (1971) advises against giving details of the natural parents, as this could lead the child to want to find his biological mother. This assumption is contradicted by Triseliotis' findings. Adoptees who had been given a fair amount of information in a positive way did not intend to meet their biological parents. Those who had not been given information or given some facts but in a hostile way, did want to meet them.

A wish to 'complete themselves' through gaining more information characterized the former group; a great difficulty in understanding themselves without knowing their origins was conveyed by the latter group.

Children are not always able to let their parents know how much they would like to learn about their biological parents. Adoptive parents interviewed by Goodacre (1966) reported that, while some children asked searching questions 'the rest showed an alleged lack of interest' (p. 115). She refers to McWhinnie's study of adult adoptees, which revealed that, as children, they had been most curious about their origins but wanted the information to come from their parents. The adopters, in their turn, awaited their children's questions and interpreted the children's feigned indifference at its face value.

Barbara Tizard (1977), whose research concerned children up to the age of 8 adopted from institutions after the age of 2, reports that some parents commented that their children never asked questions about the 'telling', and that other parents felt their children had 'shut off' after a point and did not want to know. 'The difficulties of "telling" are . . . greater than many social workers realise, and arise not only from the reluctance of the parent but also of the child' (p. 142). 'The information may be both difficult for the child to comprehend and unwelcome', she suggests, 'but the more freely it is discussed, the less mystified the child will be' (p. 143).

This points to one more difficult task that adoptive parents have to fulfil—namely, to appraise whether their child wants to know but refrains from asking, or whether at the particular stage of his development, or due to other circumstances, he is not ready to know. Forcing a child to know about his biological origins when he may not be able to cope with the information may be as great a mistake on the parents' part as their reluctance to look behind the facade of 'lack of interest' in the child.

Revelation of adoption in five case examples

Of the five children we describe here, two were reported by their parents never to have asked questions to do with their adoption. Four of the children were adopted in their infancy, and one at the age of 2. The four could conform to Wieder's 'prototypical model' of adoption, except that in two cases the adoptive parents, though childless at the time of the adoption, later produced a child.

The disturbances of the children consisted of behaviour problems: difficult relationships with parents and others and, in the case of the older children, learning difficulties. Their pathology was of varying degrees of severity, ranging from mainly neurotic disturbances to those due to distorted personality development. In the case vignettes that follow we have tried to focus on these children's reactions to disclosure of adoption. However, some overlap with their reactions to their adoption in general is unavoidable.

Only the parents of two children (Ben and William) provided us with information about reactions to the first 'telling'. In none of the cases did the parents connect the emergence of their children's emotional problems with the revelation of adoption. This is unlike the three cases reported by Wieder. It may be that the parents of the children with whom we worked were less insightful and less aware of a link between their children's disturbances and the disclosure of adoption, or less prepared to talk about it. It may also be that there were other disturbing circumstances besides the disclosure in the background in these cases, which led the parents to talk about, say, the child's reaction to the acquisition of a sibling, rather than to the 'telling'.

In our analytic material, again unlike Wieder's cases, the subject of the first 'telling' did not appear directly. What did come to the fore were memories of later occasions of being 'told' (e.g. Jacqueline), or derivatives of initial reactions (e.g. Elsie, Sophie). Each case highlights some aspects of the difficulties inherent in the process of disclosure.

William

William, adopted at 9 weeks, was referred to the clinic at the age of 8 years. Although milestones had been within the normal range, learning and behaviour difficulties appeared when he entered primary school. His referral symptoms included smearing and hiding faeces and strange, potentially dangerous behaviour at school. His parents reported long-standing difficulties in getting through to him. They had talked to him about his adoption 'even before he could understand' and read him a book about it. They said William loved to hear how he came to their home, especially how his carry-cot did not fit into their car and how he had cried the first day. The parents reported that he never asked questions about his adoption but had recently asked about his biological mother—'Was she very old?' His mother would bring up the subject of adoption whenever there was a 'natural lead' and always celebrated the day of William's arrival. Once when she had remarked that everything in their house was secondhand, William replied, 'I am secondhand, too'.

When he was 2½, his mother gave birth to a girl. William was said to have taken the birth in his stride and had apparently been very protective towards his sister.

His treatment elicited little about his adoption; wild, aggressive behaviour with physical attacks on the therapist marked many of his sessions. However, when treatment was terminated after two years, the anal symptoms had disappeared, and school behaviour had somewhat improved. The therapist considered that the main gain had been a greater freedom of communication between child and parents, which included the subject of William's first mother.

It is difficult to know how far the adoption was a cause of William's disturbance, though one knows that he felt 'secondhand'. The birth of a natural sister must have played a part in this. Though the 'telling' about the adoption had followed the adoption agencies' lines, yet William showed no willingness to ask or talk about it. Why? With insufficient material here we can only speculate along the following lines:

1. Though the 'telling before he could understand' may have been meaningless at the time, the birth of the sister must have conveyed an awareness that he had not come from this mother's womb. Perhaps he asked no questions for fear of displeasing his parents.

2. William was said to 'love' the story of how the carry-cot did not fit into the car, but one wonders whether he did not sense in this some parental anxiety that he might not fit into the family. His wish to have the story repeated may reflect efforts at mastery rather than pleasure.

3. The parents' well-intentioned frequent referrals to adoption may not have been welcome, especially with the presence of a non-adopted sibling. Similarly, he might have preferred to celebrate just his birthday, like his sister, and not the date of his arrival in their home. A wish to deny these differences could ensue, leading to avoidance of the subject of adoption and a stifling of curiosity in general.

Sophie

Sophie was adopted at 7½ weeks. When she was 2½ years old, another little girl was adopted, and when she was 5½, a natural son was born. She was referred to the clinic at age 9 because of obesity and a difficult relationship with her mother. Our Well Baby Clinic had noted that in infancy this relationship had gone well. But as Sophie grew older, the mother became preoccupied with her messiness and increasingly rejecting towards her during the anal phase, and a mutually provocative relationship developed. She had been told about her own adoption when her sister was adopted (and she herself in the anal phase). She was told that they had both been 'chosen'. However, when she became jealous and demanding, the mother would threaten, for example, that she would give her away to the dirty old woman at the end of the road.

It became apparent through her fantasies during treatment that she felt thoroughly rejected, as when after a weekend break she threw her doll at the therapist, screaming, 'She's not my baby, she's adopted; throw her in the Thames!' She saw both her mothers as bad, saying, 'I have a foster mother, my real mother is dead. She tried to kill me.'

Sophie fantasied that her (male) therapist was her biological father, but later accused him of killing a little girl with poison bombs. A fantasy that 'a baby has been stolen' came to the fore after she heard from her therapist that he would be leaving. There was a recurrent fantasy about two fathers fighting over a baby, stealing it and being punished. In the end the mother kept the baby for herself, but only to spite the fathers. These fantasies, prompted by her therapist's impending departure, reflect her desperate efforts to understand why she had been given away.

Though fantasies of being kidnapped are common in adopted (and non-adopted) children (Peller, 1961), Sophie's had an individual stamp. Her stories of a baby killed with bombs or stolen contain both anal-sadistic and oedipal determinants. They may have been linked with the timing of the disclosure of her adoption, i.e. at the height of her anal phase. To her perception of her adoptive mother as depriving her of her faeces, and of a place in the family after the sister's adoption, she may have grafted on the fantasy that she had been stolen. A shift in her fantasy, with father now the thief, may have reflected her shift to the oedipal phase.

Sophie herself occasionally 'stole' things from others; also the therapist thought that the adoptive mother had a fantasy that she had 'stolen' Sophie.

This case illustrates intense maternal conflict over the ownership of an adopted child, the wish to disown Sophie often coming to the fore. What sense could the child make of the story that she was 'chosen' if she was also threatened with being sent away? The birth of her non-adopted brother, re-opening the whole question of where she came from, proved to be confusing for her, though she had known about her adoption at least since the age of 3.

Jacqueline

Jacqueline acquired an adopted brother when she was 5. She began treatment at age 13, because of learning problems, difficult behaviour at home and at school, a chronically bad relationship with her brother, and angry battles with mother. She had been closer to father since her adoption at 6 weeks, and the fact that he found it easier to comfort the child than did the mother had always been a source of hurt and jealousy to the latter. Jacqueline was told about her adoption long before her brother's adoption, but the event confronted her with the fact of her own adoption in a new and forceful way.

Analytic material demonstrated that the 're-telling' at 5 had a marked impact on the nature of her phallic phase development. In treatment she explained that at 5 she had not even understood the true meaning of adopted but thought it meant she had once had a big toe. This image was understood to be a displacement from the perception of her brother's penis. Analysis revealed that Jacqueline felt castrated and rejected by the combined knowledge of her adoption and the feeling of losing mother to brother. This overwhelming narcissistic injury turned her away from an already difficult relationship to fantasize about an ideal biological mother. She recalled a fantasy that having two sets of parents would mean two sets of presents, and her feelings of rejection and injury when this did not occur revived in the transference.

Her adoptive parents had little information about the biological mother but felt uncertain of giving even this, and were troubled by her wish to know her previous Christian name. The mother's feelings of insecurity about her mothering capacities and fear that Jacqueline would leave her deprived her of an ability to act appropriately in response to misdemeanours, or even to communicate with the child in a natural manner.

Ben

Ben, an adopted child, had a brother six years older, who was the parents' natural son. The reasons for adopting Ben were in part, at least, an attempt to rescue an insecure marriage. However, this failed some two years later, with the father living overseas and the mother and the boys returning to financial and residential insecurity in England.

When Ben began nursery school at the age of 3½, a teacher, on learning that he was adopted, advised Ben's mother to tell him about this. Though efforts were made to do so in a considered way, it later became clear during therapy that it would have been more helpful to have given him further time to cope with the many 'shocks' to which he (and his mother) had most recently been exposed before introducing this new element of insecurity. A year later he came into treatment because of disturbed behaviour at home, hostility to adults in the nursery school, feelings of exclusion by other children, and general unhappiness. He first brought the subject of adoption into the analysis when he expressed intense envy of his brother's birthmark, which was interpreted as his wish for a sign that he had a special place with mother, like his brother had.

Ben's case suggests that if advice to parents about 'telling' is prompted by general considerations—as, for instance, that the child should know by a certain age—it may run counter to the particular needs and preoccupations of that child at that period of his life.

Elsie

Elsie, referred to the clinic when she was 6 years of age, was privately adopted (at 23 months) from a foster family with whom she had lived since she was 6 weeks old. This new family included two older adopted children, a brother and a sister. Although initially showing no overt reaction to removal from the foster-home, she soon appeared terrified of the adoptive parents, withdrawn and tearful, and on entering school appeared abnormal. In treatment one saw that this was not the case, and that for her the emotional impact of the move had created a degree of confusion that had led to a denial of realities and an incapacity to ask questions.

Within six weeks of her treatment, Elsie, remembering her foster-mother, however dimly, said, 'I have a first Mummy and a second Mummy. I like my second Mummy, but I love my first. I don't understand', she added painfully, 'why did it happen, why?' What her parents were unable to explain to her was that before the foster mother there had been the 'very first' one, who gave birth to her but was too ill and unable to keep her. She had fantasies of mothers fighting over her and of the theft of a baby. These were understood as helping her to defend against the pain of being given away by the foster mother because of naughtiness. The therapist prepared the adoptive mother for the fact that the central questions of her adoption and the issue of her biological mother would have to be faced with Elsie. Then, after a session, Elsie repeated her questions to her mother in the therapist's presence. When the mother had completed the explanation, Elsie said to her, 'I like you and I want to stay with you, though I'm glad you didn't born me, because then I wouldn't have my lovely yellow hair.'

In cases where the adopted child does not ask questions but withdraws instead into confused fantasies and develops a pseudo-backward stance, parents need help in deciphering clues that even a young child might give about his frightening version of what had happened. For a child in whose past there was a remembered previous 'mother', the question of why this mother had relinquished him is all the more frightening. Facing it with the child, as the child grows older, has to lead to the acknowledgement of the existence of a natural mother. To avoid this issue can only perpetuate confusion.

Discussion and conclusions

The various opinions on the subject of the timing of the 'telling' about adoption fall roughly into three groups:

1. The 'telling' should be done very early in the child's life.

2. It should not be done before latency.

3. It should occur as late as possible or not at all.

Some writers in the first group argue that in order to safeguard the child from the experience of finding out through other sources, very early telling is advisable, and some feel that this will produce in the child a sense of having always known, thus avoiding the shock of revelation. It seems to be this desire to spare the child the anxiety of ever learning for the first time, as much as the shock of learning from outsiders, that has pushed further and further back the age when the child should be told.

The answers cannot be ready-made—the choice of what and when it is best to tell, is, of necessity, a compromise between the child's circumstances and own *individual* needs and capacities to assimilate the information.

Most of the children discussed were told early in their lives, whether by the parents' choice or by necessity (e.g. the arrival of a sibling). Although we cannot conclude that early disclosure (or this alone) was responsible for their emotional disturbance, it should be said that none of the children could be quoted as an example of good coping with the early-acquired information. Of course, the 'what' and 'how' of it is very pertinent, and the content of some communications may leave much to be desired. In general, the younger the children, the more difficult for the adoptive parents to help them to assimilate the information cognitively and emotionally. An exception would be an older child who had previously been encouraged to believe something different. In addition, the characteristic conflicts of each phase of development are bound to affect the child's response. Disclosure during the anal phase, when ambivalence towards the adoptive mother is at its height, with characteristic conflicts over independence and issues of keeping or giving up faeces, is not a suitable time to confront the child with knowledge of adoption. As Sophie's case indicates, this information may become entangled in anal-sadistic fantasies with features such as killing the baby with bombs, stealing it, etc. Although the degree of conflict between Sophie and her mother was especially high, it seems probable that revelation of adoption during the anal phase might increase any child's ambivalence towards the mother who is there, i.e. the adoptive mother; it might also endow the child's self-representation with primitive negative characteristics deriving from anal stage fantasies (e.g. Sophie's '. . . she's adopted, throw her in the Thames').

'Telling' *is* very difficult—doing it appropriately is more difficult still. For parents to ascertain the right time for their child to learn about being adopted; to be able to discern when the child shows signs of wanting to know more, and when that readiness has not yet arrived; to accept the unreadiness but not accept at face value the apparent lack of interest—all this requires a great amount of empathy. Whether they can muster it depends on their personalities, on their marital relationship, and on other life circumstances at the time. Advice to parents tends to concentrate on when the disclosure is supposed to be right for the child, but the timing of the revelation should also feel right to the parents, in terms both of their own and their child's readiness.

If the first 'telling' is difficult for the child and the parents, the next stages of it are no less beset with problems. As the child grows older and thinks more than before about the biological parents, he or she should ideally meet with parental readiness gradually to share information, especially in adolescence. Instead, the adoptee may meet with evasiveness (e.g. Jacqueline) or more-or-less hidden derogatory remarks about the biological parents.

Adopted children's adolescence tends to be an extremely difficult period (Mackie, 1982). It is hard for the children, who are faced with the task of creating a sense of adolescent identity that has to accomodate two sets of parents and, very often, illegitimacy. It is hard for the parents, who may see their children's adolescence as a time when they might wish to leave and search for their biological parents and, in the case of girls, when they may repeat their biological mother's sexual enactments. Where parents have adopted through infertility, their adopted childrens' adolescent sexuality may pose particular problems. There are clearly very strong arguments, external and internal, against leaving disclosure until this phase.

Have we arrived, then, at a conclusion about the 'best' age for the disclosure of adoption? Like Wieder, we do not think there is a 'best age'—nor, indeed, that there is any one age that could be uniformly suggested. Very early 'telling' is beset with difficulties inherent in the child's developmental immaturity; 'telling' in adolescence is widely regarded as detrimental. There remains a wide age-range within which parents can consider how soon the child's circumstances and capacity allow him or her to cope with the information, as well as their own readiness to give it and the risk that someone else will reveal it to the child. Often this last circumstance, or others we have outlined, like the arrival of a sibling, may dictate that something be said earlier than might be indicated otherwise.

We do not think that information about adoption can be given and received without a measure of pain. The important thing is to choose the time when the child has most on his side to cope with it.

CHAPTER TWENTY

The strengths
of a practitioner's workshop
as a new model in clinical research

Margaret Rustin

In exploring and clarifying the ways in which a practitioner's workshop may provide a specifically suitable model for research within the clinical field, this chapter encourages the prospect of integrating research projects in an enriching way into the work of the child guidance clinic or hospital department. At its simplest the workshop provides a setting where a large number of cases may be considered, assessed, followed, and compared in terms of specific factors. The author explores these issues and presents some illustrations, including work on deprived children and pre-school children. Links are suggested between the theoretical underpinning of such a research workshop and recent developments in psychoanalytic thinking about social and mental structures that foster creative understanding.

(The research function of a workshop also enters in some part into the study on adoption described in chapter nineteen).

[R.S.]

As the profession of child psychotherapy has gradually expanded over the forty years since the first trainings were established, one area of growing interest has been the research aspects of individual psychotherapeutic work. Different strands combine in this developing interest: there is the gradual accumulation of clinical experience, which allows questions of a more general kind to be formulated; there is a generation of experienced child therapists reviewing the effectiveness of their work, seeing the problems of their patients in the context of social change in the wider society, and wishing to understand the interaction of internal and external factors in the changing patterns of pathology. There is also the need to demonstrate the effectiveness of child psychotherapy to health service professionals and administrators and to the broader public to ensure that the provision of psychotherapy for children and young people within the National Health Service is not only safeguarded but viewed as a priority area of expansion.

One of the clinical challenges that child psychotherapists have faced is to find ways to work with the increasingly disturbed children now referred for psychotherapy. Some of the relevant theoretical advances are described elsewhere in this book, but another consequence of the changing population of children seen for therapy is the realization that there are stressful experiences that many of our child-patients have in common, and that attention to the recurring features of work with particular groups of patients would promote effective reflection on our techniques and a better understanding of these children's inner world, and their particular cries of vulnerability.

At the Tavistock Clinic's Department of Children and Parents in the late 1970s, one such group of patients that presented a special challenge were the children and adolescents in care, at that time many of them living in Children's Homes. Increasing numbers were being referred for individual psychotherapy, partly in response to their evident difficulties, but partly also as a consequence of the consultative work done with Children's Homes, which led many residential staff to become concerned about the emotional difficulties of some of the individual children in their care. Quite a large number of these children were taken on for intensive psychotherapy, and this work was reported on in the volume, *Psychotherapy with Severely Deprived Children,* edited by Boston and Szur (1983). A research workshop meeting on a weekly basis ran concurrently with the treatment of this group of children, which provided a forum for the study of their progress in therapy.

This chapter draws on the experience of participating in that workshop, which came to be seen as a model useful in supporting clinical research. There has, in fact, been sustained growth in research work organized on similar lines; workshops focusing on the special features of psychotherapy with autistic children, physically ill and disabled children, and mentally handicapped children are current examples, as well as a workshop on fostered and adopted children, which developed directly from the original study of deprived children, with the new focus reflecting the dramatic changes in child-care policy and planning.

There has always been a potential for clinical research using psychoanalytic psychotherapy as a primary source of data. However, the possibility of gathering together a large enough number of psychotherapists working with a particular kind of case does something to offset a major difficulty in such research, which is to do with the small number of patients that any individual therapist can treat at one time. In the study of in-care deprived children it was possible to follow up eighty cases with whom there had been some sustained contact, and this embraced work in different clinics, referrals from varied sources, different boroughs, and with children of all ages and both sexes, so some of the features of more orthodox research studies could be reproduced. In one sense, any individual piece of psychotherapeutic work is a research project—patient and therapist do not know what the outcome of their exploration together will be. Therapists have some tools to make use of: a practised capacity for close observation of their own and their patients' behaviour, a range of theories that may be relevant in giving order and meaning to observations they are able to make, their experience of work with other patients, and what life itself has taught them. Insofar as it is possible to describe clinical experience in a way that differentiates the observations made and the theoretical constructions found useful in understanding them, the work becomes potentially available to the wider scientific community. There is a model here of careful descriptive writing (used in reporting the psychotherapy undertaken in the 'in care' workshop) that is very helpful in demonstrating the possibility of writing up the clinical process in a way that is both close to the experience of patient and therapist and accessible to a wider readership. The material could be approached by a reader without a psychoanalytic background. He or she would find a body of data that could be considered from other theoretical standpoints but also demonstrates the links between the object of study— namely, the particular assumptions with which deprived children are likely to approach the world and the framework of ideas that this particular group of therapists have found helpful in their efforts to comprehend these children's puzzling behaviour and attitudes.

This model of work could certainly be used more widely. While the relative wealth of therapeutic resources in a large clinic makes it easier to gather a sufficient body of people together, it is sometimes possible for people working in different settings and with varied professional tasks to set up a workshop meeting regularly and to undertake to report systematically on experience with a particular kind of case. Of course further work is certainly also needed to deal with all kinds of questions arising from this original study of working with severely deprived children—to pursue, for example, the issues of which children are most likely to be helped by psychotherapy and to explore problems of foster-placement and foster-breakdown (now part of the agenda of the Fostering and Adoption workshop). But it might also be that a quite different research focus would bring a group together and that, for example, learning difficulties, psychotic disturbance, the effects of mental illness in a parent, or sexual abuse could be investigated. It is of tremendous value in the development of appropriate services for children and families when the often wide divide between practitioners and research workers can be bridged. The relevance of research and the effectiveness of practice could both be improved by this cross-fertilization. The emphasis in the Butler–Schloss report on the events in Cleveland is on the need for working together, on co-operation between the many agencies likely to be involved in Child Abuse Cases, and this plea for close collaboration is equally relevant to research. This research workshop affected its membership and encouraged their development as researchers and therapists, and it is of interest to try to understand why this was so, and how it was achieved.

The research group defined in this way has specific functions that enable the research task to be pursued effectively. The most crucial is the support the group provides for the idea that observations that are as yet unrelated have a potential for being meaningfully linked and patterned. The state of mind that clinicians and researchers have to experience and survive is one in which one does not yet know the significance of what one is doing but has to go on doing it as best one can in the meantime. This is a difficult task because we tend to become disheartened, non-alert, or blunted intellectually or emotionally by data that cannot be organized meaningfully. Maintaining an openness to what comes our way is a prerequisite for keeping alive the capacity to be surprised at a new idea. The new idea may link together observations from a fresh perspective and is usually a harbinger of hope—the hope of things making sense—but also very often a source of disturbance, as it will be likely to challenge previous assumptions. It is the occasion of both excitement and anxiety. The steady interest of the group can enable all these experiences to be better managed. Keats' idea of the 'negative capability' required to be able to write poetry has often been applied to the problems of maintaining a frame of mind suitable for research in human relationships, and it gives one a measure of the difficulty we face that it is a poet's phrase that seems to capture the essence.

The group does, however, have to maintain its functioning as what Wilfred Bion called a 'work group' and will have to resist some processes typical of group life that would subvert the task. [A description of some aspects of group life can be found in *Experiences in Groups* by W. R. Bion (1961). Much further work has been done in developing the understanding of groups, but Bion's central idea of a working group being defined by its capacity to pursue its recognized task and to be alert to the potent distractions of other forms of life characteristic of groups is fundamental.]

The enormous amount of time required to do research in psychotherapy is hard to bear with. Clinical work needs to be recorded in close detail. The valuing of the project by colleagues is important in justifying the hours spent writing up work that may not appear of great worth, and in making tolerable the labour of this kind of minute recording. If a research workshop can be relied on to listen with a fresh ear to one's laboured and often unsuccessful efforts to get into contact with a child, it is a huge support.

The Tavistock Workshop functioned initially in a regular weekly time-slot. Attendance was regular and by and large enthusiastic. Minutes were taken of the discussion that followed the presentation and made available to the membership at subsequent meetings. This created a feeling of direction and momentum that was helpful in supporting people in making the extra effort required by the research task. It was possible for this groundswell of co-operation to continue when a smaller number of the workshop struggled to gather material together in a publishable form.

In more conventional research work, the structure of the investigation as represented by the schedules for questionnaires, the video sequences, taped interviews, etc. takes some of the strain of the doubts and uncertainties off the individual researcher. Well-established methods of gathering evidence can be pursued without too much of a sense of disabling unease about the project and its possible outcome. The function of a practitioners' workshop has some similarly helpful features. As discussed above, the group's attentiveness to the as yet unordered mass of clinical data helps to make tolerable the experience of not knowing how to make sense of things. Additionally, and bearing in mind the acutely painful prior events in the lives of most of the children being studied, the problem of how their therapists were going to cope with often overwhelming experiences of distress and confusion was a crucial one.

Therapy offered a chance that a relationship might develop that could take the strain, but the children did not approach their therapists with much basic trust, and the therapists were necessarily uncertain about how much they would be able to help. When the workshop was initiated, psychotherapy with children who had experienced serious deprivation was not an established area of work. In fact, most of the therapists had probably digested as part of their previous training and experience a received idea to the effect that these children were so damaged as a result of missing areas in their experience of basic care that they were unlikely to be helped by a psychotherapeutic approach. [Previous orthodoxy would probably have stated that such children would need residential care and an experience of good primary care before they could make use of individual psychotherapy (see B. Dockar-Drysdale, 1990). The new idea was that their difficulty in responding to available care might be modified by a psychoanalytic approach.] So there were a number of particular problems that therapists exploring this new area faced. These children were expected to be patients with whom it was difficult to work. This expectation proved quite correct. The therapists found themselves faced with exceptional technical difficulties of various kinds—how to establish any genuine contact with the kind of two-dimensional child who seemed unable to take or keep a grasp on anything really significant; how to manage levels of violent rage in sessions that threatened to destroy the thinking capacities of the therapist, to damage the room or its contents seriously, to inflict physical injury on therapist or patient, and to disturb other people working in the building; how to bear the extremely perverse, despairing, and sometimes suicidal or murderous feelings evoked in the therapeutic relationship. Most of the therapists found themselves quite often in the grip of alarming feelings about their work with their patients. Extreme states of mind, including hopelessness, hatred of intolerable humiliating experiences, and guilt in the face of the children's often truly awful early lives were frequent. In order to proceed, our expectation had to be that they might be able to discover personal resources to face the kind of inner devastation that most of us are spared. What kind of support and comfort makes it possible for work to proceed at this level of stress?

The workshop seemed a source of strength and comfort to its struggling members, helping them to avoid ways of protecting themselves from the impact that these children made on them that might reduce their upset and distress, but at the cost of making the therapy ineffective in the most difficult areas. These children seemed often like the sort of baby who can be very difficult to care for—not wanting to feed, not able to get comfortable, living in expectation of disappointment. The kind of support that mothers need in looking after particularly vulnerable babies who have had difficult births, been premature or incubated, been ill or born handicapped in some way, is rather similar to the needs experienced by the therapists. Their patients did represent a specially vulnerable and often seriously traumatized group of children, whose early experiences had left them emotionally bruised and lacking in trust. Like the mothers of seriously distressed infants, the therapists rarely found themselves approached by their patients with hope that their unhappiness could be relieved. Very long patient work was needed before this possibility could be established in the children's minds. Wanting to help, but being perceived as persecuting, is a frequent feature of psychotherapists' lives, but the unrelenting way in which this structure could persist with these children was a great burden. The workshop helped its members to gather up their courage, endurance, and persistence.

The professional and emotional range in the group was also helpful. Just as clinical work with children and families is best supported by a multi-disciplinary team, so it was found that the research task was facilitated by a group with diverse backgrounds and capabilities. The perspectives of child psychotherapist, psychiatrist, educational psychologist, field and residential social workers, teachers, and others could add up to a gradually more coherent picture of a child's situation, both inside and outside himself. This range of professional contributions was matched by the range of intellectual and emotional strengths that a group is able to provide—some members could bring a particular talent for conceptual rigour and development, others provided the kind of listening that elicits relevant thoughts and further memories from the therapist. Imaginative links between the child's inner world as revealed in sessions and the often fragmentary knowledge of early history and the present-day reality of life in children's home and school could be forged, because the clinical team involved in all aspects of the child's life were all represented in the workshop.

These ideas are, of course, very familiar in the context of the child guidance model of a multi-disciplinary team, but I am suggesting that they can also give a special quality to clinical research when the whole team actually involved in the care of the child in the widest sense can be involved. The kind of applied research reported by Isobel Menzies Lyth (1982) and the team who worked on problems in the care of children in long-stay hospitals shared some of these strengths—those who are living the problems are those who can most fruitfully struggle to identify and describe them and to explore possible avenues of change.

In thinking over what involvement in the workshop meant to its members it has struck me that this way of initiating and supporting clinical research and development is probably very relevant to tackling problems of 'burn-out' in workers exposed to constant high levels of stress. Even when a heavy case-load is being struggled with, and one in which the experiences of the clients have an emotionally disturbing impact on the workers, the creation of a space in which all aspects of this work could be investigated systematically with colleagues, over time, might make a significant contribution to the capacity of workers to think about what is happening to them and their clients and reduce the sense of functioning as a sponge whose task is to absorb distress that no one else can bear. There are, of course, other ways in which this kind of support can be arranged, and often it may arise out of supervisory or consultative relationships, but there may be a particular value in the model of a group of colleagues of varying disciplines and seniority adopting the task of furthering the understanding of a defined aspect of their work. The sense of contributing to building a store of useful knowledge and of making something of our painful experience rather than just surviving it enhances professional identity and responsibility, not in a self-congratulatory way, but by extending our conceptions of what might be managed and could therefore be attempted. It is probably relevant in understanding the research group's function that over half the sample of eighty children had unsupported mothers. The continuing trend towards one-parent families means that this is true of a large number of cases seen in many professional contexts. The group's support for a therapist who is struggling alone with a child sometimes served as a crucial counterbalance for the therapist who was exposed to the child's conviction that there was no possibility that human beings could co-operate for his benefit. The absence of a basic experience of two parents sharing responsibility leaves a profound mark, and the therapists often found themselves feeling as lonely and without resource in the session as the child believed them to be. The research project, however, could help to contain or sometimes re-establish adult companionship for the therapist who had been dealing internally with feelings of abandonment and inadequacy. The dread of chaos and personal disintegration that the workers had to face recurrently in themselves can easily lead to defensive measures to protect the worker's identity rather than further the therapy. The workshop can assist workers to stand their disturbing experiences by exploring the nature of the chaos that the therapists are being asked to know through their own experience.

CHAPTER TWENTY-ONE

Beyond
the unpleasure principle

Anne Alvarez

The author discusses the history of the development of a number of psychoanalytic theories on the imaginative play of children. She considers that in the past there has been too great an emphasis placed on interpreting such play in terms of a denial of painful realities, limitations, or anxieties. She believes that the work of developmental research has shown a greater recognition of the pleasurable aspects of play and in particular of the elements of maternal involvement and stimulation in this sphere. She feels this to be of particular importance in interpreting with borderline and psychotic children, and with those who have experienced early deprivation. For them it is as important to be helped to conceive of and experience a pleasurable reality as it is to be assisted in coming to terms with a harsh one. This has implications for technique, which are illustrated with clinical material.

[R.S.]

Some of the material in this chapter has previously been published in the *Journal of Child Psychotherapy, 14* (1988), No. 3.

The Czech novelist, Milan Kundera, in a lecture upon receiving the Jerusalem Prize in 1986, gave a definition of poetry that might be relevant to the question of play as a form of thinking: 'Poetry lies not in the action, but *there where the action stops, where the bridge between a cause and an effect is ruptured, and thought wanders off in sweet lazy liberty.*'

I would like to spend a little time comparing and contrasting some of the psychoanalytic theories of play with the theories and findings put forward by the researchers in child development. It seems to me that the psychoanalytic theories have tended to concentrate on the serious elements operating in play, whereas the child development workers concentrate more on those elements that have to do with what a surprised obsessional patient of mine once called, wonderingly, 'fun'. It is not surprising, of course, that child analysts and child psychotherapists are more sensitive to the serious motives in their patients' play, considering the level of illness and distress they tend to see in their patients. In a picture drawn by a very deprived little boy there appeared the image of a child buried alive in a grave, with his arm pushing out of the coffin and reaching up, skywards. In some ways this groping arm did seem to indicate a breath of hope, but the graveyard above was mostly filled with evil-looking old crones and witches.

Not much sweet lazy liberty and not much fun there.

Yet many chronically depressed, deprived children have great difficulty in using their imagination at all; some are hardly able to draw or play, and many are quite unable to imagine, even in their play, that life could be different, or that they could exert much control over their fate. It is essential, in my view, that we become alert to their moments of emergence from depression. We need to distinguish carefully between the narcissistic identifications of the genuinely manic patients, based on omnipotence, and the first beginnings of new identifications and new internalizations based on fantasies of potency, in children who may have been clinically depressed all their lives. Both motives may, of course, co-exist in a single patient at any one moment, but they should not be confused.

As early as 1919, Melanie Klein became interested in how learning, a supposedly intellectual activity, could be interfered with by blocks caused by unconscious phantasies and fears. This led on to an exploration of the activity of learning itself, and the view that *everything* a child did in play was an expression of unconscious phantasy. In those early years, it was particularly his unconscious sexual phantasies and their symbolic expression that she saw in the material. So, for example, a child's problems in adding or subtracting numbers could be seen as relating to phantasies about what happened when *people* came together or were separated Klein, (1932). This is not the whole story, of course. [The neurologist, Oliver Sacks, 1984, has written that for mathematicians or those amateurs who love numbers, these can involve a recognition involving warmth, emotion, personal relations. He quotes the mathematician, Wim Klein, as saying 'Numbers are friends for me, more or less. It doesn't mean the same for you, does it—3,844? For you it's just a three and an eight and a four and a four. But I say, "Hi! 62 squared."']

Subsequently, the work of Klein and her followers (Segal, 1981) on symbol development, of Winnicott on transitional objects (1958), and of Anna Freud on the ego (1986) led to an awareness of meanings and evocations beyond 'oral' breast–mouth relations and described problems of love, understanding, hatred, envy, guilt, and creative reparation. Further, Bion's (1962) work on the development of thinking emphasized the mental aspects of meaning that are now no longer seen so much in terms of phantasied bodily encounters and feelings. It is interesting that Michael Fordham, who has done so much to bring Jungian theory down to earth into the world of the infant and young child, seems to stress bodily experience even more than many Kleinians who have been influenced by Bion's ideas. My impression is that while the Jungians have been coming down to earth, we Kleinians have been trying to make our way up to heaven, and we have recently crossed somewhere in the middle (Fordham, 1976)! I think that Bion's ideas on how his psychotic patients learned to think, and his speculations on the very *birth* of thought, do correspond to many of the findings of the most modern child development research findings that suggest that newborn babies *begin life* as little abstractors and pattern perceivers (Stern, 1985). What all the analytic orientations do have in common, however, is a belief that play has meaning, and that even play of the most meaningless kind has meaning.

The first detailed example of observation of a very young child's play and a discussion of its significance is found in Freud's *Beyond the Pleasure Principle* (1920g). He describes a game invented by his 1½-year-old grandson, who was a 'good boy' who did not disturb his parents at night and never cried when his mother, to whom he was very much attached, left him for a few hours. Freud had observed that he often played a game with his toys, which Freud became convinced had to do with 'gone-ness' and his mother's departures. One day, Freud made an observation that confirmed his view. The child took a wooden reel with a piece of string tied around it and threw it over the edge of his cot, so that it disappeared, exclaiming 'o-o-o-'. He then pulled the reel out of the cot and hailed its reappearance with a joyful 'da' [there]. Freud suggests that the complete game—disappearance and return—was 'related to the child's great cultural achievement—the instinctual renunciation . . . he had made in allowing his mother to go away without protesting. He compensated himself for this, as it were, by himself staging the disappearance and return of the objects within his reach.'

Freud points out that it is no use pretending that the enactment of the joyful return was the main part of the game, because the first act, that of departure, was staged as a game in itself and far more frequently than the episode in its entirety. He emphasizes that it is the unpleasurable experience of the departure that was being played out, but that the pleasure principle still played a part because a passive experience was turned into an active one. So note that the element of pleasure does get into this early psychoanalytic theory of play, but the pleasure in the joyful return of the object, and in the control over the departures of the object, is seen as primarily *a defence against unpleasure*. Freud, in his customarily thorough and intellectually honest way, raises the problem that the joyful return might *seem* to be a major part of the play, but he insists that it is not. Perhaps he cannot help seeing it as a less significant part, because of the nature of his view of 'reality' as fundamentally frustrating, painful, and disappointing, and which therefore has to be 'faced' and come to terms with. This emphasis and this theory does not seem to be a particularly harmful one in the practical situation where we attempt to explain the play of a child from a relatively secure family situation and who seems to need to work over and play out the gaps and breaks in this security. I believe such an emphasis and such a theory can be harmful in the work with *some* psychotic and *some* deprived children who may need to work through, and come to terms with, another type of 'reality'—one that may contain hope, security, and even pleasure.

Susan Isaacs (1952) suggests, in terms fairly similar to Freud's 'mastery and turning of passive into active', that the child's play gave him evidence of his 'triumph in controlling feelings of loss' and consoled him for his mother's absence. She adds that the child 'enjoyed the phantasied satisfaction of controlling his mother's comings and goings. On this basis he could tolerate her leaving him in actuality, and remain loving and obedient.' Her language is more human and less mechanistic than Freud's and for that little boy's attempts to come to terms with an experience of loss, the theory seems mostly adequate. I think it may underestimate the importance of joyful return even in his play, but I think it certainly leaves something to be desired as a general theory of play. Working with children who cannot play, and watching them begin to play, does teach one, I think, that the coming to terms with loss is really only one half of the story. Coming to terms with, getting accustomed to, the idea of gain is, I think, the other half.

I shall raise, therefore, three questions in this chapter. Susan Isaacs says that the child's play helped him to 'control' feelings about loss and absence and to enjoy the 'phantasied' satisfaction of controlling his mother's comings and goings. My questions are: (1) Is 'control' the right word? Well, I think that Kleinian theory itself, not all of the implications of which may have been used by Isaacs when she first gave this paper in 1943, would provide an answer to that question. (2) Was the child enjoying only a 'phantasied satisfaction' in the pleasurable parts of his play? I shall discuss some very interesting comments of Bion's here, made quite late in his life, and also Winnicott's reflections on play. (3) If play does not involve only a phantasied satisfaction, then what does it involve, and what might be some of the preconditions for play? Hoxter (1977), like Winnicott and rather like Kundera on poetry, stresses that play is a bridge between unconscious phantasy and reality. I think that many of us trained in the Kleinian tradition have in the past stressed a particular carriageway on the bridge, the one that leads away from reality, so that we feel we must help the child to go back, to see what his evasions and escapes are really in flight from. Winnicott (1971) also sees play as operating in this intermediate area—he invented it—but he insists that there is a paradox involved in the use of the transitional object or transitional space, and Winnicott asks that the paradox be accepted and tolerated and respected, *not* resolved. He says that 'by flight to split-off intellectual functioning it is possible to resolve the paradox, but the price of this is the loss of the value of the paradox itself' (p. 31). One thinks here of a patient feeling that something good is happening in the room today, or even feeling that together *you and he* are having a good time. Winnicott would, I think, respect the we-ness or the general vagueness of the experience, whereas I think Kleinians in the past may have felt impelled to tell the child he felt the Mummy or Daddy therapist was giving him a good experience to-day. We, would, in the past, have tried to resolve the paradox and see it perhaps as a narcissistic 'defence' against separateness and have tried to help him to see the experience in clearer terms as a self-object relation of a separatable kind.

Winnicott says, let the child stay in the middle of the bridge, if he needs to, and I think in many situations he is absolutely right. I think many present-day Kleinians influenced by Bion's views on containment and Betty Joseph's (1975) ideas on the importance of respecting the defences would take a similar view, on the technical level, at least.

The theoretical point I wish to raise, if I may stay with the image of the bridge for a moment longer, has to do with the carriageway leading towards reality, and with the definition of reality itself. I shall question the early psychoanalytic negative view of reality and wonder whether play is even concerned with, not escape from unpleasant reality, but coming to terms with, getting to know, a pleasant one. I shall also raise the question of whether play is sometimes a preparation for even more pleas-

ant, as yet only dreamed of realities, which should not be confused with denials of current ones. Modern psychoanalytic
technique has moved a long way from its initial preoccupation
with the patient's past and the attempts to reconstruct it. Psychoanalytic technique is much more to do with constructing the
living present in the here and now. Yet in the *theory* of play we
may need to think not only of the past and perhaps not only of
the living here-and-now present, but also of the child's future.
And this may have implications for technique. I came to this
idea through something Bion said and through clinical work
with my patients, but I now know that Margaret Lowenfeld said
it in 1935.

Many psychoanalytic theories do assert, as I have said, that it
is the negative experiences in life that are the great teachers,
the great stimulators, that pleasure soothes and feeds illusion
and unpleasure awakes and alerts us to the great outside world
of 'reality'. The most concise formulation of this idea occurs in
Freud's (1911b) paper, "Formulations of the Two Principles of
Mental Functioning'. Here Freud suggested that it was the pressure of internal needs, followed by disappointment of their satisfaction, followed by the inadequacy of hallucinatory wish-
fulfilling dreams to gratify these needs in any long-term way,
that eventually drove the mental apparatus to form a conception
of the real circumstances in the external world and to endeavour
to make a real alteration in them. 'A new principle of mental
functioning was thus introduced; what was presented in the
mind was no longer what was agreeable but what was real, even
if it happened to be disagreeable. This setting up of the *reality*
principle proved to be a momentous step' (1911b).

The identification of what the negative stimulators to
thought really are has been enormously refined since the days of
Freud's insistence on the frustrations of sexual longings. For
example, the Kleinian notion of the reality that has to be faced
for maturity and character to develop is more private and in a
way more tragic than the one Freud's little Oedipus must suffer:
it is not the brute force of the power of reality that forces awareness upon the growing child—it is, rather, the force of his love,
and its influence over, the restraint upon, his hate that enables
him to tolerate and accept, rather than submit to, loss. Instead

of renunciation, there is relinquishment. Instead of control, there is acceptance. A child may play the reel game in the paranoid position in order to control and triumph over his mother's departures—in the depressive position, he may, in playing the game, be coming to terms with them.

Winnicott's notion of the transitional object is placed developmentally between the symbolic equation and the true symbol. He describes this as an intermediate area of experience between the pure narcissistic illusion that everything belongs to me and mature awareness of separateness and indebtedness to the object. Winnicott (1971) stresses over and over again that this is an area that may need to go *unchallenged*—that it shall exist as a resting place—and that the creation of the first not-me possession, the teddy bear for the baby (and sometimes the first playful thought-recognized-to-be-a-thought by the psychotic patient), may need to be respected, contained, held, and that the feeling of powerful possession—'She's mine', or 'I did it'—should not be challenged as a defence against more humble acknowledgements of dependence and gratitude.

Yet all the theories, including Winnicott's, come together in the stress on the experience of loss, separation, separateness, or what Winnicott calls disillusion, as the great stimulators of learning and intellectual growth and development. Now it is only fair to point out that it is the *balance* between illusion and disillusion that Winnicott (1958) stresses, not simply the disillusionment and pain side of the equation. It is also true that Klein, read carefully, also stresses balance rather than just the negative, although her positive is less about merging fusion than about a loving, more alert relation. She certainly stressed over and over again that the introjection of the good breast was the fundamental foundation for future development (Klein, 1937). But is it only a necessary condition for development, or is it sometimes sufficient?

Bion likewise stresses the negative experience in his great book on thinking, *Learning from Experience* (1962). 'The link between intolerance of frustration and the development of thought is central to an understanding of thought and its disturbance'—what matters is the choice the personality made between procedures designed to evade frustration and those designed to modify it.' In the latter case, the conditions for thinking exist. He goes on to some absolutely fascinating hypotheses about the nature of thinking, which I can only touch on here. He suggests that there is a function of the mind, which he terms alpha function—the function of the mind that allows thoughts to be thought about. He declares that thoughts precede thinking, and suggests (p. 57) that 'thinking is something forced on an apparatus, not suited for the purpose, by the demands of reality, and is contemporary with, as Freud said, the reality principle. . . . The apparatus has to undergo adaptation to the new tasks involved in meeting the demands of reality by developing a capacity for thought.' Bion does not seem to discuss the possibility that this same alpha function might be operating on pleasure, delight, and other experiences in a similar and equally necessary way, nor does he seem to suggest that the mother's containment might also operate on experiences of intense delight. Winnicott, on the other hand, does refer to the mother holding the baby through periods of excitement. But neither theorist seems to imagine the mother offering stimulating or delightful input as a stimulus to intellectual growth. Mothers need a capacity for reverie, but they also need a capacity for enlivening and alerting their infants to the joy of life. Pleasure, I am suggesting, may be just as thought-provoking as distress, because pleasure comes in as great a variety of forms. The test, I think, is not whether the experience is pleasurable or painful, but whether it is *interesting* and novel enough to be paid attention to and to stimulate concentration and invite attention. Perhaps we need a fresh vocabulary, one that takes us beyond the old pleasure–pain dualisms. Such a vocabulary does exist, I suggest, in the writings of child development researchers such as Stern (1985), Trevarthen (1975, 1985), and Brazelton (Brazelton et al., 1974).

To move from the psychoanalytic literature on play to the child development writings is almost funny, because the emphasis is so different. In a book on play edited by Bruner, Jolly, and Sylva (1985), Bruner's introduction begins by somehow taking for granted the playfulness of play, and he cites the common research finding that young chimpanzees seem to be able to play when their mother is nearby to provide a buffer against distraction and pressure. Corinne Hutt (1966) points out that 'Play only occurs in a known environment and when the animal or child feels he knows the properties of the object in that environment; this is apparent in the gradual relaxation of mood, evidenced not only by changes in facial expression, but in a greater diversity and variability of activities. In play the emphasis changes from the question of "what does this *object* do?" to "what can I do with this object?"' One is reminded here of Winnicott's insistence that the transitional object is the child's first not-me possession, *not* his first not-me object, and his insistence that playing is doing. It is the importance of this feeling of possession and of potency and power, of being able to *do something to someone,* or to *do something with one's thoughts,* that I want to illustrate.

Since Freud, psychoanalytic theory has been much preoccupied with the notion of the absent object (O'Shaughnessy, 1964). Many clinical studies and detailed observations of infants have suggested that a person's capacity to have confidence in the durability of the loved object when it is out of sight is extremely important for cognitive and symbolic development, for the ability to endure and survive life's painful losses and crises, and for mental health in general. Some experience of separateness, loss, and pain seems to be a vital ingredient in this development. Yet the child development research on the cognitive problem of 'object constancy' has suggested that the whole issue of when 'out of sight' implies 'out of mind' and when it does not is highly complex (Bower, 1982). There would seem to be other vital ingredients besides the experiencing of loss. Babies around 12 months of age who are unable to find an object hidden before their eyes in an inverted cup (the famous Piagetian experiment) have little difficulty when the cup has a picture of a smiling face stuck on it. They also found the task much easier if the experimenter leaned forward, caught the child's gaze, and said, 'Go on, you find it then!' The researchers point out that this seems to remind the child that the experimenter really does want them to find the toy, that she was not *hiding it away,* just hiding it for them (Freeman et al., 1980). Clearly an object that is too available might never stimulate curiosity and intellectual interest, but it seems to me that one that is too unavailable may have the same effect. For many psychotic, borderline psychotic, and deprived children the story of their lives is often filled with feelings of loss, impotence, shame, and terror. Before they can begin to symbolize this and find a way of playing it out, they seem to need some perspective from it, and this seems to be achieved partly through the development of phantasies of gain, potency, pride, and trust. I have looked for a word or concept that might stand opposite Freud's great theory of the 'work of mourning' and carry the same weight and dignity. Words such as rejoice, celebrate, or give thanks do not convey the long, slow process, akin to mourning in its slowness, of the gradual birth and development of hope in a child who may have been clinically depressed all his life. Daniel Stern's description of the slow, momentous discovery in the infant that his experience can be shared by someone else probably comes nearest the mark (1985).

Molly

Mrs Horne, a child psychotherapist, has been treating a 9-year-old girl, here called Molly, referred by the educational psychologist because of learning difficulties and withdrawn behaviour at school (daydreaming and rocking). Her mother had collapsed and died very suddenly when Molly was 2, just four months after the birth of her baby sister. She is black, and she has a loving and devoted father and close and caring older brothers and sisters. They are now in contact with warm and helpful members of the father's family in London. However, there was a period when the family was not in London, and the father had a permanent relationship with a woman who was extremely cruel and neglectful to the children. He is now separated from this woman, so I am calling Molly a deprived child for purposes of this discussion; it will be clear, however, that she was by no means as despairing and cut off as some of the institutionalized children or children who have had numerous changes of caretaker.

Molly began to weep in her third session, and it seemed as though she might go on weeping forever. At one point later on, she asked whether, if she jumped out of the window, Mrs Horne would jump out after her to save her.

The session I want to mention follows a half-term break that was unplanned. This sort of situation can easily stir up older dreads and older depression, and feelings of being let down. This is some months into treatment, and although her hope and trust are very precarious, Molly is certainly no longer withdrawn.

Molly came quickly with me from the waiting area, then delayed in the corridor some 10 feet from my door. She threw out 'Don't speak! You're *not* my friend.' I commented—from the rear—that it had been a long gap, and that she was wondering if we were still friends. 'You're not my friend.' She motioned roughly with her arm for me to go past her in the narrow passage. I said that I felt she would like me, as usual, to *be* in my room for her when she came in, and that I would do this. I went in and, sitting in my seat, was at an angle of 60 degrees or so to the door. To face her when she enters is both persecuting and terrifying, so ambivalent is her attachment.

The session begins and continues for some while, with the child being very defensive and bitter and rejecting the therapist, but gradually moving towards her.

Now here we get to the crux of things. I quote from the therapist's notes:

She climbed on to the little table and balanced with her feet on the door handle, hands on top of the open door (a quite dangerous position). Looking down on me, she laughed, 'Are you scared?' She moved the door. 'Did I make you scared?' 'Did you scare me to death?' I developed it. 'I can make you die', she asserted in quiet, convinced seriousness. I said that sometimes it was hard to hope that we wouldn't be killed—or our time together—when she was angry with me.

'Come on!' She bounced down. 'Let's play hide-and-seek.' I turned my back while she hid four times. Each time there was great delight in being discovered, and I offered the obvious interpretation about being lost (each out of sight) and found, linked to the half-term just past and the holidays to come. [The therapist then comments in the notes, not to the child, that, interestingly, this was an enactment of her *actively* seeking Molly, which of course hadn't happened in the half-term break. It was time to finish, and she seemed content.]

This piece of material is interesting, partly because of the development that follows the therapist's acceptance of the child's doubts about her goodness and trustworthiness. But it is the dangerous play on the door and the hide-and-seek game that I wished to look at from the theoretical and technical point of view. Was her hide-and-seek game only a phantasy? Do we see the child as pushing into the therapist her unwanted baby feelings of rejection and panic in an attempt to deny them and escape from them? Is the session only about facing loss, or is the child gradually trying out, playing out more and more clearly, the idea that this woman seems to have returned, and that she, Molly, seemed to have had the power to bring her back? Is she getting rid of an experience of powerlessness? In part, she may be, but is she also actually having an experience of very pleasureable power—the power to make a maternal object *seek her out*? Should we interpret to the child that she is denying what happened last week—i.e. loss and departure and let-down—or should we note that she seems to *want to be sure that her therapist is really looking for her, really concerned about her, and really has returned*. Would such an interpretation offer reassurance and denial of more painful realities? I think not. I suspect that for some people who have suffered very early in their lives or very much in their lives, joy and fun and the power to pull the object to you are elements of 'reality' that take as much digesting and learning about as their opposites. Mrs Horne described 'delight' in the game, not manic triumph.

The child development and Winnicottian question, 'What can I do with this object?' is so fundamentally different from what seems to have been the question in the early years of psychoanalysis, 'what can I no longer do with this object', or 'what can I not do that I previously imagined I could do', or 'what can I not do that my mother or father can do', that it is difficult to imagine that they are both talking about a thing called children's play. And yet the idea that play is denial of more fundamental and painful truths dies hard. When I was doing some reading and writing last year on the subject of defence, a little boy patient of mine came into a session with a mask, a sort of marine sergeant's mask with a big square jaw—it was just before Halloween—and he put it on straight away. I said that he seemed to want me to see him as strong and powerful today. I then added that I thought that we both knew this was because he was actually scared to death as his treatment was ending prematurely at Christmas, because he and his family were moving to the North of England. We had been talking about it a lot lately, and he feared, not only the cold, but violence, horror, and poverty of a nightmarish kind. When I implied, however, that the mask was a defence against his anxieties and fears of weakness, he simply shouted 'no' in terrible desperation. I thought about what I had been reading lately, and a few minutes later, when he put on the mask again, I repeated that it was clear that I was to see him as a very strong, brave, tough fellow today. But this time I left the second bit out—I did not add that underneath he was really terrified. He listened tensely, and then said slowly and with great relief, 'yesss'. Then, after a bit, he said that in fact he was worried sick about the move. I have thought a great deal about that mask since. At first, I rather implied that he *wished* he were strong, but that of course we both knew that he was not—an idea consistent with a theory that play attempts to control reality, or evade reality, or triumph over reality. And some play, much play, does precisely that. And with a less ill patient with more ego and more confidence to fall back on, such an interpretation would probably have been palatable. But supposing the child needed his object to remind him not of the current sad, frightening, pathetic reality, but of the potential possibility of being strong one day. Little 2-year-olds put a cowboy hat on, and nobody tells them, 'Now don't forget, you're not Daddy yet!' The mother says, 'Wow, what a tough guy you are today!' She 'contains' not only his disappointments, but also his aspirations. She plays the game.

Bion suggested, very near the end of his life, that we should not see dreams as only attempts to rewrite the past. We should see them as living life events—life experiences. He said, however, that we could also see them as in some ways anticipatory of the future. I had a little boy patient at the time who dreamt he had found a fossil in his garden and woke up so sad that it was 'only a dream' because, he said, he had always wanted to touch a piece of history. Bion thought such dreams were not 'only dreams'—that is, not necessarily denials of childish impotence—rather, they could be seen as anticipations of future grownupness. This prospective element is very important in the thinking of Jung, who wrote about this long before Bion. I have also learned from colleagues about two references to masks in literature, the first in *Christina Alberta's Father,* by H. G. Wells (1985), and the second in Edwin Muir's autobiography; in both cases the masks were used not as disguises but as experiments with, attempts to try on, a new identity. In both books there are references to Jungian analysts. I also found my own example. All three lead me to think that perhaps we need a term other than projective identification for such moments—something like 'anticipatory identification', perhaps. My example is from a poem, Mignon's song, by Goethe, from *Wilhelm Meister*; it begins:

So let me seem, until I am
Strip not my white robe from me
from the lovely earth I hasten
down into that sure house.

The translators (Bird & Stokes, 1976) state that the literal translation would go as follows: 'Let me remain attired as an angel until I become one.'

The emergence of Michael Fordham's model of development: a new integration in analytical psychology

James Astor

Over the last five decades Fordham has evolved a model of the mind that is congruent with Jung's attitude to the psyche while being radically different in its understanding of maturation and development. It is particularly Jungian in that it places intuition, described by Jung as 'the matrix out of which thinking and feeling develop as rational functions' (Jung, 1921), in the centre of the analyst's mental activity, intuition which is checked against the evidence in the dreams and clinical material of the analysis. This approach values the irrational fact as an aid to the advancement of understanding and knowledge.

Central to Jung's model of the mind is the idea that there is an individual self that functions also in an organizing way within archetypal forms and as the totality of the psyche. Like Jung, Fordham values abstractions as instruments in the development of knowledge. By relating abstraction to emotional experience he has traced the connections between 'individuation' in childhood and its adult form described by Jung as: 'The process by which individual beings are formed and differentiated. In particular, it is the development of the psychological individual as being distinct from the general, collective psychology. Individuation, therefore is a process of differentiation having for its goal the development of the individual personality' (Jung, 1921). Fordham maintains that the depressive position is an early step in individuation. His work on this has a central feature: *thinking about feeling*. This is a route full of pain, but also meaning, recognizing as it does that thoughts originate in the unconscious.

To understand Fordham's model of the mind it is necessary to trace the way his collection of the initial data led on to the expansion and alteration of the theory as the existing theory was no longer able to accomodate the observations.

Building on Jung's idea of the ego and the archetypes (Jung, 1954), in the 1930s Fordham began systematically collecting clinical material from his analyses of children. This material confirmed the presence of archetypal images in the inner world of children. He published his findings in *The Life of Childhood* (Fordham, 1944). He did not dare to think then that there might be images of the self, since traditional Jungian theory held the child to be contained in the mother as part of her psyche. However, in 'Some Observations on the Self and the Ego in Childhood' (Fordham, 1957) he developed his own thoughts. Starting from the belief that the ego grew out of the self (an idea later used in a very different way by Neumann), he put forward the hypothesis that there was a primary or original self present at birth which then of necessity divided into parts as its relation to the world developed, thus enabling consciousness to arise (consciousness in the meaning of 'a sense organ for the perception of psychical qualities', Freud, 1900a). He proposed the term 'deintegration' for this process and compared it to Jung's picture of consciousness arising out of the unconscious 'like an island newly risen from the sea' (Jung, 1946a). In this way Fordham linked deintegration with ego development, since his conception was that the self integrated the fragments of ego consciousness which arose as a result of the deintegration. Fordham's concept of the self as an essentially psychosomatic entity is expanded in the following passage from 'Some Observation on the Self and Ego in Childhood':

The sequence can be conceived as follows: the original self deintegrates spontaneously. . . . The deintegrates represent a readiness for experience, a readiness to perceive, a readiness to act instinctively, but not an actual perception or action. The next step is to perceive and act according to the patterns of the deintegrates; . . . there then develop reaction patterns based on archetypes which differ from instincts in their innate predisposition to represent themselves in a pre-conscious image.

It is, however, only through the integrative action of the self that these deintegrates which have grown into ego nuclei get brought together so as to contribute to a single ego nucleus or centrum as Jung calls it. [Fordham, 1957]

The fact that the fit is not always perfect is one of the principal stimuli to ego development, probably because of the constructive anxiety it evokes. The value of this idea of deintegration and reintegration as the dynamic process of the self can be seen in the number of papers published over the years in the *British Journal of Medical Psychology* and in the *Journal of Analytical Psychology*. It has also provided the dynamic for Lambert's book *Analysis, Repair and Individuation* (Lambert, 1981), and for the investigation of emerging self-representations as originally described by Jung in archetypal images, in anthropology (Layard, 1959; Gordon, 1962; Maduro, 1980), and in literature (Willeford, 1987).

Fordham himself has developed the concept in relation to the dialectical procedure, i.e. that the analyst makes available a part of himself to the patient as a deintegrate of the self. The implication of this is that the therapeutic value of analysis does not reside exclusively in the analyst's interpretative activity.

Reflecting on failures of deintegrative processes led Fordham to investigate the boundaries of the self. He hypothesised that if these boundaries are designed to preserve its existence, then any evidence of failure of deintegrative processes may impel the self towards a pathological development operating an exclusive defence system. (This exclusive defence system, with its concomitant ruthlessness, is also evident in creative people, writers for example, who need to protect themselves during periods of creative work. Or in Jung, for instance, who would take himself off to his tower at Bollingen when he was struggling with a problem.

The self and autism

Fordham's interest in disorders of childhood led him to study the pathology of autism. He published his research, theoretical ideas, and clinical evidence in *The Self and Autism* (Fordham, 1976). Like Anthony (1958) Fordham does not consider autism to be a homogeneous entity and follows him in making the distinctions, primary and secondary, while thinking about autism as a disorder of the self. The advantage of this approach is that it allows the very different cases encountered in autism to be considered on a continuous spectrum.

> The essential core of autism represents, in distorted form, the primary integrate of infancy, and that idiopathic autism is a distorted state of integration, owing its persistence to failure of the self to deintegrate. [Fordham, 1976]

This is not to say that autistic children live in an inner world; rather, that they live in a world of objects in which the differentiation is between self-objects and not-self-objects. A self-object is a part of the self merging with an object to record and focus on states of the self (Fordham, 1985b). This view challenges the barrier hypothesis of autism, which views it as a condition in which a barrier is presumed to protect an inner world in the child, and this is the reason the adult cannot communicate with him/her. Fordham is clear that the self can develop well-organized defences and that they are absolute and impenetrable. In the core of the primary autism, symbolization in its flexible and creative form does not occur. His approach does allow, however, for the development of symbolization in a child whose fantasy system is defective (e.g. in secondary autism). Concurrently came the idea that the self must have defences that are discernible in analytic practice as well as in autism. Fordham suggested that it was the not-self objects that constituted the danger and that it was the persistent destructive warding off of these not-self objects, long after they were a threat, that maintained the autistic state.

Defences of the self

Complementary to Fordham's studies in autism were his studies in countertransference and his distinguishing of this phenomenon from interaction within the analytic process. This work arose from his study of the personal affective processes stirred in him by the patients with whom he was having difficulties. Jung, in his foreword to Fordham's collection of papers, *New Developments in Analytical Psychology* (Fordham, 1957), praised his views of the transference (p. XII) and emphasized its 'central position in the dialectical process of analytical psychology'.

Fordham described patients who did away with everything he said by silence, open attack, or ritualization and by so doing made a nonsense of his interventions. He found himself in the area of primitive defences characterized by the annihilation of bad objects. Confusion, reversals, distortions dominated the interactions, so that any agreed meaning to words no longer remained. This attempt by the patient to split the analysis into a false invasive technique and a concealed real person may, if the analyst is not alert to it, generate a malignant form of countertransference. The confusion between analyst and patient can become so damaging that the analyst may consider himself to be no longer able to work with the patient. The analyst can become confused, acquiescent, masochistic, and frustrated, but

> All these states of the analyst avoid helplessness, despair and depression on his part, so he can begin to consider whether it is not these feelings that are the state of the patient contained in himself. It cannot be underlined sufficiently that the patient remorselessly plays on any weak points he may discover in his analyst, the effect being to destroy the mature, nurturing, feeling and creative capacities of the analyst. [Fordham, 1985b]

Fordham stresses the importance of maintaining an analytic attitude during this period, and he points to the value and meaning that the pain has for the patient. He asserts the importance of continuing to analyse the delusional transference and describes how by metabolizing the patient's projective identifications he was able to develop his interpretive skills in ways that were made use of by his patients. Fordham's robustness at moments such as these is in part dependent on his view arising from experience that the self is indestructible in its ultimate sense.

Jung and the self

Fordham's idea that the self functioned not only integratively but also deintegratively was revolutionary, but it was also of value in elucidating the often apparently contradictory writings of Jung on the subject of the self. Fordham investigated these writings and systematically grouped them under two main headings. The first is the totality definition of the self. In this definition Jung writes of the self as the totality of the personality outside time, space, and desire. The second concerns Jung's use of the self as an archetype. If the totality definition implies that the self combines ego and archetypes, then there is an apparent contradiction when Jung comes to define the self as an archetype only. But with the help of deintegration, Fordham's dynamic of the self, it becomes possible to reconcile these definitions since those aspects of the self that are manifestly archetypal can be accounted for as a partial expression of the self (Fordham, 1985b).

Fordham and psychoanalysis

Fordham's studies of archetypal patterns of behaviour have focussed on the maturation of the individual, rather than on the development of the cultural patterns and history of our time. His discovery of archetypal symbols in childhood led him on to study psychoanalysis. The work of Mrs Klein and her followers provided him not only with a way into the mind of the child through her play technique, but also with an understanding of the ways in which external experiences are transformed in the processes of internalization. Susan Isaacs defined unconscious phantasy as the primary content of unconscious mental processes. These earliest phantasies originated in the body, from an internal and instinctual source (Isaacs, 1952). This definition, Fordham recognized, came very close to Jung's meaning and definition of archetypes as 'a psychic expression of the physiological and anatomical disposition' (Jung, 1921, para. 748). Fordham used Mrs Klein's methodology for penetrating into the mind of the child, and this helped him acquire the clinical experience for his development of Jung's ideas about the self.

As a founder member and chairman of the first society of analytical psychology, Fordham involved himself in a regular forum with psychoanalysts (e.g. Rickman, Clifford Scott, Winnicott, Bion) in the Medical Section of the British Psychological Society. His contributions to these proceedings included both explicitly (Fordham, 1948) and implicitly the necessity for those engaged in psychotherapeutic work to heed Jung's emphasis on values. Repeatedly during those years, Fordham is to be found drawing the attention of psychoanalysts to Jung's contribution to our understanding of the individual and the group. His interest, however, in psychoanalysis, infancy, and childhood has led to Fordham being criticized by analytical psychologists for denigrating Jung's work, since Jung broke from Freud and concentrated his interest on the second half of life. This puzzling criticism seems to arise from a lack of observational and experiential data concerning the affective conflicts that centre around the different parts of the body, its contents, and functions, not only in relation to children but also to adults—almost as if 'Jungian' children do not suffer from the problems 'Kleinian' children suffer from and certainly do not carry these difficulties forward into their adult lives.

Science, mysticism, and religious experience

The mutual influence of the two groups resulted in several interesting clinical symposia (see *British Journal of Medical Psychology, 33* (1), 1960). In addition, this contact strengthened the existing tradition within the Society of Analytical Psychology of a scientific approach to the development of analytic ideas, with close adherence to observational material. This has been spelled out by Stein (Stein, 1973). He argues that Jung's approach can be understood as being similar to that of the modern physicist who works with theoretical entities and that for the analytical psychologist the entities are the archetypes. Their value to us is that when the phenomena arising from them are examined, they help us think about them; 'they do a job', much as an electron does for a physicist.

In trying to understand Fordham's insistence on a scientific approach to the psyche, I am mindful not only of his personal preference but also of the context of his professional development at the London Child Guidance Training Centre. He was the lone analytical psychologist in a department where the predominating influences were derived from psychiatry or psychoanalysis. Here Jung was thought to be somewhat mystical, in the pejorative sense of the word, not in the way Fordham uses it. He himself values mysticism, seeing in it a search by the individual for the truth of his nature through acquiring knowledge and then reflecting on it. In particular Jung's writings on the collective unconscious fuelled ideas that his approach to psychology extended the subject beyond the bounds of the human psyche. This is true but was understood as meaning 'beyond the bounds of scientific scrutiny', which it is not. Much of Fordham's writings on religious experience (Fordham, 1958, 1985b) has been directed to bringing the concept of the collective into the area of analytical psychology, where it can be subjected to the same scientific evaluation as the personal. Just as Bion has done in his work on basic assumption mentalities, Fordham demonstrates how Jung's theory of the collective unconscious mediates between religious practices and psychological analysis. The disagreements between theologians and psychologists are not indicative of a fundamental incompatibility, concerning the meaning of the experiences of the primordial images, so much as a difference in the way that they are looked at. Theologians come to conclusions about the nature of God, psychologists about the nature of man. What is important for the psychologist is to retain his objectivity; to suspend, not just his belief, but also his disbelief.

Patient–analyst interaction

Scrutiny of the patient–analyst interaction has been a fruitful area for the further investigation of the actions of the self with particular reference to the experiences on the boundaries, surfaces, and walls of the container and their impact on development. Fordham has pioneered among analytical psychologists the microscopic study of patient–analyst interaction. He has argued that if details are not brought out into the open, there develops a secret tradition inaccessible to critical evaluation. In effect, a core of unexamined transference and countertransference material mushrooms and grows, fed on infantile anxieties. To give support to idiosyncratic behaviour on the part of analysts, various appeals are made by the doubters of this view to, for instance, the *vas bene clausum* of alchemy, which is then combined with a statement by Jung on technique: 'I am unsystematic very much by intention' (Jung, 1963). Fordham (1985b) has argued that this is to misunderstand Jung. Jung's empirical studies of how the self can be made largely but not completely conscious valued an interactional procedure in which the analyst's unconcious plays an essential part. This is what Jung meant when he wrote of the disadvantage to a psychotherapist of 'knowing beforehand' (Jung, 1946b). For it to become part of the analyst's technique, however, he has to have worked on his own internal life. It is not so much the particular qualities of the analyst that are important as his ability to metabolize and manage them. Fordham's study of this in himself led to his paper on syntonic countertransference, 'Notes on the Transference' (Fordham, 1957). He showed that what he had thought of as being part of himself was part of the patient's affective life with which he had introjectively identified. The free flowing of projective and introjective identifications between patient and analyst provided the raw material for interventions. They are in effect the prima materia of analysis. In essence Fordham's ideas are a microscopic development of Jung's macroscopic statement about the need for the analyst to have an analysis, about important aspects of the transference being interactional, and about the intensity of transference increasing when the analyst is having difficulty empathizing with his patient. These ideas of Jung's are all related to his theory of archetypes. Thus Fordham argues that when Jung writes of his suspicions of the value of theories and theorizing, one should not take this to mean that Jung did not value theoretical guidelines (viz. his theories about types, archetypes, the personal and collective unconscious). What Jung was drawing attention to was the value of leaving a place for the ultimate nature of the self within the interactions that constitute the analytic process.

Fordham, in his papers on transference and countertransference, has developed a theory of analytic practice which has enriched our understanding of the unconscious processes between patient and analyst. In particular he has pointed to the dangers of acting in the countertransference (Fordham, 1957, 1974, 1978, 1985b). The value of this has been to bring into the open what analysts actually do, to study the relationship between the pathological reaction of the analyst (countertransference) and its relation to the patient's transference. He also described the transformations that occur within the analyst and patient as part of the interactional nature of the dialectical procedure. This included the study of the complex processes of identification, projection, and introjection and has been part of the work that has led to changes in his emerging model of the mind. Thus Fordham has taken an idea of Jung's, developed it, drawing on his own experience which has included his study of contemporary psychoanalysis, and then represented it in an expanded form of Jung's original idea. Countertransference illusions are shown to arise when the analyst fails to transform highly complex information received from his patient. He is unable then to digest it and feed it back to his patient so that he in turn can transform it. As Fordham writes:

Suppose a patient evokes warmth and compassion in the analyst; that needs scrutinising, because it may be a grave mistake to provide it. That is so because the supposed feeling in the analyst can be a response to his patient's projective identification, and then it is the analyst's job to feed it back to the patient so that he or she becomes capable of such feelings as well. Furthermore, if an analyst becomes identified with such experiences and believes that he can sustain them all the time, he has been caught by a defensive illusion. He has lost his shadow. [Fordham, 1985b]

This work of Fordham's on the self and its manifestations in unconscious phantasy led the way to the most recent and radical changes in the Jungian child analytic model, changes that derive principally from the impact of infant observation on his thinking.

The impact of infant observation

It was not until 1976 that Fordham initiated and took part in Infant Observation seminars. Here he was to find the evidence for what he had postulated all those years before (Fordham, 1944), drawing on abstractions and occasional observations from his own data, and later on those of Jung. In the face of observational material Fordham's postulate of the infant self changed into a description of the facts of an infant's life. The deintegrative–reintegrative process became a description of how the infant (originally integrated) comes into relation to his/her mother. The observational material led Fordham to modify his earlier view of individuation in childhood which at first followed Jung in postulating an original state of primitive identity. Later, however, he regarded this as secondary and periodic. This infant observation material, published in *Explorations into the Self* (Fordham, 1985b) and *Abandonment in Infancy* (Fordham, 1985a), provided convincing evidence for the child being an individual from the start. Thus, 'individuation becomes realisation of his condition through the development of self representations' (Fordham, 1985b). The most important distinction Fordham makes is between splitting and deintegration. In splitting, structural and pathological changes occur within the personality, whereas in the dynamic processes of deintegration and reintegration normal development occurs. From the historical Jungian point of view the alterations that Fordham has made to his model of the mind are radical. In a recent public lecture (1 February 1989) Fordham listed the major changes to his thesis. He no longer finds tenable the following preconceptions that have gradually been absorbed into his model of development, some from Jung and some from psychoanalysis:

1. that an infant is part of his mother's unconscious, leading to a state of fusion (Jung);

2. that an infant is in a state of primary identity with his mother (Jung);

3. that events take place in the space between mother and infant (Winnicott);

4. that there is a primordial relationship with mother that is different in nature from any other relationship (Jung);

5. that the mother is the carrier of the infant self or mirrors it (this proposition is theoretically impossible and observations of mothers and infants do not give evidence of it: 'It appears to me', Fordham says in an unpublished public lecture, 'that the authors of that conception are referring to projective identification of deintegrates of the self') (Jung, Winnicott, Lacan);

6. that part objects precede whole objects (Klein);

7. that there are well-defined stages, paranoid, schizoid, and depressive, called positions (Klein).

It can be seen from this that Fordham's model of development is built up around the individual's experience. It would be incorrect therefore to assume that distress following, for instance, an interrupted feed would necessarily lead to splitting. Attention in such an instance would have to be paid to the mother's capacity to metabolize her infant's pain and in this way help her infant negotiate the experience. Splitting has occurred in this model when there is an observable change in the personality of the child, expressed mainly through destructiveness and violence, the principal emotion in this state of mind to the over-whelmingly bad object (see Fordham, 1985a).

In this way the ordinary developmental processes are kept separate from pathological developments, and deintegration is kept separate from splitting and idealization. To quote Michael Fordham:

> Klein spoke of splitting, whereby she suggested that a baby, in the course of development, splits up in such a way that wholeness is violated. Deintegration, by contrast, means that the quality of wholeness permeates the baby's actions. The dif-ference between these two hypotheses may be thought about as follows. Early on in extrauterine life, a baby experiences one breast as good and another one as bad, depending on the degree of satisfaction or frustration experienced in feeding. It is believed that the baby does not know that both breasts are the same; that awareness comes later as cognitive and emo-tional development proceed. One can say that the two breasts are the consequence of splitting, or that deintegrates become classed as good or bad because emotional development has not reached the stage of being able to grasp that the two experi-ences emanate from the same source. Whether one or the other of the hypotheses be correct, the distinction becomes important in emotional development. [Fordham, 1985a]

Similarly, when an infant is observed playing with the nipple, it might seem that what was happening had something to do with eroticizing this nipple, perhaps even having some thoughts about it, but one would need many examples over time before one could say with confidence that he was thinking about it as separate from the breast and that therefore a split had occurred in his ego.

In making such a statement, I am emphasizing the view that each child is a person, separate from his parents but capable of interacting with them. In these activities what is happening is what Fordham has called deintegrating not disintegrating, and this action of the self is part of the sequences of deintegrat-ing and reintegrating that lead to ego development. One could imagine reintegration as corresponding to a rudimentary form of having thoughts. Splitting, on the other hand, refers to a pathological development that manifests itself through its fixed quality. (To those more familiar with Bion than Fordham, beta elements might be equivalent to the first deintegrates, and reintegration equivalent to the effect of maternal reverie and the development of alpha function.) In terms of my understanding of Meltzer's work on the aesthetic conflict (Meltzer & Harris Williams, 1988), most babies are born with a predisposition to be interested, +K, the desire to know and understand the object. (Meltzer's idea of the aesthetic object that has such an overwhelming impact on the infantile mind is very close to Jung's description of those experiences indicating action of the self.) In an infant observation, therefore, what we are observing seem to be principally physical acts. But they are psychic ones to our mind. The baby's world since birth seems dualistic: there is a body–mind. But is this so? Consider this exchange between Bion and Jung. Jung was lecturing at the Tavistock and Bion asked him,

'You gave an analogy between archaic forms of the body and archaic forms of the mind. Is it purely an analogy or is there in fact a closer relationship?'

Jung replied,

'You touch again on the controversial problem of psychophysical parallelism for which I know no answer, because it is beyond the reach of man's cognition. As I tried to explain yesterday, the two things—the psychic fact and the physiological fact—come together in a peculiar way. They happen together and are, so I assume, simply two different aspects to our mind, but not in reality. We see them as two on account of the utter incapacity of our mind to think of them together. [Jung, 1935]

Our ego is not splitting the physiological from the psychic, it is just not able to think of them as one and the same. You cannot think, for instance, physiologically about a mental content. (That would be like reversing alpha and beta in Bion's terminology, and in this example Jung is making just that point.)

The model

In Fordham's germinating model there is a primary integrate, the original psychosomatic self (quite different conceptually from the self of psychoanalysis with its references to ego functions and the development of self feeling). From this self we observe the infant actively deintegrating, leading through reintegration to the experience of rudimentary perceptions. These perceptions are thought of as being made up not only of what is 'out there' but also of what is put into them to give them meaning, a part of the self. Now initially these objects consist mainly of the deintegrates and so record extra- and intra-ceptive sense data. They are in Fordham's language self objects. (In my view this model in its dynamic projective part is close to normal projective identification as described by Bion.)

If we view the variable content of any perception to be on a sliding scale, then using Jung's simile of the archetypes manifesting their images within a spectrum of light from the infrared (self object) to the primary colours (real object), we can study observations. When we as observers feel the experience of the infant to be preponderantly 'bad' rather than 'good', I would suggest that there was a preponderance of self objects to which we are ascribing a 'bad self object' quality. We are here doing the thinking about the feelings, but for the infant the actions are archetypal and possibly with only rudimentary mental imagery. In terms of Jung's simile of the spectrum of light and its relation to archetypal experience, what we have been observing is at the infra-red end of the spectrum where archetypal experience merges into physical action.

As analytical psychologists, we do not assume that splitting is the inevitable developmental response to pain.

Rather, I have in mind a distinction between deintegrative–reintegrative experiences and those that fail to be reintegrated over time. Depressive concern would be an example of the reintegrative process making things all right, leading to greater appreciation of the good object, enhanced intellectual development, and a greater sense of reality. The problem for the observer seems to me to be to comprehend the significance of the experience observed. We can probably come to some measure of agreement about the meaning. In this model the language of normal development is kept separate from the language of pathology.

This idea of the original integrate, which is the beginning of Fordham's development of the Jungian model, is also an idea congruent with ordinary devoted mothers' experience of their babies as individuals. It is also what I have in mind when I think of the intra-uterine observational material now being reported. This shows infants interacting with the uterine wall and the placenta, drinking the amniotic fluid, and perhaps acquiring biochemically some notion of the mother's emotional capacity.

Infant observations led Fordham to think that the first experience is a whole object experience, followed by increasingly part object experiences. These are episodic and so not characterized by him as splitting, which refers to a noticeable change of a structural and pathological kind. The eventual bringing together of those experiences that are partial in meaning with those that are felt to be 'whole', in terms of self objects, is thought of not as a phase of development but as an achievement that comes and goes throughout life. What this would require is the establishment of the breast as a symbol, described by Jung as 'an intuitive idea that cannot yet be formulated in any other or better way' (Jung, 1922), or what Bion more precisely called the establishment of the thinking breast. In other words in order for the symbol to be created the self object (breast) has to be destroyed while the actual breast continues in existence and from this experience a symbol is created.

As Fordham has pointed out (Fordham, 1976), this way of thinking about maturation takes Jung's idea of the individuation process and treats it in much the same way as Freud treated the ego ideal, but with important differences, e.g. no primary narcissism. Whereas for Freud the ego ideal arising from primary narcissism remained desirable but unachievable, Fordham's contribution has been to link the process of individuation to the development of depressive concern. He rejects an initial state of primary narcissism on theroretical and observational grounds—this is not to deny that it is a quality of some infant experience. The Jungian ideal would be development without any splitting. I do, however, acknowledge the importance of splitting in the development of character.

Fordham, like Bion, worked from an idea and found that it enlightened his observations. Theoretical speculation and observation are interdependent in his work. Klein made clinical discoveries and developed her theory about them afterwards. Fordham's model is observable and useful and has profound implications for analytic practice. It is within the Jungian tradition of self psychology but is a radical development of it, made possible, in part, by Fordham's integration of the essential discoveries of Klein.

CHAPTER TWENTY-THREE

The institution as therapist: hazards and hope

Isobel Menzies Lyth

With this concluding chapter the theme shifts from the focus on individuals and on family groups as the author explores relationships between individuals and wider social groups, here exemplified by institutional settings. In particular, she considers an aspect of the development of the self, through identification, and the nature of this process within institutions. The dual themes that healthy development depends greatly on the availability of appropriate models for such identification, and equally on the management of identification with inappropriate ones, is illustrated with some detailed material. In her experience of consultancy in institutions such as children's homes and children's hospitals, Mrs Menzies Lyth observed the extent to which social structures, defence systems, and patterns of authority, for example, can affect the development of the self in child members. She also saw how institutions could be helped to change in ways that would improve the models offered for identification.

[R.S.]

This chapter brings together two aspects of the author's experience: (1) psychoanalytical theory and clinical practice, and (2) work as a consultant to institutions. The relevant aspect of psychoanalytical theory concerns the building of personality through introjection and identification. Personality development is influenced by the models available for identification: models of individuals and relationships; ways of thinking, feeling and behaving; settings where people are together and interact. Healthy development depends to a considerable extent on the availability of appropriate—i.e. healthy—models and the management of the relationship with inappropriate models.

As a psychoanalyst one sees this from inside the person, the models the patient has already established in his internal world. As a consultant to an institution, one sees it from the outside. What are the real models the institution makes available for introjection and identification? How can the institution develop the kind of models that will further healthy development in its members? The institutions from which my experience has been drawn have been primarily, but not only, for children and adolescents, disturbed or delinquent children in residential care, children in day nurseries, and small children making long stays in the Royal National Orthopaedic Hospital. In all of them one was concerned to mitigate the potentially harmful effects of institutionalization and promote healthy growth and development. In most of them one was also concerned with providing therapy for already disturbed children. One would not, in any case, distinguish too sharply between these objectives.

If one looks at the problem from the institutional point of view, it is not an exaggeration to say that the whole institution, its every aspect, is a potential milieu for growth, development, and therapy. So one's field of concern includes such things as the management structure, the division of the institution into subsystems and the relation between them, the nature of authority and how it is operated, the social defence system, the culture and traditions (Menzies, 1970). In three of the institutions, my formal role was that of *management* consultant. In all the institutions my colleagues and I gave considerable attention to management.

In practice, the institution's impact on its clients (I use this word as a generic term for the people who are cared for in the institution) is mediated to a considerable extent through staff who tend to stay longer, are more effectively integrated into the institution, and have more responsibility for the way it functions. Staff are key models. They have their own individual personalities, their ways of making relationships and working, their strengths and weaknesses as models, but the way they deploy these in the institution is greatly influenced by features inherent in the institution, the opportunities it gives for mature functioning, or, alternatively, the ways it may inhibit this. Consultancy may play a part in optimizing institutional development in such respects.

In the past, and still today, too many of the institutions that care for children have provided inappropriate models—as shown, for example, in the Robertsons' work concerning the care of children in hospitals, or the film *John,* about a child placed temporarily in a residential nursery (Robertson, 1969, 1970). The separation from his mother was crucial in that child's experience, but if one looks at children's institutions with a sophisticated eye, one can see that they are more damaging to the separated child than they need be. The institutional models were not good. For example, early hospital studies were done in hospitals where not only was maternal visiting inadequate, but the care-system was multiple indiscriminate care-taking, which effectively prevented the child from forming meaningful new attachments. Such experiences may have made us unduly pessimistic about the quality of care possible for children in institutions. Institutions can change to provide a better setting for growth, development, and therapy and provide better models for identification. One is entitled to be more optimistic.

The development
of appropriate institutional models

What follows describes some examples of work in institutions that may give substance to my optimism and shows how institutions can change in a desirable direction.

Delegation and its relation to the staff as models

A particular problem lies in the area of management. Staff tend to be members of the helping professions and think of themselves as professionals first and as managers only secondarily, if at all. Sometimes, indeed, they despise management and regard it as irrelevant or even detrimental to therapy. Nothing could be further from the truth. The most effective therapeutic communities I have worked in were headed by people who saw their role primarily as management and did not shirk managing. A central management issue is delegation. It is good practice to delegate tasks and responsibilities to the lowest level at which they can effectively be carried and to the point at which decision-making is most effective. Such delegation *downwards* increases opportunities for staff to demonstrate their capacity to carry responsibility for themselves and their tasks and to make realistic decisions, aspects of a good model. But this has not traditionally happened in such institutions, collectively known as humane institutions. In many of them the tasks, responsibility, authority, and decision-making are concentrated at an unnecessarily high level, with consequent diminution of the staff more directly in contact with clients. Delegation *upwards* has been common (Menzies, 1970). To give an example: the matron of one of the children's homes asked for consultancy with a problem that was troubling her. The setting was traditional and typical. The matron made all the decisions about food and distributed the food in kind to the housemothers, who organized meals for boys and staff in the houses where the boys lived. The matron virtually decided what everyone would eat, and the housemothers had little power of decision-making over food or responsibility or authority for planning.

This was a bad system, especially from the perspective of institutional functioning and the models presented to the boys. For example, since decision-making, authority, and responsibility were structurally concentrated in the matron, the housemothers tended to disclaim their responsibility and authority. They would blame the matron if things went wrong rather than feel an obligation to cope themselves. A trivial example illustrates this point. Two boys went for a walk one evening and came back hungry. The housemother gave them two of the eggs matron had given her for the boys' breakfast. She appealed to the matron for two more eggs and was disconcerted and angry when the matron would not—could not—give her two more. matron was expected to be a cornucopia, but, of course, her resources were also severely limited. The housemother blamed the matron and drew the boys with her into this rather paranoid, undesirable attitude, of which the matron was an undeserving victim.

The system gradually changed. The housemothers were given the money to buy food. With it was delegated the responsibility and authority for providing food. The matron gave up her direct authority and responsibility for food provision and became an adviser and support system for the housemothers if they wanted to use her that way.

The effect of the change was dramatic. The housemothers visibly grew in authority and stature as they accepted and faced the new challenge. They became better models. Food provision was better, and talk of scarcity began to disappear. Confrontation about shortcomings in food provision was now between the housemother, her colleagues in the house, and the boys. There was no escape and no available scapegoat. Blame could not be projected in a paranoid way. The boys learned an important fact about reality: resources are scarce, and not because someone is mean; in life, one has to cope with this. Boys could be involved with the housemother in doing so, helping her with the shopping, planning, and so on. Ingenuity and creativity were freed: staff and boys took to gardening to improve food supplies and began to keep livestock. It was a much healthier atmosphere.

Effective delegation implies more than taking responsibility for oneself. It implies accepting and respecting the authority of superiors and being acceptable to them. It implies taking responsibility for subordinates and holding them responsible for their work. This was particularly important for the clients whose relation with authority was disturbed. They had little capacity to take responsibility and authority for themselves, and, on the whole, regarded people in authority as there only to be rebelled against.

Institutional boundaries and the development of identity

Healthy development requires the establishment of firm bound-aries around the self and others across which realistic and effective transactions can take place and within which a firm sense of one's own and others' identity can be established. Young children and the disturbed young people in many institu-tions have not developed effective boundary control or a firm identity and need help in achieving this.

A danger in children's institutions is that boundaries are inadequately controlled and there is unwarranted intrusion into sub-systems and into the individuals in them. There is some-thing about residential institutions that seems to make people feel and act as though it is perfectly all right to have everything open and public and to claim right of entry to almost anywhere at almost any time. Children, it seems, are not supposed to need privacy or seclusion. Nothing could be further from the truth, nor from what the good ordinary family does. The family tends jealously to guard its boundaries, regulating entry and exit to and from the family home—in particular, protecting the children both from excessive intrusion and from excessive free-dom to go out across the boundaries. Many institutions present bad models of boundary control.

Problems appear particularly in the living-space of children in institutions, their homes while they are there. This has needed attention in all the institutions where I have worked. In the orthopaedic hospital the boundaries around the cot unit for small children were much too open (Menzies Lyth, 1982). The unit opened directly into the hospital grounds, and people walk-ing there seemed to feel free to visit the children en passant, often with kindly intentions of entertaining and encouraging the children. The cot unit provided the easiest access to the unit for latency children, and people on their way there would also visit the small children. The boundary between the two units was open, so the small children were visited a good deal by older children and their visitors. Altogether, it was an inappropriate situation. Small children cannot handle that amount of contact, especially with strangers; their boundary control is not good enough, and the excessive demands on it are likely to interfere with its development. The model presented was not likely to further healthy personal growth.

Changes were gradually made. The external door was closed to everyone except members of the cot unit. Staff and other adults such as parents had the authority and responsibility to see that the rule was obeyed. Staff let it be known that the policy was 'No admittance except on business' from the latency unit, and staff and other adults had the authority and responsibility to see that this was sustained. Later a partition was built between the two units. The benefits of this boundary control in the ongoing life of the cot unit and to the children were inestimable.

There remained the problem of the large number of people who did have legitimate business with the children. Their crossing of the boundary also had to be supervised to mitigate possible detrimental effects. In particular, their actual contacts with children needed to be monitored, since small children have not developed the capacity to mediate such contacts effectively for themselves, and in the hospital setting they may be frightened by strangers who do nasty things like taking blood samples or putting them in traction. The normal way that the child's boundaries would be protected and the transactions across them monitored would be by a known and trusted adult, who could comfort the child and negotiate on his behalf, controlling the boundary and presenting a good model. So it became the rule that staff from outside the unit who had business with a child should approach him only through his mother, if present, or his assigned nurse, or both. (The case-assignment system is discussed later.)

Effective boundary control of the living situation can have a positive effect on the development of identity in another way. It gives a stronger sense of identification with what is inside, of there being something comprehensible to identify with, 'my place' or 'our place', where 'I belong' or better still 'we belong together'. Children get their sense of identity and belongingness in an institution by secure containment in a comprehensible part. Small units greatly facilitate this process. Many children's units are too big. The children cannot 'comprehend' them emotionally or physically. Further, the number of staff may then be so big as to threaten multiple indiscriminate care-taking and inhibit the development of a stable self-image, since too many adults reflect too many disparate views of himself to the child.

There may also be problems about boundary control of a rather different kind—one that is perhaps more familiar to psychoanalysts or dynamically orientated psychotherapists. This concerns the boundaries of the self and transactions across them, with special reference to projection and introjection and their effect on the self and the sense of self. Excessive and powerful projection can and does change, sometimes in a major way, the apparent identities of both the projector and the recipient. Both can feel unreal and strange to themselves, and both can act strangely and inappropriately. Similarly, inappropriate introjections can create a false identity and an unstable sense of self. It is most important that staff should be able to control their own boundaries, so as to manage the effects of projection and introjection and hold them within realistic and therapeutic limits. This is particularly so, and at the same time is particularly difficult, when the client members of the institution are disturbed, delinquent, or psychotic children. By controlling their own projections and introjections effectively, staff will help the clients to control theirs and supply effective models of boundary control for identification.

For example, the apparent lack of conscience in the young delinquent may result from the splitting-off and projection of a harsh and primitive conscience that is unbearable to him. The deprived, inadequately mothered child may project into the care-taker an idealized mother figure, thereby trying to control him or her to behave in an idealized way. The danger for the care-taker and the child is that the projections may be so compelling that the care-taker acts on them instead of treating them as communications. His personal boundaries are breached, his identity temporarily changed, and the transaction ineffectively controlled. The model is inappropriate. The staff may act out the primitive, harsh, projected conscience and establish an excessively punitive regime. Or they may act out the projected ideal mother and establish an excessively gratifying regime. Both are anti-therapeutic, since both involve boundary breaking and avoid confrontation and real work with the problem where it belongs—i.e. in the client.

The situation is further complicated by inadequately controlled projection between staff members themselves, between children, and between sub-systems of the total institution. All such phenomena are anti-therapeutic; they present inappropriate models of boundary control and false identities. Progress can only be made in so far as individuals and sub-systems can keep inside what belongs to them, discard what does not, and work with the internal and external reality of their situation. This has always seemed to me one of the hardest tasks confronting the staff of institutions whose primary task is development and therapy. It is important for staff to be able to form a close, supportive group, able to confront together the introjective and projective systems and rescue each other when one or more are caught. It requires a degree of honesty that is not easy to achieve and courage for confrontation. An outside consultant may be useful—someone who can understand the processes and can view the situation with a 'semi-detached' eye and help others to do the same.

Provision for facilitating the development of the capacity for relationships

The theoretical basis for this section of the chapter lies mainly in the work of John Bowlby (1969) and his many co-workers. Briefly, the capacity to develop lasting and meaningful relationships is linked with the opportunities for the baby and young child to form secure attachments. The good ordinary family provides an excellent opportunity. There the child is likely to form an intense focal attachment, usually, although not always, to his mother. He forms other, usually less intense, relationships with a number of others—his father, siblings, other relatives, and friends—his attachment circle widening as he grows older. Moreover, the people in his attachment circle also have attachments to each other that are important to him for identification. He not only loves his mother as he experiences her, but he can identify with his father loving his mother and so extend his 'concept' of the male loving the female.

An aspect of disturbance in children in many institutions is that their capacity to form attachments is under-developed or already damaged. Putting children into institutions can damage this capacity, or damage it further if it is already damaged. This is clearly shown in the work of the Robertsons (1969b), for example. It is important, therefore, for the institution to be so organized that it sustains and furthers the development of the capacity for attachment.

One could formulate the questions thus: how far can an institution reproduce the conditions for growth provided by the good ordinary family? For the most part, institutions have dismally failed to provide a care situation that provides for focal attachment within an attachment circle, thus protecting and developing the capacity to make relationships. The typical institutional pattern or carer–client relationship is multiple indiscriminate care-taking, where all staff look after all clients indiscriminantly and no focal attachment is possible. The film *John* shows clearly how this system of care defeats all the efforts of John, a child capable of attachment, to attach himself to one nurse (Robertson, 1969b). Multiple indiscriminate care-taking, in my experience, also seems to inhibit the development of attachments between staff. There is consequently a dearth of attachment models for clients.

I am indebted to my colleague, Alastair Bain (Bain & Barnett, 1986), for a dramatic observation of the child's identification with an inadequate model of relationships in a day nursery and its perpetuation in his later relationships. He writes of 'the discontinuity of care provided even by a single care-taker which occurs when a nursery nurse has to care for a number of children'. He continues:

> their [the children's] intense needs for individual attention tend to mean that they do not allow the nurse to pay attention to any one child for any length of time, other children will pull at her skirt, want to sit up on her lap, push the child who is receiving attention away.

He adds:

during the periods between moments of attention, the young child experiences his fellows as also receiving moments of attention. . . . He will experience as the predominant pattern of relationships between adult and child, a series of discontinuities of attention, a nurse momentarily directing her attention from one child to another. . . . He and his moment are just part of a series of disconnected episodes.

A follow-up of these children into school showed them to have identified with and to be operating that model. They showed a series of episodic and discontinuous relationships with their world, fleeting superficial attachments to people, episodic discontinuous play activities, and difficulties in sustaining continuous attention to school work. I have called this the 'butterfly phenomenon', the child flitting aimlessly from person to person or activity to activity.

However, there are other ways of organizing institutions. It is possible to eliminate multiple indiscriminate care-taking and make the institution more like an ordinary family. If the institution can be divided into small self-contained units, it becomes more like a family, although probably still somewhat larger. The smaller setting in itself facilitates attachment—there are fewer people and more contact with each of them. All the children's homes and the orthopaedic hospital had small residential units of eight to twelve children, or even fewer.

It is also possible to provide something approximating more closely to a focal carer by assigning children to a single person for special care and attention. What this involves depends on needs and circumstances. In the orthopaedic hospital, most of the children were fortunate to have their mothers with them for a good part of the time, but there were unaccompanied children, and all children were without their mothers some of the time. So there still seemed the need to assign a nursery nurse to each child and family. The nurse helped the mother to care for the child when she was present and looked after the child herself when the mother was absent. She accompanied him to other places in the hospital if the mother could not. She comforted him in distress, talked to him if he was verbal, including talking through his problems. For example, a child was overheard having an imaginary conversation with his mother on a toy telephone: 'Mummy, I've been a naughty boy, and that's why you don't come to see me.' The nurse picked that up and discussed it with the child.

The staff of an institution cannot equal the almost total availability of the ordinary mother, since staff have limited working hours, but experience has shown that deep and meaningful relationships can be formed. A small boy came alone from overseas. The assigned nurse not only did general care, but talked to him about his family, of whom the child had photographs, thus helping to keep them alive in his mind. She helped to prepare him for going home, where he would find his mother with a new baby, by talking, by doll play, and by helping him to relate to real babies in the unit. They became very attached. It was moving to watch them together. Parting was painful for both, but for both the rewards were great, and the child's capacity for attachment was sustained.

Gaps in the availability of the focal care-taker are difficult but not impossible to manage. The cot unit had explicit re-assignment plans when the assigned nurse was off-duty. With a very small staff care-taking never became indiscriminate. In small units with well-monitored boundaries children form attachments to other adults and children, as in the ordinary family. Staff also form attachments to each other. This provides good models of attachment behaviour and facilitates re-assignment when necessary. The child accepts another adult more easily if he has seen the two adults in a good relation with each other. This is reminiscent of the ordinary family with its wider attachment circle.

The change to this new way of working is stressful, although potentially rewarding, and one has to attend to that in helping to bring about change. Case-assignment and closer attachment between the patient and his family and the nurse meant that the nurse was in closer and more meaningful contact with their distress. One cannot be effectively in contact with distressed children without suffering acutely oneself. Indeed, multiple indiscriminate care-taking can be seen as a structural social defence for staff against making deep and meaningful contact with the patient and his family—contact that frees normal expressiveness and brings the carer more effectively into contact with the whole range of feelings. It can be quite shattering temporarily for staff to move from multiple indiscriminate care-taking to case-assignment, including the disruption of concepts about what a child is like. The staff nurse said, 'I have had to un-learn everything I thought I knew about children since you've been here'.

The staff may need a great deal of help in tolerating the stress of being in more effective contact with patients—help from having a strongly attached group of their own, or possibly an outside consultant. One could say that staff need the same kind of care for themselves that they are expected to provide for others, a consistency in the institution in the way it treats people.

What I have been saying may be familiar already in Bion's words. He described the importance for the infant's development of his mother's capacity for reverie and containment (Bion, 1967). It is important that the mother can take in the baby's communications, ponder over them, and respond in a meaningful way. The distress of the children makes this a particularly important function for the staff of children's institutions. It may be reverie by an individual, in which case he needs close attached contact with the child. It may be something analogous to reverie in a group, e.g. staff talking together in an intuitive way, perhaps away from the heat of the moment. The communications with which staff must work are often massive and disturbing, and such mutual reverie may be important for bearing them. Like the ordinary devoted mother (Winnicott, 1958), staff need to be contained in a system of meaningful attachments if they are to contain their clients effectively.

The introjection
of the institution's social defence system

Institutions per se develop defence systems that are the product of interaction between the members of the institution, especially their personal defence systems. The defences affect the way in which the institution functions, its structure, its traditions, and so on. Continued membership tends to mean that members have to accept and use the social defence system as their personal defence system, at least while present in the institution, and to behave in accordance with it. From the point of view of personality development it is important that the social defence system incorporate mature defences the introjection of which will further the maturation of clients (Menzies, 1970).

The defence system is under constant threat of regression—the more so at times of crisis. It is particularly at risk when the client members are physically ill or psychiatrically disturbed children or adolescents. The impact of the clients may put pressure on staff and the institution to erect massive primitive defences against the stress they evoke.

A particular problem is that the clients may form relationships and groups that develop their own often primitive and anti-maturational defences. They develop sub-cultures of a delinquent or pathological kind, e.g. violence, perverse sexuality, criminal behaviour, excessive dependence. Staff have to contend with pressure on them to join the sub-culture and accept its defences. Or, alternatively, they may erect another sub-culture to counteract the first. It is by no means easy to resist those pressures, but it is imperative for the benefit of the clients, and for the staff themselves, that they should be resisted.

During a day's consultancy in a children's home staff were helped to tackle more effectively a sub-culture and their sub-cultural response to it, and to return to more mature defences and adaptations after a regression under stress. The professional staff described discontent among the domestic staff, who felt they could not achieve a high enough standard of work and were not getting job satisfaction. The domestic staff told much the same story.

I was not at all clear what I was supposed to do about this. It seemed remote from my usual consultancy concerns. Then I began to understand. There was much talk about violence from the boys. There had been an upsurge of violence recently, and rumour had it that unusually violent boys had just entered the home or would do so shortly. I realized that the professional staff were more than usually frightened, not only of the boys' violence but also of the impulse to counter-violence in themselves. They had not felt able to confront the violence in a therapeutic way.

Instead, they developed regressed defences and were trying to cope with it in a sub-cultural way, i.e. by attempts at appeasement and placation, such as by trying to provide a quite unrealistically high standard of living. Professional staff projected into the domestic staff the need to do so, setting a domestic standard the domestic staff accepted but could not meet, hence their discontent. In the course of a long day's work, this was sorted out. Professional staff faced their fears of violence and felt stronger to work with it directly. Projections and pressures were withdrawn from the domestic staff, who could once again feel they had a realistic job that they could carry out effectively. More effective defences and adaptations were reinstated.

One could re-formulate this incident in terms of Bion's theories of groups (Bion, 1961). The institution had mobilized basic assumption dependency to counteract basic assumption fright. The group was therefore engaged in psychotic processes of a primitive kind. The work group and progress through learning from experience were the casualties.

Conclusion

I hope my description of consultancy in institutions has justified my rather optimistic attitude at the beginning of this chapter, i.e. that institutions can change so as to provide more appropriate models for identification through which the clients of the institution can mature and develop more healthy personalities. Changes in the desired direction are possible: they have been achieved, although often at the cost of considerable turmoil, doubt, and uncertainty in the people involved. As the changes took place, clients grew and matured in ways that they had not done before, and institutionally caused damage was reduced. A follow-up of the children in the orthopaedic hospital showed that none had suffered the 'traditional' effects of hospitalization (Robertson, 1970). There was even a remarkable psychiatric improvement in a psychotic unaccompanied child with no help other than that given by the cot unit.

The disturbed children in the children's home did not do so well—the task was much more difficult—but they did notably better in personality development and subsequent life-performance than children who had been cared for in more traditional institutions.

Reflecting on such experiences in institutions for children makes it clear that the good results of such an approach are by no means limited to the children. The basis of the approach to child development was through providing opportunities for the adult carers to behave more maturely themselves and so become better models for identification, so we were not surprised to note how much the adults also matured—adults who were healthy and mature, but still had potential for further growth. Mothers who spent any considerable time in the orthopaedic hospital with their children grew in strength, confidence, and sensitivity. The same was true of the staff of all the institutions, the most dramatic development in adults being probably in the young nursery nurses, both in the orthopaedic hospital and in the day nursery, where Bain and Barnett worked (Bain & Barnett, 1986).

The approach would seem relevant also to those adults who live or work in institutions, and not only those who are ill or distressed. Alastair Bain (1982) has reported similar personal growth in the staff of a computer company as the management structure changed, responsibility and authority was delegated downwards, and so on. My own early work in a teaching hospital is also relevant (Menzies, 1970). The nature of the institution and especially its primitive social defence system was forcing regression on both qualified and student nurses and so could be said to be anti-maturational, a severe stricture on an educational institution. That made me think about educational institutions in general. This approach seems relevant, especially if one regards educational institutions as having a wider task in relation to psychosocial development than merely the inculcation of academic knowledge. Elizabeth Richardson (1973) has described developments in a secondary school which support this comment.

I do not feel it is going too far to consider that this way of thinking about institutions applies to all institutions if they are to promote growth and development in their members and facilitate fuller development of their potential. This would not deny, however, that they probably have particular importance in institutions whose primary task is the promotion of growth and development for those who have suffered physical or emotional deprivation or trauma, and for the care of the mentally or physically ill.

Changes in the desired direction are possible. Indeed, when I survey the work of my Tavistock colleagues, a great part of it has been in helping institutions to bring about such changes. Bringing about change is not easy—it requires faith. Further, change is not once and for all. Constant vigilance is needed to prevent regression, and constant adaptation is needed to meet changes in the environment and changing demands. I am not prescribing a life of ease for those of us who manage institutions.

CHAPTER TWENTY-FOUR

Some notes on the contribution of Margaret Lowenfeld to child psychotherapy

Margarita Wood

D r Lowenfeld (1890–1973) was born in England, of Polish–Welsh parentage. When in 1919, in the aftermath of the Russo–Polish war, she went to Poland as a physician, she recognized the inadequacy of words to describe the devastation, trauma, and lack of the bare fundamentals of existence, yet she also found children who, although bereft, had survived with an amazingly creative spirit. This experience and her scientific openness to new data deeply influenced her psychotherapeutic method. This centred on play as embodying the child's attempts, through both cognition and affect, to comprehend the experience of the body and the outside world, becoming then the means to the understanding and integration of original distress and inchoate idea. Fantasy, representing a child's non-verbal image of reality, by-passes defences, enabling the child to engage in a self-encounter that can be facilitated by the therapist without impingement. In 1928 Lowenfeld opened her clinic in West London, later the Institute of Child Psychology (ICP), using a holistic approach. The children created their own forms out of an enriched environment, the 'World Technique'—a sand-

tray with miniature people, animals, etc., being the most notable. *Play in Childhood* (Lowenfeld, 1953) was very influential,
and her insights were later acknowledged by Winnicott (1971).
The first training in child psychotherapy, established there in
1935, continued until the closure of the ICP in 1978. As analys-
ands in varying schools, students worked in an eclectic milieu
with children, including the severely deprived and disturbed,
accepting that 'not knowing' formed a proper part of scientific
enquiry.

Many of Lowenfeld's ideas formulated in the 1930s were
ahead of her time and ill-received: ideas on the nature of infant
experience now gain support from research (Bower, 1974); modification of interpretative technique to sensitivity arising from
deprivation are described by Boston and Szur (1983); parallels
with later psychoanalytic theory are recognized by Urwin (1988,
p. 136). However, Lowenfeld withdrew from contention into
clinical work and research, leaving many misunderstandings,
although her work continued to attract interest: Buhler (1951)
and Kalff (Bradway, 1981) appropriated the 'World Technique',
and in varying forms it is found world-wide in therapy, psychology, and research. Lowenfeld's own book (1977) and *Selected
Papers* (1988) appeared posthumously.

New developments include a brief exploration of the transference–countertransference when mediated by the image-mak-
ing process in painting (Wood, 1984) and research into fantasy
and cognitive processes in 'World-making' (Wood, in preparation).

REFERENCES

ABAFA (1980a). *Access to Birth Records*. ABAFA Research Series 1, May 1980.

_____ (1980b). *Explaining Adoption: A Guide for Adoptive Parents*. ABAFA Publication.

Advisory Council on Child Care (1970). *A Guide to Adoption Practice*. ACCC no. 2. London: HMSO.

Ansfield, J. G. (1971). *The Adopted Child*. Springfield, IL: Charles C Thomas.

Antony, J. (1958). An experimental approach to the psychopathology of childhood autism. *British Journal of Medical Psychology*, *31*: 211–225.

Anzieu, D. (1989). *The Skin Ego* (translated by C. Turner). New Haven, CT: Yale University Press. [*Le moi-peau*. Paris: Dunod, 1985.]

Athanassiou, C. (1986). Étude clinique du développement des deux aspects différenciés du concept de liens. World Congress on Infant Psychiatry, Stockholm.

Axline, V. (1966). *Dibs: In Search of Self*. London: Victor Gollancz.

Bain, A. (1982). The Baric Experiment: The design of jobs and organisation for the expression and growth of human capacity.

443

Occasional Paper No. 4. London: The Tavistock Institute of Human Relations.

Bain, A., & Barnett, L. (1986). The design of a day care system in a nursery setting for children under five. *Occasional Paper No. 8.* London: The Tavistock Institute of Human Relations.

Baker, L., Barcai, A., Kaye, R., & Haque, N. (1969). Beta adrenergic blockade and juvenile diabetes: Acute studies and long-term therapeutic trial. *Journal of Pediatrics, 75*: 19–29.

Bender, H., & Swan-Parente, A. (1983). Psychological and psychotherapeutic support of staff and parents in an intensive care baby unit. In: J. A. Davis, M. P. M. Richards, & N. R. C. Robertson (Eds.), *Parent–Baby Attachment in Premature Infants* (pp. 165–176). London: Croom-Helm.

Bender, L. (1956). Schizophrenia in childhood: Its recognition, description and treatment. *American Journal of Orthopsychiatry, 26*: 499–506.

Bentovim, A., Elton, A., Hildebrand, J., Tranter, M., & Vizard, E. (1988). *Child Sexual Abuse within the Family: Assessment and Treatment.* London: John Wright.

Berger, M. (1979). Preliminary report of the study group on the problems of adopted children. *Bulletin of the Hampstead Clinic, 2*: 169–176.

——— (1980). (In collaboration with D. Bandler, C. Elliott, & J. Hodges.) Second report on problems of adopted children. *Bulletin of the Hampstead Clinic, 3*: 247–256.

Berger, M. & Hodges, J. (1982). Some thoughts on the question of when to tell the child that he is adopted. *Journal of Child Psychotherapy, 8* (1): 67–87.

Bernstein, B. (1972). Social class, language and socialisation. In: P. P. Giglioli (Ed.), *Language and Social Context* (pp. 157–178). London: Penguin Books.

Berry, J. (1979). *Fractured Circles.* London: New Beacon Books.

Bick, E. (1964). Notes on infant observation in psychoanalytic training. *International Journal of Psycho-Analysis, 45* (4).

——— (1968). The experience of the skin in early object relations. *International Journal of Psycho-Analysis, 49*: 484–486.

Bicknell, J. (1983). The psychopathology of handicap. *British Journal of Medical Psychology, 5* (6): 167–178.

Bion, W. R. (1961). *Experiences in Groups.* London: Tavistock.

_____ (1962). *Learning from Experience*. London: Heinemann. [Reprinted London: Karnac Books, 1988.]

_____ (1967). A theory of thinking. In: *Second Thoughts*. London: Heinemann. [Reprinted London: Karnac Books, 1984.]

_____ (1970). *Attention and Interpretation*. London: Tavistock. [Reprinted London: Karnac Books, 1984.]

_____ (1990). *A Memoir of the Future*. London: Karnac Books.

Bird, G., & Stokes, R. (1976). *The Fischer-Dieskau Book of Lieder*. London: Victor Gollancz.

Bird, R. (1986). *L'adolescente, la famiglia, la comunità, quale risposta?* (edited by I. Rossi). Bologna: Cooperativa Libraria Universitaria Editioni.

Blacher, J., & Meyers, C. (1983). A review of attachment formation and disorder of handicapped children. *American Journal of Mental Deficiency, 87* (1–6, January): 359–372.

Boston, M. (1972). Psychotherapy with a boy from a children's home. *Journal Child Psychotherapy, 3* (2).

Boston, M. & Szur, R. (Eds.) (1983). *Psychotherapy with Severely Deprived Children*. London: Routledge & Kegan Paul. [Reprinted London: Karnac Books, 1990.]

Bower, T. (1977a). *A Primer of Infant Development*. San Francisco, CA: W. H. Freeman.

_____ (1977b). *The Perceptual World of the Child*. London: Fontana/Open Books.

_____ (1982). *Development in Infancy*. San Francisco, CA: W. H. Freeman.

Bowlby, J. (1951). *Child Care and the Growth of Love* (second ed.). Harmondsworth, Middx.: Penguin Books.

_____ (1969). *Attachment and Loss, Vol. 1*. London: Hogarth.

_____ (1979a). *The Making and Breaking of Affectional Bonds*. London: Tavistock.

_____ (1979b). On knowing what you are not supposed to know and feeling what you are not supposed to feel. *Canadian Journal of Psychiatry, 24*: 403–408.

Box, G. E. P., & Jenkins, G. M. (1976). *Time Series Analysis, Forecasting and Control* (second ed.). San Francisco, CA: Holden-Day.

Box, S., Copley, B., Magagna, M., & Moustaki, F. (Eds.) (1981). *Psychotherapy with Families: An Analytic Approach*. London: Routledge & Kegan Paul.

Bradway, K. et al. (1981). *Sandplay Studies: Origins, Theory and Practice.* San Fransisco, CA: C. J. Jung Institute.

Brazelton, T. B. (1970). The origins of reciprocity: The early mother–infant interaction. In: M. Lewis & L. Rosenblum (Eds.), *The Effect of the Infant on Its Caretaker.* New York: Wiley.

Brazelton, T. B. et al., (1975). Early mother infant reciprocity. In: *Parent Infant Interaction. CIBA Foundation Symposium 33.* Amsterdam: Associated Scientific Publishers.

Brazelton, T. B., Koslowski, B., & Main, M. (1974). The early mother–infant interaction. In: M. Lewis & L. A. Rosenblum (Eds.), *The Effect of the Infant on Its Caregivers.* London: Wiley–Interscience.

Brinich, P. (1980). Some potential effects of adoption upon self and object representations. *Psychoanalytic Study of the Child, 35*: 107–133.

Brodzinsky, D. (1984). New perspectives on adoption revelation. *Adoption and Fostering, 8* (2): 27–32.

Bruner, J. S., Jolly, A., & Sylva, K. (1985). *Play—Its Role in Development and Evolution.* Harmondsworth, Middx.: Penguin Books.

Buhler, C. (1951). The World Test: A projective technique. *Journal of Child Psychiatry, 2* (1): 4–23.

Burlingham, D. (1963). Some problems of the ego development in blind children. *Psychoanalytic Study of the Child, 18*: 197.

Byng-Hall, J. (1986). Family scripts: A concept which can bridge child psychotherapy and family therapy thinking. *Journal of Child Psychotherapy, 12* (1): 3–15.

Call, Justin D. et al. (1983). *Frontiers of Infant Psychiatry.* New York: Basic Books.

Canetti, E. (1983). *The Human Province.* London: Andre Deutsch.

Carpenter, G. (1975). Mother's face and the newborn. In: R. Lewin (Ed.), *Child Alive.* London: Temple Smith.

Castell, J. H. F., et al. (1963). Report of the Working Party on Subnormality. *Bulletin of the British Psychological Society, 16* (53): 37–50.

Chennells, P. (1987). *Explaining Adoption to Your Adopted Child: A Guide for Adoptive Parents.* London: BAAF.

Chidester, L., & Menninger, L. (1936). The application of psychoanalytic methods to the study of mental retardation. *American Journal of Orthopsychiatry, 6*: 616–625.

Clark, P. (1933). *The Nature and Treatment of Amentia*. London: Bailliere.

Condon, W. (1975). Speech makes babies move. In: R. Lewin (Ed.), *Child Alive*. London: Temple Smith.

Copley, B. (1976). Brief work with adolescents and young adults in a counselling service. *Journal of Child Psychotherapy, 4* (2): 93–106.

―――― (1983). Work with a family as a single therapist with special reference to transference manifestations. *Journal of Child Psychotherapy, 9*.

―――― (1987). Explorations with families. *Journal of Child Psychotherapy, 13* (1).

Corbett, J. A., et al. (1975). Epilepsy. In: J. Worris (Ed.), *Mental Retardation and Developmental Disabilities, Vol. 7*. New York: Brunner/Mazel.

Creighton, S. J. (1978). Department of Health and Social Security: *Report of the Social Work Service of DHSS into Certain Aspects of the Management of the Case of Stephen Menhenniott*. London: HMSO.

―――― (1987). Quantitative assessment of child abuse. In: Peter Maher (Ed.), *Child Abuse, the Educational Perspective*. Oxford: Blackwell.

Crome, L. (1960). The brain and mental retardation. *British Journal of Medicine, 1*: 897–904.

Dale, F. (1983). The body as bondage: Work with two children with physical handicap. *Journal of Child Psychotherapy, 9* (1): 33–47.

Davis, J. A., Richards, M. P. M., & Robertson, N. R. C. (Eds.) (1983). *Parent–Baby Attachment in Premature Infants*. London & Canberra: Croom Helm.

Daws, D. (1985). Sleep problems in babies and young children. *Journal of Child Psychotherapy, 11* (2): 87–95.

Daws, D., & Boston, M. (1977). *The Child Psychotherapist and Problems of Young People*. London: Wildwood House. [Reprinted London: Karnac Books, 1990.]

Dockar-Drysdale, B. (1990). *The Provision of Primary Experience: Winnicottian Work with Children and Adults*. London: Free Association Books.

Doll, E. A. (1953). Counselling parents of severely retarded children. In: C. L. Stacey & M. F. Demartino (Eds.), *Counselling and Psychotherapy with the Mentally Retarded.* New York: The Free Press.

Donaldson, M. (1978). *Children's Minds.* London: Fontana/Collins.

Douglas, J., & Richman, N. (1984). *My Child Won't Sleep.* Harmondsworth, Middx.: Penguin Books.

Dyke, S. (1987). Saying 'no' to psychotherapy: Consultation and assessment in a case of sexual abuse. *Journal of Child Psychotherapy, 13* (2): 65–81.

Edelson, M. (1986). Causal explanation in science and in psychoanalysis: Implications for writing a case study. *Psychoanalytic Study of the Child, 41*: 89–128.

Emde, R., & Sorce, J. F. (1983). The rewards of infancy. Emotional availability and maternal referencing. In: J. D. Call, E. G. Galenson, & R. L. Tyson (Eds.), *Frontiers of Infant Psychiatry, Vol. 1* (Chapter 3). New York: Basic Books.

Erikson, E. H. (1950). *Childood and Society.* Harmondsworth, Middx.: Penguin Books.

————— (1968). *Identity.* London: Faber.

Fain, M., & Kreisler, L. (1970). Discussions sur la genèse des fonctions representatives. *Revue Française de la Psychanalyse, 34.*

Ferenczi, S. (1921). *Final Contributions to the Problems and Methods of Psychoanalysis* (edited by Michael Balint). London: Hogarth Press, 1955.

Field, T. et al. (1980). *High Risk Infants and Children.* London: Academic Press.

Fonagy, P., Moran, G., & Higgitt, A. (1989). Psychological factors in the self-management of insulin-dependent diabetes mellitus in children and adolescents. In: J. Wardle & S. Pearce (Eds.), *The Practice of Behavioural Medicine.* Oxford: Oxford University Press.

Fordham, M. (1944). *The Life of Childhood.* London: Routledge & Kegan Paul.

————— (1948). The individual and collective psychology: Reflexions prompted by Dr Bion's address from the chair. *British Journal of Medical Psychology, 21.*

————— (1957). *New Developments in Analytical Psychology.* London: Routledge & Kegan Paul.

————— (1958). *The Objective Psyche.* London: Routledge & Kegan Paul.

————— (1974). *Technique and Countertransference. Library of Analytical Psychology, Vol. 2.* London: Heinemann Medical.

————— (1976). *The Self and Autism.* London: Heinemann Medical.

_____ (1978). *Jungian Psychotherapy: A Study in Analytical Psychology*. London: Wiley. [Reprinted London: Karnac Books, 1986.]

_____ (1985a). *Abandonment in Infancy*. Wilmette, IL: Chiron Publications.

_____ (1985b). *Explorations into the Self. Library of Analytical Psychology, Vol. 8*. London: Academic Press.

Forryan, B. (1988). The deprived and violent adolescent in psychotherapy. *Midland Journal of Psychotherapy, 1*: 1–8.

Fraiberg, S. (Ed.) (1980). *Clinical Studies in Infant Mental Health*. London: Tavistock.

Freeman, N., Lloyd, S., & Sinha, C. (1980). Hide and seek is child's play. *New Scientist, 88* (30 October): 1225.

Freeman, R. D. (1970). Psychiatric problems in adolescents with cerebral palsy. *Developments in Medical Child Neurology, 12*: 64–70.

Freud, A. (1965). *Normality and Pathology in Childhood*. London: The Hogarth Press & The Institute of Psychoanalysis. [Reprinted London: Karnac Books, 1989].

_____ (1986). *The Ego and the Mechanisms of Defence*. London: Hogarth.

Freud, S. (1900a). *Interpretation of Dreams. Standard Edition, 5*.

_____ (1901b). *The Psychopathology of Everyday Life. Standard Edition, 6*.

_____ (1905e). Fragment of an analysis of a case of hysteria. *Standard Edition, 7*.

_____ (1909b). Analysis of a phobia in a five-year-old boy. *Standard Edition, 10*.

_____ (1909c). Family romances. *Standard Edition, 9*.

_____ (1911b). Formulations on the two principles of mental functioning. *Standard Edition, 12*.

_____ (1912b). The dynamics of transference. *Standard Edition, 12*.

_____ (1920g). *Beyond the Pleasure Principle. Standard Edition, 18*.

Freud, W. E. (1975). Infant observation: Its relevance to psychoanalytic training. *Psychoanalytic Study of the Child, 30*: 75–94.

Friedrich, W. N., & Boriskin, J. A. (1976). The role of the child in abuse. *American Journal of Orthopsychiatry, 46*: 580–590.

Frith, U. (1985). Does the autistic child have a theory of mind? *Cognition, 21*: 37–46.

Furman, E. (1974). *A Child's Parent Dies*. New Haven, CT: Yale University Press.

Furman, E., & Katan, A. (1969). *The Therapeutic Nursery School.* New York: International Universities Press.

Gaddini, E. (1969). On imitation. *International Journal of Psycho-Analysis, 50* (4): 475–484.

Gardziel, A. (1986). The diagnosis of autistic and psychotic disturbances in children. Paper presented at the Eleventh International Congress of IACAPAP, Paris.

Gesell, A. (1946). *How a Baby Grows.* London: Hamish Hamilton.

Giannotti, A., & de Astis, G. (1978). Early infantile autism: Considerations regarding its psychopathology and the psychotherapeutic process. Paper read at the Eighth National Congress of the Italian Society of Infantile Neuropsychiatry, Florence (October).

Glenn, J. (1974). The adoption theme in Edward Albee's 'Tiny Alice' and 'The American Dream'. *Psychoanalytic Study of the Child, 29*: 413–429.

Goldschmidt, D. (1986). A contribution to the subject of psychic trauma based on a course of psychoanalytic short therapy. *International Review of Psychoanalysis, 13*: 181.

Goldstein, K. (1948). *Language and Language Disturbances.* New York: Grune & Stratton.

Goodacre, I. (1966). *Adoption Policy and Practice.* London: Allen & Unwin.

Gordon, R. (1962). Gods and the deintegrates. *Journal of Analytical Psychology, 8* (1).

Gosling, R. (1975). Foreword. In: S. Meyerson (Ed.), *Adolescence and Breakdown.* London: Allen & Unwin.

Gottman, J. M. (1973). N-of-one and n-of-two research in psychotherapy. *Psychological Bulletin, 80*: 93–105.

Grotstein, J. S. (1981). *Splitting and Projective Identification.* New York: Jason Aronson.

Grunbaum, A. (1984). *The Foundations of Psychoanalysis: A Philosophical Critique.* Berkeley, CA: University of California Press.

Gulatieri (1979). Quoted by M. Lewis et al. in: J. Matson et al. (Eds.), *Psychopathology in the Mentally Retarded.* New York: Grune & Stratton.

Gunther, M. (1959). Infant behaviour at the breast. Lecture delivered to a seminar at University College Hospital, London.

Haag, G. (1985a). La mère et le bébé dans les deux moitiés du corps. *Neuropsychiatrie de l'enfance et de l'adolescence, 2–3*: 107–114.

———— (1985b). Psychothérapie d'un enfant autiste. In: *Lieux de l'enfance, No. 3*. Paris: private publication.

Hamilton, V. (1982). *Narcissus and Oedipus*. London: Routledge & Kegan Paul.

Harris, M. (1966). The contribution of observation of mother–infant interaction and development to the equipment of a psychoanalyst or psychoanalytic psychotherapist. In: M. E. Harris Williams (Ed.), *Collected Papers of Martha Harris and Esther Bick*. Perthshire: Clunie Press, 1987.

———— (1975). Some notes on maternal containment in 'Good Enough Mothering'. *Journal of Child Psychotherapy, 4* (1): 35–36.

———— (1976). Infantile elements and adult strivings. In: M. E. Harris Williams (Ed.), *Collected Papers of Martha Harris and Esther Bick*. Perthshire: Clunie Press, 1987.

Harris, M., & Carr, H. (1966). Therapeutic consultations. *Journal of Child Psychotherapy, 1* (4): 13–23.

Hartnup, T. (1986a). Children and institutions, 1: The child and the professional. *Journal of Child Psychotherapy, 12* (2): 41–67.

———— (1986b). Children and institutions, 1: The professional and the institution. *Journal of Child Psychotherapy, 12* (2): 41–67.

Hayman, M. (1957). Traumatic elements in the analysis of a borderline case. *International Journal of Psycho-Analysis, 38*: 9–21.

Heaton-Ward, A. (1977). Psychosis in mental handicap. *British Journal of Psychiatry, 130*: 525–533.

Henry, G. (1983). Difficulties about thinking and learning. In: *Psychotherapy with Severely Deprived Children*. London: Routledge & Kegan Paul.

Hinkle, L. E., & Wolf, S. (1950). Studies in diabetes mellitus: Changes in glucose, ketone, and water metabolism during stress. *Research in Nervous and Mental Disease, 29*: 338.

Hobson, P. (1986). The autistic child's appraisal of expressions of emotion. *Journal of Child Psychology and Psychiatry, 27*: 321–342.

Hodges, J. (1984). Two crucial questions: Adopted children in psychoanalytic treatment. *Journal of Child Psychotherapy, 10* (1): 47–56.

———— (1989). Aspects of the relationship to self and objects in early maternal deprivation and adoption. *Bulletin of the Anna Freud Centre, 12* (1): 5–27.

Hodges, J., Bolletti, R., Salo, F., & Oldeschulte, R. (1985). Remembering is so much harder: A report on work in progress from the research group on adopted children. *Bulletin of the Anna Freud Centre, 8* (3): 169–179.

Hoffer, W. (1952). The mutual influences in the development of ego and id: Earliest stages. *Psychoanalytic Study of the Child, 7*: 31–41.

Hoffman, L. (1981). *Foundations of Family Therapy.* New York: Basic Books.

Hoxter, S. (1964). The experience of puberty. *Journal of Child Psychotherapy, 1* (2): 13–26.

———— (1977). Play and communication. In: D. Daws & M. Boston (Eds.), *The Child Psychotherapist and Problems of Young People.* London: Wildwood House.

Hoxter, S. (1986). The significance of trauma in the difficulties encountered by physically disabled children. *Journal of Child Psychotherapy, 12* (1): 87–88.

Hurry, A. (1986). Walk-in work with adolescents. *Journal of Child Psychotherapy, 13* (1): 33–47.

Hutt, C. (1966). Exploration and play in children. In: J. S. Bruner, A. Jolly, & K. Sylva (Eds.), *Play—Its Role in Development and Evolution.* Harmondsworth, Middx.: Penguin Books, 1985.

Isaacs, S. (1930). *Intellectual Growth in Young Children.* London: Routledge.

———— (1952). The nature and function of phantasy. In: M. Klein et al. (Eds.), *Developments in Psychoanalysis*: London: Hogarth.

Jaffe, B., & Fanshel, D. *How They Fared in Adoption: A Follow-Up Study.* New York: Columbia University Press.

Joseph, B. (1975). The patient who is difficult to reach. In: P. Giovaccini (Ed.), *Tactics and Techniques in Psycho-Analytic Therapy, Vol. 2.* New York: Jason Aronson.

Jung, C. G. (1921). Psychological types. *Collected Works, 6.*

———— (1922). On the relation of analytical psychology to poetry. *Collected Works, 15.*

———— (1935). The Tavistock Lectures. *Collected Works, 18.*

———— (1946a). Pyschic conflicts in a child. *Collected Works, 17.*

———— (1946b). Psychology of the transference. *Collected Works, 16.*

———— (1954). Transformation symbolism in the Mass. *Collected Works, 11.*

———— (1963). *Memories, Dreams and Reflections.* London: Collins and Routledge & Kegan Paul.

Kanner, L. (1943). Autistic disturbances of affective contact. *Nervous Child, 2*: 217–250.

Katan, A. (1946). Experiences with enuretics. *Psychoanalytic Study of the Child, 2*: 241–255.

Kaye, K. (1977). Towards the origin of dialogue. In: H. R. Schaffer (Ed.), *Studies in Mother–Infant Interaction*. London: Academic Press.

Keats, J. (1817). Letter to George and Thomas Keats. In: *Letters edited by M. B. Forman* (fourth ed.). London: Oxford University Press, 1952.

Kennell, J. H., & Klaus, M. H. (1971). Care of the mother of the high-risk infant. *Clinical Obstetrics and Gynecology, 14*: 19–26.

Klaus, M. *The Amazing Newborn*. Ipswich: Concorde Films.

Klein, M. (1930). The importance of symbol formation in the development of the ego. In: *The Writings of Melanie Klein, Vol. 1* (pp. 219–232). London: Hogarth Press & the Institute of Psycho-Analysis, 1975.

———— (1931). A contribution to the theory of intellectual inhibition. In: *The Writings of Melanie Klein, Vol. 1*. London: Hogarth Press & the Institute of Psycho-Analysis, 1975.

———— (1932). The psycho-analysis of children. In: *The Writings of Melanie Klein, Vol. 2*. London: Hogarth Press & the Institute of Psycho-Analysis, 1975.

———— (1937). Love, guilt and reparation. In: *The Writings of Melanie Klein, Vol. 1*. London: Hogarth Press & the Institute of Psycho-Analysis, 1975.

———— (1946). Notes on some schizoid mechanisms. In: *The Writings of Melanie Klein, Vol. 3*. London: Hogarth Press & the Institute of Psycho-Analysis, 1975.

Klein, S. (1980). Autistic phenomena in neurotic states. *International Journal of Psycho-Analysis, 61*: 395–402.

———— (1987). Review of Frances Tustin's book, 'Autistic Barriers in Neurotic Patients'. *International Review of Psycho-Analysis, 14*: 426–427.

Knight, R. P. (1941). Some problems involved in selecting and rearing adopted children. *Bulletin of the Menninger Clinic, 5*: 65–74.

Kornitzer, M. (1976). *Adoption*. London: Putnam's.

Krige, E. J. (1936). *The Social System of the Zulus* (Chap. 5). London: Longmans Green.

Lambert, K. (1981). *Analysis, Repair and Individuation. The Library of Analytical Psychology, Vol. 5*. London: Academic Press.

Laufer, M., & Laufer, M. E. (1985). *Adolescence and Developmental Breakdown*. New Haven: Yale University Press.

Layard, J. (1959). Homo eroticism in primitive society as a function of the self, *Journal of Analytical Psychology, 4* (2).

Lowenfeld, M. (1935). *Play in Childhood*. London: Victor Gollancz.

———— (1979). *The World Technique*. London: Allen & Unwin.

———— (1988). *Child Psychotherapy, War and the Normal Child: Selected Papers*, edited by C. Urwin & J. Hood-Williams. London: Free Association Press.

Ludvigsson, J. (1977). Socio-psychological factors and metabolic control in juvenile diabetes. *Acta Paediatrica Scandinavica, 66*: 431–437.

Lynch, M. A., & Roberts, J. (1982). *Consequences of Child Abose*. London: Academic Press.

Mackie, A. J. (1982). Families of adopted adolescents. *Journal of Adolescence, 5* (2): 167–178.

MacFarlane, A. (1975). Olfaction in the human neonate. In: *Parent–Infant Interaction*. CIBA Foundation Symposium 33. Amsterdam: Associated Scientific Publishers.

Maduro, R. (1980). Symbolic equations in the creative process: Reflections on Hindu India, *Journal of Analytical Psychology, 25* (1).

Mahler, M. (1968). On human symbiosis and the vicissitudes of individuation. *Infantile Psychosis, Vol. 1*. New York: International Universities Press.

Mahler, M., et al. (1975). *The Psychological Birth of the Human Infant*. New York: Basic Books.

Malan, D. H. (1963). *A Study of Brief Psychotherapy*. London: Tavistock.

Mannoni, M. (1967). *The Child, His 'Illness' and the Others*. Harmondsworth, Middx.: Penguin.

———— (1973b). *The Retarded Child and the Mother*. London: Tavistock.

Markova, I., et al. (1984). The use of tools by children with haemophilia. *Journal of Child Psychology and Psychiatry, 25* (2).

Martin, H. P., & Beezley, P. (1977). Behavioural observations of abused children. *Developmental Medicine and Child Neurology, 19*: 373–387.

Mason, M. (1985). *Women's Health and Disability*. London: Women's Health Information Centre.

McDougall, J. (1974). The psychosoma and the psychoanalytic process. *International Review of Psychoanalysis, 1* (Part IV).

McWhinnie, A. M. (1967). *Adopted Children: How They Grow Up.* London: Routledge & Kegan Paul.

Meltzer, D. (1967). *The Psycho-Analytical Process.* London: Heinemann.

———— (1973). *Sexual States of Mind.* Perthshire: Clunie Press.

———— (1986). *Studies in Extended Metapsychology* (Chap. 14). Perthshire: Clunie Press.

Meltzer, D., et al. (1982). The conceptual distinction between projective identification (Klein) and container–contained (Bion). *Journal of Child Psychotherapy, 8* (2): 185–202.

Meltzer, D., Bremner, J. Hoxter, S., Wedell, H., & Wittenberg, I. (1975). *Explorations in Autism.* Perthshire: Clunie Press.

Meltzer, D. & Harris Williams, M. (1988). *The Apprehension of Beauty.* Perthshire: Clunie Press.

Menzies, I. E. P. (1970). The functioning of social systems as a defence against anxiety. *Tavistock Pamphlet No. 3.* London: The Tavistock Institute of Human Relations.

Menzies Lyth, I. (1982). The psychological welfare of children making long stays in hospital: An experience in the art of the possible. *Occasional Paper No. 3.* London: The Tavistock Institute of Human Relations.

Miller, L., Rustin, M., Rustin, M., Shuttleworth, J. (1989). *Closely Observed Infants.* London: Duckworth.

Milner, M. (1957). *On Not Being Able to Paint.* London: Heinemann.

Minuchin, S. (1974). *Families and Family Therapy.* London: Tavistock.

Minuchin, S., & Fishman, H. C. (1981). *Family Therapy Techniques.* London: Harvard University Press.

Minuchin, S., Rosmon, B., & Baker, L. (1978). *Psychosomatic Families: Anorexia Nervosa in Context.* Cambridge, MA: Harvard University Press.

Moran, G. S., & Fonagy, P. (1987). Psychoanalysis and diabetic control: A single-case study. *British Journal of Medical Psychology, 60*: 357–372.

Mrazek, P. B., Lynch, M., & Bentovim, A. (1981). Recognition of CSA in the United Kingdom. In: P. B. Mrazek & C. H. Kempe (Eds.), *Sexually Abused Children and Their Families.* Oxford: Pergamon.

Muir, E. (1987). *Autobiography.* London: Hogarth Press.

Muir, R. C. (1975). The family and the problem of internalization. *British Journal of Medical Psychology, 48*: 267–272.

Muir, R. C., & Lewis, P. J. E. (1974). The family as an operating model for the adolescent inpatient unit: Experiences in an New Zealand setting. *Australian & New Zealand Journal of Psychiatry, 8*: 173–179.

Murray, L. (1988). Effects of post-natal depression on infant: Direct studies of early mother–infant interactions. In: R. Kumar & I. F. Brockington (Eds.), *Motherhood and Mental Illness, Vol. 2: Causes and Consequences*. London: John Wright.

Newson, J. (1974). Towards a theory of infant understanding. *Bulletin of the British Psychological Society, 27*: 251–257.

——— (1978). Dialogue and development. In: A. Lock (Ed.), *Action, Gesture and Symbol: The Emergence of Language*. London: Academic Press.

Novick, J. (1977). Walk-in Clinics for Adolescents. *Journal of Child Psychotherapy, 4* (3): 84–89.

Office of Health Economics (1973). *Mental Handicap*. London: OHE.

Olin, R. (1975). Differentiating the psychotic child from the mentally retarded child. *Minnesota Medicine, 58* (June): 489–492.

Oliver, C., Murphy, G. H., & Corbett J. A. (1987). Self-injurious behaviour in people with a mental handicap. *Journal of Mental Deficiency Research, 31*: 147–162.

O'Shaughnessy, E. (1964). The absent object. *Journal of Child Psychotherapy, 1* (2): 34.

Palazzoli, M. S. et al. (1978). *Paradox and Counterparadox*. New York: Jason Aronson.

Palombo, S. (1978). *Dreaming and Memory*. New York: Basic Books.

Peller, L. (1961). About 'Telling the Child' of his adoption. *Bulletin of the Philadelphia Association for Psychoanalysis, 11*: 145–154. [Reprinted in: E. N. Plank (Ed.), *Lilli E. Peller on Development and Education of Young Children: Selected Papers*. New York: Philosophical Library, 1978]

——— (1963). Further comments on adoption. *Bulletin of the Philadelphia Association for Psychoanalysis, 13* (1): 1–14. [Reprinted in E. N. Plank (Ed.), *Lilli E. Peller on Development and Education of Young Children: Selected Papers*. New York: Philosophical Library, 1978]

Phillips, I. (1966). Children, mental retardation and emotional disorder. In: *Prevention and Treatment of Mental Retardation*. New York: Basic Books.

Piaget, J. (1953). *The Origin of Intelligence in the Child*. London: Routledge & Kegan Paul.

Piontelli, A. (1987). Infant observation from before birth. *International Journal of Psycho-Analysis, 68*: 453–463.

Porter, R. (1986). Psychotherapy research: Physiological measures and intrapsychic events. *Journal of the Royal Society of Medicine, 79*: 257–261.

Rayner, E. (1971). *Human Development*. London: Allen & Unwin.

Raynor, L. (1980). *The Adopted Child Comes of Age*. London: George Allen & Unwin.

Registrar General. (1975). *Classification of Occupations and Coding Index*. London: HMSO.

Reid, A. (1982). *The Psychiatry of Mental Handicap*. London: Blackwell Scientific Publications.

Rexford, E. N., Sander, L., & Shapiro, F. (Eds.) (1976). *Infant Psychiatry*. New Haven, CT: Yale University Press.

Richardson, E. (1973). *The Teacher, the School and the Task of Management*. London: Heinemann.

Rimland, B. (1964). *Infantile Autism*. London: Methuen.

Robertson, J. (1953). Some responses of young children to the loss of maternal care. *Nursing Times, 49*: 382–386.

―――― (1969a). *Guide to the Film 'John'*. Ipswich: Concorde Films Council.

―――― (1969b). *John, 17 Months: For Nine Days in a Residential Nursery*. Ipswich: Concorde Films Council; New York: University Film Library.

―――― (1970). *Young Children in Hospital*. London: Tavistock.

Rutter, M. (1976). Infantile autism and other child psychoses. In: M. Rutter & L. Hersov (Eds.), *Child Psychiatry: Modern Approaches*. Oxford: Blackwell.

―――― (1979). Autism: Psychopathological mechanisms and therapeutic approaches. In: M. Bortner (Ed.), *Cognitive Growth and Development*. New York: Brunner/Mazel.

Rutter, M., Shaffer, D., & Shepherd, M. (1975). *A Multi-axial Classification of Child Psychiatric Disorders*. Geneva: World Health Organization.

Rycroft, C. (1968). *Imagination and Reality*. London: Hogarth Press.

Sacks, O. (1985). *The Man Who Mistook His Wife for a Hat*. London: Picador.

Salzberger Wittenberg, Isca (1988). Counselling young people. *The*

Child Psychotherapist & Problems of Young People. London: Karnac Books.

Sander, L. (1976). Issues in early mother-child interaction. In: E. N. Rexford, L. Sander, & T. Shapiro (Eds.), *Infant Psychiatry*. New Haven, CT: Yale University Press.

Sandler, J., Kennedy, H., & Tyson, R. (1975). Technique in child analysis. Discussion on transference. *Psychoanalytic Study of the Child, 30*: 401–441.

Sandler, J., Kennedy, H., & Tyson, R. (1980). *The Technique of Child Analysis: Discussions with Anna Freud*. London: Hogarth Press. [Reprinted London: Karnac Books, 1990.]

Sartre, J. P. (1965/1982). 'Huis clos' [In camera]. In: *Three Plays*, translated by S. Gilbert. Harmondsworth, Middx.: Penguin Books.

Sarwer-Foner, G. J. (1963). The intensive psychoanalytic psychotherapy of a brain-damaged pseudo mental defective fraternal twin. *Canadian Psychiatric Association Journal, 8* (5): 296–306.

Schade, D. S., Drumm, D. A., Duckworth, W. C., & Eaton, R. P. (1985). The aetiology of incapacitating, brittle diabetes. *Diabetes Care, 8*: 12–20.

Schafer, R. (1974). Early social behaviour and the study of reciprocity. *Bulletin of the British Psychological Society*, No. 27.

Schechter, M. D. (1960). Observation on adopted children. *Archives of General Psychiatry, 3*: 21–32.

———— (reporter) (1967). Panel on psychoanalytic theory as it relates to adoption. *Journal of the American Psychoanalytic Association, 15*: 695–708.

Schilder, P. F. (1950). *The Image and Appearance of the Human Body*. New York: International Universities Press.

Schlichtkrull, J., Munck, O., & Jersild, M. (1965). The M-value, an index of blood sugar control in diabetes. *Acta Medica Scandinavica, 177*: 95–102

Scott Clifford, W. (1963). The psychotherapy of the mental defective. *Canadian Psychiatric Association Journal, 8* (5).

Segal, H. (1975). Notes on symbol formation. *International Review of Psychoanalysis, 38* (6).

———— (1981). Notes on symbol formation. In: *The Work of Hanna Segal*. New York: Jason Aronson.

Segal, S. S. (1967). *No Child Is Ineducable*. London: Pergamon.

———— (1971). *From Care to Education*. London: Heinemann.

Sendak, M. (1970). *Where the Wild Things Are*. Harmondsworth: Puffin Books.

Shaffer, D. (1977). Brain injury. In: M. Rutter & L. Hersov (Eds.), *Child Psychiatry: Modern Approaches*. London: Blackwell.

Shengold, L. (1967). The effects of overstimulation: Rat people. *International Journal of Psycho-Analysis, 48* (3): 353–367.

Sinason, V. (1986). Secondary mental handicap and its relationship to trauma. *Psychoanalytic Psychotherapy, 2*: 131–154.

_____ (1988a). Dolls and bears: From symbolic equation to symbol. The use of different play material for sexually abused children. *British Journal of Psychotherapy* (Summer 1988).

_____ (1988b). Smiling, swallowing, sickening and stupefying. The effect of abuse on the child. *Psychoanalytic Psychotherapy* (Summer 1988).

Sisters against Disability (1985). *Newsletter*. London: Women's Health Information Centre Publication.

Spensley, S. (1985). Mentally ill or mentally handicapped? A longitudinal study of severe learning difficulty. *Psychoanalytic Psychotherapy, 1* (3): 55–70.

Spitz, R. (1965). *The First Year of Life*. New York: International Universities Press.

_____ (1983). Life and the dialogue. In: R. Emde (Ed.), *Dialogues from Infancy*. New York: International Universities Press.

Stein, L. (1973). Analytical Psychology a Modern Science. Library of Analytical Psychology, Vol. 1. London: Heinemann Medical Books.

Stern, D. (1985). *The Interpersonal World of the Infant*. New York: Basic Books.

Stern, D., Barnett, R. K., & Spicker, S. (1983). Early transmission of affect: Some research issues. In: J. D. Call, E. C. Galenson, & R. Tyson (Eds.), *Frontiers of Infant Psychiatry*. New York: Basic Books.

Stevenson, J. (1986). Evaluation studies of psychological treatment of children and practical constraints on their design. *Association of Child Psychology and Psychiatry Newsletter, 8* (2).

Stokes, J. (1987). Insights from psychotherapy. Paper presented at International Symposium on Mental Handicap. *RSM* (25 February 1987).

Storr, A. (1983). *Jung: Selected Writings*. London: Fontana.

Symington, N. (1981). The psychotherapy of a subnormal patient. *British Journal of Medical Psychology, 54*: 187–199.

_____ (1986). *The Analytic Experience*. London: Free Association Books.

Szanto, A., (1981). À propos de la position ventrale des nouveaux-nés. *Le Pediatre, 17*: 75.

Szur, R. (1977). Working in a hospital. In: D. Daws & M. Boston (Eds.), *The Child Psychotherapist and Problems of Young People*. London: Wildwood. [Revised ed., London: Karnac Books, 1981.]

Szur, R., Freud, W. E., Earnshaw, A., Bender, H., & Elkan, J. (1981). Colloquium: Hospital Care of the Newborn. *Journal of Child Psychotherapy, 7* (2): 137–159.

Tattersall, R. B. (1977). Brittle diabetes. *Clinics in Endocrinology and Metabolism, 6*: 403–419.

———— (1985) Brittle diabetes. *British Medical Journal, 291*: 555–556.

Tischler, S. (1979). Being with a psychotic child: A psycho-analytical approach to the problems of parents of psychotic children. *International Journal of Psycho-Analysis, 60*: 29–38.

Tizard, B. (1977). *Adoption—A Second Chance*. London: Open Books.

Tizard, B., & Hughes M. (1984). *Young Children Learning*. London: Fontana.

Tramontana, M. G., & Sherrets, S. D. (1983). Assessing outcome disorders of childhood and adolescence. In: M. J. Lambert, E. R. Christensen, & S. S. De Julio (Eds.), *The Assessment of Psychotherapy Outcome*. New York: Wiley.

Trevarthen, C. (1975). Early attempts at speech. In: R. Lewin (Ed.), *Child Alive*. London: Temple Smith.

———— (1979). Instincts for human understanding and for cultural co-operation: Their development in infancy. In: *Human Ethology: Claims and Limits of a New Discipline*. Cambridge: Cambridge University Press.

———— (1985). Facial expressions of emotion in mother–infant interaction. *Human Neurobiology, 4*.

Trevarthen, C., & Hubley, P. (1978). Secondary intersubjectivity: Confidence, confiding and acts of meaning in the first year. In: A. Lock (Ed.), *Action, Gesture and Symbol: The Emergence of Language*. London: Academic Press.

Triseliotis, J. (1973). *In Search of Origins—The Experiences of Adopted People*. London: Routledge & Kegan Paul.

Trowell, J. A. (1986a). Child abuse. Prevention and intervention. Unpublished paper.

_____ (1986b). Court work: How do child psychiatrists arrive at their recommendations? Unpublished paper.

Tustin, F. (1966). A significant element in the development of autism. *Journal of Child Psychology and Psychiatry, 7.*

_____ (1972). *Autism and Childhood Psychosis.* London: Hogarth.

_____ (1980). Autistic objects. *International Review of Psychoanalysis, 7*: 27–39.

_____ (1981). *Autistic States in Children.* London: Routledge.

_____ (1984). Autistic shapes. *International Review of Psychoanalysis, 11*: 280–288.

_____ (1986). *Autistic Barriers in Neurotic Patients.* London: Karnac Books.

_____ (1988). Psychotherapy with children who cannot play. *International Review of Psychoanalysis, 15*: 93–106.

_____ (1990). *The Protective Shell in Children and Adults.* London: Karnac Books.

Urwin, C. (1986). Developmental psychology and psychoanalysis: Splitting the difference. In: M. Richards & P. Light (Eds.), *Children of Social Worlds.* Cambridge: Polity Press.

_____ (1988). Child psychotherapy, war and the normal child. In: C. Urwin, & J. Hood-Williams (Eds.), *Child Psychotherapy, War and the Normal Child: Selected Papers of Margaret Lowenfeld.* London: Free Association Books, 1989.

Urwin, C., & Hood-Williams, J. (Eds.) (1989). *Child Psychotherapy, War and the Normal Child: Selected Papers of Margaret Lowenfeld.* London: Free Association Books.

Victor, G. (1986). *The Riddle of Autism.* Toronto: Lexington Books.

Warnock Report (1978). *Special Educational Needs: Report of Enquiry into the Education of Handicapped Children and Young People.* London: HMSO.

Wells, H. G. (1985). *Christina Alberta's Father.* London: Hogarth.

Wieder, H. (1977). On being told of adoption. *Psychoanalytic Quarterly, 46* (1): 1–22.

_____ (1978). On when and whether to disclose about adoption. *Journal of the American Psychoanalytic Association, 26* (4): 793–811.

Willeford, W. (1987). Feeling, imagination and the self. Edmondton: North Western University Press.

Williams, A. H. (1975). Puberty and phases of adolescence. In: S. Meyerson (Ed.), *Adolescence* (p. 37). London: Allen & Unwin.

Wilson, P. (1987). Directors' Report. London Youth Advisory Centre.

Winnicott, D. W. (1949). Birth memories, birth trauma and anxiety. In: *Through Paediatrics to Psychoanalysis*. London: Hogarth Press, 1958.

―――― (1958). *Collected Papers: Through Paediatrics to Psychoanalysis*. London: Tavistock.

―――― (1960). The theory of parent–infant relationship. *International Journal of Psycho-Analysis 41*: 585–595. [Also in *The Maturational Process*, 1965b.]

―――― (1965a). *The Family and Individual Development*. London: Tavistock.

―――― (1965b). *The Maturational Processes and the Facilitating Environment*. London: Hogarth Press. [Reprinted London: Karnac Books, 1990.]

―――― (1971). *Playing and Reality*. London: Tavistock.

Wittenberg, I. S. (1970). *Psycho-Analytic Insight and Relationships*. London: Routledge & Kegan Paul.

Wolff, P. H. (1963). Observations on the early development of smiling. In: M. B. Foss (Ed.), *Determinants of Infant Behaviour*. London: Methuen.

Wood, M. (1984). The child and art therapy. In: T. Dalley (Ed.), *Art as Therapy*. London: Tavistock.

―――― (In preparation). A comparative study of the imaging process in readers and non-readers using the Lowenfeld World Technique. University of Nottingham.

Wright, H. L. (1968). A clinical study of children who refuse to talk in school. *Journal of the American Academy of Child Psychiatry, 7*: 603–617.

INDEX